Australian &
New Zealand Edition

Being a Great Dad FOR DUMMIES®

by Stefan Korn, Scott Lancaster and Eric Mooij

WILEY

Wiley Publishing Australia Pty Ltd

Being a Great Dad For Dummies®

Australian & New Zealand Edition published by
Wiley Publishing Australia Pty Ltd
42 McDougall Street
Milton Qld 4064
www.dummies.com

Copyright © 2010 Wiley Publishing Australia Pty Ltd

The moral rights of the authors have been asserted.

National Library of Australia
Cataloguing-in-Publication data

Author:	Korn, Stefan.
Title:	Being a Great Dad For Dummies/Stefan Korn.
ISBN:	978-1-742-16972-9 (pbk.)
Notes:	Includes index.
Subjects:	Fatherhood Father and child. Parenting.
Dewey Number:	306.8742

Cover image: © iStockphoto.com/Bondarenko Liliya

Typeset by diacriTech, Chennai, India

Printed in Australia by
Ligare Book Printer

10 9 8 7 6 5 4 3 2

About the Authors

DIYFather.com has become one of the most recognised organisations promoting active fatherhood in Australia and New Zealand. DIYFather.com was brought into this world by Wellington-based dads Stefan Korn, Scott Lancaster and Eric Mooij, who recognised the need for social innovation in the fathering space. DIYFather is a social enterprise that aims to help men become the best fathers they can be. The directors of DIYFather have been recognised for their work by winning the 2009 New Zealander of the Year award in the education category.

Stefan Korn is a New Zealand-based internet entrepreneur. He is passionate about e-commerce and the web, and in general loves getting involved in new businesses. His wife Raquel gave birth to their son Noah in May 2007 and the experience of becoming a father, as well as the challenges of looking after Noah, prompted him to join DIYFather. Stefan has a PhD in Artificial Intelligence and an MBA in international business. Before becoming an entrepreneur Stefan held senior management roles for large international corporations in the IT, Telecommunication and Hospitality sector. In addition to DIYFather, Stefan runs an investment company for online startups, WebFund. Stefan is also actively engaged in community projects and enjoys tutoring for Wellington Community Education.

Scott Lancaster is the founder of DIYFather.com. He is married to Renee, who gave birth to their daughter Pyper in July 2007. After discovering what little parenting information was available for fathers, Scott approached the other two directors, who helped him build DIYFather. Scott looked after Pyper full-time for the first two years of her life and experienced being a stay-at-home dad (SAHD). Scott has an Applied Science degree majoring in Agriculture and comes from a farming background.

Eric Mooij is married to Andrea, who welcomed baby Ava into the world in April 2008. Eric is also father to Nastassja (16), Christian (15) and Amber (14). Although he is not living with his three older children, Eric has regular contact with them and supports them in every way possible. Eric is keen to make a stand for separated families. Coming from a broken family himself and having relived this experience with his first three children, he works hard to be a positive role model. Outside of DIYFather, Eric works in IT and project management.

Dedication

We'd like to dedicate this book to all dads.

Authors' Acknowledgements

First and foremost we would like to thank our children Pyper, Nastassja, Christian, Amber, Ava and Noah for giving us the opportunity to be fathers in the first place, and for putting up with us writing a book when we could have played with them! Special thanks of course to our partners Renee, Andrea and Raquel for their continuing support and encouragement, and special thanks to Raquel for proofreading the manuscript. Thanks also to our families and friends who helped out with baby-sitting duties at crucial times.

Huge thanks to the team at Plunket who provided a lot of the research material this book is based on and helped us ensure the content of the book is safe and sound. Special thanks to Erin Beatson and Claire Rumble who have been a fantastic source of wisdom and inspiration.

A very special thank you also to Kimberley Rothwell who has been the most wonderful support we could have wished for in getting this book together.

We'd like to thank our publisher Wiley and especially Bronwyn Duhigg for taking on this project, and Catherine Spedding for doing such a great job at editing our manuscript!

And last but not least we would like to give thanks to the worldwide community of dads who have contributed content and encouragement over the years. There are too many of you to list everyone individually, but if you've checked out our site, have participated in our classes or have been in touch with us — thanks heaps from Stefan, Scott and Eric!

Publisher's Acknowledgements

We're proud of this book; please send us your comments through our online registration form located at http://dummies.custhelp.com.

Some of the people who helped bring this book to market include the following:

Acquisitions, Editorial and Media Development

Project Editor: Catherine Spedding

Acquisitions Editor: Bronwyn Duhigg

Editorial Manager: Gabrielle Packman

Production

Graphics: Glenn Lumsden (pages 101, 106 and 109), various artists and the Wiley Art Studio

Cartoons: Glenn Lumsden

Proofreader: Miriana Dasovic

Indexer: Karen Gillen

Contents at a Glance

Introduction 1

Part I: From Here to Paternity: Conception to Birth 7

Chapter 1: Fatherhood 9
Chapter 2: Getting Pregnant 27
Chapter 3: Pregnancy: A Drama in Three Acts 39
Chapter 4: Preparing for a Baby in the House 55
Chapter 5: Birth..77

Part II: The First Year 93

Chapter 6: Being Dad to a Newborn 95
Chapter 7: The First Three Months 115
Chapter 8: Months Three to Six 135
Chapter 9: Months Six to Twelve 155

Part III: The Toddler Years 175

Chapter 10: Toddling Towards Two: Months 12–24 177
Chapter 11: Charging Towards Three: Months 24–36 197
Chapter 12: More Babies: Brothers and Sisters 211

Part IV: The Preschool Years 221

Chapter 13: Fun and Games...223
Chapter 14: Health and Nutrition..237
Chapter 15: Education 257

Part V: What Happens When 269

Chapter 16: Stay-at-home Dad..271
Chapter 17: Serious Illness and Losing Your Baby 281
Chapter 18: Disabilities, Disorders and Special Conditions 299
Chapter 19: Divorce and Separation..311

Part VI: The Part of Tens 333

Chapter 20: Ten Ways to Improve Your Partner's Pregnancy Experience.............335
Chapter 21: Ten Ways to Bond with Your Newborn Baby 341
Chapter 22: Ten Ways to Engage with a Toddler 347

Appendix: Resources for Dads 351

Glossary 371

Index 381

Table of Contents

Introduction 1

About This Book 1
Conventions Used in This Book 2
What You're Not to Read 2
Foolish Assumptions 3
How This Book Is Organised 4
    Part I: From Here to Paternity: Conception to Birth 4
    Part II: The First Year 4
    Part III: The Toddler Years 4
    Part IV: The Preschool Years 5
    Part V: What Happens When 5
    Part VI: The Part of Tens 5
    Appendix 5
    Glossary 5
Icons Used in This Book 6
Where to Go from Here 6

Part I: From Here to Paternity: Conception to Birth 7

Chapter 1: Fatherhood 9

Dispelling Common Myths about Fatherhood 10
    The pros and cons of fatherhood 12
    Knowing what to expect 13
    Trading in your lifestyle (but not the sports car) 14
Only Fools Rush in 16
    Hey, I'm not ready for this 16
    My partner wants a baby 17
    Timing isn't always everything 17
Introducing the New-Generation Dad 18
    Dadhood: A good time to man up 18
    Joining the movement 18
    Exploring care routine strategies 19
The Seven Habits of Highly Successful Dads 21
Help, I'm a Dad! 23
    Asking for directions 23
    Finding trusted organisations and sources of information 23

Internet research...24
Turning to friends, colleagues and family 25
Starting your own group 26

Chapter 2: Getting Pregnant 27

Here Comes the Fun Part...27
Conceiving naturally...28
Improving the odds — pregnant tips and tricks...................29
Conception's not happening..30
Understanding What Can Go Wrong 31
Working out why conception hasn't happened 31
Exploring other ways to get pregnant...............................32
OMG, You're Going to Be a Dad 34
Getting confirmation...34
Knowing what to do next 35
Choosing a carer 36
Things to do before morning sickness starts.......................37

Chapter 3: Pregnancy: A Drama in Three Acts 39

Act One: The First Trimester..40
Eating for two — or how to gain 15 kg in 40 weeks 40
Understanding the medical stuff.......................................41
Dealing with common side effects in the first trimester.........42
What's your baby up to? 44
Act Two: The Second Trimester 45
Enjoying the golden trimester..46
Understanding more medical stuff 46
Dealing with common side effects in the second trimester 47
What's your baby up to now?...48
Act Three: The Third Trimester...49
Making choices about the birth 49
Understanding even more medical stuff.............................51
Dealing with common side effects in the third trimester.............51
Preparing for Project Push — are we there yet?...................53

Chapter 4: Preparing for a Baby in the House. 55

Getting the Right Gear..56
Clothes and shoes...56
Toys 59
Strollers, prams and buggies...60
Car seats...61
Other accessories 63

Making Room for the Baby 64
  The nursery 64
  Decorations 66
  Animals in the house 66
Finding the Right Consumables 67
  Nappies 67
  Crème de la crèmes 69
  Shopping for your baby's health and first aid.................69
Stuff You Tend to Forget 71
  Upskilling 71
  Transport 72
  Birthing equipment...73
  The hospital bag(s) 73
  The baby shower 75
  Checklists...76

Chapter 5: Birth . . . .**.77**
The Final Countdown...78
  Discovering what you need to know about labour.........78
  Understanding your role in labour 79
  Getting ready — last minute preparations 81
Action!..83
  When you think you're in labour 83
  When you're really in labour 84
  Helping your partner through childbirth 84
  Keeping sane 85
  Giving nature a helping hand 86
The Big Moment's Arrived..88
  Cutting the cord 88
  When time stops — meeting your baby......................88
  Keeping your cool 89
Welcoming Your Baby to the Real World......................89
  What happens immediately after birth......................89
  The first few hours...90
  The first few days..91

Part II: The First Year **93**

Chapter 6: Being Dad to a Newborn . . . .**.95**
Dealing with the Aftershock.......................................95
  It's life but not as you know it 96
  Meet the baby..97
  You've got the blues 99

Looking after a Newborn 99
  Getting your hands dirty.. 100
  Feeding 104
  Sleeping — you and the baby.. 107
  Crying — you, your partner and the baby 109
  Daddy time.. 110
Juggling Your Other Priorities.. 111
  Making time for yourself.. 111
  Looking after your partner 112
  We are family 112
  Managing the work–life balance.. 113
  Sex.. 114

Chapter 7: The First Three Months **115**

Getting to Know Your Baby.. 115
  Groundhog day.. 116
  Practical solutions to common problems........................... 117
  Non-trivial care jobs 122
Hands-on Dad 123
  Baby massage.. 123
  Baby activities... 125
  Keeping baby safe and sound 125
Your Baby's Development 128
  Growth and weight 128
  Hearing, sight, taste, smell and touch............................... 128
  Your baby's amazing brain 131
Male and Female Postnatal Depression.................................. 132
  Do you feel like screaming?... 133
  Support organisations 134

Chapter 8: Months Three to Six **135**

Your Growing Baby... 135
  Baby's new tricks 136
  New challenges for dads 137
  New adventures for dads 138
  Adjusting to your baby's changing needs........................... 140
Getting on with Life 143
  Out and about with your baby 143
  Baby-proofing the house.. 145
  Wading through the necessary paperwork 146
  Doing things together: You're still a couple 148
Leaving Your Baby with Others 149
  Family and friends 149
  Nannies.. 150
  Babysitters.. 151

Day care centres 151
In-home care or family day care............................ 153

Chapter 9: Months Six to Twelve.......................155
Keeping Up with Baby.. 155
Your baby's changing diet 156
Don't forget the toothbrush 159
Your little explorer.. 159
The routines, they're a-changing 159
Parenting styles.. 160
You're good at this.. 161
Playtime with Daddy 162
Sitting, crawling, walking 162
Talking the talk 164
The life aquatic... 165
Playgroups 166
Toys you already own 167
Here Come Some Milestones................................. 168
Preparing to return to work.............................. 168
Going on holiday 169
Wow, that's strange: Addressing your concerns.... 171
How time flies 173
One today!.. 173

Part III: The Toddler Years 175

Chapter 10: Toddling Towards Two: Months 12–24 177
Hey, You've Got a Toddler Now 178
Sleeping update... 178
Eating update.. 179
Health update.. 180
Safety update.. 182
Conscious Fathering.. 182
A Busy Year for Your Little One 183
Toddler development 184
Say 'daddy'... 186
Dad, I need a wee 187
Can we play football yet? 189
It's All About Me, Dad!... 190
Understanding discipline.................................. 190
Tantrums, biting and hitting............................. 192
Sharing — what a nice idea 194
Setbacks 195

Chapter 11: Charging Towards Three: Months 24–36. . . . .**197**

    Exploring the World with Dad...198

        Helping your toddler grow up 198

        Developing skills and confidence 199

        Fun and games..201

        Some words for worried mums 202

    You've Created a Genius 202

        Development update 202

        Giving your toddler choices...203

        Setting boundaries and rules to match.....................................204

        Stimulating your toddler's interests..205

        Talking to your child so he understands 206

    Exploring Different Opportunities...207

        The fathering road less travelled...208

        TV, videos, computers and games 208

        Next stop — kindergarten..209

Chapter 12: More Babies: Brothers and Sisters **211**

    Having Another Child..211

        Is having another child worth it?...212

        What to expect 213

        Budgeting and finance..213

    Looking after Another Family Member...215

        Taking a practical approach 215

        Keeping two or more healthy and safe 215

        Juggling activities...216

    Sibling Discipline 217

        Understanding sibling rivalry...217

        Coping with jealousy and fighting 218

        Fighting and setting boundaries 219

        Discovering different personalities 219

Part IV: The Preschool Years **221**

Chapter 13: Fun and Games **223**

    Your Active Preschooler...223

        Mapping the next two years 224

        Building self-sufficiency and self-esteem 224

        Father worries 227

    Keeping Your Preschooler Busy 228

        'Dad, I'm bored' 228

        Bad weather busters 229

        Bringing out your child's talents without going OTT...................230

Being a good sport..231
The great outdoors...232
Lifelong Learning Starts Here..233
Fathers as first teachers..233
Kindergarten happiness...234
Learning objectives 235
Learning for the whole family 235

Chapter 14: Health and Nutrition **237**
Food, Nutritious Food 237
Cooking and baking for busy dads 238
Avoiding the wrong foods...239
Introducing different foods...240
Leading by example..240
Curbing fussy eaters...241
Coping with special dietary requirements 242
Exercise..245
Getting your child (and yourself) into exercise...................245
Working-out routines..246
Practising yoga and meditation 247
Common Health Problems...248
Childhood illnesses 248
Recurring health problems: Where to from here? 254
Alternative medicines and remedies..................................255
Child obesity: Honey, we're spoiling the kid 256
A word on health insurance 256

Chapter 15: Education **257**
Exploring Education Philosophies 257
Getting your head around education choices.......................258
Alternative education philosophies 259
Private versus public..260
Same-sex versus co-ed 261
School Begins This Summer...262
Preparing for school...262
Checklist: Things kids need to know..................................263
Homework with dad 264
Special dads for special needs...265
When schools don't meet your expectations.......................266
Complementary Education...267
Languages 267
Music 268
Sport 268
Religious education 268

Part V: What Happens When *269*

Chapter 16: Stay-at-home Dad 271
Daddy's in Da House 272
   Debunking some myths about guys as primary caregivers 272
   Coping with your new career 273
   Getting organised 274
My Daddy Just Cares for Me 275
   Upskilling 275
   Healthy bodies and active minds....................................276
   Keeping mum in the loop 277
   Working from home 277
The Brotherhood of Dads 278
   Networking as a SAHD 279
   Being the only guy in the room 279

Chapter 17: Serious Illness and Losing Your Baby 281
Avoiding Health Problems....................................282
   Protecting against diseases 282
   Providing a violence-free home....................................282
   Keeping accidents at bay....................................283
   A healthy start to life....................................283
   Birth options to reduce the risk of fatality 286
   Reducing the risk of SUDI and SIDS 287
   Calling all dads — creating a healthy and safe home....................................288
Coping with Illness and Injury 289
   Spotting injury....................................289
   Diagnosing a serious illness 291
Preparing for the End....................................292
   Taking care till the end....................................292
   Where to care for your little one....................................293
   Letting family and friends know....................................294
   Seeking help....................................295
Dealing with the Unthinkable....................................295
   What to do, what not to do....................................296
   Saying goodbye....................................296
   Is there such a thing as 'moving on'? 297

Chapter 18: Disabilities, Disorders and Special Conditions 299
What Is a Disability, Anyway? 299
   Knowing when something is wrong with your baby 300
   Physical disabilities 301
   Intellectual disabilities 302
   Multiple disabilities 303
   Getting formal confirmation 304
   What comes next?....................................304

Help, My Child is Disabled!...305
  Adjusting your expectations 306
  Finding help, assistance and resources 307
Access for People with Disabilities 308
  Your special baby 308
  Working with health professionals 308
  Living with a disability 309
  Changing your lifestyle..................................310
  Sharing the love 310

Chapter 19: Divorce and Separation.....................311

Marriage on the Rocks! 312
  What you can do 312
  What you can both do 313
  Where to go if all fails 314
Splitting up 315
  Out the door, with the shirt on your back! 315
  Understanding the divorce process 315
  Making separation easier on your children........315
  You're not just another statistic 316
  Finding good support 317
  Separating being a husband from being a father 318
Are You Still Dad?...318
  Who'll look after the kids? 318
  Being a remote or part-time father 319
  Understanding contact arrangements 321
  Paying child support 322
  Seeking guardianship of your children 323
  Getting advice..325
She Left Me but I Got the Kids 326
  Getting to grips with being a primary caregiver............327
  Supporting your children's mother 328
  Seeking help and assistance 329
  Having fun 330
Introducing a Stepmum.......................................330
  Talking about a new partner to your children 331
  Meet and greet..331
  Getting remarried..332

Part VI: The Part of Tens **333**

Chapter 20: Ten Ways to Improve Your Partner's Pregnancy Experience....................................335

Take Care of Your Lady 335
Get on the Wagon..336

Give Your Partner Some 'Me' Time Every Now and Then 336
Be There for the Medical Stuff 337
Get with the Program 337
Go on a Babymoon 337
Be Excited about Becoming a Dad 338
Celebrate! 338
Record That Beautiful Belly 339
Keep Telling Her How Beautiful She Is 339

Chapter 21: Ten Ways to Bond with Your Newborn Baby 341

Be 100 Per Cent Committed 341
Be at the Birth 342
Up Close and Personal 342
Ready, Set . . . Read! 343
Tummy Time 343
Be Hands-on — Literally 344
Be the Paparazzi 344
Get Creative 345
This Stroller Was Made for Walking 345
Get Your Hands Dirty 345

Chapter 22: Ten Ways to Engage with a Toddler 347

Obstacle Course 347
Get Handy 348
Playing Chase and Tag 348
Jigsaws 348
Balloons 349
Balls 349
Water Games 349
Art 350
Reading 350
Stacking Blocks and Building 350

Appendix: Resources for Dads 351

Glossary 371

Index 381

Foreword

*I*n recent years an increasing number of fathers have been looking to take more time with their children, and searching for the resources and tools to help them do so. And who better to write a new book for fathers than dads themselves?

Attitudes have relaxed around previously strictly defined parenting roles and now there is more flexibility about how different family members — including dads — can care for their children.

Plunket has long recognised and encouraged the importance of a father in a child's life. Evidence shows that children's development benefits in many ways when fathers are involved in their lives. It benefits them emotionally, physically and intellectually. Research also shows that fathers and mothers play and interact differently with their children.

As the face of modern fathering is constantly changing, Plunket strives to look for new opportunities to support fathers to take part in their children's lives. In underlining the importance of the fathering role, we are committed to helping dads. Plunket will always support making a variety of resources available to suit a multitude of parents and families.

No parent has a manual to help with the most challenging and rewarding job in the world — but having the right tools is a great start and Plunket is happy to welcome *Being a Great Dad For Dummies*, Australian & New Zealand Edition, as a new tool in the parenting toolkit.

Jenny Prince, CEO, Plunket

Introduction

*T*his book is the first *For Dummies* book on parenting specifically written for dads in Australia and New Zealand. We believe a quiet revolution is happening among men who want to become more involved in the upbringing of their children. Historically fathers have taken a bit of a passive role in looking after babies and young children, and many a father would have felt out of place, not knowing what to do or what he was there for. Fortunately, things are changing. Lots of guys now want a piece of the baby action and are rolling up their sleeves to muck in with everything that needs doing — from nappy changes to baby baths, and tummy time to toilet training.

The number of stay-at-home dads (SAHDs) is constantly rising in almost all developed countries, a sure sign that the parenting world is changing and that staying home looking after the kids is no longer a reason to hand in your man card. In fact SAHDs are leading the way for all other dads to show the world how brilliant dads can be at looking after babies and children. Countless studies have been done by fatherhood institutes around the world to provide scientific evidence about the difference a dad makes in the lives of his children. Unfortunately many problems our children experience these days are linked to absent or uninvolved fathers. So, to experience the 'coming out' of active dads and the rise of a new generation of fully involved dads is truly inspiring.

With *Being a Great Dad For Dummies*, Australian & New Zealand Edition, we would like to do our bit in helping along this peaceful revolution and to help every new dad or dad-to-be walk his journey to active fatherhood. The great news is, being an active dad is not difficult. Dads can do everything mums do except give birth and breastfeed. So if you're worried about becoming a dad, relax, read on and know that everyday blokes make fantastic dads. Above all, enjoy the wild ride to fatherhood — being a dad is the best time of your life!

About This Book

This book is your guide to dadhood. In *Being a Great Dad For Dummies*, Australian & New Zealand Edition, we share the collective wisdom from dads and parenting organisations gathered through DIYFather.com over the years. We wrote it all down in this book, so that you can become the best father you can be. Here are some of the important pieces we pull together for you.

✔ Much has changed over the last three decades and the previous generation's approach to having children. Modern dads want to be involved and they want to find out for themselves what it means to be a dad.

✔ Your kids, your family and the world at large need strong dads. Fathers have been somewhat absent from childcare and upbringing because of work, family situation or a limited understanding of the role of a father. It's about time that changed.

✔ You may find it hard to even approach the topic of babies and children. Worry no more.

✔ You may be missing out on the best moments of your life if you feel you don't know what to do with babies or children — so we tell you.

✔ You have everything you need to be a fantastic dad, you just don't know it yet, or perhaps lack a bit of confidence to demonstrate your dad skills.

✔ After flipping through the pages of this book, you'll impress your baby and your partner with all the cool things you know and are able to do with and for them.

Conventions Used in This Book

All web addresses appear in monofont, which looks like this. When this book was printed, some web addresses may have needed to break across two lines of text. If that happened, rest assured that we haven't put in any extra characters (such as hyphens) to indicate the break. So, when using one of these web addresses, just type in exactly what you see in this book, pretending as though the line break doesn't exist.

What You're Not to Read

Although we hope you read every word we've written, we understand your life is busy and you want to read only the need-to-know info. You can safely skip the sidebars, which are shaded grey boxes containing text. These provide supporting or entertaining information that isn't critical to your understanding of the topic.

Throughout this book, we give you the website addresses of a number of dedicated parenting or fatherhood sites where you can find more information on some of the topics we've discussed, such as buying sensible baby gear and toys, parenting styles, effective behaviour management, illnesses and special conditions, childcare and child education. Although you don't have to go to these websites, having a browse through them is well worth your while.

Foolish Assumptions

We assume that you're reading this book because you've just been told that you'll be a dad soon or you've decided it's about time you became one. You may also have been told by your partner to 'skill up' and read about parenting so she doesn't have to do all the work around the baby. Good — because you don't want your partner to do all the work around bub anyway.

We assume you're somewhat puzzled by the prospects of becoming a dad and would like an easy and comprehensive guide. So, to make sure we're all on the same page, this book is for you if you're

- Freaked out about becoming a dad
- Concerned about your lack of knowledge and experience around all things babies
- Three months into your partner's pregnancy and feel like it's all getting a bit too complicated
- Looking for an alternative to being told everything you need to know about babies by your partner
- On your way to the delivery suite and have missed all the antenatal classes
- Already a dad and want to skill up and find out what you can do to help your baby develop his full potential
- A dad to one or more children but feel like you could be doing more with your kids
- Going through a difficult time in your fatherhood journey and would like to read up on stuff

Lastly, we assume you haven't had much exposure to or experience with babies and children up to now.

How This Book Is Organised

This book is divided into six major parts. At your fingertips is everything you need to guide you through the first five years of your fatherhood journey.

Part I: From Here to Paternity: Conception to Birth

Part I covers all aspects of your fatherhood journey before your baby is born. Naturally it all begins with conception, so Chapter 1 contains tips on how to improve your chances of conceiving and what to do if conception doesn't happen. After that we give you a man's guide to pregnancy and share some secrets on keeping your pregnant partner happy and healthy. We also give you the no-bull guide to getting the house, nursery and your life ready for the imminent arrival of your little addition to the family. Finally we help you get ready for the big moment when your baby arrives in this world.

Part II: The First Year

This part is really where 'the rubber hits the road' in terms of your fatherhood experience. Your child's been born and plenty of upskilling is required on your part. So we break down all the baby care skills for you in a dad-friendly way. As your baby grows and develops, amazing experiences are to be had for every dad. We provide practical tips, activities and inspirations so you can help your little champ develop her full potential and have lots of fun with her along the way.

Part III: The Toddler Years

This part covers years two and three when the little person in your house is referred to as a 'toddler'. Lots of fun is to be had with children this age. You may have heard of the 'terrible twos'. While a few challenges need to be mastered during this period, we believe that keeping your family happy and healthy isn't rocket science. In this part we describe some useful principles you can use to help with behaviour management, to master the development of skills and to get organised if you want to return to work or have another child.

Part IV: The Preschool Years

In this part we give you a helping hand to get through a particularly active period of your little champ's development. The first chapter in this part is packed with ideas, activities and games to avoid the one sentence every father dreads, 'Dad, I'm bored!' We also give you a full update on all health- and nutrition-related information you need now that your child is testing his physical and mental capabilities (and your nerves). We round off this part by demystifying the various choices you've got for your child's education.

Part V: What Happens When

This part is for all dads who have chosen the road less travelled and have become a stay-at-home dad (SAHD). In Part V we also tackle some of the more difficult journeys of fatherhood, including helping your child through a serious illness or losing a child, parenting a child with a disability or special condition, and sharing care of your child following separation and divorce.

Part VI: The Part of Tens

This part is perfect for all super busy dads. In these chapters we give you ten tips on making pregnancy a nicer experience for your partner, on really connecting with your newborn baby, and on how to engage with your toddler. If during your fatherhood journey you find yourself stuck for tips and need some inspiration, Part VI is your friend when in need.

Appendix

The Appendix is a list of support organisations on all topics covered in the book, including general childbirth education and parenting, pregnancy and birth, multiple births, childcare and education, child development, child safety, postnatal depression, sudden unexpected death in infants (SUDI), disability, divorce and separation, playtime, health, grief and loss of a child, illness and special conditions, palliative care, and general fatherhood.

Glossary

The glossary defines the most commonly used terms you'll hear during pregnancy or when visiting a paediatrician.

Icons Used in This Book

Icons are those little pictures you see sprinkled in the margins throughout this book. Here's what they mean:

This icon denotes critical information that you really need to take away with you. Considering the state of our own overcrowded memories, we wouldn't ask you to remember anything unless it was really important.

This bull's-eye alerts you to on-target advice, insights or recommendations that we've picked up over the years.

This icon serves as a warning, telling you to avoid something that's potentially harmful. Take heed!

The internet is a wonderful place to access information on being a great dad. This icon highlights some helpful sites for you to check out.

Where to Go from Here

You choose what happens next. This book is packed with information to help you at whatever state you are on your fatherhood journey. You can go directly to the topics of most interest to you, or you can start at the beginning and take it from there. With the information in *Being a Great Dad For Dummies*, Australian and New Zealand Edition, we're confident that you can handle any challenges fatherhood (or your little champ) throws at you. Most importantly, this book will help you become a confident dad and have fun along the way.

Part I

From Here to Paternity: Conception to Birth

Glenn Lumsden

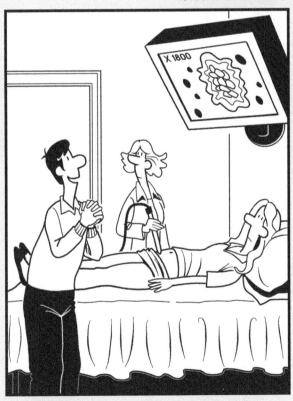

'She's cute now, but I can't wait to
see her once her cells have divided
a few more times.'

In this part ...

The way each man reacts to the news he's going to become a father is as individual and unique as his fingerprints, but all men share one thing — your lives will never be the same. Being a dad doesn't start the day you meet your newborn child, it begins much sooner than that, in some cases even from before your child is conceived. In this part, we look at what it means to be a dad and prepare you for the hurdles you may face on the way to meeting your baby: From your partner getting pregnant to understanding pregnancy and dealing with the biggest event of all — the birth of your child.

Chapter 1

Fatherhood

In This Chapter

▶ Being a dad — you're in good company

▶ Weighing up the biggest decision of your life

▶ Exploring dadhood

▶ Understanding what it takes to be a great dad

▶ Knowing where to go for guidance

Right now, somewhere across the globe, someone is becoming a father. He may be suited up in scrubs as his child is delivered by caesarean in a high-tech delivery suite, or holding his partner's hand as she gives birth in a pool at home. He may be pacing at the neighbours' hut in a village somewhere in the third world as his wife gives birth surrounded only by women, or heading through rush hour traffic to get to the hospital on time. Wherever these dads-to-be are, they all have one thing in common. When they clap eyes on their new little baby, they know life will never be the same.

There's something about becoming a father that's universal. For ages, you've been just yourself: Building a career, buying a house, perhaps travelling and seeing the world. You've concentrated on becoming a person in your own right — an individual. You've had wild days and adventures, you've been places. Those are all great things to do with your life. But when you have a child, you begin a whole new adventure — one that doesn't end when your visa runs out or the bar closes. Your new adventure is lifelong. Being a father will make you think of your own father and all the fathers who came before him, and you'll realise you're something bigger than just a stamped passport and some good stories around the campfire — you're a bona fide member of the human race, a piece in a puzzle that has been put together over millions of years. And there's a part of you that will go on into the next generation, and then hopefully the next and the next.

In this chapter, we explore what it means to be a father and talk about the reality of being a dad. The role of fathers has changed a lot in just the generation between our fathers and us. We're more involved, but we also have a lot more stress on us — work commitments, financial pressure, separation from our partners and information overload. But fear not — in this chapter and in the rest of the book we keep fatherhood real with practical information, useful explanations and a bit of humour. After all, children are lots and lots of fun, so why make the journey to fatherhood more serious than it needs to be?

Dispelling Common Myths about Fatherhood

Towards the end of the 20th century we experienced a revival of fatherhood and the dawn of a new generation of dads. A generation of dads who are no longer content playing a supporting role in the upbringing of their children. Dads who want to experience parenting fully, warts and all. Some brave dads are even taking over and sending mum back to the workforce. The number of stay-at-home dads is increasing year by year in most Western societies, a clear sign that something fundamental is changing about how we bring up our children and organise our lives. If you're thinking about becoming a stay-at-home dad, we have lots of advice and practical tips for taking on your new role in Chapter 16.

However, despite the generation of new dads, many dads are still faced with a few persistent stereotypes:

✔ **Fathers are completely useless when it comes to looking after babies and children.** That's poppycock. Yes, dads parent differently from mums, but male ways of doing things are just as valid and important. Research shows that fathers are just as good as mothers at caring for babies, responding to their needs and temperaments, and learning how to read babies' cues. Research also shows that children with involved dads do better in school and are more confident and independent later in life. Unfortunately, fathers have effectively been cut off from getting involved through preconceived ideas about parenting, peer pressure or the demands of the modern workplace. The good news is most dads in the 21st century now have the option to do it differently and show the world that dads make fantastic caregivers.

✔ **Fathers don't have to do any of the day-to-day care that babies and children require.** This may be true if you want to remain in the dark ages of fatherhood. Twenty-first century dads do care-giving because there's an important reason for it: The best way to bond with your newborn child is by taking part in all that day-to-day stuff. Changing a nappy, trimming his nails and tucking him into bed each night aren't just jobs that need to be done, they're a way for your baby and children to spend a bit of time with you and get to know you. Your child will learn that when he needs something, you're there to take care of him, make him feel better, and comfort him when he's ill or teething, or just because he needs a cuddle. He'll learn words from you as you chat to him while he's in the bath, learn how to put clothes on from the way you dress him each morning, and learn all sorts of other good qualities simply from the way you are. You also brighten up his world no end with all the silly things you do.

✔ **Mums laugh at dads when they're out with babies by themselves.** Maybe — but mostly because they probably find you really cute with your little one strapped to your chest! In most cases, women will flock from all corners of the room when you walk into that playgroup with bub on your shoulder. If you get the occasional overly 'helpful' mum in the supermarket who doesn't think you quite know how to handle a crying baby, be confident that you can demonstrate who's daddy by settling your little one in one minute flat.

✔ **Fathers don't have a social life.** Wrong — fathers (and all parents) have a different social life. You may have to invest a bit of time and thought into how you'll manage going out or taking part in sport. But these things can all be organised. After all, dads are fantastic at organising. It takes a while getting used to having an extra person in your life, but that doesn't mean you'll never be able to go out again. Chapter 8 provides hints and tips for getting out and about, with and without your wee one.

✔ **As a dad you don't have a sex life anymore.** Actually that one is kind of true, but only temporarily. The birthing experience, sheer exhaustion and practicalities of looking after a newborn can make it somewhat tricky to get back to your pre-baby sex life with your partner. The word here is patience. Your sex life will return (check out Chapters 6 and 8 for more on this subject). But you might just have to be a bit more creative now that your little one is in the house.

The pros and cons of fatherhood

As with every life decision or change, there are good things and challenges. If you want to take a rational approach to fatherhood, consider the following.

On the plus side:

- Fathers report their lives are more meaningful than before they had a child.
- Fatherhood can make you a more compassionate, mature and confident person.
- You get to be a child all over again (yes, you get to play with cool toys and teach your child lots of silly tricks).
- Being a father is a chance for you to hand down skills and values from your family. This will feel very good when you're nearing your final days.
- You'll probably for the first time in your life truly understand your own father.
- You get a real kick out of raising a child well and seeing them achieve lots of things.

The challenges:

- Until around three months of age, newborn babies are full on. They cry, sometimes for no apparent reason at all, and you feel like the sound is piercing your brain. There's a reason recordings of crying babies are used as torture. Chapter 6 provides helpful hints about settling a newborn and coping with crying.
- Sleep deprivation is also a well-known torture technique. Fathers of babies under a year old typically have 42 minutes less sleep a night than other men. Doesn't sound like much, but it adds up. For ways to deal with sleep deprivation, see Chapter 8.
- You'll have less time for yourself and making plans really does mean making plans — spontaneity goes out the window a bit at the beginning. Check out Chapter 8 for ways to get out and about.

We think the upsides of fatherhood far outweigh the downsides, especially because most of the really annoying aspects (like sleep deprivation) get much easier the older your children get.

A sad reality for a small percentage of New Zealand and Australian fathers is that they may not get the chance to experience all the joys that fatherhood has to offer. Though we don't often talk about it in our society, miscarriage, stillbirth, premature birth and death in infancy are terrible losses for some fathers to bear.

Others have to deal with the fact that their child, so full of promise and hope, has a serious illness or disability that forces them to shift expectations of what being a father is all about. We talk more about these issues in Chapters 17 and 18 with lots of information and support for parents.

Knowing what to expect

Asking someone to tell you what being a father is like is a bit like asking 'how long is a piece of string?' Answering that question is impossible. Like the uniqueness of your child's DNA, every father's experience is different. A good way to get an idea of what fatherhood is like is to spend some time with friends who have recently had a baby. Talk to your own parents too.

Here are some common factors that most fathers face:

✔ Sharing your partner's body with your child before and after birth can feel a bit weird. Sex during pregnancy can be brilliant or a bit challenging, depending on your partner's experience. See Chapter 3 for more about sex during pregnancy. In addition, after giving birth some women aren't into sharing their boobs with you if that's where junior's getting his tucker.

✔ Sleep becomes a big issue. Babies don't understand that day is for being awake and night is for being asleep. Over time, your baby will adjust and eventually 'sleep through the night' — the holy grail for most parents. But a baby who does this before six months of age is rare. Babies also need nutrition every few hours to grow, so if your baby is waking up in the night for feeds, consider it a good thing that he's thriving and growing. Chapters 6, 7 and 8 discuss feeding your baby and getting him to sleep.

✔ Expect to feel frightened, scared, overwhelmed and sometimes lost as you navigate fatherhood. Just changing a nappy for the first time or getting clothes on a newborn feels awkward and wrong when you're new at it. So what — mums and all other dads who get involved have the same experience.

✔ You'll do things that you never thought you'd do, you'll laugh at things that seem completely ridiculous to you right now, and you might cry at times that you least expect. You'll also learn lots about yourself and experience things that you cannot experience any other way. Fatherhood is truly an adventure.

Being a father is a lot about acceptance and going with the flow. A useful mantra to remember is 'this too will pass', as every illness, teething episode, period of sleep deprivation or colic *will* pass. Looking after a baby teaches you a lot about life and you may find that you're more relaxed, confident and happy as a result of having a child.

Parenting, for both fathers and mothers, requires a certain amount of letting go. When a baby is born, we want things for our child: The best of everything; every opportunity and good thing in life that may come her way. You naturally want her to avoid the mistakes you made in your own life. But it doesn't work that way.

Your child is not an extension of you, your baby is her own person. She'll grow up to have her own ideas, her own interests, her own strengths and they may be vastly different from yours. You may want her to be a lawyer so she has money to pay for things you could only dream of, but what really makes her happy is working with animals, or in a charity. Sometimes you just have to admit that father *doesn't* know best. You may be disappointed, but it's her life and only she can live it. Support her — that's what great dads are for.

Trading in your lifestyle (but not the sports car)

Well, actually, we hate to say it, but you *may have to* trade in the sports car too. Becoming a father is about changing your state of mind and changing the idea of what's important to you. As a dad the car's less about the ultimate drive and more about keeping your child safe and fitting the buggy in the back. Chapter 4 helps you negotiate safe transport for your baby, as well as what sort of pram, stroller or buggy to get.

If you want a baby but not to change the way you live your life, you're probably better off waiting for a while to have children. Some things will inevitably change:

- ✔ **Your work.** If you want to spend time with your family, you may consider working fewer hours, or changing to a flexible working arrangement that you can negotiate with your employer. See Chapter 6 for more about finding a work–life balance.

  You may even decide to give up work and be the primary caregiver to your child, making you a stay-at-home dad (SAHD). If this sounds like you, see Chapter 16 for more information. This book is written with the philosophy that dads, just as much as mums, take part in the day-to-day care of a child, so we've left out nothing about how to look after your little one.

✔ **Your freedom.** Doing things when and where you want doesn't work when you've got a baby. If the swell is perfect and you just feel like going out for a surf, you may have to wait until bub is asleep, or take him and mum along with you. It's the same with spending time out and about with your partner. Going out to dinner and a movie is no longer a spontaneous activity, it requires planning. Finding time for yourself alongside work and family commitments is one of the biggest challenges fathers face. Chapter 8 gives you ideas for getting out and about after your baby arrives.

✔ **Your finances.** If you both had an income before your child came along, you'll be down to one income for a while. If you lived in a one bedroom flat, it's time to find somewhere bigger, and a way to pay for it. We offer some tips on how to reduce the cost of caring for your child in Chapter 12.

✔ **Your friends and family.** Your relationship with friends and family will change. If you live away from your parents, you'll probably find yourself having to spend a lot more time travelling to visit them more often. Some of your childless friends will really embrace you having a child and will become the fun aunt or uncle your child gets excited about seeing. Others will not be so keen and you'll see them less as a result.

✔ **Your holidays.** Going on holiday takes on a whole new meaning. You'll definitely have to postpone that backpacking trip around South America for a few years, at least until your kids are big enough to trudge alongside you. Family holidays are different — great fun, but unlike any holiday you've had since you were a child. Chapter 9 gives you some great ideas for how to manage a trip or holiday with bub in tow.

✔ **Your lifestyle.** Risky lifestyle or sport activities like base jumping and free climbing are no longer just about risking your own life. You now have to consider the future of your child and family.

✔ **Your health and behaviour.** A child is one of the ultimate reasons to change some unhealthy habits like smoking, heavy drinking, eating junk food and being a slob. Children need a smoke-free environment to breathe in, good healthy food, clean clothes and nappies, and good hygiene to prevent illness. And who needs to grow up hearing language that might make a sailor blush? If you're a little lost when it comes to health and nutrition, we give you the goods in Chapter 14, where you'll find everything you need to know about, from what junior should be eating, to exercising together.

Only Fools Rush In

Sometimes you can plan when you have a child, sometimes nature has her own ideas. Either way, fatherhood is a big deal — fatherhood's not like buying a new pair of shoes or getting a plant. Your child, if you decide to have one, has only one shot at life and he deserves the best start you can give him. A committed, involved and reliable father is a big part of that. If you're being pushed into having a child by your partner, talk it through with her, don't just go along with it because you're afraid of the discussion. Becoming a dad is an important step in life, so take some time to figure out how you feel about it and share your thoughts with your partner.

Hey, I'm not ready for this

How often in your life can you say you're really ready for something? Not often. Fatherhood, of all things, is probably the most difficult to feel truly ready for. Even if you've been planning to have a child, spent months going through IVF (see Chapter 2 for more about this) and been dreaming of the day you hold your child in your arms, the sledgehammer of reality will probably whack you over the head the day you find out you're really going to be a dad.

If your partner is already pregnant but you don't feel ready for fatherhood, you've got time on your side. In the coming months, as your baby grows and gets ready for birth, spend some time with other people's children, talk to other fathers and let yourself ease into the idea of fatherhood. Think about the kind of father your dad is and what you've learned from him. Think of all the things you would do differently.

If you're really, truly not ready for fatherhood as the birth approaches, it may help if you talk to someone about your fears. Your midwife or GP can put you in touch with a counsellor.

You can find a counsellor yourself through these organisations:

In Australia:
Family Relationship Services Australia www.frsa.org.au/site
Relationships Australia www.relationships.com.au

In New Zealand:
Relationship Services www.relate.org.nz

Don't forget to talk to your partner about what you're feeling. After all you are in this together, so it helps to share your feelings and thoughts with her.

Although having children can be the most amazing and joyous adventure, the strains of work, family and other commitments can put a lot of pressure on a relationship. Unfortunately, many relationships don't survive this extra pressure. In Chapter 19, we talk about how fathers can cope with divorce and separation and still continue to be great dads.

My partner wants a baby

You're faced with a sticky situation — your partner is ready to have a baby, her biological clock is ticking, all her friends have babies and she's eager to join the club. But you're not.

Here's our advice: Rather than fight the idea of becoming a parent — moan, whine, or try to ignore it until it goes away — give the idea of fatherhood some serious thought. Talk about it together with your partner, explain why you're not ready, but equally, listen to her point of view. Imagine yourself as a dad — how does that feel?

Mull it over. Where do you want to be in ten years? Dad to a litter of children with the rewards that brings? Or still living a childless life with the freedoms that brings? When you look back on your life in your old age, do you want children and family to be part of it?

You may feel like there's never a good time to have children or you just don't feel ready. Perhaps you're quite clear that you definitely don't want children. Cool, but then you also owe it to your partner to let her know.

Timing isn't always everything

Sometimes, despite thinking that you'll wait to have a family until after a big project is completed, or you've found a bigger house, or until you've been on that trekking trip to Nepal, nature jumps the gun. Your partner sits you down and says she's pregnant. Blimey — you're going to be a dad. The key is to not panic. Freak out maybe, but don't panic (mostly because it takes a while for the baby to arrive). Okay, so you haven't painted the roof or done a skydive yet. Well, you never wanted to be one of those 'boring older people' anyway, so there are still plenty of opportunities to do whatever you want to do, perhaps even with your children. Fatherhood doesn't mean you suddenly have to stay home every night whittling on the front porch, it just means the pace of life you live ticks along to a different clock.

Introducing the New-Generation Dad

Fathers today are a quantum leap from the previous generation of fathers. Twenty-first century dads push buggies, get up for night feeds, change nappies, and have tried and tested burping techniques. We do it all — except for being pregnant, giving birth and breastfeeding. As for the rest of it, there's nothing we can't tackle. Dare we say it, we can even do some things better than mums.

Dadhood: A good time to man up

All your life you've had just one person to take care of — yourself. You've made choices, taken risks and shouldered the consequences. But becoming a father is 'the big stuff'. You have a vulnerable, dependent, helpless child on your hands who needs you for the most basic aspects of her survival, such as food, warmth and love.

Becoming a dad can add a profound sense of meaning to your life. Your views on life, priorities in the world and aspirations for your own future are forever altered. This is a good thing. By becoming a dad you become part of the circle of life that has been going for eons. You're passing on the baton to your child, packed with all your wisdom and skills, to send bub off on his own journey. You've got so much you can share with your offspring.

Children need dads. A Canadian study showed that having a father in a child's life helps her develop empathy. Another long-term study showed that a father's involvement with his child from birth to adolescence helps build emotional stability, curiosity and self-esteem.

If you're going to have a child, be involved, committed and passionate about your new role. Your child deserves nothing less.

Joining the movement

By becoming a father, you join the ranks of men for thousands of generations before you. You've come from a long line of fathers! In New Zealand, the average age of a first-time father is 33, four years older than a generation ago. According to figures from 2006–07, more than 4,500,000 Australian fathers are over the age of 18. So you're in good company.

So as a soon-to-be-dad we'd like to encourage and inspire you to join the movement of involved and active fathers. Our children need involved fathers in their lives and you also owe it to yourself. If you're going to be a dad, be a 100 per cent dad and experience it all. You wouldn't do other things in your life half-hearted, so get with it and give it your best shot. Make an effort, skill up and spend as much time as possible with your child.

Exploring care routine strategies

The question of how best to raise a baby is one of the most hotly contested subjects today. The rows of parenting psychology books on bookshop shelves attest to that. We've become disengaged over the last few centuries from listening to our instincts. We've let medical science overrule our hearts and minds, and slavishly followed rigid routines and overbearing doctor's orders that demanded that mother's convenience came first and baby's needs came second. We've joined the rat race and let work dictate our daily and weekly schedules.

Families are also smaller than they used to be, so children can grow up never having to help mum wash the nappies, or settle a baby like they did back in our grandparents' day, when there were as many children in a family as you could find names for.

In recent years, there's been a swing back to letting the child's needs lead the way as well as research that backs up this method of parenting. Parents caught in the middle of grandparents' ways, their own instincts and the swing back to gentler parenting methods can find deciding on a parenting method confusing. Media reports shower us with research that says everything under the sun is bad for our kids, and we're stuck between experts who promote their particular technique and the latest trend from celebrity parents. Chapter 10 has lots of great tips for raising your child in a warm, loving relationship, as well as making discipline work.

Keep in mind that the way you want to run things in your family is up to you. Whether you adhere to a strict routine, or are a bit more laid back about it, as long as your little champ is clean, fed and thriving, happy and cheerful, gets enough sleep, and is shown love and affection, he'll be okay. Don't get caught in a trap of constantly comparing your baby to other babies; it generally leads nowhere and just adds to your frustration. Have confidence in the way you bring up your children and trust in your child developing in his own unique way.

These are some of the care routine strategies you may have heard of as you contemplate fatherhood, and how you'll cope with a newborn:

- ✔ **Strict routine.** In our mums' day, a strict routine with feedings and sleeping by the clock was promoted as being the best way to bring up a baby. Today, advocates of this method claim that having a strict routine or schedule establishes good habits early so you can detour sleepless nights and excessive crying. For some parents, this routine works a treat and their baby easily slips into line. For others, their baby resists and parents end up even more stressed out that their little one won't play by the book.

- ✔ **A routine, but not by the clock.** Babies need to feed and sleep at regular intervals but rather than let the clock determine when that might be, reading your child's cues is the key to making the routine work. There's a pattern or routine of waking for a feed, feeding, having a nappy change, some play or awake time, and then back down for a sleep that continues throughout the day, but at night there's no play or awake time. Chapter 6 has more about establishing a routine.

- ✔ **Attachment parenting.** This form of parenting mimics parenting styles found in developing countries, where cots, bassinets and strollers are rare. Your child is in contact with you at all times of the day, is carried around in a sling or baby carrier, and sleeps with you at night, so that she builds a strong bond and attachment with you.

Many other strategies for raising a newborn exist. Do you leave him to cry when you put him down in order to teach him to fall asleep on his own, or rock him to sleep in your arms every nap time? Do you have the baby sleep in your bed, or have him in a bassinet in his own room? These are questions that you and your partner have to ponder and come up with your own answers to. You have to live with whichever strategy you come up with, so the strategy has to work for *you*. Chapter 6 gives you lots of ideas for raising a newborn.

Another minefield you're going to have to get your head around is your child's education. Private, public, Steiner, Montessori — these are all terms you're going to hear bandied about as your child gets older. Luckily for you, we've done some of the hard yards in Chapter 15 so you can figure out the educational maze for yourself.

As your baby turns into a toddler, you'll have to start thinking about discipline. People often think of discipline as the way you punish your child for being naughty. But in our books, that's not what discipline is about. Discipline is about creating an environment where your child can learn to adjust her behaviour and understand what's okay and what's not. Discipline's about clear boundaries, consistency and consequences. We talk about discipline in more depth in Part 3.

The Seven Habits of Highly Successful Dads

Here's a collection of seven habits we observe in amazing dads — a collection of traits that each and every bloke can develop on his journey to becoming a father.

✔ **Confidence:** It takes time to feel truly confident about handling a newborn, but you gain confidence by doing things and getting your hands dirty (literally in some cases), even if at first things don't go right. Looking after a newborn, baby and toddler can seem daunting at times, but isn't actually that hard. It just comes down to being attentive to the needs of your little one, making an effort and learning a few tricks.

No matter how hard things get — you're stressed out at work and the baby's waking up every three hours at night, your partner's sick and you're doing all the housework — you'll get through it and you'll be a more confident dad (and person) as a result. So don't be afraid to muck in because it will give you a great sense of achievement, lift your spirits and build your self-esteem when you don't have to rely on mum for anything to do with the baby (other than breastfeeding).

✔ **Creativity:** Sometimes you truly have to think outside the box when you're looking after babies or spending time with children. Children are very lateral in their thinking, which can work to your advantage as you can easily turn an empty water bottle into a spaceship. Children have no trouble with pretend play and let their fantasies run wild, so just go with it. Sometimes you'll also have to find creative solutions to some basic problems, such as when you've run out of nappies. An old tea towel may have to do while you take bub to the shop to get disposables.

✔ **Endurance:** Sometimes the only way to cope with a situation is to endure it. When your baby is colicky, or wakes every few hours at night, or is teething and cries constantly, you may be at the end of your tether trying to work out how to put a stop to that noise. Often there's no solution, there's nothing you can fix or do to make a difference. It's just the way it is and you're going to have to suck it up. But understanding that everything in parenting comes and goes — that one day, your little one will sleep through, one day, your child will have all his teeth, and one day, he will grow out of colic will help you endure the bad times while they last.

Like patience, endurance can be hard to muster when you're tired, you've had little sleep and you see no end in sight. The early weeks of a baby's life are a little like an endurance sport — just surviving the sleep deprivation, the crying that grips your brain and shakes it about, and the never-ending rounds of feeding, burping, changing and settling can seem impossible. But even marathons end sooner or later, so take every day as it comes and before you know it you'll be celebrating your champ's first birthday.

If you're having a hard time coping with a crying child, and feel like lashing out — stop right now. Put your baby in a safe place, such as her cot, and take a breather. Count to ten. Even better, go outside for a minute or two, take some deep breaths and calm down. When you go back, comfort your baby and call your Well Child provider, midwife, GP or someone who can come and take over for a while, while you take a break.

✔ **Optimism:** Your life as a dad will be much easier if you try to see the funny side of things and take the 'glass is half full' position. At times you may be overwhelmed, stressed or totally exhausted and then it's easy to slip into thinking nature's way of organising procreation totally sucks. When you get annoyed and you're feeling negative, your child is likely going to pick this up and he might actively participate in making the situation even more difficult to handle. So shake yourself up and snap out of negativity. Try a different approach or do something to get in a better frame of mind. Chances are you'll get a more positive response from your child if you're more positive.

✔ **Passion:** Immerse yourself in all the tasks that need doing around your baby, toddler and child. By doing that you'll develop a passion for being a dad and you'll love being a dad with all your heart. Your child picks up on your passion and will be inspired to learn, develop and grow with you at an amazing pace. In Chapter 7 you find more information about your baby's amazing brain, how babies develop and how you can help their development as a dad.

✔ **Patience:** Patience is a virtue — especially for dads! Patience is your friend and makes things a lot easier when you've got kids around. Without patience, you would just pop with anger and there'd be tears all round, even for you. Most of the learning in the early years (and perhaps even throughout life) is achieved through constant and frequent repetition. As a father, you're in the business of facilitating that learning, which means repeating yourself a lot, such as reading *Where the Wild Things Are* for the fifty-third time, or telling your little champ not to pour his milk in the fish tank for the seventeenth time. As adults we're often not great at dealing with constant repetition because it's deemed boring or frustrating. By fostering your own patience you'll be able to elegantly deal with constant repetition and keeping your calm. As a result your child will get the support and encouragement he needs to learn. By being patient you avoid putting unnecessary pressure on your child to achieve something, which helps reduce frustration or feelings of inadequacy on his part.

✔ **Presence:** Taking time to be with your child and partner in a family is important. How you spend that time with your family is also important. Children have a finely tuned awareness of your attention. They can tell right away if you're actually engaging with them or merely present physically, with your mind miles away. Being present means you devote 100 per cent of your attention to your child and you focus on what he's doing. You don't watch TV, read the newspaper or get a bit of work done at the same time as playing with your child. If you're hanging out with your child, be fully present and 'in the moment'. For those dads who don't live with their children anymore, hanging out with your kids isn't as easy as it used to be, so we've included some info in Chapter 19 about spending as much time with your kids as possible. Also check out Chapter 9 for ideas on playing with your little champ.

Help, I'm a Dad!

We wrote this book because we were once new dads like you, starting out with mysterious new babies, wondering which way the nappy went on. Being a dad is a scary, wonderful, adrenalin ride of a trip and one many of you will judge your lives on. But at first it's hard to know where to turn and who to ask on the way.

Asking for directions

Okay, we know, men don't like asking for directions. That said, it helps to have a map or some cool navigation gadget. That's why we created www.diyfather.com. Think of www.diyfather.com as your Google Map to fatherhood and this book is your journey planner. So you're off to a good start. In some cases you might need specialist information which is impossible to cover in a general book or website, so we've compiled a list of resources (see the Appendix) and general tips for finding information.

Finding trusted organisations and sources of information

The people who know your baby best are you and your partner. You know what he likes and dislikes, what his little quirks are and when something doesn't seem right with him.

It can be tempting to want to 'fix' a particular problem a child has. Perhaps your baby is a bad sleeper during the day, or is colicky, or just won't take a bottle no matter how much you try. As adults we're used to having quick fixes and instant solutions for many problems in our day-to-day lives. For better or worse, with babies and children it's different. Many aspects of babyhood and childhood can't just be fixed. Things take time, perseverance and a laid-back attitude. To overcome a particular issue, you may have to try lots of different approaches until you find one that fits.

So where do you find these different approaches? Your first stop should be your Well Child provider or child health nurse. They have experience with all kinds of children, and can spend some time with your little one getting to know him and finding out what's going on. Another good place for information is the booklet that you would've been given when your baby was born. Depending on where you live, your health service would've given you a guide for basic baby and toddler care. These booklets often have good strategies for things like starting to feed your baby solid food, coping with crying and dealing with nappy rash, along with local services you can call in times of need. This book too has invaluable information on these topics.

See the Appendix for more organisations you can get in touch with should the need arise.

Internet research

The internet's a pretty handy thing. With just a few keystrokes, you can search for anything your heart desires. But beware — anyone can build a webpage, run a blog or comment in a forum, but may not have the expertise you're looking for. Gauge the quality of the information provided on websites by checking the organisation or individual who's responsible for it, their credentials, affiliation with recognised authorities and any ulterior motives they may have, such as financial, political or religious reasons.

On the other hand, checking out forums where other dads are sharing their problems and offering solutions can be handy. Just don't take as gospel that everything they say is authoritative. Remember that what works for one baby may not work for yours and vice versa.

As a starting point you can always check the following sites for useful and trustworthy information:

 ✔ **DIYFather** (www.diyfather.com): Written by dads for dads, the site contains information about all aspects of fatherhood from newborns to teenagers.

✔ **Plunket (**www.plunket.org.nz**):** Plunket in New Zealand has been looking after children under five for more than 100 years. Not only are Plunket nurses the most popular Well Child providers in New Zealand, Plunket runs parenting courses, can hook you up with a coffee group (called a PIN group, or 'Plunket in the neighbourhood') and has a car seat rental service.

✔ **Raising Children Network (**http://raisingchildren.net.au**):** This non-profit site is supported by the Australian government, the Royal Children's Hospital in Melbourne and the Parenting Research Centre. The site has articles on all aspects of looking after kids, from changing a nappy to the tricky questions of spoiling a baby and spotting allergies. There's a special section for dads.

If your baby or child is sick, avoid diagnosing her by searching the internet. After phoning a health service (listed in the Appendix), a real live GP is your first port of call should you be concerned about your baby's health. For more about common health problems, check out Chapter 14.

Turning to friends, colleagues and family

When you're a new father, everyone in the world is excited for you and gets a bit nostalgic for when their own children were little. They'll want to share with you their hard won pieces of advice and have an opinion on just about every aspect of looking after junior. Some of it will make sense to you, other gems will seem bizarre. You'll just have to add each pearl of wisdom to your pile of approaches to try should you need to. Ultimately you'll find out yourself whether something makes sense for your situation or not.

Turning to people who are close to you is an invaluable way to stay sane. If you're struggling, go hang out with a dad who's been through the wars himself. Looking at dads who've been through the crazy first weeks and months, and then come out the other side and want to have more kids, is a great way to get inspired and motivated for your own journey. You may at first think they've lost the plot, but really, these dads are no different from you. They've survived and as many dads say, 'every day just gets better'. And no, they haven't joined some terrible cult and become brainwashed — they've just had children and one way or another that tends to have a big impact on everyone.

Not long from now it will be you sitting down with a new dad, hearing tips and advice flow forth from your own mouth!

Starting your own group

We all know a new dad, or someone who's about to enter into the realm of fatherhood. Lots of dads meet at antenatal classes and keep in touch after that. Getting together to talk and share your experiences doesn't need to be a formal affair, with chairs in a circle and 'feelings'. It can be a beer while junior snoozes in his stroller or a coffee at a café with the little ones clamouring over each other on the floor. Getting together can be just a gathering at the park or watching a cricket match. Finding new dads to join you should be easy, but if you're feeling a bit isolated, give your midwife, Well Child provider or child health nurse a call to see if they have any dads living nearby on their books who you could catch up with. See Chapter 16 for great networking ideas.

Another easy way to get together with other dads is to use the mum networks. Ask your partner about speaking to other mums about a dad get-together. Before you know it a BBQ, picnic or stroller walk will have been magically arranged and you can take it from there.

Chapter 2

Getting Pregnant

In This Chapter

▶ Conceiving — the fun part

▶ Understanding what can go wrong

▶ Celebrating you're going to be a dad!

Deciding to start a family with your partner is one of the biggest decisions you'll make in your life (yes, bigger even than how to eat a cream egg or which footy team to support). For some, starting a family's not even a decision — it just happens. For others, just getting on the starting line of fatherhood is a journey, and there's still the pregnancy and birth to get through before you earn your dad wings.

Getting pregnant can be as easy as a few rolls in the hay or it can be a long struggle. But the important thing is that you approach the journey to parenthood together, and even if talking about fallopian tubes and sperm counts isn't your thing, you'll get through.

In this chapter you'll learn all about the adventurous and treacherous journey your sperm has to make before reaching his lady-in-waiting, the egg, and then the mission underway to get that egg into its safe haven, the uterus. You'll find out tips and tricks to getting pregnant, and what options are out there if things just aren't coming together. And finally, once things are underway, we'll guide you through the process of getting sorted for the coming months.

Here Comes the Fun Part

You've probably worked out where babies come from by now. Making babies is fun — we admit it and so it should be! There aren't many projects in life that start with a little nooky with your best girl. The rest of the journey may be exhausting, challenging or even frustrating at times, but at least this one first step can be all about a good time.

So go on, have sex, and lots of it. There aren't many manuals that tell you to do that, are there?

Conceiving naturally

Of course, in an ideal world, just making the decision to 'start trying' would result in an instant pregnancy. But nature didn't make it that easy. No sirree. There are lots of barriers between your sperm and her egg; in fact, it's a miracle any of us were born at all.

Of the millions of sperm a man ejaculates during sex, only about 100,000 make it past his partner's cervix at the entrance to the uterus, having run the gauntlet of acidic vaginal secretions (Figure 2-1 shows the female reproductive system). Of the 100,000 sperm that get past the cervix, only a measly 200 make it into one of the two *fallopian tubes* where a ready-to-be fertilised egg is waiting for a date — IF your timing is right and your partner is *ovulating* (producing an egg). Luckily there are many sperm to start with because such a small percentage of them survive the journey. In the end it's a merciless race to see which one of your sperm emerges as the champion and fertilises the egg by breaking into it.

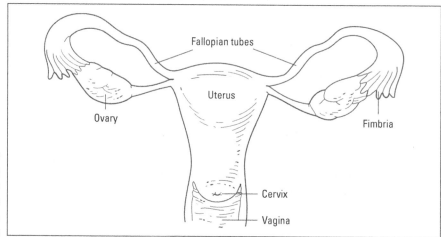

Figure 2-1:
The female reproductive system.

Once the egg is fertilised, it moves down the fallopian tube and into the *uterus* or womb. Cell division starts and before you know it (literally) the tiny cluster of cells begins nestling into the lining of the uterus wall, also known as the *endometrium* (see Figure 2-2). The cluster of cells then starts another long journey transforming into an *embryo*, and after eight weeks *gestation*, into a *foetus*. Bingo — your baby is on his way.

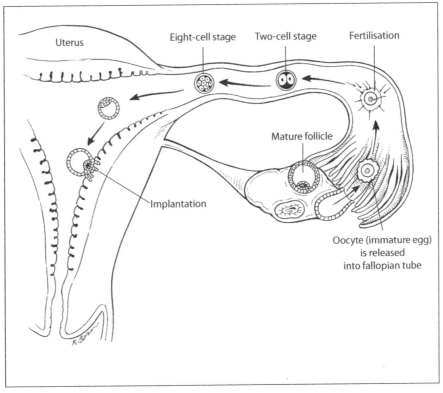

Figure 2-2:
The journey of the fertilised egg from the fallopian tubes to implantation in the lining of the uterus wall.

Improving the odds — pregnant tips and tricks

Like a lot of things, getting pregnant is a matter of having quality equipment and good timing. Nail those, and your chances of getting pregnant are pretty good.

But you can help things along by:

- ✔ **Being fighting fit:** It goes for prospective fathers as well as mothers that the healthier you are, the better for conception. Now's a good time to stop smoking, lay off the booze and other recreational drugs, get an exercise routine and eat well. It can't hurt to do those things anyway.

- ✔ **Letting gravity help:** Try to ensure your partner doesn't get straight up for the 'loo routine' after! Help those precious sperm get to their destination by keeping your partner horizontal with her pelvis tilted upwards. So cuddle up or do whatever it takes to keep her in the bed! Remember — every little bit helps.

✔ **Making a date:** *Ovulation* is when an egg is produced ready for fertilisation. It occurs on approximately day 14 of a 28-day menstrual cycle, with day one being the first day of your partner's period. So plan for that time to be your 'business time'. If your partner's cycle is irregular or you just need more reassurance, try an ovulation test kit to tell you if the time is right for lurve. Ovulation test kits are urine tests that detect hormones, like a pregnancy test kit.

✔ **Making sure your little fellows are in tip top shape:** Have a health check. Your doctor can check for any signs of sexually transmitted disease, any anatomical problems such as an undescended testicle and any other issues you may not be aware of.

✔ **Medication:** Prescribed medication as well as over-the-counter drugs can have a negative effect on mum or baby, so check with your doctor before taking anything during pregnancy.

✔ **Practising:** Have sex at least once a day when your partner is ovulating. If you feel a little put off by scheduled sexy time, just do it all the time — even in the off season. You never know what might happen. Being 'in the mood' for sex should also help conception! Finally, do some research on positions that aid conception and try them out — now that's an assignment you will enjoy!

Stress can affect your partner's ovulation, so try not to get too worked up about not getting pregnant straight away. Good things take time and worrying about it won't make things happen any faster! Wanting to get pregnant is a great excuse for having lots of sex, so just enjoy it for a while.

Your GP will probably advise your partner to take *folic acid* if you tell him you are trying for a baby. Taking folic acid won't improve your chances of getting pregnant but it will improve your chances of conceiving a healthy baby. See Chapter 3 for more information about the effects of taking folic acid on your unborn baby.

Conception's not happening

You've been trying for months. And trying. And trying. But conception's just not happening. You're getting sick of sex — as if you ever thought that would be a problem. But yep, you may be feeling exactly like sex is the last thing you'd like to do. As they say, too much of a good thing, etc. So don't beat yourself up over feeling sex-tired.

Couples under 35 years of age who have been having regular unprotected sex for a year and haven't become pregnant are said to be infertile, and those over 35 years old are deemed infertile after six months. If this is you, it could be time to talk to your doctor about getting some help.

Understanding What Can Go Wrong

Approximately one in six Australian and New Zealand couples have an issue with getting pregnant. There are a lot of factors in both partners that can cause infertility, but let's just look at what factors could be affecting you for the moment. Around one in six guys across Australia and New Zealand experiences infertility, and problems on the male front can account for 40 per cent of 'infertile' couples not being able to get pregnant. Low sperm counts, blockages to the sperm being ejaculated, poor sperm motility and sperm with an abnormal shape account for most fertility problems among guys.

Working out why conception hasn't happened

The following factors can contribute to infertility in men:

- ✔ **Anatomical problems** such as erectile dysfunction or blockage caused by a varicose vein, called a *varicocele*, that connects to the testicle

- ✔ **Exposure to harmful substances** and heavy metals

- ✔ **Lifestyle**, such as smoking and drug taking, which can slow sperm

- ✔ **Overheating sperm** by having frequent hot baths or wearing tight fitting underwear or tight trousers (even jeans have been blamed for this)

- ✔ **Sexually transmitted diseases** like gonorrhoea and chlamydia.

In 40 per cent of cases of male infertility, the cause may not be known. Either way, going for a checkup is a good thing to do. So be a man and own up to this task — if there's a problem at least you know and chances are you can do something about it. This reduces stress overall and your partner will definitely love you even more for having a checkup.

If the issue is not with you, but your partner, try to be aware that this can be a rather rough time for her and she's probably feeling like a bit of a failure. A lot of women believe that being able to carry and nurture a child is an essential part of being a woman and not being able to do this will leave her feeling inadequate. As her partner you're in the best position to help her feel just as whole a woman no matter what.

Exploring other ways to get pregnant

If your partner is having trouble falling pregnant, the first step is to talk to your doctor. In some cases, lifestyle factors may be what's holding you back and if the problem is a blockage, surgery could help. But in other cases, it may be time to consider *assisted reproductive technologies*, otherwise known as calling in the baby-making experts.

These are some of the treatments you may want to talk about with your doctor or specialist.

- **Artificial insemination (AI):** Semen is collected, given a bit of a clean up, then inserted into your partner's vagina, uterus or fallopian tubes. And yes, there may be a plastic cup and some dirty magazines involved — but hey, it's all for a good cause! For example, treatment is available for sperm with poor motility, meaning they can't get to the egg on their own and need a little help.

- **In vitro fertilisation (IVF):** Aka making a 'test tube' baby. Your partner will be given hormone treatments to kick start her ovulation. When she is ovulating, your partner will go through a procedure where her eggs are harvested. The collected eggs are then mixed with your sperm and given a chance to be fertilised. The fertilised eggs are then put into your partner's uterus, then you wait to see if they settle into the uterine wall.

- **Intracytoplasmic sperm injection (ICSI):** Sounds sexy doesn't it? Rather than mix sperm and egg and wait to see which eggs are fertilised, sperm is injected straight into the egg. As with IVF, the fertilised eggs are placed into your partner's uterus, where hopefully one implants.

Assisted conception

If you use IVF or other assisted reproductive technology, be aware of the increased chance of multiple births. According to a recent report in the UK, on average one in four IVF treatments result in multiple pregnancies compared with one in 80 naturally conceived pregnancies.

With IVF, sometimes two embryos are placed into the uterus, increasing the chances of having twins. In New Zealand, publicly funded IVF for women under 35 allows for only one embryo to be transferred at a time and some clinics in Australia won't allow you to transfer more than two embryos. This is because the chance of complications during pregnancy and birth, such as premature birth or *pre-eclampsia* is higher with multiple pregnancies than with a single baby.

Adopting

You've been having sex on schedule for years now and had the tests to make sure your little guys are not only plentiful but frisky as well. Your partner has been through multiple cycles of IVF but it just hasn't worked out and all the trauma of not getting pregnant is way past its use-by date. Perhaps you have decided to give up on having a child of your own.

Being unable to conceive a child doesn't have to mean you can't be a father. Adoption is another option you can look at.

Adopting a child means you take on the parental rights and responsibilities of looking after that child as you would if you were his biological father. That's a lifetime's responsibility. It can be easy to love your own child unconditionally and you have to decide if you're able to do that for a child who's not biologically yours. Most adoptions these days are open adoptions, which means the child and his birth parents stay in touch with each other.

The number of babies who are put up for adoption in New Zealand and Australia is much lower than it was a generation ago, and some couples look at adopting a child from overseas.

In New Zealand, adoptions are arranged through Child, Youth and Family. The adoption process is a lengthy one — there are police and background checks, information evenings to attend, and visits to your home from social workers. Once you have jumped through all the official hoops, your profile is put into a pool waiting to be selected by birth parents. This can take up to a year. Once you are chosen by birth parents, you have to wait at least 12 days after the birth of the child before you can take your new baby home with you.

- **Child, Youth and Family:** www.cyf.govt.nz/adoption
- **The Adoption Trust:** http://adoptionoption.org.nz
- **Open Adoption New Zealand:** www.opan.org.nz

In Australia, each state has different departments that look after adoption services. Check the service in your area:

- **ACT:** www.dhcs.act.gov.au/ocyfs/services/adoptions
- **New South Wales:** www.community.nsw.gov.au/parents_carers_and_families/fostering_and_adoption/adoption.html
- **Northern Territory:** www.health.nt.gov.au/Children_Youth_and_Families/Adoption/index.aspx
- **Queensland:** www.childsafety.qld.gov.au/adoption/
- **South Australia:** www.dfc.sa.gov.au/pub/Home/Familiesandyoungpeople/Adoption/tabid/199/Default.aspx
- **Tasmania:** www.dhhs.tas.gov.au/service_information/services_files/adoption_and_information_service
- **Victoria:** www.cyf.vic.gov.au/adoption-permanent-care
- **Western Australia:** www.community.wa.gov.au/DCP/Resources/Adoption

About two-thirds of couples dealing with infertility do have a baby through medical intervention, so medical intervention's definitely worth finding out about. Ask questions, even if it can feel a bit embarrassing at the start. By the way this is good training for going through birth — many more embarrassing moments to come!

OMG, You're Going to Be a Dad

Partner's boobs sore? Check. Period missed? Check. Thrown-up for no reason? Check. That could mean you're going to be a dad (either that or your partner just had a really stressful week). Either way — don't panic. If your partner is really pregnant you've got around nine months to sort out your new life. Say goodbye to how you currently live, farewell the days of tidy living rooms, sleeping-in and endless hours of self-indulgence, and say hello to fatherhood! So with that in mind it's really a good thing a baby takes around 40 weeks to grow from a tiny cluster of cells into a living, breathing, crying baby so you can get a few things in order, like confirming the pregnancy and figuring out the next steps.

Getting confirmation

Your partner will have no doubt raced off to the next pharmacy on the first suspicion of being pregnant. Over-the-counter pregnancy tests can sometimes give inaccurate results, so even if you have a positive result from a test, the first thing you'll want to do is make sure the pregnancy thing is actually happening.

Make an appointment with your GP, who will probably give your partner a urine test to see what levels of the hormone human chorionic gonadotropin (HCG) are present — that's the hormone responsible for the morning sickness and bone crunching tiredness your other half has to look forward to. If the test shows increased levels of HCG (that is, a positive result), your doctor may perform a gynaecological examination on your partner to check the physical signs of pregnancy more closely. But even your GP will only be able to provide a definite answer when the pregnancy symptoms are clear, which is around four weeks after fertilisation. So it might be a good idea to hold off telling the world — in fact, you may want to wait until the first scan anyway. Find out more about ultrasound scans and breaking the news to others in Chapter 3.

Once you've got confirmation of your pregnancy, a quiet (or loud) celebration with your partner is in order. However, it will have to be a celebration unlike most you've had in the past because alcohol, cigarettes and other drugs are definitely off the menu. But hey — you'll find plenty of other ways to have a good time!

Knowing what to do next

Welcome to the exciting new world of _antenatal_, or pre-birth, care. This was once strictly the domain of the pregnant woman and her doctor (usually male for some reason), but things have changed. For starters you as the dad are going to be much more involved (say yes!). But you also have more choices about who you team up with for the journey to parenthood. Your GP can refer you to maternity services in your area and generally you'll have the choice of paying for care from a private obstetrician or midwife, or staying in the public health system with a hospital or independent midwife.

The role of your carer of choice (known in New Zealand as a lead maternity carer or LMC, but not given a fancy name in Australia, though each state is slightly different) will guide you through the pregnancy, birth and early weeks of your baby's life. They monitor the baby's growth and wellbeing, and check for conditions such as pre-eclampsia and _gestational diabetes_ (see the Glossary for help with terms used in pregnancy). They also work with you to come up with a birth plan (see Chapter 3 for more details on birth plans), deliver your beautiful new baby and help you in the first few days after birth. This may include getting your partner started with breastfeeding or helping with basic baby care tasks such as bathing or changing a nappy. In general your lead maternity carer will be your 'go-to guy' if you have any questions, health issues or just need someone to talk to during the pregnancy. So check with them first before contacting other services or professionals.

Yes, a lot of attention during this time will be on the mum-to-be. But that doesn't mean you can't ask questions and have a say in the kind of care your partner and unborn child receive. You, as dad, have a very important role in the making of your family, so don't feel embarrassed or afraid to ask about anything you're not sure of.

Choosing a carer

You'll find a maze out there of midwives, birthing centres, obstetricians and hospitals. Knowing who does what can help you decide where you would like your baby to be born, and what kind of care you would like to receive during and immediately after birth.

- ✔ **GPs** are your general family doctor. They aren't specialists in antenatal care or childbirth, but in rural settings, they can work with the local hospital to provide maternity care.

- ✔ **Midwives** are trained health professionals who give antenatal care, deliver babies, help establish breastfeeding and stick around for about four to six weeks after the birth to help when you're unsure about your baby's health and wellbeing. Midwives also ensure the recovery of mums to a healthy state. Midwives take a holistic approach to pregnancy and birth, and often counsel you as a family, acknowledging not just the physical challenges of becoming new parents, but also your mental and social wellbeing. They see pregnancy and birth as a natural process, not a medical one, and can sometimes deliver your baby at home. While they are trained in their field, they are not doctors and do not perform *caesareans* or prescribe medication (although they can prescribe some specialist drugs). If you choose to go with a midwife and complications arise during the pregnancy or birth, they will most likely arrange for you to see an obstetrician in the public health system.

- ✔ **Obstetricians** are doctors who specialise in *obstetrics*, or the health of women and babies during pregnancy, birth and after the birth, called the *post partum* or *postnatal* period. They generally work in hospitals and are often the choice of couples experiencing complications during pregnancy, or who have had trouble getting pregnant. If you choose to use an obstetrician as your carer, you have to pay for it. In Australia the fees are around $2,000 for antenatal care, with extra fees for an initial consultation and postnatal visits. Some of the fees can be claimed back through a Medicare rebate. In New Zealand, expect to pay $120–150 for each consultation or a lump sum of around $2,500.

During the birth, midwives or hospital nurses will be on hand to monitor your baby's progress, but the obstetrician arrives only for the late stages and delivery itself. Obstetricians are primarily concerned with the physical health of the baby and mother, and won't help you with any non-medical baby care issues after birth. For example, they won't come to your house to show you how to best change your little nipper's nappy.

Talk with whoever you choose as your maternity carer about the options for where your baby can be born: At home, in hospital or in a birthing centre. The availability of birthing options depends on where you live and the carer you have.

Take time to find the right maternity carer for you. As well as getting referrals from your GP, a good place to start is with recommendations from your friends and colleagues. Make sure you're really happy with your carer and that you've got 'good chemistry'. Things can get pretty hectic during pregnancy or birth so make sure you're in good hands and you're comfortable with your carer's personal and professional style. If you're not happy with your carer, consider changing. Both of you must be 100 per cent comfortable with your choice of carer.

To find out what services and carers are available in your area, check out www.healthdirectory.org.au in Australia, or call toll free 0800 686 223 in New Zealand.

Things to do before morning sickness starts

Your life is about to change forever, so there's no time like the present to do some of those things you might have to trade in when your child is born.

Here's a bunch of things we suggest for celebrating your impending fatherhood while you still have the time:

- Get in loads of unprotected sex (with your partner!)
- Have the holiday of your lifetime. Holidaying won't be the same for the next 18 years or so — make the most of it now.
- Ponder your own experience growing up and which things you would like your child to experience
- Sleep in late, cook a leisurely brunch for you and your partner, or go for picnics
- Splurge on something indulgent, like going to a fancy restaurant or a day spa

✔ Start a journal, scrapbook or blog to document the months leading up to your child's birth and make it a memento to give your child when she's older (yes — plenty of good material for an embarrassing 21st birthday slideshow)

✔ Swot up on massage and practise on your partner. Invest in a few good quality aromatherapy oils and some sweet almond oil.

Chapter 3

Pregnancy: A Drama in Three Acts

In This Chapter

▶ Getting through the first trimester

▶ Enjoying the golden trimester

▶ Preparing for birth

*P*regnancy is a bit like *The Lord of the Rings* trilogy: It has a beginning where the scene is set and there's a bit of chaos, a middle where things calm down a bit and an end where everything comes to a head. The three distinct parts are called *trimesters* and each has its scary and great bits (just like in the films), such as the first time you hear your baby's heartbeat at a checkup, feel your baby kick inside mum's belly, or see your baby's squashed up body twisting and turning on an ultrasound screen.

The easiest part of becoming a dad is the pregnancy bit. Fortunately us dudes don't get the morning sickness and leg cramps, and we're not the ones who can't get out of bed without a crane. By the end of the pregnancy, you're probably going to be a bit over hearing about what aches this week, or what ridiculous food your partner has to have right now. But that's not to say there's nothing for us to do during pregnancy. Apart from all the preparations (which we talk about in Chapter 4) there's all the stuff you can do with your partner to help her out a bit and to get to know your offspring (yes — before he's even born!). Your partner definitely needs a strong man for the finale, 'birth' (which we cover in detail in Chapter 5).

In this chapter we take you through the three trimesters and show you what your baby is up to on the inside. We also take the mystery out of morning sickness and explain why your partner can't sleep even though she's exhausted.

Act One: The First Trimester

After the initial excitement that you're going to be a dad, the hard yards of supporting your partner through pregnancy begin. Of course supporting your partner's not actually 'that' hard, but you get to demonstrate your commitment to your new role when the initial ultrasound scan clashes with an all-important meeting you had arranged for that day.

Eating for two — or how to gain 15 kg in 40 weeks

During pregnancy your partner is literally 'making the baby' (in an assembly line kind of way) so good ingredients are essential for a quality end product, meaning that your unborn baby needs good food. Mum's healthy diet during pregnancy has a profound impact on the wellbeing of your little sprat even later in life, so encourage mum to eat well. For you this may mean laying off unhealthy options as well — there's nothing worse than tempting a pregnant woman with food she can't or shouldn't have.

Mum also needs good food to help her deal with the physical, mental and emotional changes and challenges she faces until your baby is born. The female body requires 10–12 per cent more energy when pregnant.

So, what is 'good food'? Your partner needs:

- **Six servings of fruit and vegetables:** An apple or tomato is a serving, so is half a cup of salad. Leafy green vegetables are particularly good as they contain folic acid, which helps prevent birth defects such as spina bifida (see Chapter 18 for more about birth defects).

- **Six servings of grains:** A cup of cooked pasta or rice, or a slice of wholegrain bread or a bread roll makes a serve. Wholegrains are particularly useful because — you guessed it — they contain folic acid. (On 13 September 2009 Australia introduced folic-acid enriched breadmaking flour. New Zealand has decided to stick with a voluntary system for increasing folic acid intake.)

- **Three servings of dairy:** A large glass of milk, a tub of yoghurt, or two slices of cheese are each a serve. Low fat milk helps control weight gain.

- **Two servings of protein:** An egg, or two slices of lean red meat, or two chicken drumsticks are one serving. Vegetarians can also get protein from nuts and seeds, legumes and tofu.

Folic acid, also called folate, is a B vitamin that is important to help prevent birth defects like spina bifida. Eating folate rich foods such as wholegrains, chickpeas, leafy green vegetables, and Marmite or Vegemite helps you reach the recommended daily allowance of 500 micrograms (0.5 milligrams). You can also top up your folic acid intake by using vitamin supplements. Check the recommended amount of folic acid as some women in a high-risk category need more.

Mum shouldn't eat certain foods because of the risk of bacteria, such as listeria, to which pregnant women and unborn babies are extremely vulnerable. So don't go treating your sweetie to:

- Any cooked food that's been in the fridge for more than 12 hours
- Cold deli meats or pâté
- Ready-made salads
- Soft cheeses like brie, ricotta and blue vein
- Sprouted seeds
- Sushi
- Unpasteurised milk.

Ask your GP, obstetrician or midwife for a comprehensive list of foods to avoid.

By the end of her pregnancy your partner may be really hanging out to eat a good bit of brie again, so a great way to celebrate the baby's birth may be to put together a platter of the things your partner's been missing out on for nine months. Start a 'foods to remember after birth' list.

Understanding the medical stuff

During the next nine months you're going to learn a whole new vocabulary and get to know your partner's insides more than you may want to. The Glossary lists terms to help you decipher what your carer of choice is talking about.

If you're unsure of where the various parts of the female reproductive system are located, refer to Figure 2-1 in Chapter 2.

Dealing with common side effects in the first trimester

For some unfortunate mums, the first three months of pregnancy are a downright drag, and can feel like an illness rather than the beautiful natural process of creating life. There's no glow and there's no bump to show off. Instead, as your baby makes itself comfy in your partner's uterus, he's making his presence known in other ways. Symptoms vary wildly from woman to woman, so there's no way of exactly knowing what's going to hit your partner. Here's a list of common complaints.

Morning sickness

Morning sickness typically involves feeling nauseous and vomiting. It's a common condition usually experienced during the first three months of pregnancy. Morning sickness doesn't pose a risk to the baby unless it's very severe. Morning sickness is caused by those crazy pregnancy hormones and usually subsides after 12 weeks. It can come on anytime but is usually worse in the morning because your partner's stomach is empty. At its worst, morning sickness is like having a hangover and being seasick at the same time, so no wonder your partner is off to the bathroom once again. Get used to it — bathrooms also become a prominent feature in the last trimester, albeit for different reasons (your partner needs to wee every ten minutes because the baby puts pressure on her bladder).

One thing that makes morning sickness worse is getting up on an empty stomach, so try having a plate of dry crackers or toast with Marmite or Vegemite ready for your partner to nibble when she first wakes up. Other tips include eating smaller portions more often during the day, increasing intake of carbohydrates and reducing intake of fats, and stimulating pressure points on the inner arm just above the wrist crease.

Morning sickness can get so bad that your partner may become dehydrated. The symptoms aren't always easy to spot so double-check with your midwife, obstetrician or GP if your partner is having a really rough time with morning sickness.

Exhaustion

Your baby's growing rapidly and taking a lot of your partner's energy. Getting through a day at work may be more than your partner's up to, so you can score lots of points if you take on more of the household chores, prepare meals and do the things your partner's not up to doing.

'Dog nose'

Pregnancy does strange things to a woman, not least of all her ability to smell everything. Your partner can walk into a room you left three hours ago and smell your aftershave. She'll be sensitive to most smells, especially things like perfume, food and petrol fumes — they may even make her vomit — so if you're heating up your favourite garlic bread (the one with extra garlic and blue cheese), open a window or put on the rangehood.

Tender breasts

If you have ventured into the odd strip bar in your student days you should be familiar with the following concept: 'You can look, but you don't touch'. For many expectant dads the same concept now applies to their wives' breasts. Pregnancy hormones cause your partner's breasts to become a bit bigger, but they'll be sore and tender. So while you may be admiring your partner's new shapely form, it may pay to wait until she invites you to party before gatecrashing her bra.

Moodiness

Blame it on the hormones, because your partner hasn't turned into a grumpy, unpredictable monster, she's just at the mercy of her body. Go easy on her if she's a little ratty right now. Talk to your partner and figure out a way to communicate when she's in one of her moods, because *progesterone*, the hormone responsible for all this, isn't going to go away for a long time yet.

Though your partner's feeling crap, this is your chance to shine. You can treat your partner and make her feel special in lots of simple ways at this difficult stage. Come home with a little gift (baby socks are great), shout her a pregnancy massage (along with some nice oils to battle stretch marks), or get a nice DVD for the night. If your partner bites your head off for trying, don't take it personally. Try again next week.

Activities to avoid

Some activities are not recommended for mums-to-be, such as:

- Going on rides in theme parks (because of the acceleration the body experiences during the ride)

- Extreme sport and adventure sport (such as bungee jumping, parachuting and wild water rafting)

- Dyeing her hair (because of the chemicals used in dyes)

- Travelling on a plane (in case the baby decides to arrive early, although this is mostly relevant towards the end of the pregnancy)

For a comprehensive list of things to avoid, ask your GP, obstetrician or midwife.

What's your baby up to?

Between 6 and 12 weeks, your baby grows from 6 millimetres long to 5.5 centimetres long (see Figure 3-1). In other words your baby has grown 900 per cent in six weeks. No wonder your partner is so tired.

During this time, your baby's organs take shape, with the heart beating from about six weeks. Though neither you nor your partner can feel it yet, your little tadpole (they look like that at the beginning) is moving around in there. She's floating in amniotic fluid in her amniotic sac. The placenta is developing to act as life support for your baby.

Your first ultrasound scan, which typically happens between 6 and 12 weeks after conception, is a pretty big deal for a number of reasons. First you get to see your baby for the first time ever and it's an amazing sight. Second in some cases your doctor may unfortunately advise you that something isn't quite right. This happens in about one in six cases and may result in miscarriage or termination of the pregnancy for medical reasons. Your doctor typically prepares you before the scan, but talking about this scenario with your partner before you have your first scan is a good idea.

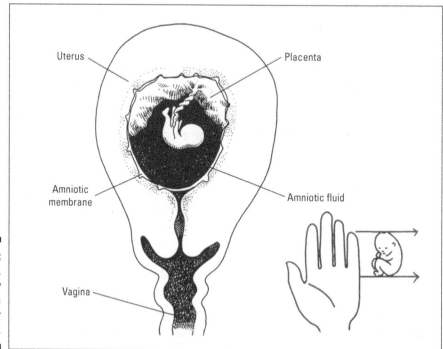

Figure 3-1:
At 12 weeks, your baby is about the size of your little finger.

The above material has been reproduced with the permission of the NSW Department of Health from its publication Pregnancy and Birth.

Two (or more) for the price of one

You've just found out, through the magic of an ultrasound scan, that you're going to be a father of not one, but two babies at once. You're freaking out. Being dad to two at the same time is hard work, but of course not unmanageable. Being dad to two at the same time is a great opportunity to be twice the man (at least) of what you are today!

Having twins, triplets or more babies at once is called a *multiple birth*. Multiple births happen in two ways. Identical or *monozygotic* twins are formed when the fertilised egg divides into two very early on, and two separate embryos develop. Non-identical twins, also known as fraternal or *dizygotic* twins, occur when two eggs are fertilised at once in the fallopian tubes. Triplets can sometimes be a combination with two identical twins and a fraternal twin, but not always.

In pregnancy, twins are more at risk of arriving prematurely (38 weeks for twins is considered full term) and having a low birth weight. Your carer will guide you through the intricacies of multiple birth and will probably monitor your partner's wellbeing throughout the pregnancy more carefully.

Unfortunately it means that the side effects of being pregnant are more pronounced, so morning sickness may be more intense, weight gain faster and earlier in the pregnancy, and things like varicose veins, heartburn and shortness of breath more pronounced. See 'Dealing with common side effects' for the last two trimesters in the rest of this chapter. See also Chapter 2 about IVF and multiple births.

Act Two: The Second Trimester

The morning sickness is waning, your partner is feeling a little less exhausted and she's beginning to show a bit of a bump — welcome to the second trimester. Weeks 13–28 are usually the best period of pregnancy. You start to see your partner's body change as the baby grows and feel the baby's first kicks by putting your hand on her belly — a pretty amazing feeling.

Because 80 per cent of miscarriages happen in the first 12 weeks, many parents don't announce they're pregnant until the second trimester.

Now is also the time to ask about a *nuchal fold* test to check for potential birth defects, especially if your partner is older than 35. A nuchal fold test aims to determine the likelihood of your baby being born with *Down Syndrome*.

Enjoying the golden trimester

Most pregnant women feel a lot better throughout the second trimester. As your partner's belly is getting bigger, the reality that you're going to have a child really sets in. Exciting times! Towards the end of the second trimester your partner probably also starts feeling those first kicks and bumps. Typically this happens around 18–20 weeks. They may be hard to spot at first, as that little foot tries to get in touch with you through all those abdominal muscles, but feeling those kicks for the first time is a pretty magic moment.

You see your partner transform as the baby grows, and she may start planning what to buy (not more clothes!) and how to decorate the baby's room. This is called 'the nesting instinct' and you pretty much have to go with it. When it comes to purchasing things for the baby, however, dads are hugely important as we tend to 'keep it real'. Many household budgets are under a lot of pressure when the baby arrives and with your partner being high on hormones you should go shopping together to avoid a local financial crisis. See Chapter 4 for an overview of what you actually need to buy.

Around 20 weeks, your midwife, obstetrician or GP may send you for an ultrasound scan to make sure the baby's bits are all in the right place and that things are progressing smoothly. If you can't wait another 20 weeks to find out your baby's flavour, you can usually find out at this scan, unless junior has his legs crossed!

Sex during pregnancy is absolutely OK and apparently is even good for the baby as well. Bonus! The second trimester might be the best time to share a bit of passion although it depends greatly on how your partner is feeling throughout pregnancy. By the way, it's not out of the question to have sex almost up until labour, depending on how your partner feels. Couples have been known to use sex to bring on labour (see Chapter 5 for more about bringing on labour).

Understanding more medical stuff

Your caregiver will start to feel for the baby at each checkup by asking your partner to lie down. They also use a *Doppler* or a foetal heartbeat monitor to listen for the baby's heartbeat, which at a remarkable 120–160 beats per minute sounds like a dance party's going on in there. Your caregiver also checks the *fundal height*, or the length of the uterus as it progresses into the abdomen.

Your midwife, obstetrician or GP also routinely asks your partner for a urine sample to check for protein in her urine. Blood pressure also gets the once over too as high blood pressure and protein in urine are both indicators of pre-eclampsia.

Dealing with common side effects in the second trimester

Most changes during this trimester are a result of the growing size of your baby. They include:

- **Back pain.** This is perhaps one of the most common complaints of pregnant women and is caused by the growing weight of the baby, additional strain on the spine and a change in the centre of gravity which the body needs to adjust for.

- **Constipation.** This is a common problem during pregnancy. The main reason for constipation in the second trimester is an increase in the hormone progesterone, which slows the movement of food through the digestive tract. Later in pregnancy the problem of constipation is likely to be made worse by the pressure of the growing uterus on the intestines. Taking iron supplements, which many pregnant women take, can also make constipation worse.

- **Heartburn.** This burning sensation in the middle chest is caused by the hormone progesterone which softens the uterus so it can stretch, but also softens the oesophagus, allowing acid to come back out. So if your partner complains about heartburn, don't be offended — your cooking isn't the cause.

- **Leg cramps.** These seem to plague pregnant women more at night, but no-one's sure what causes them. Blame the hormones, we reckon.

- **Softening ligaments.** The ligaments in the pelvis stretch, which widens the pelvis to prepare for birth. It can give your partner a floating sensation in the joints and cause sharp stabbing pains when she stands up too quickly or rolls over in bed. This is called *round ligament pain* and is nothing to be worried about, although knowing about this pain is good.

You can't do much about these things, other than continue to be a superstar with your support, love and encouragement.

What's your baby up to now?

At 24 weeks, your baby is about 21 centimetres from head to bottom (see Figure 3-2). She also has her calendar full doing these amazing things:

- ✔ **Getting her eyes done:** Pigmentation in the iris develops. If your baby is of European descent, she'll be born with blue eyes that may change colour in the months after birth. Maori, Aboriginal, African, Indian, Pacific Island, and Asian babies can be born with brown or blue eyes, and eye colour can also change with time.

- ✔ **Having a facial:** Your baby's using the world's best moisturiser, *vernix*, a waxy coating that keeps her skin from getting wrinkled as she floats around in fluid all day. She'll also grow fingernails, hair and eyebrows.

- ✔ **Listening to music and your voice:** Your baby can hear now, but won't know what she's hearing for a long time yet, though research suggests that babies know their parents' voices when they're born from what they hear in the womb. Amazing isn't it?

- ✔ **Preparing to rock and roll:** At the end of the second trimester your baby is almost done growing and developing all external and internal organs.

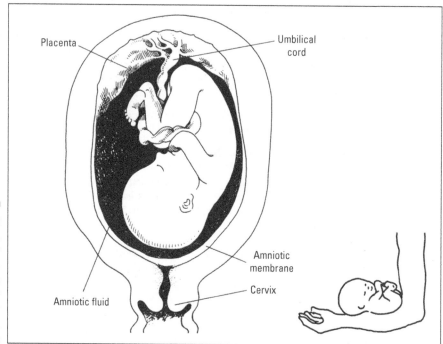

Placenta

Umbilical cord

Figure 3-2: At 24 weeks, your baby is about the length from your elbow to your wrist.

Amniotic membrane

Cervix

Amniotic fluid

Act Three: The Third Trimester

You're on the final lap now. Don't get too excited though, you still have some hoops to jump through. Start thinking about childbirth education classes, which your carer can refer you to. These classes can be extremely valuable in terms of educating you about the process of birth, can answer any burning questions you might have and you can meet other prospective dads who are just as excited — or terrified — as you are. Lots of people go on to keep in touch with their classmates as their babies grow. In New Zealand antenatal classes are mostly provided by Parents Centre and Plunket or your local hospital.

A range of public and private providers exist in Australia. If you're having your baby at a hospital, check if they provide antenatal classes. Ask your carer, check with Medicare or speak to your friends or colleagues who have already been to one.

Checking with someone who has already attended an antenatal class you are interested in is definitely a good idea. Some classes are more dad-inclusive than others. For example, some providers split the group into mums and dads to talk about specific issues or situations. Having a guys-only session as part of an antenatal class is great as it provides the ideal opportunity for some 'man talk' about pregnancy, babies and fatherhood.

Making choices about the birth

The time's come to start looking forward to the The Birth. That baby is going to have to come out. In ye olde days, birth was a straightforward thing — woman goes into labour, sheets are torn into strips, water is boiled, there's a lot of yelling, then baby comes out. These days, with our technology and greater awareness of the anatomy of birth, you'll be faced with a lot of choices concerning how junior enters the world. Home birth or hospital birth? No drugs, or all the drugs you can get? With lots of family, a video camera and updates on Twitter? Or just your partner, the person delivering the baby and you?

First up to think about — and possibly foremost in your partner's mind right now — are pain relief options. There's a swing towards having as little intervention or to be as natural and drug-free as possible during labour and birth. But ultimately the pain relief options really depend on your partner's preferences. Towards the end of pregnancy she's probably grappling with the idea of what labour is going to be like and the pressure to be as stoic about it as possible. Supporting your partner and standing by whatever decisions she makes regarding her body and the birth of your baby goes a long way towards making it easier on her.

Let's have a look at what's on offer:

- ✔ **Drug-free:** Heat packs, massage, breathing exercises and being in water may help relieve the pain of labour. Keeping active during the birth and avoiding lying on her back can also help your partner manage the pain.

- ✔ **Epidural:** An epidural is a local anaesthetic injected into the spinal column. It blocks out all pain and is often used during caesareans so the mother can be awake when her child is born.

- ✔ **Gas:** A mix of laughing gas or nitrous oxide and oxygen has been used for decades and is a safe way to relieve pain during labour. It sometimes makes women feel a bit nauseous.

- ✔ **Pethidine:** A strong pain reliever, pethidine can cause drowsiness in both mother and baby, though usually without any long-term effects. Pethidine can also cause nausea.

Another big decision is where and how to have the baby. No doubt your partner has researched all options by now. Unfortunately the 'I just want to wake up in the morning and my baby will be here' option doesn't exist. She'll probably let you know what her next best option is — or you might ask her about it. The most common scenarios are:

- ✔ **Birth centres or free-standing birth centres:** Having your baby in a special birth centre run by midwives might provide you with additional options to try particular birthing techniques or varying positions during labour. However, birth centres generally take a non-interventionist approach and don't provide epidurals.

- ✔ **Home birth:** This option has become more popular. You need the support of a community or private midwife. If your partner wants a water birth you can hire special equipment to facilitate the birth at home.

- ✔ **Hospital birth:** Most women in Australia and New Zealand opt for a hospital birth. Some hospitals provide extra facilities for water births or natural (as in no pain relief) births.

 Talk with your carer about your options and discuss the pros and cons of each one. Don't be afraid to ask questions and be sure you know everything you need to be confident about the upcoming birth. As your lady's number one support person, you need to know what's going on just as much as she does.

 Your birth option may also depend on whether you go through the public health system or use private health insurance. In many states in Australia home birth is available only for low-risk pregnancies and through private health care.

Understanding even more medical stuff

As you head into the home stretch of pregnancy, you have more checkups with your midwife, obstetrician or GP, and you and your partner work out a *birth plan*. This sounds like an oxymoron, as birth is one process that you just have to surrender to — you have very little control over what happens. Lots of pain relief options and delivery methods are available, so be clear with your midwife, obstetrician or GP about which of these you're keen on and which you're not. That's what a birth plan is — a clear understanding of how you would like things to go so that the person delivering your baby knows your wishes.

Keep an open mind about how the birth will go. If you've planned for a nice water birth at home, be prepared that if things don't go as smoothly as you would like you may have to be transferred to hospital. Or if you've said there's absolutely no way my woman needs pain relief, she may be yelling for an epidural in the first five minutes. The ultimate aim is delivering your baby safely into the world with the least amount of anxiety and trauma on your beloved so you set off on your parenting path on the healthiest and safest foot.

Your midwife, obstetrician or GP checks the baby's position and makes sure she's in the right place. During this trimester your baby makes her way down head first towards the cervix ready for birth, a process called *engaging*. If she has her feet pointed down towards the cervix, she's in a *breech* position. If she stays breech until the birth, chances are your carer will recommend a caesarean birth.

Your caregiver may also take swabs from your partner's vagina to test for *group B strep*, which is a bacteria that can infect your baby as she's being born. If traces of it are discovered, your partner will probably need to be on an antibiotic drip during labour.

Dealing with common side effects in the third trimester

By now the golden glow of the second trimester is getting a bit tarnished. As your partner nears her due date, your baby is starting to take over her body — literally. Her internal organs are getting pushed and shoved all over the place and her abdominal muscles have split in the middle to make way for that wide load she's carrying. Your partner may even waddle already, as her relaxed ligaments widen her pelvis.

Some common complaints during this time include:

- ✔ **'I've got baby brain':** Pregnant women often feel like they're losing their marbles. They tend to forget stuff, don't remember simple or frequent activities, and appear to be running around like headless chickens. These symptoms are believed to be caused by hormones, lack of sleep and the general toll pregnancy takes on the body.

- ✔ **'I can't sleep but I'm so tired all the time':** Insomnia is one thing most mothers-to-be in the third trimester agree on. Her joints might be sore, back aching, with a baby that kicks all night and heartburn to boot. Your partner may also need to get up for a wee every five minutes. Lying on her back to sleep can put pressure on the *vena cava*, an important artery feeding the heart, so she has to lie on her side at night, and turning over in bed can be a little trying. You could suggest she try a pillow under her right side, where the vena cava is, which tilts the weight of her body off the artery.

- ✔ **'I've got varicose veins, and worse — piles':** The third trimester can be hard on a girl. She's getting rounder by the day, may waddle, she's tired, and not getting enough sleep is making her grumpy. And then haemorrhoids — also known as piles — turn up and make her feel downright miserable. She's not feeling like a radiant mother-to-be anymore, she's feeling like a veiny, fat frump. Varicose veins and piles can be caused or made worse by the weight of the baby on her body, so get her to take it easy and rest lots.

- ✔ **'My ankles are swollen and I'm big as a house':** As well as carrying a rapidly growing baby around, your partner's retaining fluid and has more blood flowing through her body. In hot weather or after standing for long periods this blood collects in her ankles. Your partner should put her feet up whenever she can and avoid salty foods. A few foot rubs from dad wouldn't go amiss either. Calling her 'fatso' or 'chubby' does not go down well even if you think she looks hilarious.

- ✔ **'Why doesn't anything I eat taste right?':** Blame that pesky progesterone — along with everything else it causes food cravings. Finding anything that tastes just how she wants it to be may be very hard for your partner, and predicting what she needs is almost impossible. We suggest that you roll with it and keep up your partner's spirits by suggesting lots of different options.

Taking slow walks together, reading or singing to the baby in bed at night, making lists of potential names together, and taking photos of that burgeoning belly make for a good time and help support each other as the big day approaches. These are some of the last days that your family numbers just the two of you, so take time to be with your partner right now.

Preparing for Project Push — are we there yet?

Yes, almost! Your baby's just putting the finishing touches on before making his glorious entry into the world. He's been keeping busy by:

- **Beefing up:** At the start of the third trimester, your baby weighed about 750 grams, but by the end, he's his birth weight — an average 3.4 kilograms. The most rapid weight gain happens in the final few weeks.

- **Getting in position for take-off:** All going well, your baby is head down with his feet under your partner's ribcage (see figures 3-3 and 3-4). No wonder she's uncomfortable.

- **Practise makes perfect:** He's been rehearsing for his big entrance by practising breathing. He's also developing his bones to be ready for action, opening his eyes and sucking his thumb.

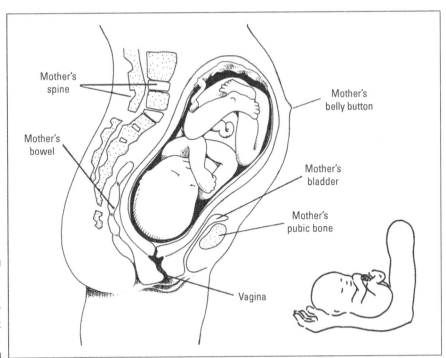

Figure 3-3: At 32 weeks your baby is about 25 cm long.

The above material has been reproduced with the permission of the NSW Department of Health from its publication Pregnancy and Birth.

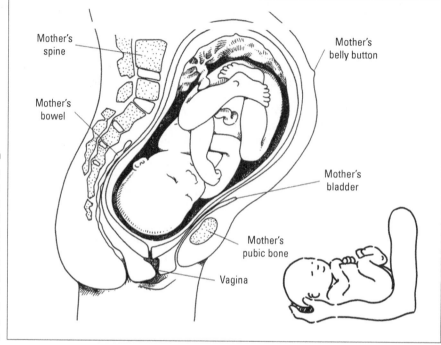

Figure 3-4:
At 40 weeks your baby is about 33 cm long from head to bottom and is head down, ready to make his entry.

Mother's spine

Mother's belly button

Mother's bowel

Mother's bladder

Mother's pubic bone

Vagina

The above material has been reproduced with the permission of the NSW Department of Health from its publication Pregnancy and Birth.

Chapter 4

Preparing for a Baby in the House

In This Chapter

▶ Finding out what to buy

▶ Getting organised around the house

▶ Choosing nappies, creams and baby consumables

▶ Making sure you're all set for the big day

*F*ew things change the way you live as much as welcoming a baby into your life. Having a baby is like having a house guest who never cleans up after himself, cries a lot and has more needs than the two of you put together. Adding a baby to the family is not as simple as clearing out the spare room for him to sleep in. He needs stuff: clothes, bedding, nappies, all sorts of things you need to think about that become part of your daily life as a father.

As you count down to your baby's birth, you need to get things done to avoid hassles down the line — get those bags packed ready for the hospital, get the bassinet and a car seat sorted and be ready to go at a moment's notice. When he arrives, chances are you won't have a lot of time for decorating the baby's room, or shopping for socks, so it's best to get those things out of the way now.

In this chapter you discover the ins and outs of what to look for when buying things like nursery furniture, strollers, nappies, clothes and toys. You find out what nappy rash is and how to prevent it, and how to help your baby when he's teething. We give you lots of checklists for everything you need to do before the birth and what you need to take with you to the hospital or have prepared for a home birth.

Getting the Right Gear

Who would have thought a baby would need so much stuff? Getting set up for a new person in your house takes a bit of thought — and a mountain of cash if you're not careful. Rather than going out and buying every bit of gear the baby shops say you must have, we tell you what you really need.

To keep costs down, send the word around among your co-workers that you're having a baby. They may have cots, bassinets and strollers they're no longer using. You can completely kit out a nursery for very little or even for free.

Clothes and shoes

Baby clothes come in more shapes and styles than you would have thought possible. Check out what works for you before you spend up large. As well as the usual T-shirts, singlets, jerseys/jumpers and trousers that children and adults wear, babies have these kinds of clothes to keep them decent.

- **Bodysuits** are long or short sleeved T-shirts that do up around the baby's crotch with domes (clips or press-studs). They are handy for keeping everything tucked in so bub's tummy doesn't get chilly. They're also great during the summer months when a short sleeved bodysuit can be worn by itself without pants or as pyjamas. The only drawback with bodysuits is that if your baby is fully dressed and has a nappy leak, you have to take everything off to change her, rather than just her pants or skirt.

- **Stretch-n-grows** are all-in-one trousers and tops that either dome up the legs and front, or zip up. They're like an overall with socks. Some dome up the back, which is really inconvenient and we recommend steering clear of them. Most have feet, but you can get stretch-n-grows without feet for summer.

- **Sleeping bags** are like stretch-n-grows with sleeves but no legs, just a sack covering your baby's legs and feet. They're handy in winter when your child is able to roll over and kick around in bed. Your child inevitably kicks off her blankets so having her wear a sleeping bag means she can't get cold. Sleeping bags are also good because if her legs are bare under the sack, you can get to her nappy more easily and disturb her less at night.

The following list is a guide to what you should have ready to go for your newborn baby. You can customise your list as you find your dad-legs and suss out which items work well for you. You can also tweak the list to suit the seasons. As a general rule, baby clothes should be loose-fitting, made with breathable and soft fabric, and easy to open and close. Remember you can go through three to four sets of clothes in a day because of nappy leaks and baby spew. You need:

- ✔ Lots of singlets, either cotton or woolly for winter.

- ✔ Four bodysuits, both long and short sleeved, or long or short sleeved tops if bodysuits don't appeal.

- ✔ Four pairs of trousers. Overalls are pretty cute but make sure they have openings in the legs so you don't have to take the whole lot off to change her nappy.

- ✔ Four stretch-n-grows or sleeping bags for night time. Check that they are cotton, rather than polarfleece or microfleece, as those fabrics aren't breathable and she may get overheated.

- ✔ Two jackets for going out.

- ✔ Two cardigans or wraparound jerseys that don't need to go over her head.

- ✔ Lots of pairs of socks — one is always getting lost.

- ✔ Four hats, preferably made of a lycra cotton mix so they stretch, or lovely soft wool if they're handmade.

- ✔ Lots of bibs with either domes or Velcro. Bibs with ties can prove too fiddly.

- ✔ Two pairs of slippers that have elastic around the heel. In our experience these stay on better than other slip-ons. Babies don't need shoes until they're walking.

- ✔ Two pairs of gloves or mittens. Get some that you can tie around the wrist because babies tend to lose them (intentionally and unintentionally).

Here are some tips for selecting clothes and getting your baby all dressed up.

- ✔ Most babies get grumpy at having clothes pulled over their heads. Avoid anything that doesn't have a few domes opening at the shoulder or an envelope-style neckband (two overlapping pieces of fabric that stretch easily when put over her head) to make pulling the clothing over her face painless.

- ✔ When putting on a stretch-n-grow, cardigan or any other top that doesn't go over your baby's head, it's a good idea to lay it on the surface you're dressing your baby on before you lay her down. Then all you have to do is slide her arms into the sleeves, dome her up and you're good to go.

- ✔ Avoid anything that has a back opening. Your baby spends a lot of time lying on her back in the early months and it can't be comfortable having domes under you. They're also tricky to get on when you're getting her dressed.

- ✔ Avoid anything that looks too fiddly. Some babies really dislike getting dressed and trying to do up silly little ribbons when she's having a meltdown isn't our idea of a good time.

- ✔ If your baby arrives in winter, look for clothes that have folds sewn into the ends of sleeves — they're actually mittens. These are great to keep your bub from scratching herself with those needle-like newborn nails.

- ✔ If in doubt on sizing, buy clothes that are too big. At least you know junior will grow into them.

- ✔ If you've been given a lot of hand-me-downs, be aware that the fire retardant in some clothing may be worn and will not be as effective as it is in new clothes.

- ✔ You will be given a tonne of new clothing as presents, so if you find you have too much, don't be afraid to take it back to the shop and swap it for something you can use in the future, like the next size up.

- ✔ Dark colours show baby spew much more than light colours, but light colours show baby poo much more! Just go with what colours you like.

Handling a baby during the first few months can feel a bit tricky because she can appear really fragile. So think about what steps you need to go through to put on a particular item of clothing. If the clothes seem complicated to close or open, don't buy them. Don't be afraid to try out the garment in the shop with a baby doll.

How many 0s can you go?

If we lived in a perfect, logical world, clothing labels would give an age range to show the size of the item, but until he's one, your little one will be less than zero, or many zeros. Here's how it works:

- ✔ 0000: birth to three months, or newborns under four kilograms

- ✔ 000: three to six months, or babies four to six kilograms

- ✔ 00: six to nine months, or babies between six and eight kilograms

- ✔ 0: 9 to 12 months, or eight to ten kilograms

- ✔ 1: 12 months, or babies over ten kilograms

If your baby is premature look for more 0s when you're buying clothes. Clothes are often labelled '00000' or the label says 'premature'.

Your baby won't need shoes for a while yet. A good time to start looking for shoes is when your little champ starts crawling. Studies show that going barefoot is best — but that's not always practical. For a baby who isn't walking yet, soft soled shoes with an elasticised heel work well and protect toes from being scraped on the floor or ground. But as he starts walking, his footwear needs to change gradually towards firmer shoes.

Here are some tips and tricks for buying your toddler's first pair of shoes:

- ✔ Let your baby walk around in the shoe just like you would if you were trying on new shoes for yourself.

- ✔ Choose shoes with one centimetre of wiggle room at the front and end, but no more than that — he'll trip over his own feet.

- ✔ Look for shoes that are as similar to bare feet conditions as possible. He doesn't need arch support at this stage!

- ✔ Babies' feet get hotter and sweat more than adults' feet, so choose natural breathable materials rather than synthetics.

- ✔ Many cheap children's shoes give out in the toes — toddlers are always crawling on the ground, then are up on their feet, using their toes to leverage themselves. Make sure the shoes have extra sturdy stitching in the toes for long wear.

- ✔ Soles that grip are important too, as junior needs all the help he can get to not slip when he's learning to walk.

Toys

When your baby is born, all he does for a while is poo, pee, eat, cry, sleep and gaze benignly at things. So he doesn't need an electronic ABC, or a racing car set, or a mini piano. What he needs are things that give him a real sense of the world he's just come into — new sights, shapes, textures, smells, sounds and sensations. These can easily be provided by spending time with your baby, singing to him, and touching his skin and fingers with textures like an old comb, fabric, your hair, leaves, the cat's fur — you get the idea. As he begins to grasp and brings his hands together, things like a rattle or a chain of plastic rings can keep him fascinated for ages.

When your baby starts teething, he looks for things to put in his mouth to push against his gums to relieve the discomfort. Many toys double as teething rings and aids.

Some good ideas for baby toys include:

- ✔ **Cloth books.** Look for ones with flaps or textures sewn into them.

- ✔ **Plastic keys.** For some reason babies love your car keys, so give them their own set. These are great for teething too.

- ✔ **Play gyms.** Play gyms are mats with arms curved over the top where you can attach colourful objects like paper flowers, branches from the garden, soft toys and strings with shells for your baby to look at as he lies on the mat. Just make sure he can't pull anything down that he shouldn't be chewing on. Nothing is safe from his gummy mouth once he's got the hang of his hands.

- ✔ **Rattles.** You can buy rattles or make your own from old plastic containers filled with rice. Ensure the lid is on securely.

- ✔ **Soft toy animals.** Avoid fluffy toys with long hair or fur.

Less is more when it comes to toys — no matter what the toy manufacturers tell you, nothing beats spending time playing and exploring with your baby. Brain development is assisted by appropriate stimulation and human contact.

To make sure toys are safe for your little one, check for any parts that may come off and become a choking hazard, as well as toxins, such as toxic paints. Inevitably your little champ will try to put all toys (and most other things) into his mouth, so make sure they're safe to put in his mouth.

Strollers, prams and buggies

Prams have evolved into high-tech, fold-at-the-touch-of-a-button contraptions that can double as shopping trolleys, have water bottle holders, be taken off-road and cook you lunch (just kidding). Baby stores are packed with different models of prams and strollers. A pram and/or stroller is often one of the bigger purchases you make in this fatherhood game, so shop around.

Some research suggests that babies in buggies that face towards you rather than out into the world are better as your tyke is less stressed. Facing each other encourages more talking, laughing and social interaction.

These are some of the things you need to look out for:

- ✔ Can you dismantle the pram and put a car seat or bassinet attachment on it in the early months, making it easier to transfer junior from bed or car seat?

- ✔ Does the stroller come with a fitted sunshade and fitted weather cover?

✔ Does the stroller fit through the door of your favourite café? Can it be easily manoeuvred through a packed supermarket? If you're looking at three-wheeled buggies, make sure the front wheel isn't fixed so you can manoeuvre it easily.

✔ How easy is it to adjust the back of the seat? Can bub lie down flat in it for sleeping? Can the back be raised up high for a growing child to see more of the world around them?

✔ How easily will the pram fit in your car boot or in your house? Some models can be bulky.

✔ How easily does the pram fold down? The last thing you want is to be pulling levers all over the place when you've got a fussy baby to deal with. If you're travelling by bus, strollers that can be folded down with only one hand are ideal so you don't have to hand your baby to a total stranger while you wrestle with getting the stroller onto the bus.

✔ How well does the stroller support your child's growing spine and neck?

✔ How well will the stroller survive if you want to take it on unpaved walkways or bush walks?

Car seats

Getting a cute mobile for your baby's cot is optional, buying a stroller that you can take mountain running is optional — but using a car seat for your most precious cargo is not. Yeah sure, you free ranged in your parents' car when we were little and lived to tell the tale, but sadly some children haven't. So take advantage of the fact things have evolved somewhat since our day and use a car seat for every journey you take in the car with your baby.

There are different sizes for the age and weight of your child, generally falling into these categories:

✔ **Baby capsule:** This is a car seat shaped like a cradle that is used for newborns up to six months or weighing eight kilograms. The capsule is strapped into the car using the car's existing seatbelts and is rear-facing.

A baby capsule can be taken out with your baby in it and attached to the top of special shopping trolleys, sets of wheels and some strollers that have mechanisms to which a baby capsule can be attached. Baby capsules also have a movable handle so you can carry your bub around in it like Red Riding Hood's basket of goodies.

✔ **Child car seat:** From 6 to 12 months (weight 8 to 12 kilograms), babies should still be in rear-facing car seats. Many rear-facing models can be converted to front-facing after bub's first birthday. Car seats usually have a strap that attaches to a bolt in the back of the back passenger seat. If your car doesn't have a bolt, they can be purchased and put into the car by a mechanic for very little money.

✔ **Booster seat:** When your child reaches 18 kilograms or his shoulders are too wide for his car seat, he can move to a booster seat.

As an alternative to buying a car seat, check out Hire for Baby (http://hire forbaby.com) in Australia and Plunket's (www.plunket.org.nz) car seat rental scheme in New Zealand.

Infants should stay in rear-facing car seats until they are 12 months old and are in the 9–12 kilogram weight range.

Knowing your buggy from your pram

Confused about what's a pram, what's a buggy and what's a stroller? Then read on!

In Australia, most people refer to baby carriages as prams; in New Zealand, most people call them buggies. Whatever you call them, they're substantial beasts, sometimes with three wheels, sometimes four. Prams are quite cosy and comfortable for your child, and have an adjustable back so that your tyke can lie down or sit up. Some models face out to the world, others face you (and the position can usually be adjusted depending on the baby's age). Many models also have a carry cot-type set up, so you can sling a bassinet on top when your baby's still wee.

A stroller is not so heavy and can be folded width-ways quite easily. Strollers don't have a push bar at the back, but two handles like the handle of an umbrella, which are really handy if you travel by bus and have to fold the stroller when you get on, or if you're a frequent flyer. Some people even refer to them as 'umbrella strollers'.

Whatever mode of transport you choose for your baby, make sure that it meets Australian/New Zealand standard AS/NZS 2088:2000. Prams and strollers are designed to move freely, so always ensure that you are holding onto the pram or that the brakes are on when you've stopped moving. In Australia, prams and strollers are now fitted with a tether strap to help you keep control over the pram (you can also buy tether straps where you buy prams). The Australian Competition and Consumer Commission pamphlet 'Prams and strollers' provides helpful information on pram/stroller safety and is available on its website, www.accc.gov.au.

If you're still not convinced about the need to be really vigilant around prams, buggies and strollers, check out www.diyfather.com/content/check-the-brakes-on-your-stroller-buggy-pram.

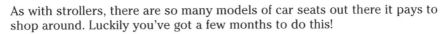

As with strollers, there are so many models of car seats out there it pays to shop around. Luckily you've got a few months to do this!

If you're buying a secondhand seat, check the safety regulations with the road safety authority in your country, state or territory to make sure it's up to scratch.

Other accessories

You find most of these things lurking in homes where kids live:

- ✔ **Baby bath or tummy tub:** You need something to wash your baby in and most parents go with a traditional tub that you can have on a table or sturdy bench. It means you don't have to fill up a normal sized tub and break your back leaning down into it. While your baby is still really small and unable to sit up by herself, it can be handy to have a bath support. A bath support is a ramp that baby can lie back on that holds her at a 45 degree angle so her head is safely kept out of the water. Another option for bathing is to use a tummy tub which looks a bit like a wastepaper basket but is said to replicate being in the womb. Baby 'sits' upright in it and is held snugly in place by the tub's walls. They are pricey though, so shop around.

- ✔ **Bouncinette or baby chair:** Most kids have spent time in a bouncinette, those ramp-like baby chairs that bub can lie in and watch you go about your day from a better angle than lying on the floor. They're portable, easy to clean and she can even sit outside in one while you're gardening or pegging out washing.

- ✔ **High chair:** When bub starts solids, you're going to need somewhere she can sit and be fed. A wide range of high chair models is available, from chairs with an ergonomic design made of timber that hasn't been treated with chemicals to chairs with more levers and straps than a space shuttle. Having a detachable tray that you can take off and clean regularly (after every meal!) is handy, as are safety straps so you can be sure bub isn't going to wriggle her way out of it and get hurt. As an alternative to a high chair you may want to use models that attach to your table. Later on you can use little booster seats that you strap to a normal chair.

Take a look at Chapter 8 for information about baby slings, front packs and carriers.

Making Room for the Baby

When you were growing up, do you remember how important having your own room was? It's more than the place where a child's bed is, or where his clothes are stored. It's a child's sanctuary, his own special space that has all the things he loves close by. Although he won't know this for a wee while yet, you can start creating that individual, happy space for him before he's born. But first we cover what you need to have.

The nursery

Cot, bassinet, drawers, change table, rocking chair, bookshelves, toy boxes — the nursery is one place you can spend a whole bunch of money on all new stuff if you're not careful.

Here are some of the basic items you need to set up a nursery.

Somewhere to sleep

For the first few months most bubs sleep in a bassinet or Moses basket. A bassinet is like a basket on legs. If the bassinet is on wheels, you can move it from room to room easily during the day for naps (babies can sleep anywhere when they're newborns) and wheel it into either your room or the nursery at night. When bub has outgrown the bassinet he can graduate to a cot, where he'll sleep until he's about two, or has worked out how to climb out of it.

If you're getting a secondhand cot or bassinet, check it thoroughly to make sure there's nothing that could fall apart and injure your baby. To find out more about ensuring your baby's safety when sleeping and reducing the risk of SUDI (Sudden Unexplained Death of Infants) check out Chapter 17.

Somewhere to be changed and dressed

A lot of nurseries have change tables — tables at the right height so you don't have to lean a lot to change bub's nappies or get her dressed. Some experts advocate that babies should be changed on the floor to avoid having baby roll off a change table, but others just stand by the rule that baby is never left on the table unsupervised — even for a second. Whichever you choose, having a change mat or a load of cloth nappies to have under her to catch any rogue poos is essential.

We believe cloth nappies are an essential accessory — and not only for covering your baby's bum. They can act as change mats, be put over your shoulder to catch any baby spew when you're burping her, be put on the floor during nappy-free time to catch any accidents and can be slung over the handle of a baby capsule to act as a sun shade. They're inexpensive, washable, very hardy and every nappy bag should have one.

Somewhere to store clothes

You would think that so small a person wouldn't need much room for her clothes, but she grows so big so fast she needs room to store not only the clothes she currently fits, but also the ones she grows into. Hand-me-downs and presents from well-meaning friends and family mean clothes are rarely in short supply. Child-sized hangers for her wardrobe can be bought from a homeware or discount store.

If you're given too many hand-me-down clothes, having a system in place for sizing stops you feeling overloaded. Have designated boxes for each size and store them in your baby's wardrobe. As they grow out of one size, you've got another size ready to go. This is a great job for dad when your partner goes through a period where she can't organise herself out of a paper bag because of all the hormones going crazy during pregnancy or after birth.

Bits and bobs

Other things that are handy to have include:

- ✔ A nappy bucket with tight fitting lid for soaking soiled clothing, bedding and cloth nappies.

- ✔ A washing hamper or washing basket.

- ✔ A rocking chair or armchair where mum can breastfeed or you can give the last bottle of the day before bed. An armchair or rocking chair is also somewhere to share stories, songs and cuddles as your baby gets bigger. Some mums find chairs without arms most comfortable, so have a few options available for your good lady.

- ✔ A pedal rubbish bin with a lid — big size if you're using disposable nappies. Yes, the pedal is essential!

- ✔ Something to house toys and books, such as a bookshelf or toy box.

- ✔ Nappy cream or powder, wipes and other toiletries in arms' reach of where you change your baby.

- ✔ A lockable medicine box where you store health items like pain relief, thermometer and nail clippers (see 'Shopping for your baby's health and first aid' later in this chapter).

Decorations

Decorating your baby's room is another way to clean out your wallet in a hurry, as there are thousands of things to put in a little person's room. Expectant mums have been known to get carried away, so you might have to display a bit of good old male shopping rationale. Babies spend a lot of time gazing into space when they're really small, as if they're tuning into a radio show you can't hear, and like looking at high-contrast objects around them, such as black and white shapes. Keep the decorating simple. As your baby develops his taste and his needs change, transforming the nursery into a little child's room won't be a drama.

Here are our tips for keeping it simple.

✔ Keep the colours neutral, so that the room can easily be redecorated as your baby grows. Baby blue may be cute when he's a few months old, but not when he's seven.

✔ Use pictures of close friends and family on the walls so your baby can grow up knowing who the important people are.

✔ You or your partner may want to make something special for the baby's room, like a painting or piece of embroidery.

✔ Mobiles hanging from the ceiling don't need to be fancy. A string of shells hanging from driftwood can entertain a wee bub.

✔ Use removable decals on the walls, so they can be easily taken off as bub grows up and won't damage the wallpaper or paint.

✔ Involve your child in the decoration of his room as he gets older. After all, his room is his space.

Animals in the house

A lot of couples have a cat or a dog before baby comes along. The change a little person brings affects the pet's life as well as your own. Your pet will find itself a long way down the pecking order once your cherub is on the scene, and will have to put up with pulled fur, loud noises and being chased in the not-too-distant future.

Show your child how to be gentle with animals and people from the get-go, as well as how to approach dogs with caution. A child should always hold her hand out for a dog to smell and stay still when it comes near so the dog doesn't see her as a threat.

Teach your child not to touch strange animals (almost impossible until she's a bit older) and to wash her hands afterwards as animals can carry all sorts of nasties in their fur.

Don't leave your child alone or out of sight with pets. Cats can react badly when your baby decides it's time to 'ride the kitty' and may even give junior a scratch or two. If the mantra of being gentle to the cat doesn't warn your child that felines are not to be messed with, then a scratch on the nose most certainly will.

Dogs and cats can feel neglected when a new baby joins the family, so spend time making them feel settled and happy. Don't move your pet's special sleeping areas or toys away to make room for baby. Try to keep your pet's routines as settled as possible so it doesn't feel left out.

A great way to keep cats out of your baby's cot is to fill it with balloons during the day. If your cat hasn't encountered balloons yet, chances are it'll only go near them once until the first one bursts.

Finding the Right Consumables

There's a reason you see a whole aisle of the supermarket dedicated to baby stuff — there's a lot of it and a lot of things to choose from. Parents also make for really easy prey for marketing people. A few sleepless nights and sheer desperation does amazing things to your shopping habits. So having a good nose around all the stuff you can buy before the baby arrives makes the shopping-in-a-hurry experience easier on you later on. Don't worry about buying the wrong nappy cream, teething gel or nappies. You go through lots of them and have plenty of opportunities to try out different options. But we can help you get a head start.

Check out Chapter 12 for some great money saving tips for homemade versions of baby stuff.

Nappies

As proper males you don't think about nappies of course. Until you become dads that is. Get used to nappies ... they will become your friends, because they are between you and a whole lot of pee and poo.

You can select from three main options when choosing what to wrap your baby's bottom in — cloth nappies that can be washed and used over and over, disposable nappies that you throw away after each change, and hybrids where you throw away some bits and keep the main bit.

Of course, you can go nappy free and practise *elimination communication* if that's your thing (see Chapter 6).

Cloth nappies have come of age. No longer are cloth nappies those scratchy, leaky, bulky cloth things that require a degree in origami to fold into the right shape and are held together with safety pins. Now cloth nappies come already shaped with domes, and Velcro to make putting them on and getting them off as easy as a disposable nappy.

New Zealand's Nappy Network can help you choose which type suits you best. Have a look on thenappynetwork.org.nz. In Australia, see ozclothnappies.org.

Cloth nappies do require a bit more money upfront and require time and energy washing them, but some comparisons show cloth nappies to come out cheaper than disposables. Modern cloth nappies can also be used on more than one child and can be bought in good condition secondhand. Eco-conscious dads can rest assured your child's nappies aren't clogging up landfills for years to come.

But if you think just changing a nappy is gross, having to clean them may be a step too far for you. Disposable nappies mean you never have to clean a nappy. They can be a better option if you're on holiday, or for use in the day-to-day nappy bag so if your baby needs a change when you're out and about, you don't have to carry a dirty nappy around until you get home. Recently eco-friendly disposables have entered the market in Australia and New Zealand. They're now available in most supermarkets at comparable prices to the major brands. They're typically made from corn starch and other sustainable resources, and often don't contain any of the chemicals that keep babies dry but which may cause nappy rash, as well as being bad for the environment. All in all a sound alternative we think.

Hybrid nappies are made of a washable underpants part and a disposable pad. Hybrid nappies generally require upfront investment in the pants but tend to work out cheaper in the long run.

Disposable nappies may be right for you if you live in an area where water is scarce. Cloth nappies use a lot of water in rinsing and washing.

Crème de la crèmes

Nappy rash is a big concern for most babies from time to time. Nappy rash is a condition where the ammonia from bub's poos and wees irritates his skin, making it red and tender, and making him pretty unhappy with life. The easiest way to stop nappy rash in its tracks is to expose the bottom to air and sunlight for a good half an hour a day. Changing his nappy regularly and using a barrier cream or powder can protect his bum from a nasty rash too.

Like all things baby, you can find an enormous range of nappy creams on the market and your partner might have a few ideas of what to get. Don't feel overwhelmed by the vast choice of products available. At the end of the day anything from the supermarket that has zinc oxide in it will do the trick. Castor oil and zinc oxide cream is very effective and cheap, but it can be thick and sticky, so you might want to use it at night and have a lighter cream in the day, or use a powder with zinc oxide in it. You can also try out Vaseline as a barrier cream.

Manufacturers want you to buy all sorts of other crèmes to make your little champ smell good, have nice skin, relax, fall asleep better and so on. By all means try them out and if you find one that works really well, keep using it. In general we recommend keeping it simple and using natural oils, which are cheap and effective. Olive or almond oil have been known to be particularly effective for most temporary skin irritations and even cradle cap (see Chapter 7 for more about oils and cradle cap).

Shopping for your baby's health and first aid

Having an arsenal of potions and lotions on hand in the early months and years is essential. Here's what we think every dad should have in his baby fix-it kit.

- ✔ **Almond or calendula oil:** Your baby doesn't need moisturisers or scented lotions. If she has dry skin, pure oil is best without all the toxins and fillers big companies use to preserve their products. Calendula oil is really great for massage, and almond oil is great for dry skin and *cradle cap*, a condition common in babies where flakes form on the scalp like baby dandruff.

- ✔ **Antibacterial cream:** Stop infections in cuts and grazes by treating them with antibacterial cream.

✔ **Arnica cream:** As he grows, your baby is going to get his fair share of bumps on the head and scrapes on the knee. Arnica cream applied to the bruise can assist with the healing.

✔ **Child's sunscreen and insect repellent:** Essential if you live in tropical climes, but the best form of protection is clothing and keeping out of the sun. Babies' skin is a lot more sensitive than adults' skin so junior can burn even when he is not exposed to direct sunlight. Mosquito nets can be bought to go over the cot or bassinet too.

✔ **Digital thermometer:** If junior is sick with a cold or flu, you can tell when it's time to whip him off to the doctor by using a digital thermometer to check his temperature. Take your baby's temperature by putting the thermometer under his arm, called the *axillary* temperature. 'Normal' temperature is 37 degrees Celsius. Unfortunately some babies don't enjoy having a thermometer stuck under their arm for long enough to get an accurate reading. If your little one is like that you may want to consider getting an ear thermometer which takes the measurement in seconds.

✔ **Gripe water:** In the first six months or so, your baby's digestive system is still pretty immature. He'll need help bringing up wind in his stomach whenever he eats. Some babies really struggle with bringing up wind, which causes them a lot of upset. Gripe water helps babies bring up wind more easily.

✔ **Karvol, Vicks Baby Balsam and Euky Bearub:** Karvol is a decongestant that can be applied to the baby's clothes to clear nasal passages as he sleeps. Vicks Baby Balsam and Euky Bearub are applied to the chest and back when he's congested. Check these medicines are suitable for your baby's age.

✔ **Nail clippers or baby nail scissors:** Babies can scratch themselves easily so you need to keep their nails short and neat. This is easier said than done. Try clippers or special baby scissors to see what works best for you.

✔ **Pain reliever:** Children's Panadol (Pamol) or Nurofen for kids is used for pain and fever after immunisations, teething, and fever when your baby has a cold. Use a plastic syringe with measurements marked on the side to dispense the medication and check with your doctor for the correct dosage (which is worked out by baby's weight). Aspirin is not suitable for young children.

✔ **Teething relief:** Teething powder and gels like Bonjela can help soothe a teething baby's gums.

Check with your GP before giving your baby Panadol (Pamol) if he's younger than six months old. Always check the labelling on any medical product (or any product in fact) to make sure it's suitable for your baby's age. If you're unsure whether it's suitable, check with your GP.

Be prepared to keep adding to your household first aid kit with bandages, band aids, scissors and tweezers as your little one gets older and encounters more little accidents.

Stuff You Tend to Forget

There's so much to do and only nine months to do it in. Along with watching your partner's belly grow and preparing for the biggest change in your life yet, you can do a whole bunch of things to minimise the chaos in your world right now and to save yourself a bunch of grief down the line. Here are some ideas.

Upskilling

If you thought your school days were over, think again. Parenting education is upon you, and your partner might send you to birth school (also known as antenatal classes)! While most childbirth education or antenatal classes focus on the birth of your baby, it's a good idea to pick up some tips and tricks about getting through the first few weeks and months. Fortunately there are now many inclusive courses available where as a guy you feel less of a spare wheel. In New Zealand check out Parents Centre and Plunket for courses from pre-birth to school age. In Australia visit www.bubhub. com.au/servicesantenatal.php for classes in your state. Even better, DIYFather.com offers dedicated courses just for dads (for guys only). Depending on the type of course, these are delivered in collaboration with Parents Centres or Plunket. Check out www.diyfather.com/courses for more information.

You may wonder whether you *really* have to go to antenatal classes. The answer is yes — not necessarily because you learn amazing things, but because your partner appreciates it and you can network with other couples and dads who are in the same boat.

Antenatal classes can also help you decide whether to go for a home birth, hospital birth or *elective caesarean*, where you choose to have a caesarean on a particular day.

Class content varies wildly so try to shop around early if you can and check what's on offer before you sign the dotted line. Apart from the standard options we mention earlier, you can also find alternative classes or providers by asking your carer, and checking with your friends who have had babies or with your local hospital.

If you want to go beyond skilling up on the basics of baby care and childcare you can also check out courses that teach baby massage, baby sign language and activities with babies.

Transport

You've no doubt all seen the movie where Mrs Pregnant goes into labour and Mr Pregnant drives like a crazy man to get to the hospital before the baby's born. If you're having a hospital birth rather than a home birth, then some variation of the movie scene will happen to you. We don't advise driving fast or tearing around corners like a Formula One driver — after all, you want to all arrive in one piece at the hospital. Unlike the movies, a parking space will not magically appear right outside the delivery suite doors, so it pays to do a little investigative work before the big day about where you can park.

Have some cash in the hospital bag for parking, or check with the hospital when you do your hospital tour to see if they have any special parking for families in the maternity ward.

You may also want to check some time in advance of the birth that you know how to get to the hospital. Some people do a test run to see how long it takes them. You don't want to be mucking around with maps on the way there. Your partner might not thank you for having to spend anymore time squashed in the backseat than she has to.

You might also want to consider the following.

- ✓ Has the car got all the necessary bits and pieces of paperwork such as an up-to-date roadworthy certificate (Australia), or warrant of fitness (New Zealand)?
- ✓ Is the car accessible night and day, or is it blocked in by other cars sometimes?
- ✓ If your car is out of action, is there someone you can call as a back-up?
- ✓ Is there enough petrol in the tank to get you there?
- ✓ Have you got a capsule or car seat to transport your baby home?

Birthing equipment

If you're having a hospital birth, you don't need to bring anything to the delivery suite other than your beloved and her hospital bag, which in some instances can be pretty big indeed. But if you're having the birth at home, you need some bits and bobs to prepare for the big day.

- ✔ A birthing pool: These can be hired from private companies or through your local homebirthing association. Some can even be used as a paddling pool for your child afterwards.
- ✔ A container for the placenta.
- ✔ Towels: For cleaning up and wrapping the baby in after birth, and for mum and dad if you've both been in the pool.
- ✔ Waterproof mats to cover your carpet: A tarpaulin covered with newspaper and an old blanket or sheets should do it.

Your midwife will give you a full list of everything you need to have prepared.

The hospital bag (s)

The old conundrum of knowing what to take on holiday and what to leave behind is nothing compared to the quandary of what to take to the hospital when your baby is on her way. Packing the hospital bag is often broken down into three sections — things needed for mum during the birth, things needed for mum after the birth and things needed for the baby. Things needed for dad often get a bit neglected, because fathers weren't welcome anywhere near the action for a long time. Fortunately times have changed and chances are you are the best man for the job to get organised about Project Birth. Here are some suggestions for a mum, baby and dad friendly hospital bag:

What the parents need during the birth

You'll need some or all of the following items for the big event:

- ✔ **Camera and batteries**
- ✔ **Mobile phone and charger:** Check with the hospital before making phone calls to announce your little one's arrival because some don't allow mobiles to be used in the ward.

✔ **Music, incense, candles:** Take anything that you and your partner think will make the labour easier by setting a nice mood. Check with your carer first because some hospitals may not allow candles or incense in the delivery suite.

✔ **Snacks and drinks:** Some labours can take a long time (24 hours is not unusual), and it's hard work on mum doing all the pushing and dad doing all that supporting. Nuts, chocolate, energy drinks, muesli bars, crackers or whatever you like can be packed in a lunchbox to nibble on during the labour. Many mums prefer drinking through a straw so have a couple handy if you can.

✔ **The appropriate clothing:** Mum's feet might get cold during a long labour, so pack a pair of nice comfy soft socks. If you're having a water birth, you might want to pack a pair of shorts so you can get in the pool too.

There may be a lot of waiting around, so pack a book or something to keep you occupied.

What mum needs after the birth

In all likelihood, you'll be spending a few hours with your new baby, calling everyone you want to call and feeling a little giddy. You'll probably head home for a shower, something to eat and a sleep. But mum needs at least these things to help her settle into her stay at the hospital:

✔ A change of clothes for coming home

✔ Herbal or homeopathic remedies such as arnica for bruising, or Rescue Remedy for stress

✔ Lanolin nipple cream that doesn't need to be washed off before breastfeeding

✔ Maternity bras and nursing pads in case of leaking breastmilk

✔ Maternity pads, though these can be supplied by the hospital

✔ Pen and notebook for recording a few things after the birth

✔ Pyjamas or a nightie that opens at the front for breastfeeding, a dressing gown and slippers

✔ Soft cotton undies

✔ Usual toiletries your partner would take on holiday, such as a toothbrush, shampoos, cleanser, deodorant, moisturiser, lip balm, contact lens supplies, hair bands and brush, and any medications.

What bub needs after the birth

The little person you'll be taking home will need:

- Disposable nappies. Even if you are going to use cloth nappies, *meconium*, the sticky tar-like poo your baby expels in the first few days after birth, is best handled by disposable nappies as meconium can be hard to get out of cloth ones. Many hospitals won't give away free nappies anymore, so be prepared and take a few extra.

- Dummy or pacifier. While a pacifier is probably one of the most commonly known baby accessories, lactation consultants may not be that happy about you giving your little champ a pacifier if you're experiencing breastfeeding difficulties because pacifiers are believed to cause 'nipple confusion' in some cases.

- Formula (labelled 'from birth'), bottles, teats and sterilising equipment if you're going to bottle feed

- Muslin wraps or blankets

- Something to wear. A couple of newborn sized all-in-ones with feet and long sleeves, some hats and some socks or booties. Newborns are used to being in a nice hot spa pool and have no way to control their temperature yet, so even in summer they need to be kept warm. You may also have a special 'coming home' outfit picked out.

- Wipes and nappy rash cream for cleaning and protecting your baby's bottom while changing her nappies.

If you want to go the extra mile to ensure you've got everything you could possibly need for your newborn, check with a midwife. Check with a lactation consultant for any breastfeeding equipment, aids or remedies your partner may need.

The baby shower

It's no longer strictly true that baby showers are all about mum, where a bunch of women sit around drinking tea and playing games like 'guess what mess is in that nappy'. Dads are getting in on the act too. No, not sitting around eating sandwiches and oohing over Aunty Vera's knitted booties, but getting together to mark your transition into fatherhood. It could be a game of pool with mates, a day out fishing, a game of ten pin bowling, a joint occasion with mum's mates, or a boys' night out on the town. We definitely recommend having a 'man shower' to celebrate the occasion (and no, your man shower's unlikely to be similar to your stag night).

Checklists

In all the excitement of becoming a father, it's really easy to forget stuff, so devise a comprehensive list of everything you think you'll need and put it somewhere you can't miss it. Don't leave it up to your memory — you're bound to forget something.

Your checklist should include:

- ✔ **Car seat:** Have you got a car seat sorted and know how to fit it into your car?

- ✔ **Home birth list:** Mats to protect floors, home birth pool if you want it, towels for yourself and the baby, any other requirements your midwife needs.

- ✔ **Nursery:** Baby has somewhere to sleep and bedding to sleep in, baby has clothes to wear, you have something to store clothes in, baby has nappies and bum protection, you have something to change baby on.

- ✔ **Pet care:** Who will look after any pets during the birth while you're not at home?

- ✔ **Phone list:** Should include emergency numbers, your lead maternity carer, friends, family and work.

- ✔ **Your hospital bags:** For during the birth, for the hospital stay and for bub.

- ✔ **Your transport:** Ensure your car has all its paperwork and petrol, you know your way to the hospital, you have parking money, and you know where parking is.

If you've decided on a hospital birth, check out your options (if you have several hospitals to choose from) because standards and facilities vary significantly. Most hospitals offer special 'tours' for pregnant couples to see what the facilities are like and where you need to go on D-day. This tour is really useful because you can check out details and take lots of time to ask everything you ever wanted to know about giving birth in a hospital.

Chapter 5

Birth

. . . .

In This Chapter

▶ Getting ready for labour

▶ Knowing what to do during labour

▶ Helping nature to deliver your baby

▶ Enjoying the first few moments with your baby

. . . .

*B*eing born is, ironically, the most dangerous thing you probably do in your life. In third world countries, just being born or having a baby is still a precarious thing to do. That said, infant mortality rates are at the lowest in history and constantly dropping. In Australia and New Zealand we're lucky because problems during birth are rare and plenty of help is available if things get a bit tricky.

But that doesn't mean you can take everything for granted. You need to know what's going on during birth. Knowledge is power, so we've put together this chapter to keep you in the loop. That said, no two births are the same and no-one can tell you what's going to happen during the birth of your child. The process may seem a bit random and very drawn out, but usually that's just part of the journey to dadhood.

In this chapter you find out about the different phases and stages of labour, when real labour starts and when to call your carer. You discover strategies for making labour less of a pain for your partner and how to keep both of you sane during this trying time. We also give you some advice on keeping your cool at the big moment when your child is born, and guide you through the heady first minutes, hours and days as a father.

The Final Countdown

The nursery is ready, the freezer is stocked with meals, the car seat has been fitted and the mother of your child is pacing around the house waiting for it all to start happening. It's like sitting in a reception room, waiting for your name to be called so you can finally become a dad. Keep yourself occupied with some last minute tasks, and a bit of brushing up on what happens during and immediately after labour.

Discovering what you need to know about labour

You can't be too prepared for labour. And as you're number one in the pit crew, understanding what's going on is essential. To help you get your head around this momentous occasion, the Glossary outlines terms used in labour and birth to help you understand what's going on.

There's a lot to take in, so here's a quick guide to what generally happens during labour.

Like all good things in life, labour happens in three stages.

- The **first stage** is when your partner's cervix softens, then widens, called *dilation*, making space for the baby to come through and out of the uterus. The uterus *contracts* at regular intervals allowing the baby to come through. The contractions become increasingly painful. These are *those* contractions you've heard so much about on movies and TV. The cervix is fully dilated at ten centimetres. For a first birth, the first stage takes an average of 6 to 14 hours (but can take a day or more), so you can see that your presence with a strong shoulder and heat packs galore will really help.

- The **second stage** is the bit where your partner pushes the baby out. The second stage is also helped along by contractions that increase in length and intensity during this stage. Finally, your little one is born!

- The **third stage** is a little less glamorous (as if birth is at all glamorous) and involves the placenta, that lifeline to your baby, being born. The placenta is also called afterbirth. It takes between five minutes to an hour to come out. Most women are too knackered by this stage, or energised by finally meeting their baby, to notice much about expelling the placenta.

Think that's all there is to it? Nuh-huh. The first stage also has three phases and your partner will probably be too caught up in the moment to recognise them as they happen to her:

- ✔ **Latent phase:** Contractions are 5 to 20 minutes apart and become more frequent as they progress. The cervix dilates to about three centimetres.

- ✔ **Active phase:** This phase is characterised by the cervix dilating from about three centimetres to fully dilated. Contractions increase in length and intensity and come every three to five minutes, so your partner doesn't have a lot of downtime to get herself a pillow or make a cup of tea. That's your job, mister. This is usually when getting to the hospital or opening the door for the midwife to deliver your baby at home is right up there on your to-do list.

- ✔ **Transition:** Okay, your partner's allowed to lose it now — and probably will. This is the point just before the pushing starts. Contractions are very intense, sometimes overwhelming and your partner may say things like 'I can't do it!' (plus a whole lot of swear words we don't need to list here).

One of the more obvious signs that things are about to kick off is when your partner's waters break. This usually happens in the most inappropriate situation — but hey, it's all natural. However, this doesn't mean your partner's in labour. She may be, but in some cases labour starts up to 24 hours after the waters break. Either way it's a good idea to call your carer or midwife to inform them that the waters have broken. Read about more signs of the first stage of labour later in this chapter.

Understanding your role in labour

We've talked a lot about supporting and being there for your partner. So what does 'being there' really mean? Ask a lot of dads who have been through the birth of their children and the answer that might spring to mind is 'stand around like an idiot and feel guilty and inadequate'. It's easy to feel sidelined when the focus is on your partner and she's in kind of a crabby mood with you, which you would be too if you had three kilos of person coming out of an orifice. She's focusing on what her body is doing, listening to the coaching and advice of her midwife or obstetrician, and coping with pain, hormones and emotions you can't even begin to imagine (or don't want to).

In general your partner relies on you to sort out a long list of support tasks which you can do with dignity and humility. So if your partner needs a shoulder to hang onto for leverage when she's pushing, give it to her. If she needs a drink in a cup with a straw and three ice cubes, get it organised. If your partner says she can't do it anymore, tell her with conviction that she can. Being there means taking care of your partner when she needs you to and most importantly taking charge when she needs you to. Labour can be totally overwhelming for your partner and she's vulnerable to every emotion in the book. She's also vulnerable to being pushed around by the hospital system: an obstetrician who may be angling for a caesarean birth when your partner is dead set against it and wants to keep pushing for a bit longer, or an over pushy *lactation consultant* who is stressing out your exhausted partner. If something doesn't feel right, you have to make a decision for the good of your partner and baby and advocate on their behalf. It's all about your family so you get to be 'the man who calls the shots' when push comes to shove.

Dads can really make their role count during labour by being:

- ✔ **A link to the outside world.** Let friends and family know what's going on because they'll be anxious to hear how the birth's going. You can also be the first to announce to the world that your new son or daughter has arrived — a very special thing to be able to do!

- ✔ **Strong.** Help out where you can by making sure your partner is as comfortable as she can be, is well stocked with food and water, and is warm or cool enough.

- ✔ **The rational calm voice in the hustle and bustle.** Even when things get stressful or hectic try to keep your cool on your partner's behalf and advocate for her if things are slipping out of control.

Take your cues from your partner. Her needs are pretty specific and she'll let you know about them. But don't try to tell your partner you know how she feels, because you don't. Any complaining (to her) of any sort from your end may not be received well.

Have a standby support person in case labour goes on for a long time, or you desperately need some rest. Talk about who would be suitable with your partner. Perhaps her sister or mother could fill in for you while you have a meal or take a breather.

iPhone apps during labour

If you are the proud owner of an iPhone you'll be amazed that 17 applications are specifically designed to monitor the duration and frequency of your partner's screaming (read contractions) during labour. Here's a selection of them with a DIYFather.com recommendation for a free app:

- Baby's Coming (free) — DIYFather recommended
- Contraculate (free)
- Contractulator (free)

- TapTimer Lite (free)
- Contractions (commercial)
- Contraction Master (commercial)
- iContraction (commercial)
- Labor Mate (commercial)
- Birth Buddy (commercial)
- Contractions Alert — Baby Boy (commercial)
- Contraction Tracker (commercial)

Getting ready — last minute preparations

As you count down the days to your partner's due date, you could be feeling all sorts of things — excitement about meeting your baby for the first time, or absolute terror about the reality of your new responsibility. It's okay, we've been there. You may also be a bit worried about how you'll handle the labour, about your role in it and how well your partner will cope. Worrying is okay and yes, lots of guys cry, pass out or throw up during labour, which is all part of the journey. Basically just ride it out.

Before the fun starts double-check (or triple-check) a few things, such as ensuring you've:

- Arranged for someone to look after your pets/plants and clear your mail. You may be gone some time.
- Briefed people at work, or left handover notes or contact details if you need to leave suddenly
- Charged your camera batteries
- Got the hospital bags packed and ready to go, even if you're planning a home birth, in case you need to transfer to a hospital in a hurry

✔ Made sure the car seat is ready to go and have practised putting it in and taking it out of the car

✔ Stored phone numbers of friends and family on your mobile phone and that the phone's charged with plenty of credit if you use a prepaid model.

The checklists in Chapter 4 will help you remember anything you may have forgotten.

Bring it on!

Though only five per cent of babies are born on their due date, passing that magical day without a babe in her arms will probably weigh on your partner's mind. She may have been viewing the due date as the finish line and to go over it without a result may push her to the end of her tether. By now, the less desirable effects of pregnancy like fluid retention, heartburn, insomnia, weight gain, shortness of breath, waddling and having that baby kick her insides won't be such a novelty. Your partner wants her body back and your baby out.

There are techniques you can try to help bring on labour and some can even be fun, but none can guarantee results. No doubt everyone you meet who has asked you 'Is the baby here yet?' will follow up with one of these ideas.

✔ **Drink castor oil.** Drinking castor oil to cause diarrhoea is an old fashioned way of bringing on labour. We don't recommend drinking castor oil because it makes the contractions pretty nasty.

✔ **Have acupuncture or acupressure.** Some people swear by the results of having acupuncture needles or pressure applied to certain points of the body. Others think it's coincidental when labour naturally happens soon after the procedure's done.

✔ **Have sex.** The *prostaglandin* in your semen may help to *ripen* the cervix, making it ready to dilate.

✔ **Make your loved one a spicy meal.** The aim is give your girl diarrhoea, which can start contractions. It may just give her more heartburn.

✔ **'Sweep the membranes' or 'strip and stretch'.** Sometimes called having a 'sweep' done, during this rather uncomfortable procedure the midwife or doctor puts their fingers inside the cervix. Once inside, they stretch open the cervix and strip membranes away from it.

✔ **Take a walk together.** The rocking motion may help stimulate contractions.

Your partner isn't considered overdue until 42 weeks and three days after conception. If labour hasn't happened, you can discuss with your carer when or if to induce the baby. This involves using prostaglandin to ripen the cervix, rupturing the amniotic sac and using *syntocinon*, a synthetic form of *oxytocin*, to start contractions.

Action!

Your partner thinks something may be happening. Don't panic. It may be launch time, or it may be a false alarm.

When you think you're in labour

You will have signs that the birth of your baby is not far away, but it can be days or weeks before full-on labour really starts.

Here are some indicators that things are about to get interesting, but you shouldn't get too excited yet.

- A bloody **show** or mucous plug. The mucous plug that blocks the cervix during pregnancy comes away, along with blood from broken capillaries in the cervix.

- **Braxton-Hicks contractions.** These are mild contractions, like a strong period pain or cramps. They're not 'real' contractions, but may be confused with them.

- Intense or increasing **back pain** can also be a sign that things are beginning to happen.

- **Loose bowel motions.** A few days before labour, the body releases prostaglandins which help soften the cervix ready for dilation. Prostaglandins also cause things to be a bit lax in the bowel department.

Don't worry if none of the things in the preceding list happens before the contractions start. Every labour, birth and woman is different, so call your carer if you're not sure about what's happening.

When the first stage of labour begins it may feel like birth is really happening, but it isn't yet. The difference between the latent phase (also sometimes called early labour) and the active phase (sometimes called active labour) of the first stage of labour is the length and intensity of contractions. If you're still a bit confused about the various stages and phases of labour, check the definitions earlier in this chapter.

Call your midwife, obstetrician or GP for support. They can give you guidance on whether you need to grab the car keys, or if you can settle in for the evening.

When you're really in labour

All aboard the rollercoaster, get buckled in, because you're in for a real treat. The birth of a child happens everywhere around the world thousands of times a day. And you can bet that every birth happening right now is unique. Lucky you — you get to be part of your baby's story right now. The high of seeing a child born is like nothing on Earth — and you're about to meet *your own* child. How cool is that?

First things first. You'll know your partner is in labour because:

- Contractions are regular, lasting 45–60 seconds, and increasing in frequency
- Contractions are getting stronger and your partner may not be able to speak during a contraction.

Time to call your carer if you haven't already.

Helping your partner through childbirth

Many women spend the *latent phase* of labour at home, where they're more comfortable and have lots of room to move around. Even if you're planning a hospital birth it may pay to stay at home for as long as is feasible. Some mums who go to the hospital too early tense up because they're at the hospital and later on experience fatigue earlier than if they'd stayed at home for longer. Contractions shouldn't be too unmanageable and you can try these techniques to relieve whatever pain your partner is feeling.

- Apply a wheatpack or hot water bottle to your partner's bump or lower back where she feels the most pain.
- Give your partner a gentle back rub with some almond or olive oil.
- Keep your partner moving. Movement can help labour progress and gravity means the baby's weight puts pressure on the cervix, helping it to dilate.
- Run a bath or turn on the shower for your partner.
- Turn down the lights.

I'll have what she's having

Meg Ryan may have been faking an orgasm in the hit movie *When Harry Met Sally*, but we doubt the handful of women starring in the documentary *Orgasmic Birth* were. Yes, you heard us. Natural birth advocates Ina May Gaskin and Sheila Kitzinger have long said that birth doesn't have to be about pain and can be so pain free as to be 'ecstatic' or even orgasmic. Giving birth at home, in an intimate setting like one in which you'd make love, can be quite a different experience from giving birth in a hospital under bright lights knowing some stranger could walk in at any moment. Women who've had orgasmic births report feeling waves of pleasure with each contraction, which peak again and again. During labour oxytocin and endorphins flood the body. These hormones are also released during sex.

Having an orgasmic birth shouldn't be the goal for women, advocates say, but it's worth recognising that labour doesn't have to be a pain. If it happens to your partner — lucky you!

As contractions get stronger and you move into the *active phase, transition* and the *second stage* of labour, you can carry on with these pain relief techniques. Let your partner guide you as to what she needs. At some points your partner won't have any energy in her body to do anything other than ride out a contraction, especially in the second stage when she's putting everything into pushing the baby out. Holding up your partner's body and letting her lean on you in whatever way she needs helps your partner a lot.

Keeping sane

Labour can take a long time. You may get a chance to have a breather between contractions, or you may not. Giving all your energy to your partner is exhausting, so try to take some time out for yourself as well if you can.

It may help to have some people on speed-dial that you can call if it all becomes too much. Check with your partner before the big day because it would be terrible to have a person turn up during labour who your partner really didn't want to see there.

Acceptable things for dads to do during labour include:

✔ Crying when the baby is here

✔ Doing some stretching exercises to keep fresh and fend off sleep

✔ Drinking water

✔ Eating snacks

✔ Fainting

✔ Getting some fresh air

✔ Going to the toilet (as long as it's not too often and doesn't take too long)

✔ Leaving the room because you're about to be sick or faint

The following actions are really in stark contrast to the future super dad you're aiming to be:

✔ Bringing your mates into the delivery suite

✔ Doing work on your laptop

✔ Leaving the hospital to participate in your weekly pub-quiz at the local

✔ Playing video games on your mobile

✔ Sneaking into the birthing suite next door to have a kip

✔ Taking photos of other women in labour

✔ Telling your partner to keep it down because you're negotiating a business deal on the phone

✔ Watching your favourite show on a portable TV (unless your partner wants to see it too while she is riding out the contractions)

✔ Weeing in your pants because it's all too emotional

Giving nature a helping hand

Sometimes during labour nature needs help to get your baby out into the world. There are lots of reasons for this: The baby may be in distress, or your partner's health is in jeopardy, or she's exhausted and wants the baby out immediately! None of these interventions can really be anticipated. Keep in touch with your partner and if she's adamant she doesn't want any intervention, be her advocate.

When the medical equipment comes out, try not to freak out. Some of it can look scarier than it really is. The equipment's going to help you meet your baby sooner rather than later.

Ventouse

A *ventouse* is a vacuum extractor that helps pull the baby out of the *birth canal*. A ventouse is used when the baby's head is low in the birth canal but needs an extra bit of oomph to help him along. The baby's heart rate may indicate he's in distress, or his position is making it tricky for him to be born naturally.

A suction cup is put onto the baby's head and your partner may have to have an *episiotomy*, which is a cut to the vaginal opening to make room for the cup to go in. A ventouse can cause swelling to the top of the baby's head, but usually causes little or no trauma to the mother and baby.

Forceps

Forceps look like a scary pair of tongs. They are used to grip the baby's head on both sides and pull him out of the birth canal. Forceps aren't used as often as ventouse these days because of the risk that the mother's insides can be damaged, not to mention the bruising and risk of damage to the baby's head. An episiotomy is routinely required as well.

Emergency caesarean

The big daddy of medical interventions during labour is the *emergency caesarean*. They're called 'emergency' to distinguish them from elective caesareans where you opt for birth this way. All caesareans take place in an operating theatre, and you have to wear a gown and cover your hair. Your partner is given an *epidural* to numb pain (although in some cases the caesarean has to be performed under general anaesthetic), and an incision is made in your partner's belly, usually near the pubic bone, known as a bikini cut. The abdominal muscles are parted and the *peritoneal cavity* is opened to make way for the uterus. The uterus is then opened, and the baby and placenta are brought out.

Having a caesarean isn't an 'easy' way of having a baby, it's major surgery, and you may not want to look behind the sheet that stops your partner from seeing her insides come out. Having a caesarean also means your partner will take weeks to recover, and she won't be able to drive or lift anything heavy for up to six weeks. She will also be on pain medication and will have to rest a lot as she recovers, and will stay in hospital for four or five days.

If your partner had her heart set on a vaginal birth, or a natural drug-free birth, and it hasn't worked out that way, she'll be feeling disappointed and upset with herself. Add this to the hormones rampaging through her body and you have one sad little mummy. Give her all the love and support you can muster right now, she needs you.

The Big Moment's Arrived

The moment your child is born is a peak experience that's difficult to describe — totally unique, beautiful and out of this world. Enjoy it. You may find yourself shedding a tear or two at this important moment. Don't hold back, being emotional is totally cool and you're definitely not a lesser man for it (quite the opposite in fact, we think). Cherish this snapshot in time because the moment you clap eyes on your child for the first time can't be rehearsed or repeated.

Cutting the cord

Dad — because that's what you are now — this is your chance to shine. You now have another important job to do, should you choose to accept it. After the placenta is born and your baby is coping on her own without help from mum, the umbilical cord is clamped and set up for you to cut. This small task can take on several significant meanings for your new family. For your partner, cutting the cord can represent the end of her pregnancy and the start of motherhood. For you it might symbolise your part in your new family. Most importantly for your little one, cutting the cord symbolises a point in time where all life support systems from mum are cut off and his body has to sustain him. Cutting the cord is a big deal, so embrace the significance and enjoy the procedure.

The cord is really rather thick and gnarly, so apply some elbow grease and give it a good strong cut. You may want to ask your midwife or other support person to take a photo.

When time stops — meeting your baby

So you're looking at your child for the first time. It can be incredible, scary, bewildering and amazing, all in the space of a few seconds. Time seems to stop as you feel all these emotions washing over you.

Take a moment now to have a good look at what's been cooking for nine months — little fingers, little toes — as mum may have her hands full being taken care of by medical staff right now.

Notice all his little features and enjoy the amazing sight of a newborn baby. Typically there is no rush anymore once your baby has been checked and is handed to you. So you can easily take some time out to make your first acquaintance with the little one. What a great start to a lifelong bond. As dads you often get to spend time with your little ones first! How cool is that!

Keeping your cool

It's been a long day or two. You've let your partner and your midwife or doctor guide you through the process and you have to admit to yourself you've been a pretty damn awesome support crew. You've advocated for your partner, you've kept her well stocked with food and drink, and she's right now looking forward to a cuddle with your baby and a good rest. But you may find the demands of the system — the midwife needs to zip off to another appointment before you're ready, you can't be transferred from the delivery suite to the ward because of paperwork — will override you right now, so keep advocating for your partner and child if they need it.

Welcoming Your Baby to the Real World

It may be tempting once bub has finally arrived to think that the hard yards are over. You may be gazing blissfully at your new baby, frantically calling family or may be tempted to run to the shop for cigars. Cool it for a few minutes more because there's more stuff to get through yet.

What happens immediately after birth

Making sure your new baby is in good health is top priority. Most likely, your baby has come out a rather scary shade of blue or grey, but within a few minutes of breathing actual air, she starts to take on a rosier complexion. She's covered in vernix, the waxy coating that protected her skin in the womb. Your baby may even have a pointy head, caused by her soft baby skull plates moving as she came down the birth canal. Yes, babies can be a bit of a sight when they first emerge into the world! Some babies howl the house down when they're born. Others just like to take things a bit more quietly and have a look around first.

If your baby needs a bit of help breathing, your carer may massage her back with a warm cloth, or suction fluid from her mouth or nose. Don't worry, she'll be right as rain soon.

At one minute after birth and five minutes after birth, your carer does an *Apgar test* on your little one, giving her an *Apgar score* on a scale of one to ten, one being lowest and ten being highest. There are five criteria for your little miss to jump through: colour, pulse rate, reflexes, muscle tone and breathing. This test alerts your carer to any concerns about the baby's health. After her first test, your carer dries baby and hands her over to mum for some skin-on-skin time before anything else.

Within a few minutes, your baby is breathing and surviving on her own. The umbilical cord stops pulsating, which means your carer will clamp it in two places and get it ready for cutting. This is your turn to shine, dad.

Your carer measures your baby's length and head circumference and weighs your baby. Those details go into your child's personal health book. Some practitioners in some states and countries take a footprint as well. Check with your carer if you would like one to keep.

While bub is having a wee snuggle with mum (or dad if mum's too knackered), your carer puts a plastic band around her ankle with your names, date of birth and weight. These can become mementos of your baby's birth when they come off a few days later.

The first few hours

Once all the commotion has died down, there are a few practical matters to attend to. Have you started ringing friends and family yet? Mum and bub usually have a bit of skin-on-skin time and get to know each other a bit first, then have some grub. Yep — feeding your baby is going to be mum's number one priority for some time, so they may as well get stuck into it now. Your carer helps mum and bub get comfy with a first breastfeed, or if you've decided to bottle feed, help with the mechanics of getting your little one taking her bottle.

Once that's all taken care of, getting bub dressed and getting mum into a nice warm shower are next on the agenda. Mum will be pretty knackered, so you may need to give her a hand standing up and getting about, or it may be your turn to get to know your baby a bit better while your partner's occupied.

A bit of food and drink wouldn't go amiss now either. It's been a long time since either of you had a decent meal. Taking care of any food cravings your partner couldn't eat while being pregnant are also high on the agenda. That said, all you may feel like is some well-deserved rest. If you are in a hospital, see to it that any formalities are dealt with quickly so you, your partner and your brand new little one can get some rest.

The first few days

Many parents have been lulled into thinking their baby is an angel in the first 24 hours. Babies can be very sleepy and settled for the first day, and you may be fooled! But it's also a very busy time getting feeding established and finding your feet in your new role as dad. Your baby should be having about six feeds in a 24-hour period to start off with, so supporting mum by taking care of nappy changes, burping or anything else that needs attending to can help her out a lot. If mum is still in hospital, you can be a real hero dad for spending as much time as possible with the baby so mum can rest some more.

Meconium

Your perfect, cute, little bundle will produce the foulest, stickiest, goopiest poo imaginable in the first few days of life. This black tar is called meconium and it's perfectly normal. Meconium is nature's way of flushing out all the various fluids and contents of your baby's intestines. The meconium is gone within a few days. After that your baby's poo should turn to a strange orangey-yellow colour. The great news is a newborn's poo hardly smells, easing you gently into the changing soiled nappies routine.

Going home

If your baby was born in hospital, your carer and the hospital decide when your partner and baby can go home. For some new mums going home can't come fast enough. Other mums may feel they need longer in hospital for the support a 24-hour on-call midwife brings, or they might not feel physically up to leaving hospital, depending on how the birth went. Don't let the hospital push you out if you're not ready for it. Talk about your concerns with your carer, but keep in mind that you can't stay in the relative safety of the hospital forever!

Blues

About day three after birth, mum might be feeling a bit low. This is perfectly normal and will pass. Your partner may burst into tears for no reason (that she can tell you anyway) or just feel overwhelmed by responsibility. If your partner had a hard pregnancy and is looking forward to getting her body back, finding it isn't 'back' yet may be very disappointing. Chances are your partner will also be sore in all sorts of places and performing simple personal hygiene tasks or even just going to the toilet can be really tricky. Do your dad thing and try to support your partner by helping out, telling her she's awesome and enjoying your baby. By the way, this initial blues has nothing to do with postnatal depression, which is likely to come later if you or your partner end up experiencing it. See Chapter 7 for more on postnatal depression.

Part II
The First Year

Glenn Lumsden

*'It was the happiest day of my life until
I started to ask: "Will she like school?
Will she make friends? Will she find
a decent partner and settle down?"
Haven't had a moment's peace since ...'*

In this part ...

After months of wondering about who your new baby is, she's finally here. When she's born, she's completely vulnerable and dependent on you for everything in her life. But over the next year she will uncurl, smile, open her eyes wide, laugh, become mobile and may even take her first step. It's an incredible year of highs (her first smile) and lows (sleepless nights). In this part, we guide you through what you need to do to make the most of the journey.

Chapter 6

Being Dad to a Newborn

In This Chapter

▶ Welcoming a new baby into your life

▶ Learning basic newborn care tasks

▶ Organising your day around the baby's needs

*Y*our baby is finally here. Does being a dad feel 'real' now? If not, don't worry. The first few days and weeks after birth can feel surreal. It does get better though. If you felt a bit left out during pregnancy and birth, now is your time to get stuck in. Your baby is here and needs time with dad as often as possible. Realising that your baby is an actual person and that you're responsible for her now can also be quite daunting.

Every baby is different and every family is different. While *Being a Great Dad For Dummies* is designed to take some of the mystery out of your mysterious newborn, no-one can tell you how to take care of your baby like you can. In the coming days, weeks and months, you'll learn how to read your baby like no childcare professional, doctor or midwife ever will. Yes, babies have similarities and outside help is there if you need it, but learning to read your baby is a skill you develop on your own. Every dad does.

In this chapter we give you some shortcuts on your journey to being a great dad with guides to the practical aspects of baby care, like changing nappies, dressing and bathing your baby. You get the lowdown on feeding, sleeping, burping and dealing with crying. We also talk about how having a baby shakes things up in your life like nothing else can and look at ways to cope with that change.

Dealing with the Aftershock

Starting out with your new baby — a vulnerable, unfathomable being — is a scary experience. Stepping through the door with your little bundle as you come home from the hospital, or waving goodbye to the midwife if your baby was born at home, are momentous steps on the path to becoming a family. You may feel overwhelmed flying solo with your partner and the new baby, but that's quite normal. Every parent in the world is probably feeling the same. Don't stress and simply take each day as it comes.

It's life but not as you know it

Remember last week when you slept in on Sunday, had a leisurely brunch with your partner and then went for a walk taking just the house keys and some money to stop off at the shop on the way home? You'll be able to do that again, but not for many years. Getting your head around how life works now can be a struggle, but that's where dads can shine once more. As dads, we're great at adapting quickly to new situations and making the best out of any challenge we face (say 'YES!').

Looking after a newborn is literally a 24-hour, seven-day-a-week job and is exhausting. Expect your baby to sleep a lot in the first couple of days, but she needs a feed every two to four hours, so even at night she'll be waking up. Even if mum is breastfeeding, you don't get off night duty. You can help by doing any nappy changes and burping so mum doesn't feel she's doing everything. If you're bottle feeding, you can take turns so at least one of you gets a decent stretch of rest.

You may already be tired from supporting your partner after a long labour and birth and because your baby is waking every few hours, you're not getting a good eight hours sleep like you used to. You can't catch up on the sleep you've missed, but you can minimise your own exhaustion by resting when the baby sleeps. This goes for both you and your partner in these heady first days. It may pay to get used to the idea of taking turns for everything. While one of you is busy the other should rest or catch up on some much needed sleep. Here's a perfect opportunity to shine as a dad by sharing the load with mum. Remember — apart from breastfeeding, dads can do everything around a baby and there is no natural disadvantage or disposition. You are just as qualified at handling a newborn as mum. In other words, you both don't know much and are learning as you go.

Any information you've read about caring for babies tells you there's lots of chores to do in the first weeks. That's not necessarily true. On days where everything goes smoothly — baby wakes, has a feed, is burped, gurgles cutely for a bit then goes down for a nap without a whimper — you may wonder what all the fuss was about and sit around twiddling your thumbs. But not every day goes smoothly. And not every cycle of feeding, burping and sleeping goes smoothly in a day. At any point the following may happen:

- Bub's nappy overflows or leaks
- Your baby shows symptoms you decide to have checked by a midwife or doctor
- Your baby spills (vomits) — called *positing* — after a feed.

This means you suddenly have to deal with something unexpected and your plan for the day is disrupted. Get used to it as it happens a lot with children. Life becomes a lot less predictable and plans go awry. But we think unpredictability's a good thing and you can enjoy it rather than choose to be a victim of it. Expect to have to change your baby's clothes (and yours) frequently, clean the carpet or furniture, or visit the after hour clinic. Your baby also may have days where she just refuses to sleep, or cries incessantly — which is a special kind of torture — and you could end up spending an entire day or night rocking her, walking her in a stroller, or carrying her in a sling just to get some peace. If there's one thing you can count on with newborns, it's to expect the unexpected.

Take offers of help whenever you can. Having a person close to you who you can call when things are trying and understands you're running on empty is very handy. You could ask the person to drop over a meal for the two of you, take over pushing the stroller while you sit in the backyard away from the crying, or hang out the washing. A few hours break from the baby can make all the difference.

If you feel you're at the end of your tether, don't despair. Get someone to give you a break for a couple of hours and chances are you'll feel much better.

Meet the baby

It can be easy to fall into the trap of letting mum take care of everything to do with the baby. This is really easy to do as some mums have a tendency to 'take over' and secretly or unconsciously harbour the belief that dads are somewhat inadequate when it comes to dealing with babies. Of course this is not so. There's no competition to see who is better at looking after bub. In some cases you may have to tell mum to go away and do something else while you look after the baby. We highly recommend you take care of bub early on so you become more and more confident at handling your baby. You can consider yourself 'graduated' from dad school when you are perfectly happy to spend an entire day alone with bub.

If you develop a mindset of seeing your baby as a developing person who needs your help every step of the way, rather than a source of work and chores, you're already onto a winner in becoming a future super dad. If you've decided to adhere to a strict routine, or the baby is unsettled or unwell, seeing him as a problem that needs to be fixed, or a timetable that needs to be met, can be tempting. He may seem like a blob that just eats, poos and sleeps, but a lot's going on inside that little baby right now. Although he can't show you quite yet, he's getting to know you.

Babies don't generally smile until six weeks although they can appear to be smiling, which is nice even if it is uncontrolled. You'll know when the smile is intentional. He'll look you in the eye and his face will light up like you're the best thing he's ever seen, which of course you are. In the early weeks your newborn will stare at you, sussing out your face, learning the sound of your voice and snuggling into you for snoozes. These are important bonding times.

When your baby holds your gaze and checks you out in detail, a lot of developmental work is happening in his brain. Give him every opportunity to look at you. Breastfeeding mums have the advantage that this happens naturally during feeds, so you need to carve out some extra time with bub to get your fair share of baby time.

Be a 100 per cent dad. Do the full spectrum of care tasks — changing your daughter's nappies, bathing her and wiping spew off your shoulder — in the first few days as that is how your baby bonds with you. Performing these tasks tends to give you a different perspective on life and after a while you might find that little dramas like baby poo on the carpet are really no big deal.

Young dads

Being a father, no matter the age when you become one, is about commitment; commitment to being there for a new young life, guiding that new person towards adulthood and independence. For young men who find themselves becoming fathers, the commitment is no different, although without the advantages of age and maturity, fatherhood can be even more of a challenge.

In addition, your relationship with the mother may not be a stable one, your parents may think you're too young and therefore not prepared to be a father, and there may be tension between your family and the mother's. Some people may think it's better not to have the baby at all.

But the more you show you're committed, the more people will respect your determination, and the more your baby will feel the love and security having a father brings. You can show your commitment by being involved with your baby from the day you find out your partner is pregnant. Go to pregnancy checkups and antenatal classes, start making arrangements for how you'll financially support your partner and child, and show that you're man enough for this very important job. Enlist the support of both your and your partner's families.

To be legally recognised as the baby's father, you need to have your name on the child's birth certificate. Doing so makes it easier for you to have access to him if your relationship with his mother breaks down.

For resources for young dads, take a look at teendads.fatherandchild.org.nz.

You've got the blues

Expect mum to shed some tears in the first week. Hormones are playing war games in her body right now and she'll be up and down like a yo-yo. Sometimes the best you can do is to listen, remain calm even if she has a go at you and stay positive at all times. These are just clouds passing and chances are her mood will change in a few hours. So don't sweat the small quarrels, emotional outbursts or little annoyances.

What you may not know is that dads can get the blues after birth too. At these times communicating well with your partner about what you're going through is really important.

Sometimes the blues can morph into postnatal depression or PND, a serious mental health issue for new parents. Have a look at Chapter 7 for more about PND.

Looking after a Newborn

So now that you've got the baby, what do you do with him? How do you look after him? Feeling responsible for a new person can be hugely overwhelming, but babies are pretty straightforward. All they really need is love, food, warmth, sleep and a clean pair of undies.

In general, newborns exist in a 24-hour cycle of sleeping, feeding, being awake and sleeping again. Your baby tires very easily and is awake for only about an hour or so at a time. A large chunk of that time he's being fed, burped and changed if necessary, but there's time for a bit of interaction with dad, like story time (tell him anything you want — he loves to hear your voice), a few songs or even a walk outside together before the next nap time.

Depending on where you live, your midwife or carer visits you or you'll visit her in the first few weeks after the birth to monitor your baby's growth and your partner's wellbeing, and to see how you're getting on in your new lives as a family. If you live in New Zealand you then pass into the care of your Well Child provider (Plunket). So if you ever feel you don't know where to turn or who to turn to, your carer, midwife or Well Child provider should be your first port of call. If you live in New Zealand you'll have regular appointments to visit your Well Child provider as your child grows, and in some cases they can come and see you. They also have day clinics where you can take your little one if you're having problems in a particular area, such as sleeping or feeding.

In Australia, many pharmacies provide midwives you can consult for free. Check with your local pharmacy if they provide this service and if you need to make a booking to see the midwife. You can discuss with the midwife any concerns you may have, such as feeding your baby, as well as having bub weighed to check that he's putting on weight.

See the contact details in the Appendix for people to call in your area. Help isn't far away.

Get a fridge magnet (or make yourself one) with phone numbers of your community health nurse, organisation or Well Child provider. In New Zealand you can get a Plunketline fridge magnet with the number 0800 933 922 prominently displayed. Phone numbers of community health organisations are listed in the Appendix.

Getting your hands dirty

In your role of dad you get to master a few practical jobs that are probably entirely new to you — until now.

Nappy changing 101

There's no magic to changing a nappy, they're actually really easy (see Figure 6-1). Being prepared before you start is the key, as is keeping cool when the nappy you're taking off is fuller than you thought it may be. To change a nappy, you need:

- A change table or change mat on the floor, bed or sofa where you have lots of space around you and good access to your baby lying in front of you
- A clean nappy, changing mat and barrier cream or powder ready to go
- A nappy bag (small plastic bag) to put the soiled nappy in
- Baby wipes or a bowl of warm water and some cotton wool or cloth standing by to wash down bub's bum
- Towels or extra cloth nappies within reach just in case there's a last minute explosion or leak while her nappy is off.

To minimise the risk of your baby falling from the bed or change table while you change him, either keep a hand on him *at all times*, or change him on a mat on the floor.

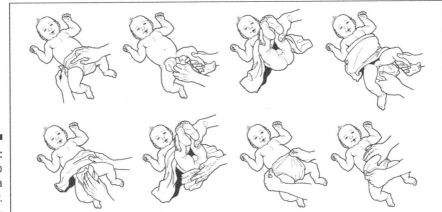

Figure 6-1:
How to
change a
nappy.

If you're a gadget dad you may want to check out baby wipe warmers. Often baby wipes can feel really cold to a baby so these devices help to warm the wipes.

As we talk about in Chapter 5, your baby's first poos are called *meconium* and they're unforgettable — sticky, greenish-black and tar-like. Your baby's poos gradually change colour as her digestive system is cleaned out and she adjusts to her new food.

- ✔ **Breastfed baby poos** are runnier than meconium, and are an orange-yellow colour.
- ✔ **Formula-fed baby poos** are firmer and a green-mustard colour.

If you are reading this before you've had your baby, it may seem very odd to be talking about the colour and consistency of baby poo. You'll probably find poo discussions become part of your new social chitchat with your partner and other parents.

To help prevent nappy rash, give your baby some pants-free time each day. Leave the nappy off so the skin can be exposed to the air and light. Use a barrier cream or powder when she has a nappy on to protect her skin. See the section about creams in Chapter 4 for more information.

Elimination communication

The practice of elimination communication (EC), also known as infant potty training or natural infant hygiene, means dispensing with nappies, and reading your baby's cues telling you when he needs to relieve himself. You simply learn when junior needs to go and pop him on the potty. Using sounds like 'ssss' and getting him used to specific places where he can 'go potty' can also act as a cue that triggers your child to relieve himself.

Those who practise EC say it empowers children by letting them take charge of their own toileting, encourages a stronger bond between parent and child as you learn to understand your child's needs and cues better, and makes your baby feel more secure because she knows you'll take care of her when she needs you to.

Practising EC doesn't mean you have to go the whole hog and be nappy-free completely — many parents try EC only when they're outdoors, or only during the day. Others encourage potty use at set times of the day, such as right after waking up, or before or after a bath. If you're interested in giving EC a go, take your time and see what works for you. Being watchful and conscious of your child's cues is the first place you'll need to start. Be prepared with a potty and some old cloth nappies to take care of accidents.

Take a look at `www.thepottyshop.com.au` or `www.organicbaby.co.nz/articles/diapers/US_pottybabies.aspx` for more information.

Bathing

Babies don't need baths every day, but a regular clean around their bottoms to prevent nappy rash, and the face and neck where dribbled and regurgitated milk can collect, is a good idea. Some babies don't like to be naked for long, others love being in the water.

For babies who aren't fond of a bath yet, 'topping and tailing' is an option. This practice is when you wipe his face, neck, hands and bottom with damp cotton wool or a soft cloth.

Holding your newborn securely at all times when you're bathing him is important. The best way is to hold him around the shoulders so that your forearm is supporting his head and your hand is holding the shoulder furthest away from you. Hold on tight — he can be a wriggly little monster even at this young age.

Here are some tips for bathing your little one.

- Check the temperature of the bath with your elbow. The water should be lukewarm; that is, if the water feels hot, it's too hot, if it feels cold, it's too cold. You can also check the temperature with a bath thermometer.

- Ensure the room temperature is quite warm. Your baby is naked and wet, so she can feel quite cold even when you feel perfectly fine in your clothes, especially when her head is wet for extended periods (try washing the head last).

- Collect everything you need before you start — cloth or cotton wool and a towel. Bub shouldn't need soap, shampoo or cleanser yet, let the natural oils in her skin do the work.

- Gunk can collect in all those rolls he's sporting on his legs and arms, so give them a wipe. The same goes for his hands, so unfurl his little fists to wipe his palms. Pay particular attention to the neck. Spilt milk rolls down the neck and can sneak into that chubby triple chin he's got at the moment.

- Wash his face, hair and neck where milk often collects with a soft cloth or cotton wool.

- When cleaning baby girls' bottoms, wipe from front to back. You don't need to pull back your little boy's foreskin to wash underneath either.

- When wiping junior's face, wipe his eyes from inner to outer using cooled boiled water and cotton wool. This helps prevent an eye infection. If he has a sticky eye, as is common in the first weeks after birth, you can also use cooled boiled water and gently wipe his eyes from inner to outer. You may want to do this before giving him a full bath, while he's still got his clothes on.

Take a cordless phone or mobile phone with you when you bathe your baby. You can never leave a baby unattended in the bath (they can drown in a few centimetres of water). Sometimes you might find you've forgotten something or need help. A phone is really handy if your partner or another person is elsewhere in the house.

Your baby sports a little stump of *umbilical cord* for about five to ten days after birth. The stump is kind of shrivelled and not that appealing to look at, but it needs to be kept dry and clean to prevent infection. All you have to do is wash with cotton wool and warm water when bathing baby or changing her nappy and pat it dry. Fold down the front of her nappy to stop the nappy rubbing against the cord and irritating it. If in doubt about the cord, call your midwife or doctor.

Dressing

Newborns aren't big fans of getting dressed and undressed, so keep clothing simple. Having a swag of sleepsuits with domes or a zip down the front are perfect for these early days when bub is in and out of bed or having his nappy changed a lot during the day.

In general, your baby should be wearing one more layer than you. If you're not sure how hot or cold your baby is, put a finger down the back of his neck. He needs to feel warm rather than too hot or cold.

If your newborn seems irritated by something, it can be as simple as a scratchy label rubbing her neck, or a thread wrapping itself round her toe. It may be a good idea to cut off labels, especially if they feel rough or scratchy.

Feeding

Feeding your baby to help her grow and be healthy is an absolute given. But how do you feed her and when?

Breast or formula?

The World Heath Organization recommends breastfeeding as the best way to provide nutrition for a baby. Breastmilk's the ideal food for your baby for the first six months of her life, providing targeted nutrition for her age and boosting her immunity. Breastmilk's always at the right temperature and generally readily available. Breastfeeding encourages bonding between mother and baby, and last but not least, breastmilk's free.

However, this isn't an ideal world and sometimes the situation just doesn't allow breastfeeding to work. Breastfeeding may not work for your family for many reasons. That's okay — there's an alternative to breastfeeding. Formula is a milk powder with added vitamins and nutrients to support growth and development, and plenty of babies thrive on it.

Whatever you and your partner decide to feed your baby, there are pros to both breastfeeding and formula. In some cases, both breastmilk and formula can be fed to your baby, which means dads get more time in the feeding seat. Breastfeeding mums can also *express* milk using a breast pump, which means you can help with the feeding even if there's not a can of formula to be seen.

As a dad, you can get out your advocating shoes again and support your partner in whichever method of feeding she prefers. If your partner's given breastfeeding her best shot but it hasn't worked out, it can be tough emotionally for her. Your partner may feel like a failure, or less like a 'real' mother to her child. She may be sensitive to the opinions of others around her, family and health professionals included, who don't understand the decision. Don't worry about the opinions of others; you don't have to justify yourself to anyone. Be confident that you're doing the best for your family.

Before deciding what and how to feed your baby, get as much information as you can so you're fully informed of the choices and their implications.

Bottle feeding

If you're bottle feeding you need the following gear:

- Bottles and teats
- Something to clean the bottles and teats in, such as a bottle steriliser unit for use in the microwave, a large bowl and sanitiser tablets, or a large pot that you can boil everything in, and a bottle brush.

Formula should be made up right before a feed according to the instructions on the tin or packet. Have a supply of bottles and teats ready to go for when your baby's next feeling peckish to save you mucking about.

Even if your partner's breastfeeding, getting the bottle feeding equipment anyway is a good idea. Your partner may wish to express breastmilk so you'll need the equipment listed for bottle feeding. Bottles and feeding equipment used with breastmilk need to be sterilised and cleaned just as thoroughly as feeding equipment used for formula.

Feeding your baby is about creating a nurturing relationship between you and your child, as well as food. Your baby is held close when being breastfed and the same should go for bottle feeding too. You can hold your baby in the same loving way as if she were breastfed, sing to her, or have a little chat while she feeds. You'll find she gazes up at you adoringly and checks out every little nook of your face.

How much and when?

Newborn babies love to eat. They grow rapidly and their stomachs are small, so they need regular feeds to keep them tanked up. Having regular feeds also encourages milk production. If your partner is breastfeeding, her milk supply adjusts to meet baby's demand.

Your baby tells you when she is hungry by:

- Opening her mouth and thrusting her head to the side, as if rooting around to find your partner's breast
- Sucking her fists or clothing
- Crying, which is a late sign of hunger and means feed me now or else!

A good sign that you're on the right track with feeding your baby is that he's putting on about the right amount of weight for his age. Babies usually lose weight in the first two weeks after birth. After the first few weeks bub usually gains around 200–300 grams per week. Don't worry, this rate slows as they get older.

Newborns usually need to be fed every two to three hours, or about eight to ten times in a 24-hour period. You'll know your baby is getting enough to eat because she'll have at least six to eight wet nappies a day, her wee will be light yellow, not dark, and her poos will be soft. If you're concerned, telephone your health nurse, Well Child provider, midwife or doctor.

Burping

Bringing up a good hearty belch may come naturally to you, but for bub, whose digestive system is still immature, a bit of air caught in her tummy or gut needs help to come out or it can be very painful. Usually a gentle pat on the back or a gentle rub counterclockwise does the trick. Your demure little princess will come out with a burp to make you proud.

You can use three good positions to burp your baby (see Figure 6-2):

- ✔ On your lap with bub facing down
- ✔ Sitting on your thigh facing out
- ✔ Over the shoulder, with bub's head held upright on your shoulder

Don't forget to support bub's wobbly head. To protect yourself against any positing (white milky spew), drape a flat cloth nappy or muslin cloth over your shoulder or lap.

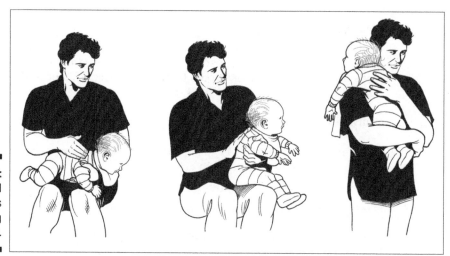

Figure 6-2:
Three good positions for burping your baby.

If your baby is difficult to burp, she may need a spoonful of gripe water, a mixture of water with various ingredients including alcohol, a bicarbonate, ginger, dill, fennel and chamomile. Gripe water is available over the counter in most pharmacies. A baby who writhes and cries after a feed may be suffering from reflux, a painful sensation caused by the regurgitation of gastric acid. See Chapter 7 for more information about reflux.

Sleeping — you and the baby

Newborns wake regularly in the night and day for food, so getting a good eight hour stretch of sleep is unlikely at this stage. As he gets older, your baby will sleep for longer chunks at night and will stay awake for longer in the day.

Your baby tells you he's tired by:

- Grizzling
- Jerky, tense movements
- Rubbing his eyes
- Staring into space
- Yawning

Crying is a late sign of tiredness and may mean your baby is overtired. When bub is overtired, he may be more difficult to settle as he's wound up about being tired.

It's all a matter of style

When you feed your baby can be just as controversial as *what* you feed your baby. Some organisations like Plunket in New Zealand and the Australian Breastfeeding Association advocate *demand feeding,* which is letting the baby determine when she is fed rather than feeding her to a schedule. Demand feeding may not work for your situation and feeding your baby at specific times may work best for you. A wide range of books is available with feeding plans to match your baby's age, including Gina Ford's *Contented Little Baby* books and Tizzie Hall's *Save Our Sleep.*

Teaching your baby about night and day

Babies don't have a sense of day and night when they're born, so part of your role as dad is to teach them the difference. Babies usually follow a cycle of sleeping, feeding, burping, changing, playing and sleeping again during the day, but you can leave out the playing at night. Where you are animated and chatty in the day, you are all business at night, keeping their room dimly lit for feeds and nappy changes, and straight back to bed when you're done. Changing your baby into day clothes during the day can help signal that night is over.

Having a bedtime routine can help signal that night is on the way and that's the time for sleeping (see Chapter 8).

Settling your baby

There are as many approaches to getting bub to sleep as there are children! How you get your baby to sleep is perhaps *the most* controversial topic. Strategies range from the *cry-it-out* approach where you put your baby down for a sleep in a bassinet or cot and let him cry until he falls asleep, to the *attachment parenting* philosophy of keeping bub in close contact with a parent in a sling or pouch to sleep and having him sleep in bed with you at night.

Other parents use a technique called *controlled crying*, where baby is left to cry for a short period of time, say a couple of minutes, before being soothed and comforted, then left for a slightly longer period. The length of time between visits is stretched out and eventually baby goes to sleep.

Some parenting experts warn against rocking your baby to sleep or doing anything where she falls asleep as a result of parent intervention, as bub becomes dependent on that technique to sleep. Putting your baby down sleepy but awake and letting her fall asleep on her own teaches her good sleep habits.

The settling approach you and your partner use is up to you. Decide what approach works best for your family.

Reach agreement with your partner before deciding which technique, method or routine to follow. Using different approaches tends not to work.

If you're having severe trouble settling your baby for days or weeks on end, calling your midwife, community nurse or community health care organisation may be helpful. Some organisations run special day centres where you can drop off your baby for a couple of hours to get some rest.

Swaddling

One technique for helping babies to sleep is swaddling, which involves wrapping a light blanket around the baby to keep him snug (see Figure 6-3). Swaddling also helps control the *Moro reflex*, which is when your little one seems to startle or jump out of his skin for no reason at all!

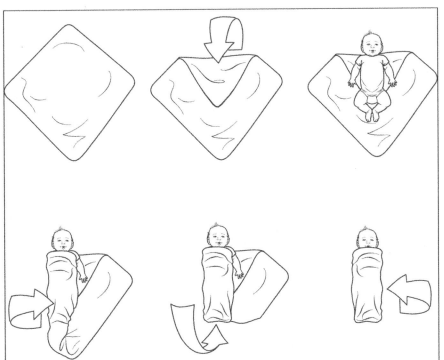

Figure 6-3: How to swaddle a baby.

Crying — you, your partner and the baby

At some stage crying is bound to take place in your household. A healthy baby may cry for several hours a day (or more). Crying is your baby's way of telling you he's hungry, lonely, tired, has wind, is too hot, or needs a nappy change. Sometimes he cries for no apparent reason at all.

Trying to figure out what the problem is while your baby howls can be stressful. Sometimes you may find yourself wanting to stop the noise whatever way you can. Crying can make you feel angry and frustrated, and you may want to lash out physically.

If you feel the crying is getting too much for you, put your baby in a safe place like her bassinet or cot, then take a few minutes to calm yourself outside. A very short but demanding exercise can help get rid of some excess adrenalin as well, so 'get down and give me 20'.

Whenever your baby starts crying get into the habit of checking three things: Is he hungry, has he got a dirty nappy, and is he comfortable and well (does he have a high temperature, are there any signs of vomit, and are there any other obvious signs of a health problem)?

After you've checked your baby, do one (or all) of the following to try to calm and comfort your baby:

- ✔ Burp him or give him some gripe water to help him bring up wind (if he's just had a feed)

- ✔ Cuddle and sing to him in a calm soothing voice, or put on a CD of gentle lullabies

- ✔ Give him a warm bath

- ✔ Put him down for a nap, he may just be tired (no kidding)

- ✔ Put your baby in the car and go for a drive around the block (not the most environmentally friendly alternative but sometimes driving's the one thing that works)

- ✔ Switch on a household appliance that makes a monotonous sound, such as a hairdryer, vacuum cleaner or washing machine. Or download some 'white noise' sounds from the internet and play the noise to your baby.

- ✔ Take him for a walk in the stroller or baby carrier (at any time of the day or night)

- ✔ Try a gentle soothing massage (see Chapter 7 for tips on baby massage)

Daddy time

Spending time with your baby doesn't have to be all work and no play. Every nappy change is an opportunity to have some fun with your little one.

Besides the usual chores and jobs you do with your baby, you can hang out together in other ways that are just good old-fashioned fun. Try these out for size:

- ✔ **Bathe or shower together.** Bathing can be a little nerve wracking at first. Make sure mum is standing by with a towel when you're ready to get out. Hold the soap — you don't want things to get slippery!

✔ **Enjoy some tummy time.** Tummy time is where your baby lies on the floor on her stomach and tries to lift her head, which helps develop junior's core strength. Read more about tummy time in Chapter 8.

✔ **Have a chat.** Babies coo from a few weeks old and delight in having their sounds repeated back to them.

✔ **Read to your baby.** It's never too early to turn him onto reading. He'll delight in the experience of being near you and seeing magical shapes and colours in the pictures.

✔ **Sing to your baby.** You can sing a tonne of good songs with your baby, but you can always make up your own. And bub doesn't care if you can't hold a tune. He'll just adore you more for it.

✔ **Take a trip to the park.** Your champ's a little too young for slides and flying foxes, but he'll love sitting on your lap with you on the swing for a gentle swing back and forth. He'll also love being outside and around other children.

Juggling Your Other Priorities

Before your baby came along, you were a partner, son, brother, friend, employee or boss and a member of your extended family. Now that bub has arrived and your priorities have changed, fitting in all those aspects of your life can be a struggle. Not only could you jeopardise the relationships you have with people in your life by letting fatherhood take over everything, but you could also lose your relationship with yourself and find your own wellbeing at risk.

Making time for yourself

You don't stop being the person you were before bub came along. You still need to take care of yourself so you can be the best father — and partner and so on — you can be for a long time. Just as mums need time to themselves, dads deserve some time off too. Having a chat with your partner about continuing to fit in sport or time with mates is important.

Making time for yourself may make you feel a little guilty and can be tricky to manage, but you need to take care of yourself before you can take care of anyone else.

Looking after your partner

There is a tendency for childcare organisations to hammer the message 'baby comes first', which is of course important. However, taking care of the baby can't be at the constant expense of your relationship. After all, if your relationship goes down the drain, there's a lot more trouble ahead. If you're the primary caregiver you know what it means to look after a baby all day and sort out the household at the same time. Being primary caregiver is a lot of hard work, so get your partner to help out when she gets home. If you're the main provider, make sure you chip in and do whatever needs to be done when you get home. Yes, working all day then helping out at home with looking after the baby is tough but you'll get through it. Looking after a baby and child does get easier over time — promise!

Above all, you and your partner need to have 'us' time and spend quality time together. You can do this by getting friends or family to look after the baby for a few hours while you go out, or even making a big deal out of a special occasion and celebrating at home when bub is asleep.

Here are some more ideas to keep your relationship alive and kicking:

- ✔ Invite some friends (especially those you are both friends with) over to cook dinner for you. Yes, inviting people to cook you a meal is cheeky but most people are only too willing to help out. This way you two get to see your friends, have a classy meal and don't have to do any work!

- ✔ Surprise each other with little gestures like leaving messages, buying a little treat or present, or getting out a DVD.

- ✔ Take a walk together with bub asleep in the pram. That way the two of you can get some gentle exercise and spend time together.

We are family

Your newborn isn't just your pride and joy, but the pride and joy of your entire extended family. There is nothing like having a child to help you realise what your own parents went through when you were a kid. They will undoubtedly want to be part of your new child's life. So share the love!

Having a lot of interaction with his grandparents, cousins and other close relatives is invaluable for your baby — the more love coming at him, the better. Having your baby feel comfortable and safe with family members also means having a lot of babysitters on hand and extra pairs of hands when you or your partner are finding things tough. It also helps your baby develop his social skills and builds confidence.

Dealing with visitors

They say it takes a village to bring up a child. When your baby has arrived you might realise that at least half of that village wants to drop in to check out the new addition to your family. Apart from your immediate family, expect to see neighbours you didn't know you had, uncles and aunts you haven't seen since you were a kid, old colleagues, acquaintances and of course all your and your partner's friends. Although you may want to show off your greatest creation, the demands of looking after a newborn (the sleep deprivation, the unfolded washing, the plates that are piling up everywhere) and your own anxiety about parenting don't make a great mix for entertaining. But you can turn a horde of visitors into an army of helpers:

✔ Don't serve tea or coffee when visitors come over. Point them to the kettle, or the vacuum cleaner, or the washing machine.

✔ If someone rings and says they're coming over, get them to pick up any supplies you're too busy or exhausted to get from the supermarket yourself.

✔ People love to help and contribute in any way they can, so make the most of offers.

✔ Put a sign up on your front door with something like 'Parents and baby sleeping, please phone to let us know when you're coming over'. Screen calls — that's what answering machines and voicemail are for.

✔ Don't be afraid to say 'no' when you just don't feel like having people over. People are generally quite understanding, especially if they've got children themselves.

Managing the work–life balance

Managing your commitments at work and your life outside paid employment is often a tricky one in this fast-paced society. Technology that allows you to work and be contactable 24 hours a day doesn't help you separate work from leisure time. Even before becoming a father, finding time to do the things you love may be a stretch. Now you have the extra demands of a family, it may be time to readdress your work–life balance and take some steps so you don't burn out.

In Australia and New Zealand, 'flexitime', or working more flexible hours, is becoming more accepted, especially for men. In some workplaces, you may be able to design your own hours, bank up hours worked to take days off in lieu, or add a no-overtime clause to your contract.

To find out how to go about setting up flexible working hours and what rights you have, see www.deewr.gov.au/workplacerelations in Australia, or www.dol.govt.nz/worklife in New Zealand.

Sex

Having a little nooky is probably the last thing on mum's mind for a few weeks after birth and this can be rough on a new dad. The lack of lovin' isn't because you smell bad or have suddenly become repulsive. Blame it on the hormones, lack of sleep, leaky breasts and the time it takes to recover from birth.

Women who've had a rough labour and some kind of intervention like ventouse or forceps should wait longer and may not want to resume intimate activities any earlier than 8 to 12 weeks. A tear or an episiotomy (see Chapter 5) can take six weeks or more to heal. On top of that, your partner may not feel very sexy having been through the birth and seen the look on your face as baby's head emerged. Your partner may feel self-conscious about her postpartum body. There's also the mental attitude required for having a sexy time. The memory of what birth felt like may last longer than the stitches, making the idea of sex unappealing.

You need to be a bit patient. Take cold showers and do plenty of exercise if need be. Most doctors recommend waiting at least six weeks after birth before having sex. That's the length of time it takes for the uterus to get back to pre-baby size after a vaginal birth.

But things get better. Your lovely lady is really just taking time to heal, get her head around things and regain some of her mojo. It may take a few months, but her appetite for sex will return. So in the meantime continue to support and love her, and show intimate affection for her in other ways with massages, foot rubs and cuddles.

When you're both ready to resume sexy time again, take it slowly. Let your partner control the pace and position, so things are comfortable for her. And don't forget contraception. It's a myth that breastfeeding stops another pregnancy and are you really ready for #2 yet?

Chapter 7

The First Three Months

In This Chapter

▶ Learning about your baby's needs and preferences

▶ Stimulating your baby's senses

▶ Understanding how your baby develops

▶ Dealing with postnatal depression

*N*ow you're really into the business end of fathering. You've got through the birth, know which end of your baby the nappy goes on and have an idea or two about how things are shaping up in your new family.

The first three months are possibly the most challenging in your new role as dad, as you come to grips with a vulnerable new life who is slowly learning more about her world and learning that you are there for her all the way.

In this chapter we deal with chores that need to be done to maintain your baby's health and hygiene, and tackle some problems that you may be facing, such as colic and reflux. We explore your baby's rapid development and how you can make the most of these important early learning stages. We also revisit postnatal depression and who you can turn to for help, and learn how to make your home a safe environment for your soon-to-be-curious, mobile baby.

Getting to Know Your Baby

There's no substitute for spending time with your baby and getting up close and personal. Babies are funny creatures and grow faster than you expect. They are kind of blobby one day, and all cute and big-eyed the next. You'll be stunned at how much they change in the first three months.

Your baby is unique in hundreds of ways, such as the way he yawns, the way he coos at the radio and the way his hair sticks up like an orang-utan's. These are all special things that will probably disappear as he grows up, so make time to absorb them as much as you can, because they won't always be there.

Everything in your baby's life is new and she doesn't have the experience to interpret situations or sensations. Watching your baby feel sand under her feet or see a dog for the first time can be hilarious. Things that we take for granted are totally new and bizarre to your wee one. Spending time with your baby is a great way to rediscover the world and sometimes can lift your spirits when you've had a rough day at the office.

When your baby was born you probably didn't know which way to hold up your little prince. Now you know which way he likes being burped, his favourite toys, the best times of day to go out and about, what songs he responds to and the best methods for settling him at night. If you don't feel you're getting any more of a grip on this fatherhood lark and still can't get him to sleep or bring up wind, don't worry. Good things take time and babies are quite random. Sometimes what works one day won't work the next. All you need is a bit of determination to stick with it. Don't give up being an involved father if you haven't had the amazing experiences we describe in this book. Your baby hugely benefits from every moment you spend with her, whether you feel you are making progress with her or not.

Groundhog day

Doing the same thing day in and day out is boring for adults, but babies love routine. If you haven't established some sort of routine or rhythm to your day with bub, establishing a routine soon is a good idea. We highly recommend having some sort of structure to your day so you and your little one know what's coming.

A pattern of sleeping, feeding, changing, having some playtime or awake time, then back to sleep is pretty standard. You don't have to run things on a clock if you don't want to, but some people love that rigidity. As he approaches his three-month birthday, your baby can stay awake for about one and half hours before getting tired and needing a sleep (again every baby is different so we are simply going by averages here).

Here are some thoughts about routines and how they may work for you.

- ✓ Anticipate how long you have out and about before bub gets tired and grizzly.
- ✓ Arrange visits from friends and family around your schedule, not theirs.

✔ Organise your day around your baby's naps, including getting some sleep while she does.

✔ Schedule time away from the baby each day, or time together as a family.

✔ Work out when to do those pesky chores, like laundry and cooking, going to the doctor or baby's checkups around when you think bub will be awake, asleep or needs a feed.

 Even if your baby is on a strict schedule and seems to have settled into his timetable well, try to take each day as it comes. Babies love to keep things interesting by filling their nappy as you step out the door, spewing just as you've got them into a smart new outfit, or demanding an early dinner when you're out without mum or a bottle to give them. Try not to see the world falling down around your feet if they don't conform to your idea of what they should be doing. Take a deep breath and get used to life on bub's time. Things will settle down again into a new routine soon.

Practical solutions to common problems

You're not alone in thinking that babies are a bit mysterious. They can't talk, so if there's something wrong, they can't tell you straight out what's going on. They have different, unfathomably fragile bodies compared to an adult's body and are sensitive to things adults wouldn't even notice, so babies suffer from 'problems' different to adults. By taking time to get to know your baby, you get more of an idea about what makes your infant tick. You may even have solved the mystery of what kinds of cry your baby makes to communicate with you. Trial and error is often the only way to work out what's going on with your baby, or what to do to achieve a particular outcome.

Here are some suggestions for dealing with common problems experienced by babies (and parents) during the first few months of your baby's life.

Jaundice

A common condition in newborns, *jaundice* refers to the yellow colour of the skin and whites of the eyes. Jaundice clears naturally in around one to two weeks. If the jaundice continues for any longer, your physician may recommend phototherapy, which is treatment with a special light that helps rid the body of bilirubin (the cause of jaundice) by altering the bilirubin and making it easier for your baby's liver to get rid of it.

Wind

Your baby lets you know he has wind by wriggling after a feed or arching his back. He may get upset and cry too. See the three main burping positions in Chapter 6 for starters, but if you're having trouble getting your boy to burp, try giving him a bit of diluted fennel tea or gripe water to drink after feeds. You can get both from your chemist or health food store.

Colic or infantile colic

Doctors often disagree about what causes infantile colic or which parts of the body are affected. Some doctors say colic's caused by trapped wind, others say a nerve condition's to blame. You will know if your baby suffers from colic. Your little one usually gets pretty ratty in the evening, crying inconsolably for around three hours. Colic generally starts at a few weeks of age and typically disappears when your baby is three or four months old. There is no magic cure for colic, we're sorry to say, but you can try all the various tricks to distract your baby so she falls asleep.

Some babies seem to be comforted by being held tummy down on laps or forearms. Colic doesn't seem to have any long-lasting effects on the baby, but hearing their baby scream night after night can be terribly traumatic for parents.

If the crying is getting too much for you, put baby in a safe place like her cot or bassinet and have a breather. You can also call your community health nurse or Well Child provider. The numbers are in the Appendix.

Surviving colic is really hard on parents, but the love and patience you show during this time won't be forgotten by your little one. Hang in there. Seek help from your child health nurse or Well Child provider if you think there could be some other problem.

Cradle cap

Cradle cap is a kind of baby dandruff, a condition in which flakes appear on the scalp. Cradle cap's not harmful and won't cause your little one any distress. You can get rid of cradle cap by massaging the scalp with almond oil or olive oil and rinsing with water. Cradle cap can sometimes become dark or crusty, or spread to the face, in which case you should talk to your community health nurse, Well Child provider, or doctor about more treatment options.

Reflux

The valve where your baby's oesophagus and stomach meet should close to keep food and stomach acids inside. In babies with reflux, this valve doesn't close properly yet. Most feeds end with your baby's milk and stomach acids coming back up again, either by being vomited up or catching in his throat and hurting him.

Your baby may have reflux if he:

✔ Has sour smelling breath

✔ Has a wet sound in his throat, or has wet-sounding hiccups. This is caused by regurgitated milk in his throat.

✔ Writhes, arches his back, vomits and cries after feeds.

Parents of babies who suffer from reflux worry if their baby is getting enough to eat, or if their baby is suffering a lot of pain from the reflux. Here are some ways you can minimise reflux symptoms.

✔ Avoid bouncing your baby.

✔ Change your baby's nappy by rolling her to the side rather than lifting her legs higher than her head.

✔ Feed your baby in an upright position, to help the milk stay down.

✔ Give your baby a dummy to suck. Sucking a dummy can help him swallow and clear the milk from the oesophagus.

✔ If using formula, try one of the anti-reflux varieties on the market. Talk to your doctor before trying anti-reflux formula.

✔ Keep baby upright as much as you can to help gravity keep the milk and stomach acids in her stomach where they should be.

✔ Put bub in a baby chair at an angle rather than placing her flat on the floor under a play gym when she's awake.

✔ Raise the mattress in baby's bed so her head is slightly higher than her stomach and the mattress is on a slight angle. Don't raise the mattress too much or she will slide under the covers, which may be dangerous.

Reflux can be the result of an allergy to cow's milk protein. In some instances having mum change to a dairy-free diet if she's breastfeeding, or switching to a non-dairy formula such as goat or soy, may help. Speak to a medical professional or a dietician first.

Treatments for reflux include thickeners that hold milk down, such as infant Gaviscon. You can also ask your chemist for specialised anti-reflux formula. Medication may be prescribed if your baby's case is particularly severe and she isn't putting on as much weight as recommended.

Your baby will remember the love and comfort you give her as she deals with reflux long after she's forgotten how reflux felt.

See www.reflux.org.au in Australia or www.cryingoverspiltmilk.co.nz in New Zealand for more on reflux management and support networks.

Colds

Even though you've bundled up your little precious and protected him from everything you can think of, he'll still fall prey to a common cold. Until he's two, there's not a lot you can do for a baby with a cold except give him infant pain relief (always check the right dosage for your little one's age), extra feeds and lots of cuddles. You can also try the following:

- Clear the mucus out of your wee one's nose with wet cotton wool rolled into a cone. Don't use a cotton bud because a sudden movement from bub can cause the cotton bud to get stuck up his nose. Use a fresh piece of cotton wool for each nostril.

- Keep up the feeds so he doesn't get dehydrated. If he's been sleeping through the night (which would be a miracle at this age) expect him to wake up more, so top him up with more fluids then.

- Saltwater drops can help unblock her nose and sinuses. Dissolve some salt in warm water and apply up her nose, drop by drop, from some dampened cotton wool.

- She may have to stop to breathe when feeding if her nose is blocked, so take your time and let her control how much she takes.

- Use a humidifier to moisten the air, which can reduce baby's congestion.

- You can also try a nasal bulb, which is a plastic bulb attached to a nose piece which goes up baby's nostril. You squeeze the bulb before inserting the nose piece and let the bulb go when the nose piece is in there, sucking out mucus. In most cases your baby will sneeze a lot which clears the mucus, so you don't need to get overly zealous about clearing your baby's nose with a nasal bulb. A nasal bulb is just handy when you can see that some mucus is stuck in the nose and you can't get it out any other way.

If your baby suddenly comes down with a fever, or your instincts tell you something more than a cold is going on, call your local health hotline or get down to your doctor. If anything, a trip to your GP can rule out anything more serious and put your mind at ease. A temperature of 36.4 degrees Celsius taken under your baby's arm is normal.

Infant acne

Some babies develop a pretty unfortunate pimply face the first days and weeks after birth. The spots are caused by hormones from the mother and fade away once those hormones are out of your baby's system. You can't do anything to make them go away, but keep baby's hands under wraps (for example, in mittens) to stop her scratching the spots accidentally. A gentle wash of warm water will keep the spots from becoming infected. Pat dry afterwards.

Nappy rash

Nappy rash is a flat red area on your baby's bum or genital area caused by ammonia from his wees and poos staying on his skin. Nappy rash is very uncomfortable and you may meet some resistance at nappy changing time if your baby has nappy rash.

The best cure for nappy rash is prevention, so make sure the bottom is washed with warm water and a soft cloth or cotton wool every time you change his nappy. Gently pat everything dry and apply your barrier cream or powder before the nappy goes on. Give him some time each day without a nappy to expose his skin to the air and sunlight.

If your poor bub should come down with a case of nappy rash, a cream like zinc and castor oil or calendula cream can help heal the skin. Be vigilant about baby hygiene. Wash cloth nappies in hot water and dry them in the sun to kill any bacteria lurking in the fabric. Some babies react badly to disposable nappies, others flare up at the sight of a cloth nappy, so be flexible and experiment with different products in your nappy routine until you figure out what works for your baby.

Nappy rash tends to flare up when your champ is teething, but not all babies experience this.

If nappy rash persists despite all your efforts, see your GP, Well Child provider or child health nurse for more advice and treatment.

Teething

Most babies younger than three months old haven't started teething, but some babies are eager to grow up and may have a few teeth bothering them. Some babies are even born with a few gnashers!

See Chapter 9 for tips on helping bub deal with teething.

Skin irritations and scratching

If your girl's skin is dry or she's scratching herself, soothe her skin with olive or sweet almond oil and put some mitts on her hands. You can get shirts and sleepsuits with fold-over ends that become mittens.

Non-trivial care jobs

Like you, babies have growing nails and snotty noses, and get stuff in their ears and eyes. Babies need ongoing body maintenance. Funnily enough that's often when frustrated mums hand over to dad. Some of these jobs require real men, so time to get stuck in. By the way if, as part of your fatherhood journey, you haven't been vomited on, had poo squirted on you, or been christened with pee yet, you're not trying hard enough.

A compilation of jobs for real men includes:

- ✔ **Administering medicine.** After vaccinations or during an illness, your baby may need paracetamol or antibiotics. Medicines for babies are usually prescribed as a liquid suspension and are most easily given in a plastic syringe (no needle attached). Dosages are typically measured in millilitres (mL) and getting the dosage right is important. Get your GP or nurse to show you the correct dose when your baby's given his vaccinations or he's prescribed medicine.

- ✔ **Cleaning ears.** Earwax is a good thing because it protects the ear canal, so don't get too worked up about it. Wiping the outer ear and neck area where milk can collect should do the trick, but be careful not to get water in the ear canal. If you're concerned about the cleanliness of your baby's ears, leave it to the professionals and see your doctor.

- ✔ **Mopping up bum explosions.** Every baby has at least one bowel motion that truly tests the limits of what you thought a small person could excrete. Babies also get the odd bout of diarrhoea if they eat something that disagrees with them or if they catch a gastrointestinal bug. The result is the mother (or father) of all poos, also called the 'backsider' as poo goes all the way up the nappy and into the bodysuit.

If your little one has a tummy bug or diarrhoea you can minimise the mess by doubling up on nappies, so if he's wearing a newborn size nappy, put a nappy the next size up over the top. That should contain any unforeseen leaks. You may want to invest in an apron to protect your clothes at these times.

✔ **Trimming finger and toe nails.** Get yourself one of those dinky little manicure sets for children, which include a pair of scissors with rounded ends, a tiny pair of nail clippers and some emery boards. Approach your baby when she's asleep or feeding so she's not focused on having her fingers dealt with. The clippers are probably easiest to start with, but failing that try special baby scissors. If you've done a pretty rough job, smooth off craggy nail edges with an emery board so she doesn't scratch herself with them. This job is likely to get harder as your baby gets older, so get some early nail cutting training in while she is still pretty helpless and can't move about much.

✔ **Wiping away sticky eye.** Many babies have a build up of mucus at their eye corners, and this can be easily removed by wetting a piece of cotton wool with lukewarm water and wiping the mucus gently away.

Hands-on Dad

The days of fathers coming home from work and disappearing behind the evening paper while mother tended to the baby are long gone. Twenty-first century dads are rolling up their sleeves and are fully involved in all things baby, which doesn't just include chores. In this section we explore ways to have fun with your new playmate and pick up new skills along the way.

Baby massage

We're not talking about being pummelled by a masseuse, but a gentle rub with a light oil, much like a hairdresser shampooing your hair or giving you one of those funny head massages. Baby massage has lots of benefits, not least of all getting his skin nicely moisturised. Touch is the most developed sense in a newborn and sensory receptors in his skin help him learn about his body. He's not really aware of where his hands, feet and tummy are yet.

Baby massage is a gentle way to express care and nurturing for your baby and is a time for you to engage and chat, or sing a song. Baby massage is total bliss for your little one and helps his development tremendously. So if you can give your little champ a massage a day that's fantastic!

A good time to massage your baby is after his bath and before bed. He'll be warm from the bath and massage will further relax him for a good night's sleep (fingers crossed).

Here's how to massage your baby:

- Make sure the room you're in is warm and that your hands are warm as well.
- Set up a flat, comfortable surface, like a change table or firm mattress.
- Use a massage oil like calendula, sweet almond or olive oil. Warm the oil in your hands before touching bub.
- Take your time. This isn't a chore like washing nappies or getting dinner on the table. Use this time to connect and enjoy being with your baby.
- Have a wee chat, or sing a song, but keep the tone of the massage calm, peaceful and low key. You can also name the body parts you are massaging. Although speech development is a while off, naming the body parts establishes vocal patterns your baby will recognise over time.
- You can roll baby over and rub her back. First, roll bub onto her side, then put a hand under her torso and the other hand on the leg closest to you. Ease her onto her chest by removing your hand as she turns over.
- To massage feet, have bub on her front and use slow gentle circles on her tootsies.
- To massage legs and arms, hold baby's foot or arm with one hand while massaging the limb in one long, gentle stroke with the other from the hand or foot and up.

Avoid massaging bub straight after he's eaten. Pressure on his belly might not agree with him.

Try to have one hand always touching your baby while massaging, even when reaching for more oil.

Baby activities

You can encourage brain development by playing with your baby. Try these activities:

- ✔ **Lying him on his tummy.** Also known as 'tummy time', a few minutes a couple of times a day on his tummy helps strengthen his back and neck muscles. On the floor you can do some visual activities like blowing bubbles or slowly moving a ball in front of his eyes. Place some objects such as toys just out of reach. He'll try reaching them as he develops his physical skills.

- ✔ **Moving him around.** Movement is good for getting those *synapses* or brain connections firing and linking with other parts of the brain. Try some gentle rocking, or have him lie on your lap facing you as you move your legs up and down. Or you can have bub on your shins while you lie on the floor. Hold his hands and lift your legs. He'll love it.

- ✔ **Reading to her.** You can't start the book habit too early. Picture books with clear contrasting colours are a big hit.

- ✔ **Talking to him — a lot.** He can't understand your words, but he's listening and learning and picking up language faster than he ever will again. You don't have to discuss Shakespeare or politics, just talk about what you're doing or seeing.

Even a mundane task like changing a nappy is an opportunity to learn for your baby. Repeating phrases like 'lying down' or 'off comes your nappy' each time connects the words and action for your child. As his language skills develop you may find him pointing to his nappy, or lying down when you ask him to.

Sport and Recreation New Zealand have put out some pamphlets with activities for under-fives which use 'active movement' skills to help your child develop and learn. See www.sparc.org.nz.

Keeping baby safe and sound

Your baby is pretty helpless physically and oblivious to danger. Keeping bub safe is up to you. The buck stops with the parents; nobody else keeps your baby safe for you. So keep up the good work by always:

- ✔ Checking the temperature of formula by sprinkling a little on your wrist

- ✔ Ensuring your baby's breathing isn't obstructed by objects such as blankets pulled too high or bumpers in her cot (remember to keep your baby's face clear and her face up when putting her down for a sleep)

- ✔ Having a smoke-free home and car

Scalding

Did you know that an average sized cup of tea or coffee can cover up to 70 per cent of the skin surface of your baby? This means up to 70 per cent of the skin of your baby could be scalded if the liquid is accidentally spilled on the baby. Unfortunately scalding is a common occurrence as any accident and emergency nurse will tell you. So always place hot beverages on safe surfaces (not near the edge) and well away from the baby.

- ✔ Keeping a hand on her when she's on elevated surfaces like a bed or change table

- ✔ Keeping your cups of tea, coffee and other hot beverages well clear of the baby (see the sidebar 'Scalding')

- ✔ Providing age appropriate toys. Toys for older children have small parts that may break off and choke your little one.

- ✔ Supervising the baby when she's in the bath, even if she's using a bath support

- ✔ Using a car seat for car trips

Right now, he can't move or prod his fingers into electrical sockets, so you can get a head start and baby-proof your house now for when he's on the move. A good place to start is to get down on your hands and knees for a baby's-eye-view of the terrain and see what jumps out at you as potentially dangerous.

Table 7-1 provides ways to help you rectify any trouble spots.

Table 7-1	Baby-proofing room by room
Room	**What to do**
Living areas	Secure bookshelves and other unstable furniture like tall CD racks to the wall with anchors to stop them toppling on your baby.
	Put childproof locks on china cabinet doors to prevent your sweetie getting into granny's heirloom china.
	Use a guard around your fireplace or heater. Teach your child to stay away by saying 'hot' when he is near the heat source.
	Tuck cables away or put cushions and furniture in front of them.
	Hide any remote controls you don't want slobbered on.
	Put barriers across any stairs or steps.

Room	What to do
Kitchen	Keep appliance cords from hanging over the bench or stove. Your baby could easily pull a kettle of hot water on herself.
	Keep pot handles tucked in over the stove.
	Use guards on your stove elements and around the top of your stove to prevent hot food spilling onto your child.
	Erect a barrier across your kitchen's doorway to prevent your child entering while you cook.
	Forget using table cloths with really small children — one tug and everything goes overboard.
	Keep cleaning products and detergents in a cupboard with a childproof lock, preferably in a high cupboard.
	Never store poisons in food containers. Junior can't tell the difference between disinfectant and a bottle of juice.
	Use a childproof lock to secure any cupboard or drawer that has precious china, knives, or equipment you don't want becoming one of your baby's favourite toys.
Laundry	If you use a nappy bucket, make sure the lid is securely fitted and is always stored out of bub's reach.
	Keep cleaning products and detergents in a cupboard with a childproof lock, preferably in a high cupboard.
	Make sure all buckets are left empty.
Bathroom	Make sure your hot water thermostat is set to less than 50 degrees Celsius.
	Keep all electrical appliances out of the bathroom to prevent accidental electrocution.
	Consider getting a lock or keeping the lid down on your toilet to prevent anything, like your car keys, being deposited in the toilet.
	Keep a lock on the medicine cabinet, and keep cleaners and detergents — even your shampoos — in a locked cupboard, preferably out of reach.
Outdoor areas	Make sure pools and balconies are fenced. Fences should have gaps of no more than 50–85 millimetres between pickets to prevent baby becoming trapped between them or falling through.

Your Baby's Development

Watching your offspring transform from a curled ball of wrinkled, angry-looking baby into a wide-eyed smiling bundle of delight is a joy. In the first three months of life, your baby changes so fast, you may have forgotten what they were like in those first days.

Growth and weight

Newborns typically lose up to ten per cent of their body weight in the days immediately after birth, but can put that back on in the following one to two weeks. Your midwife, child health nurse or Well Child provider will keep track of your baby's weight and plot it on a growth chart, usually found in your baby's record book. Unless bub is not putting on any weight, is distressed, lethargic or seems undernourished, weight is not usually a cause for concern, but is a useful way to track his growth.

Babies usually have growth spurts at around 6 and 12 weeks, when they wake more at night for feeds and take more food during the day.

During the first three months, your baby will:

- Blow lots of dribbly bubbles.
- Coo, baby's first form of non-crying verbal communication.
- Learn to lift her head without help — the result of all your tummy time endeavours.
- Reach out and try to 'bat' objects in her vision.
- Smile. The first heart-melting smiles usually appear around six weeks.

Hearing, sight, taste, smell and touch

Your baby's senses, just like the rest of his body, need time to develop. He learns by experiencing the world and interpreting what's going on, using his senses to gather information. Here's the lowdown on what your baby can sense already and what you can do to encourage further development of his senses.

Hearing

Your baby can hear from before she's born. Already she's had months listening to mum's stomach gurgle and the distant rumble of you talking to her. Your baby may settle to the sound of the vacuum cleaner or washing machine because those noises are like the white noise of being in the womb.

Your baby will respond to the high pitch of baby talk which you'll find yourself automatically using when you talk to him (some say we are genetically programmed to speak this way, so don't worry about handing in your man card when you hear yourself talk like a girl). Your little one can't understand English yet, but she can understand your tone and is soothed by soft gentle sounds. She listens when you speak and even though your speech is gibberish to her, keep going, talking is good for her language development.

If you live in a household where more than one language is spoken your child is in for a treat. Not only do children with a multilingual upbringing perform better academically (across all subjects), but seeing a child master two or more languages with absolute ease is great. In some cases multilingual children come in very handy as translators between various parts of the family. So by all means speak to your child in as many languages as you can. A baby can produce any sound of any language in the world. If she's exposed to a particular language before she reaches about nine months she'll be able to speak it like a native tongue.

Your child health nurse, midwife or Well Child provider does a simple hearing test during the first few weeks. If for some reason this hasn't happened, have your child's hearing tested right away because hearing problems can be diagnosed early. As your child grows, hearing checks are important, because hearing loss can be caused through things like ear infections, trauma and high noise levels.

Sight

The world is fuzzy for a newborn, whose eyes are only just working out how to do their job. Your newborn sees best at a distance of 20–35 centimetres, which is a good distance to check you out when she's in your arms. In the early weeks, she'll gaze at contrasts like the folds in your curtains or car lights shining on a wall as it passes your house. She'll look at something for a short time then look away. Looking at something for a long time — apart from you and her mum — is hard work for newborns. You and your partner are your baby's favourite sight.

In these early weeks, your baby learns how to focus both eyes and follow a moving object and likes to look at contrasts rather than similarly coloured objects.

You can help your champ's vision by showing her a variety of brightly coloured and contrasting images. Use one item at a time so she isn't overloaded. A nice game to play is to move in and out of your baby's focus range. She'll smile when you come into focus and concentrate on your face.

The saying 'out of sight, out of mind' is particularly true for babies up to the age of around four to nine months. If bub can't see something, it doesn't exist, which comes in handy when he wants something, such as a toy, but you need him to focus on something else. Hide the toy and you're good. However, bub eventually works out that things continue to exist even when they're not in sight. This signals the beginning of establishing a short-term memory. For example, if mum leaves the room bub starts crying because he remembers his mum and she's no longer there. This phenomenon is referred to as *object permanence*.

Smell and taste

Bub comes equipped with a pretty developed sense of smell and taste. He knows you by your smell as well as your voice and what you look like, and can recognise changes in the taste of breastmilk or a different brand of formula. Bub can already taste salty, sweet, sour and bitter flavours. When he's introduced to solids in a few months, you'll learn even the blandest foods can taste wild and exotic to a baby.

Touch

At birth, your baby's sense of touch is fully developed and she loves to be in close contact with you as much as she can. Your baby's favourite thing is to be cuddled or snuggled by you and you can't cuddle her too much. Your baby's sensitivity is also why baby massage is such an effective tool in bonding, nurturing and settling.

One of the first ways your infant discovers the world of touch is through his mouth. Even in these early weeks he investigates rattles, blankets, his fingers and all manner of objects by gumming and lolling them in his mouth.

The flipside of this incredible sensitivity is that babies can feel pain and are sensitive to scratchy clothing labels, temperature and uncomfortable nappies, so if bub is upset check if she is uncomfortable or overheated because of her clothing. A baby's skin is several times more sensitive than an adult's skin so an unintentionally firm grip can be quite painful. Rugby dads — watch the pressure you apply.

Your baby's amazing brain

By three months of age, your baby is almost unrecognisable from the helpless little bundle you first met at birth. As new connections, called synapses, form between different parts of her brain, she displays new skills and understands more of what's going on around her. Synapses are formed very quickly in the first six months of life, but as the brain works out which are worth hanging onto, those synapses that aren't used frequently are abandoned. Repetition of words, songs, sights, sensations, routines, movements, sounds and tastes helps your baby's synapses develop and make sure they're retained.

Research shows that stimulation in these early months and years of your child's life enhances brain development. Conversely, no stimulation leads to a loss of brain function. Researchers who study brain development found that brain development happens in patterns but not at the same pace. The researchers generally talk about 'development windows' being open for a particular period. During this time your baby is particularly interested in developing a certain sense or skill, or grasping a concept. If you find your baby is particularly interested in something, such as rolling over, give him lots of opportunities to do more of it and ensure he can explore his interest safely.

Stimulating your baby's brain is easy. Give him lots of safe opportunities to explore what he's interested in and keep offering new experiences. See earlier in this chapter for ideas to get your baby's brain's abuzz with new information.

Babies learn new skills at different stages and ages, so don't worry if your baby isn't doing what everyone else's baby in your coffee group is doing — he'll get there. If you're concerned, talk to your Well Child provider or child health nurse.

There's a big 'nature vs nurture' debate about how or how much you can stimulate or influence your child's development. Nobody knows how much influence *nature* (the genes your baby has inherited) and *nurture* (parental input and the learning environment) have. However, neither nature nor nurture is 100 per cent responsible for your child's development; they both have a certain degree of influence.

The next few months are about your baby discovering that he has a body. Newborns don't recognise their limbs or body as their own. Hands are a particularly big part of your bub's life in the coming months. Make sure any toys he has contact with are suitable for his age because toys for older kids may have parts that can break off and become a choking risk. Toys with different textures and surfaces expose your baby to different sensations when he plays with the toys in his hands.

Between one and three months, your baby is probably:

- ✔ Discovering her hands, perhaps sucking her thumb or fingers
- ✔ Smiling in response to your smile
- ✔ Uncurling her fists to grasp a rattle. She probably won't be able to look at the rattle, as she won't connect what her hands and her eyes are doing yet and the rattle may be too close for her eyes to focus on.

Male and Female Postnatal Depression

Feeling 'the blues' is one thing, being in a black hole is another. That's how some people describe postnatal depression (PND). The condition is associated with mothers for the most part, with an estimated 10–15 per cent of mothers suffering from postnatal depression. What's less well known is that three to ten per cent of fathers can suffer from PND too.

While many men report feeling left out of their partners' lives as mothers deal with the constant needs of their babies and their own exhaustion, others feel overwhelmed by the demands of work and hectic situations at home. At worst, you may even have negative or guilty feelings about your baby and feel you're a bad father or partner.

Knowing about and recognising some of the signs of PND can assist you to seek help for yourself or someone else with PND. Some of the signs of PND to look for include:

- ✔ Anxiety or panic attacks
- ✔ Feelings of hopelessness
- ✔ Frequent crying spells
- ✔ Loss of energy and appetite
- ✔ Loss of enjoyment in everyday activities, and in your baby
- ✔ Loss of sex drive
- ✔ Mood swings
- ✔ Problems sleeping even when baby is settled
- ✔ Prolonged feelings of sadness and hopelessness, with nothing to look forward to
- ✔ Suicidal thoughts

Every case is different. If you feel you or your partner may have PND, talk to each other about how you're feeling and see your GP.

If your partner has PND, supporting her may seem like a pretty impossible task and you may feel out of your depth. You can help in lots of ways. Try some of these ideas:

✔ Arrange things so you can spend time together with your partner — alone. Regular 'us' time helps de-stress both of you and helps you to find and share some common ground again.

✔ Let her talk while you listen, or involve a friend she feels comfortable talking to.

✔ Take over more of the housework and baby care, and try to let her get some sleep. If you can't take on everything, call in some support like family and friends so you're not swamped as well.

✔ Treat her in some way, with a night at the movies, a massage voucher, a bunch of flowers, or a special gift.

Postnatal depression in men, though not as common as PND in women, is just as serious. Admitting there's a problem is difficult. You may find the following helpful:

✔ **Talk to your doctor:** He can offer you a range of options including counselling and medication.

✔ **Talk to family and friends:** This step can be a biggie, but you're likely to be amazed at how keen people are to help. Chances are some of your mates have gone through the same thing.

✔ **Find support in your community:** In Australia talk to PANDA (www.panda.org.au). In New Zealand contact Plunket (call PlunketLine on 0800 933 922 or visit www.plunket.org.nz) or the Father & Child Trust (www.fatherandchild.org.nz).

✔ **Get some exercise:** Feeling fit and active can lift your mood. Around 30 minutes of daily activity is all you need to release mood-enhancing hormones.

Postnatal depression is temporary, and you can find a way through it. If you feel lost, take stock and get some help.

Do you feel like screaming?

If everything's getting too much for you and you need time out, here's a tip. Take time out from your partner and baby, go into another room or leave the house for a bit and let it all hang out. Scream the room, house or street down if you want. This works wonders at releasing tension and you'll feel like a new dad. Doing a quick, high energy exercise like push-ups to release excess adrenalin can also be really useful. Listening to a baby crying is one of the most stressful things you can expose a human body to (nature's cunning way of making sure the offspring is well looked after and gets priority treatment). So don't be surprised if the baby is stressing you out.

All your baby wants to do is please you. You are a rock star in his world, you're the bee's knees. When things are getting tough, you're sleep deprived, damp nappies are hanging on the clothes rack, it's 2.00 am and bub won't settle, remember that your baby isn't crying for the hell of it.

Support organisations

For practical advice on fathering go to www.diyfather.com. Other good support places to start are:

Australia:

- ✔ www.lonefathers.com.au
- ✔ Mental Health Services 1300 785 005
- ✔ Post and Antenatal Depression Association www.panda.org.au. Call 1300 726 306
- ✔ SANE Australia 1800 688 382
- ✔ The Bub Hub www.bubhub.com.au/servicesdepression.php
- ✔ www.menstuff.org/resources/resourcefiles/fathers.html

New Zealand:

- ✔ Marriage Guidance Services www.marriageguidance.org.nz
- ✔ Mothers Matter website has information for fathers suffering from PND and ways to support women with PND www.mothersmatter.co.nz
- ✔ Post and Ante Natal Distress Support Group based in Wellington www.pnd.org.nz
- ✔ Plunket www.plunket.org.nz
- ✔ Relationship Services www.relate.org.nz

Also see *Postpartum Depression For Dummies*.

Chapter 8

Months Three to Six

In This Chapter

▶ Looking after your growing baby

▶ Getting on with life

▶ Leaving your baby with others

Congratulations — you've survived the first three months! Remember those first days when you didn't even know how to hold your precious new baby? By now, things in your household are probably settling down a bit, and the adrenalin rush (read 'chaos') of the first weeks is dropping away behind you. Your baby is spending longer periods awake and is engaging with you and her surroundings. So now you two can really get to know one another!

The next three months are also a period of great change developmentally, as your 'helpless' three-month-old, who can barely hold up her head, transforms into a six-month-old bundle of activity, capable of moving around, downing solid food and using her hands for all sorts of things (some of which you don't want her to do). Hey, she may even have a few gnashers already!

In this chapter, you find out what you can do as a dad during the next three months to interact with your little champ. You also learn about any paperwork required for your baby, what you need to know before you can leave your baby with others and doing things with your partner as a couple.

Your Growing Baby

Your baby is changing — and fast. Commonly, at around three months, he undergoes a growth spurt and if he's been suffering from colic or other problems with digestion, these may mercifully start to subside over the next few months. Check out Chapter 6 for more information about burping a baby and Chapter 7 for more about digestive problems.

Baby's new tricks

Over the next three months your baby will start to:

- Clasp objects, bring his hands together and reach for toys
- Develop stronger neck muscles and be able to hold his head up more steadily
- Gnaw on everything she can get her hands on
- Make babbling sounds
- Recognise familiar objects and people, and start to look for toys
- Roll over from her back to her front
- Sleep for longer stretches at night (. . . in some cases)
- Smile (intentionally) and squeal

If your baby isn't doing these things, don't panic. All babies are unique and develop at their own pace. If you're concerned with delayed milestones, talk to your doctor, check with your midwife or talk to the community health organisation in your state or territory (Australia), or Plunket (New Zealand). Table 8-1 lists community health organisation contact details.

Table 8-1	Community Health Organisations	
Australia		
Australian Capital Territory	Australian Capital Territory Department of Health	www.health.act.gov.au/c/health
New South Wales	New South Wales Department of Health	www.health.nsw.gov.au
Northern Territory	Northern Territory Department of Health and Families	www.health.nt.gov.au
Queensland	Queensland Health	www.health.qld.gov.au
South Australia	South Australia Health	www.health.sa.gov.au
Tasmania	Department of Health	www.dhhs.tas.gov.au
Victoria	Victorian Department of Health	www.health.vic.gov.au/doh
Western Australia	Western Australia Health	www.health.wa.gov.au
New Zealand		
Ministry of Health		www.moh.govt.nz
The Royal Plunket Society		www.plunket.org.nz

The three-month mark — a milestone in Balinese life

When Balinese babies reach the grand old age of 105 days (three months in the Balinese calendar), they undergo the ceremony of Tutug Sambutan — a naming ceremony. The ceremony is a big deal in Bali, where the locals practise a unique form of Hinduism. During the ceremony, the baby's hair is cut for the first time, but not on the crown, which is left until the baby is a year old. Also, the Balinese bubs touch the ground with their feet for the first time, and have their feet blessed to help them learn to walk faster. Celebrated with family, friends and even the entire neighbourhood, this event can take weeks to prepare.

New challenges for dads

After the first three crazy months, you and your partner are probably more confident parents and are getting your heads around how your new family works. But, as with every stage of being a great dad, you get a few more hurdles to jump.

Experiencing postnatal depression

Did you know that *postnatal depression* (PND) affects dads as well as mums? Postnatal depression is a form of clinical depression which can affect women and men following childbirth. See Chapter 7 for lots of useful information about PND.

Helping your partner survive postnatal depression

Riding out the storm of your partner's depression can be tough, so your patience, communication and support are vital. She may be irritable — mad at you one minute for trying to do too many things with the baby, then mad at you for not doing enough. Stay strong and make the effort to listen to her. Offer to take the baby off her hands for a while, even if she protests, and be patient. Encourage her to talk to you and others, or to find professional help from her GP. This is where you can really demonstrate that you're super-star dad material.

Dealing with sleep deprivation

Even if your partner is breastfeeding and you're not getting up at night, you may still wake up when she tends to the baby. So, broken sleep remains a given for dads in these early months when your baby is growing and feeding like an insatiable beast. If your partner is the main caregiver and you're back at work, having to get up in the morning as well as spending eight hours with a new boss when you haven't had a good night's sleep can really get to you. You need to do something about this situation (other than drinking lots of coffee), so get organised. Take turns, sleep when the baby sleeps during the weekend or sleep at a friend's house for one night. Don't forget to give your partner a break as well — things often start to look up after you get a decent night's sleep.

To help you to top up your sleep, try using ear plugs (or headphones with white noise playing) to cancel out the baby's crying.

Your baby waking in the night for feeds is a good thing — she needs fuel to grow. The trade-off is coping with the lack of sleep, which is temporary. Bub sleeps for longer during the night as she gets older.

Missing out when you're at work

The first time your child rolls over, works out a toy or takes some other momentous step towards independence, is probably going to happen when you're stuck at work.

Stay up to date with your little person's development. Have your video camera or digital camera parked in the living room or baby's room so your partner can capture a few minutes of your child's day for you to watch when you get home. Even better — get a web cam going: They're really easy to set up and operate these days.

New adventures for dads

Now that your baby is spending less time sleeping or napping, you, dad, get to 'lift the game' and have some fun with your wee one. Okay, you may have to wait a few more years until you can kick a ball around the backyard with junior, but you have plenty of things that you can do together right now.

Research shows that playing with your baby, even when he's this size:

- Develops his social skills
- Enhances his relationship with you (and vice versa)
- Helps with hand–eye coordination
- Raises his self-esteem
- Stimulates his brain development

Best of all, playing with your baby is great fun!

Some ideas for spending time with your baby:

- ✔ **Moving around:** Movement helps your baby establish and grow connections between different parts of the brain. These connections are vital in fine tuning your child's senses, learning new physical skills and developing the ability to think and reason.

  A good way to do simple movement is by rolling your baby over. Help junior to roll over from his back to his front by lying him on his back, and crossing one leg over the other so he slowly rolls onto his tummy. Ideally you would do this on the floor on top of a blanket so he can't fall if he rolls suddenly. Make sure his head is supported if he's still a bit unsteady.

- ✔ **Singing!** With your baby in a bouncinette or baby chair, she loves being sung to along with lots of touch. Songs like 'Twinkle twinkle little star', 'Incy wincy spider', and 'Head, shoulders, knees and toes' can delight your little one. Make corresponding movements when you sing; for example, touch her 'shoulders' when you sing that word.

  One thing you never have to worry about with all babies is your level of vocal talent — they enjoy any attempt at singing. Humming or whistling is also a great alternative.

- ✔ **Stretching and growing:** Blowing bubbles during tummy time helps your little one's eyesight and gets him looking up, strengthening that neck. You can also place toys just out of his reach so he looks up or stretches his body trying to reach them.

- ✔ **Taking tummy time:** This activity is about lying your baby on her tummy so she can learn to push up and lift her head. This exercise is so important because it strengthens the muscles in your baby's back, neck, legs and arms in preparation for crawling and walking.

  Some babies really don't like tummy time — and can heartily let you know about it — so try lying down and having her on your tummy facing you. Or raise her up on your shins as you hold her hands.

The best place for your baby (and you) to play and explore is the floor. Being low makes it very safe from falls and floor contact teaches your baby about his body because he can feel a firm surface at each touch point.

Adjusting to your baby's changing needs

Looking after your baby or child is great fun — seems that every time you finally master a particular situation, he just moves on to the next challenge. Welcome to nature's way of ensuring you're not bored as a parent! Now that you're through the first three months, keeping up with your baby's development and adjusting your parenting skills accordingly is very important.

Looking a bit famished?

As your little champ gets on towards the six-month mark, you start to notice she's chowing through the milk and starting to look for something a bit more substantial. Your baby may be ready to start eating solid food. Until now, breastmilk or formula has sustained her, but now her digestive system is more developed and her growth needs have a bit more oomph.

Your baby's probably ready for 'solids' if:

- ✔ He's taking quite an interest in you eating. Look for little chewing motions or for him to be reaching out for your mouth.

- ✔ She's able to take food onto her tongue from a spoon and swallow it. *Note:* She's not ready if she pushes food away with her tongue.

- ✔ He still seems hungry after a milk feed.

- ✔ She's a bit more unsettled at night, maybe requesting an extra night feed.

 Be patient with introducing solids and don't 'force' feed ever. You can try introducing the same food several times over until your baby likes it. Don't offer too many different foods at a time — stick to a few over a period of two or three weeks.

First foods can include:

- ✔ Baby rice or cereals
- ✔ Cooked and pureed carrot, pumpkin, avocado, marrow or potato
- ✔ Mashed banana
- ✔ Strained and cooked apple and pear.

The same old routine?

Most experienced dads agree on one thing — just when you think you've a handle on things, everything changes. Got junior going for a nap every three hours? Sleeping through the night? Don't get used to it — it's bound to change! Growth spurts, mastering a new skill or teething can unsettle your baby, and just as he gets ready to start eating solids, he may wake more often at night.

Your baby loves predictability, it gives her a sense of comfort to know what's coming up in her day. So if you haven't got your prince or princess into a routine, introduce one now. You don't have to do everything by the clock, rather, just have a cycle (or a rhythm), so that your little champ knows what's coming up next. Check out DIYFather (www.diyfather.com/routines) for a selection of common routines by age. Repetition is also a primary mechanism for how babies learn, so routines and repeating things help on many levels.

If a strict schedule stresses you out because you don't work like that or your baby doesn't adhere to it, relax and do whatever works for your situation and your family. Trying to introduce some structure to your baby's life is a positive step, but not at the cost of your sanity.

Having a solid bedtime routine can help settle your baby for a good sleep pattern at night. The most popular version of a bedtime routine goes something like this — and if mum's not breastfeeding, you can be in charge of the whole thing:

- **Bath:** A nice warm soak in the bath can lull most adults to sleep and on babies it usually works a treat. Your little tyke will like it even more if you're in the tub with him for some good ol' skin-on-skin time — make sure the bathroom is nice and warm. Hold your baby on your chest or tummy, or on your propped up thighs so junior can get a good look at you. Babies are slippery little beings, though, so hold on tight — and make sure mum's on hand to scoop up your little one when it's time to get out.

- **Massage:** Babies love touch — it's the first sense they develop — and spending a little time soothing your baby with massage, and engaging them with smiles and songs can be a pretty magic time of the day for both of you. Make sure her room is warm and be ready with the sleepwear so she can be wrapped up cosily soon afterwards. Natural oils such as almond, olive or calendula are great to use. If you have any fears about nut allergies, give almond oil a miss.

✔ **Top-up feed:** This is where you need mum if she's breastfeeding. If your little one is onto formula, get in touch with your nurturing side, and grab that bottle and tank them up for a long sleep. Another slice of 'dad time' your baby can't help but love.

✔ **And into bed:** With a little song, a kiss and a final wrap (if you're into *swaddling* — a form of snug wrapping to restrict the movement of your baby's limbs), your little one soon learns that after a bath, massage and a last feed, it's always time for some serious sleeping.

A bedtime routine works even when you're on holiday, going to friends' houses or staying at grandma's.

You can adjust your bub's sleep-time routine as he gets older, with reading stories, taking favourite toys to bed or singing a special song together. It's never too early to read or sing to him. (You'll be amazed at what he picks up in the early days and 'plays back' at you when he's a bit older.)

Toys, toys and more toys

No doubt your baby was given mountains of toys when she arrived. Now that she's a bit older, she may enjoy playing with them even more. Make sure you keep some all-time favourites handy:

✔ Fabric books or Lamaze toys

✔ Rattles, squeaky toys and bells

✔ Small balls and hoops

✔ Stacking toys, boxes and wooden rings

You don't need to buy lots of toys — less is definitely more at this stage. Make sure your baby is exposed to different materials and surfaces. Plastic toys and battery operated toys should be last on your list because they typically don't offer a variety of textures and don't encourage inventive play. They're also expensive and you then need to buy batteries constantly.

Many objects your baby will be interested in at this stage can actually be found in your household. A set of keys on a key ring, empty cardboard boxes, wooden clothes pegs or fruit and vegetables can keep your little one entertained for hours.

Getting On with Life

Life doesn't stop just because your sweet, wee babe has joined the world. You still need to go out, visit friends or frequent the odd café from time to time. The more people your baby meets, places he sees and surroundings he experiences, the better for junior's rapidly growing brain. So, get out there!

Out and about with your baby

Choosing the gear is of course an area that lots of dads enjoy! You get to choose from a wide range of options for carting your baby around, and you can try all of them, depending on your situation. Popping junior in a sling can suit a quick stroll to the shop for the paper, but a jog through the park may be better taken with bub in a stroller.

Strollers and buggies

During the first three months, your baby lies reasonably flat in the stroller. Now that she's a bit older, you can prop her up a bit so she can see what's happening. You may also want to invest in a lightweight umbrella stroller, which is great for short trips and travelling. Check the model to make sure it's suitable for your baby's age. Check out Chapter 4 for the lowdown on getting the right gear.

Slings and baby carriers

If you haven't already, check out baby slings and baby carriers. They're great for short trips around town. Proponents of baby-wearing, like those that practise *attachment parenting* — in which a caregiver maintains contact with the baby at all times — swear by the benefits of having their baby in a sling or baby carrier. Babies carried in slings often sleep wherever you go and you don't have the potential hassle of trying to find a spot to park the stroller in a café or shop.

A tonne of different baby carrier models are out there, each with different pros and cons — so shop around. Get your salesperson to fit them correctly to ensure you're not squashing your precious bundle and that your back isn't damaged.

The most common types of slings and baby carriers:

- ✔ **Asian slings** are a rectangular shape with straps around both shoulders that can be worn in front or behind.

- ✔ **Frontpacks** are like the backpacks you take tramping/hiking only you put a baby in them! They have lots of padding and are usually made of canvas with adjustable straps. They can be worn with your bub facing in to you or out to the world.

- ✔ **Open and close tailed ring slings** are adjustable and fit over one shoulder.

- ✔ **Pouches** are pockets of fabric worn over one shoulder, and are very easy to get bubs in and out of. They aren't adjustable though, so can only be worn by the person they fit.

- ✔ **Wraps** are a three to five metre piece of fabric that ties around the body. They take some getting used to, but are said to be more comfortable in the long run than other slings.

Ask yourself these questions when choosing a sling or baby carrier:

- ✔ How well is the weight of the baby spread over my back and shoulders? Will I get tired after wearing it only a short while?

- ✔ Will it just be me using the sling, or is my partner getting in on the act?

- ✔ How easily do I need to be able to get junior in and out of the sling?

Travelling by car

In general, when taking your little person with you in the car, you need to use the rear-facing capsule position until your baby is at least 12 months old (or your baby weighs more than ten kilograms). Check the instruction manual for details of your model. If you haven't bought a car seat yet, check out the following options for hiring:

- ✔ **In Australia:** Hire for Baby (http://hireforbaby.com)

- ✔ **In New Zealand:** Plunket's car seat rental scheme (www.plunket.org.nz).

Check out Chapter 4 for a list of all the gear you need for your little one.

Getting out and about

So you've got the latest stroller, your baby is in his flashest gear and you're all keen to go. What can you get up to together?

- ✔ **Music and movement classes**, like Gymbaroo, are great for getting those brain connections going, but can be expensive. Expect to pay around A$170 per course in Australia and NZ$200 in New Zealand.

- ✔ **Playgroups** are community run groups of parents who get together to let their kids play while the adults mingle. Some have music sessions, and provide lots of books and toys. They can be invaluable for perking you up on a bad day — having other people ooh and aah over your baby goes a long way to putting a big grin on your face. Depending on the organisation that runs the course, expect to pay anything from a gold coin donation to around A$20/NZ$20 per class.

- ✔ **Story time and music sessions** at your local library are another tonic for isolated parents, and babies adore them. There is nothing like sitting among 30 other parents and babies singing 'The Grand Old Duke of York', and having all 30 babies laughing in delight. And these sessions are usually free.

Don't be intimidated by female dominance in some of these social settings — you're just as good a parent as the next mum. So wear your 'dad and I'm proud of it' face and enjoy the attention.

Baby-proofing the house

Junior is only just beginning to get her moves on, but watch out — in just a few short months your little person is going to be crawling and pulling up on everything and open season will be declared on cupboards, bookshelves and cables. What was out of reach one day is fair game the next. So now's a good time to take baby-proofing to the next level and ensure everything dangerous and precious in your house is either locked down or locked up. If you're unsure whether you're covering all safety aspects, you may want to double-check the baby-proofing tips in Chapter 7.

We don't want to sound like molly coddlers here, but every year many children in Australia and New Zealand are injured. Child safety is something to take seriously. Check out Chapter 7 for more about common safety hazards by room or area in your baby's adventure playground and what to do to make these hazards safer.

It's only money

Babies and children have a unique way to expose you to different points of view. For example, you're sure to come to a different understanding of what's valuable to you, mostly because your baby may eat, destroy, wee on or draw on something that you hold dear. When that momentous event happens (and yes it is 'when' not 'if'), remember not to blame your little one. Until he's much older your baby isn't going to understand the concept of material value — so if something is really, really precious, make sure you keep it out of reach (using a bank vault isn't a bad idea!).

You can never take your child's safety for granted:

- ✔ Keep any potentially lethal substances like pet litter, garden fertilisers, cleaners, pest poisons, alcohol, fire starters and paints in a high cupboard with childproof locks.

- ✔ Young children can drown in a small amount of water, not to mention the hygiene risk of touching dirty areas like the toilet, so you're best to keep the bathroom out of bounds.

You may not think so now, but when your baby is crawling and walking, she can move very, very quickly, and get herself into trouble fast. The time spent baby-proofing your house (continuously) can save your child's life or prevent her being seriously hurt.

To make sure you've got everything covered, get down to your bub's height and see what is likely to tempt your curious child.

Wading through the necessary paperwork

By now you most likely have registered your baby's birth, but you still have other bits and pieces of administration to take care of.

Insurance

Give some thought to getting life insurance if you haven't already. If something happens to you, you're going to want your family to be taken care of financially. Shop around for the best deal and to understand the various types of personal insurance. You can try your bank or home insurer as a first approach.

Give your health insurer a call to add your baby to your policy.

Savings accounts

Many parents set up bank accounts for their new child, and start saving for big purchases like a new bike or sports fees, or for far-off expenses like university fees or a deposit on a first house. Most banks have savings accounts for children with low or no fees.

Tax and benefits

To be eligible for many government schemes like New Zealand's Working for Families and KiwiSaver, your baby must have an IRD number from Inland Revenue.

In Australia, parents must have a Tax File Number (TFN) to claim the Family Tax Benefit.

Wills and guardians

Make sure both you and your partner have updated your wills to take into account your new status as parents, and have thought about who can look after your baby should something happen to you. When thinking about who should be guardian if you and your partner dies or is unable to look after your baby, make sure you ask the person(s) first before naming them in your will, and check whether they're equipped financially and emotionally to add a new child to their family.

You may want to make special mention in your will of any sentimental belongings that you want to hand down to your child, like special clothing, photographs, or family heirlooms.

Immunisation records

Keep a record of your baby's immunisations — they may be required when your child starts childcare, kindergarten or school. In Australia Medicare keeps a central immunisation record that you can check online (www.medicareaustralia.gov.au) or at your local Medicare branch. In New Zealand, a record is kept in your baby's Well Child book. If you haven't received a Well Child Book from Plunket yet, contact them on 0800 933 922 to order your copy — it's free!

Doing things together: You're still a couple

Your relationship as a couple impacts on your little one. Happy parents, happy baby, they say. As a role model to your child, the relationship you have with your partner acts as a guide when he embarks on his own romantic endeavours. But all your energy these days seems go into bub, and with the lack of sleep going on right now, just collapsing on the couch at the end of a long day may seem like the easiest way to recharge. And, with all the attention your new bundle is getting from mum, you may not be feeling 'the love'. So both of you have to work hard to ensure your relationship isn't forgotten about.

Make an effort and make time for each other. Schedule some time in the evening when bub is asleep and prepare a special dinner, or hire a babysitter and head out for the night. It doesn't have to be Bollinger and foie gras, just do something you both enjoy.

You're probably wondering when sex returns to your relationship. Chances are you're both pretty knackered most days or the baby is actively preventing you from getting it on. Your partner may also not feel like having sex at the moment. The aftermath of the birth on her body combined with leaky boobs and that all-consuming tiredness may leave her feeling less than 'bootilicious' right now. Well — basically, you just have to take it easy. Definitely bring up the subject and ask her how she feels about sex. Ask her to let you know when she's ready to resume 'relations' again. You may have to be a bit patient but pressuring her is unlikely to speed things up.

It's the (other) little things …

Sometimes, simply doing things together is what helps you feel good. Here's a list of suggestions:

- Foot massages and back rubs
- Take-away dinner for two
- Taking a shower or bath together.

Leaving Your Baby with Others

Inevitably the time comes when you and your partner need to hand over your precious baby to others. You may just need a break from the baby routine or you may want to get back to working. This is a big deal and many dads feel unsure about leaving bub with someone else (even grandparents or close relatives). Don't panic — you can put your mind at ease (or at least you can try) with advance planning.

As with most things, the key to making this process work is effective communication. A key principle is to make sure the person who looks after your baby knows how you want things done.

Let your baby's carer know:

✔ Your baby's routine, generally.

✔ Your baby's bedtime or naptime routine including any songs or stories that are part of putting your child down to sleep.

✔ Which foods are allowed and which aren't.

✔ Any specifics about your little one such as tired signs, signs that junior's got a full nappy or is overstimulated. You're an expert on this after all.

✔ What creams or powders you use (and of course any medication if applicable).

✔ How you deal with the baby crying.

✔ Any safety issues around the house.

Family and friends

Those closest to you are possibly the easiest choice of carer if you need to take some time out and/or attend appointments. Make sure you feel totally comfortable with this arrangement, and be sure to brief them in the same way you would with non-related helpers. Family members are most likely going to be stoked to spend some time with junior, and some one-on-one time is a great way to build an attachment with relatives. Just ask the relos how often they may want to do it, because you don't want babysitting to become too much of a chore for them.

Create a babysitting club with likeminded dads, where you take turns looking after each other's babies.

Nannies

A nanny is a professional who is trained to look after children in your home, and hiring one can be expensive — you're paying the person's income. Some nannies look after multiple children in the one house, so you can team up with friends and split the cost. Expect to pay an hourly rate of around NZ$14–20/A$15–24 plus a placement fee from the agency (anything between $50 and $250).

Make sure you go with a reputable agency who has done all the necessary checks on the nanny, one that can guarantee your nanny has qualifications, basic first-aid and has been vetted by the police. If in doubt, ask to see your prospective nanny's paperwork. Most importantly, check references.

A nanny should:

- ✔ Take care of your child's physical, intellectual, emotional and social needs — that is, feed them, play with them, and be someone they feel safe and secure with

- ✔ Take care of your child's (not your) laundry, cloth nappy cleaning, cooking, and bottle washing

In Australia and New Zealand, nannies can ordinarily work without any specific qualifications. So you can use online services like finda nannyonline.com.au, careforkids.com.au, www.kiwioznannies.co.nz or a nanny agency (just enter **nanny agency** + your city/state into your favourite online search engine) to find a nanny. Either way, you're best to read up on the Australian Institute of Family Studies Child Protection Clearinghouse website (www.aifs.gov.au/nch) about police checks and references for nannies.

Some agencies can also provide nannies from abroad (in some cases they're referred to as 'au pairs'). This may be a good way to expose your child to another language. However, au pairs usually stay with you for only up to 12 months and you may not be able to relate their qualifications, training and references to Australia/New Zealand.

While nannies are experienced carers, make sure you leave special instructions about your baby and the house. Also, nannies aren't maids — so don't expect them to do your washing and cleaning or to look after your household at the same time.

When choosing a nanny, interview the person with your baby there, and see how they interact together. *Hint:* The nanny should spend more time chatting and playing with the child than talking to you.

Some questions to ask prospective nannies:

- ✔ What's your family situation?
- ✔ What are your qualifications?
- ✔ How do you feel about me working from home from time to time?
- ✔ Why do you like children?
- ✔ What do you dislike about looking after children?
- ✔ What is your philosophy on boundaries and discipline?
- ✔ What is your philosophy on play and stimulation?
- ✔ What do you do when a baby is sick, and you can't wake them up? (Correct answer — call an ambulance!)

Babysitters

Babysitters are different from nannies in that they usually just look after children for a few hours — that is, a morning, afternoon or evening. The majority of sitters are cheaper, too, than nannies. Expect to pay an hourly rate of $15–$25 an hour in Australia, or upwards of $14 in New Zealand. If you go through an agency, you have to pay a placement fee.

In most cases you don't need to worry about being late back (but check beforehand) — after all, they're paid by the hour.

Teenage babysitters might be cheap but they should still have access to adult help and a car with an approved safety car seat restraint.

Interview your prospective babysitter just like you would a nanny (refer to the previous section). You're leaving this person in charge of the most important person in your world!

Day care centres

Sending your wee one off to day care can be a heart-breaking experience for a dad. It can be really hard on mum, too, so be there with a cuddle and some reassuring words if she's upset.

You're essentially entrusting your child to strangers in a strange place, so don't hold back from getting to know your crèche or centre well. The more confident you are about the place, the more confident junior is likely to be as well. Make sure to visit the centre more than once to get a good feel for it.

You can find a range of different types of childcare facilities — community, not-for-profit and commercial. In Australia, a day care centre, whether it be a kindergarten or crèche, is called a *long day care centre*.

Centres must have special programs for each age. Some take babies from six weeks old, and others don't take under-twos. Some have half-day attendance, others don't. Some provide meals, others don't. Shop around for what works best for your family. Expect to pay between $50 and $80 a day for a full day in New Zealand, while some centres in Australia charge more than $100 a day.

Childcare in Australia and New Zealand is in high demand. So register your interest early if you want to make sure of a place for your little one when you need it. Waiting lists in bigger cities or popular neighbourhoods can be up to two years.

You may be eligible for some government assistance, so check with your local centre:

- ✔ **In Australia:** Contact the Family Assistance Office to see whether you qualify for Child Care Benefit. Call 13 6150 or visit `www.familyassist.gov.au`.

- ✔ **In New Zealand:** Contact Work and Income to see if you're eligible for Childcare Assistance. Call 0800 559 009 or visit their website `www.workandincome.govt.nz`.

Here are a few things to look out for with day care centres:

- ✔ Do their opening hours work with your schedule?

- ✔ Do they charge if you're late picking up your child?

- ✔ Do they check a permissions list for whomever is picking your child up? Do they ask for identification?

- ✔ Do they open during holidays, and if so, how much do they charge?

- ✔ What are the teachers like? Are they bubbly and fun to be with? Do they have a rapport with the children, and communicate with them well? Is one particular teacher assigned to look after your child more than the other teachers?

- ✔ What qualifications do teachers have, and are they trained in first-aid?

- ✔ What philosophy does the centre have on activities, play, discipline and behaviour? How do they handle children's behavioural problems such as hitting other children?

- ✔ What medicines do they have on the premises, and what is their policy on giving medicines to children? What happens if your child is hurt?

- ✔ Does the centre have fire extinguishers, exits, alarms, smoke detectors? What are their policies in case of emergencies such as earthquakes or fire?

- ✔ What foods are the children given? Can you request special food, like gluten-free or organic? Is the centre nut-free?

- ✔ What happens at sleep time? Does the centre have a policy on dummies (pacifiers), or special blankets and toys? What happens to children who don't have a nap? Most centres usually have a dedicated sleep room, with a teacher checking on children every few minutes. Some centres provide bedding, others encourage you to bring your own.

- ✔ Is there a service for picking up children?

- ✔ What activities are available at the centre?

- ✔ Does the centre take the children on trips outside the centre?

- ✔ Are under-twos kept separate from the bigger kids, or do they all muck in together?

- ✔ Who should you speak to if you have any concerns?

- ✔ How do teachers keep track of your child's progress? Most centres have a book with stories and pictures of your child's activities.

 Check with the National Childcare Accreditation Council (NCAC) (www.ncac.gov.au) in Australia, or with the Education Review Office (ERO) in New Zealand (www.ero.govt.nz) about your centre. Both bodies evaluate childcare centres, and publish their findings.

 After a few weeks, assess how well your child has settled in. Does your little champ have special friends, is she forming bonds with any of the teachers, and is she generally happy? Also, drop in unannounced to see what your child is up to. Make a regular appearance at lunchtimes — most centres offer days where parents can come in to eat with their children.

In-home care or family day care

In-home care with a trained carer looking after several children at the same time is a different set up from a day care centre but, in principle, you can still ask the same sorts of questions. With *in-home care*, also known as *family day care* in Australia, your child is usually placed with one carer, who looks after your little one (and other babies/children) in the carer's own home.

Because you're dealing with just the one carer, you can often get to know the person better than the teachers at a day care centre, and can be a little more flexible in hours.

To avoid both you and junior feeling anxious about the daily routine and other issues, you're best to take the time and energy to build rapport with the carer.

Go with a reputable company when choosing in-home care; they will have vetted your carer's house for safety, given them training, and done police checks.

So what's important when choosing in-home care?

- ✔ Does your child get one-on-one attention?
- ✔ What learning program is in place?
- ✔ What foods are provided?
- ✔ What are the sleeping arrangements? (Single bed, bunk beds, floor space: Be sure you're happy with the safety aspects.)
- ✔ What are the other children under the carer's wing like?
- ✔ What happens if my carer gets sick?
- ✔ What happens when my child is sick?
- ✔ What happens if I'm late picking up my child?

Chapter 9

Months Six to Twelve

In This Chapter

▶ Helping your baby grow and develop

▶ Exploring the world through play

▶ Recognising developmental milestones

*Y*ou've firmly got a handle on this fatherhood business now, haven't you? The next six months are all about your baby becoming more aware of her body and using it to get around, from rolling on the floor to getting up on her feet and doing that amazing thing babies do, walking. Witnessing your small, vulnerable child set out on the path to independence is amazing.

Of course, she needs you, her dad, to hold her hand as she makes her way. So keep up the good work, you're doing a fantastic job!

But wait — there's more to learn! In this chapter we show you how to cope with your baby's ravenous appetite and what you need to feed her now that milk's not cutting it anymore. And speaking of cutting, we let you in on tips so teething is less of a trauma for your baby. We show you the amazing changes your baby is going through to become a mover and shaker and how to manage a trip or holiday with bub in tow. And last but not least, we conclude with a little party — your child's first birthday.

Keeping Up with Baby

If you thought your baby changed a lot in the first six months, hold onto your burp cloth, because things don't slow down just yet.

Your baby's changing diet

Until now, breastmilk or formula has been all the food your baby needs. But to keep up with her growth, she needs to move onto solid food. Most health professionals and childcare organisations recommend waiting until bub's around six months old before trying solids, which aren't really that solid, more puree and mush. But you may find your little one is ready to start a few weeks earlier than the six months mark.

Your baby gives you some signs he's ready for solids by:

✔ Looking a bit famished after a milk feed — he's waiting around for more

✔ Paying attention to what you eat, perhaps following your fork going into your mouth and making little chewing faces

✔ Pointing at food on the table or trying to grab food that's within reach

Your wee champ can hold his head up for long periods at a time and is able to take food onto his tongue. If he's not ready for solids, he'll push the food out again, called the *extrusion reflex*.

As your baby's digestive system is still pretty undeveloped and he doesn't have any teeth with which to break down food, first solid foods have to be pureed or mashed thoroughly so they're almost runny. Some good first foods to try include:

✔ Cooked and pureed apple, pear, apricot, peach, carrot, pumpkin, potato, kumara (sweet potato), kamo kamo (squash) and marrow.

✔ Iron-enriched baby cereal or baby rice. You can use breastmilk or formula to mix these.

✔ Uncooked and mashed banana and avocado.

Here's how to feed solids to your baby for the first time:

✔ Give your baby a milk feed first. Solid food comes after milk feeds until about eight months of age.

✔ Try one food, such as carrot, for three to five days in a row to make sure your baby has no reaction to that food.

✔ Try your first food when baby seems relaxed and happy, not when she's super hungry, tired or grumpy. Lunchtimes or early afternoons are often good times.

✔ If she's not into her carrots at first, that's okay. Try again tomorrow and if she's still not into it, give her a few days before trying again. It can take ten attempts before your princess discovers her passion for a particular food.

✔ Let bub decide how much she needs to eat. Force feeding her is not likely to make eating vegetables something she looks forward to. Let her appetite guide you. It may be only a few teaspoons at first.

A few things to remember about feeding solids to your baby are:

✔ A baby's sense of taste is very sensitive and he won't need salt, sugar or spices to flavour a food.

✔ Some people insist on heating their baby's food, but this is more a matter of adult taste than baby's. If you do heat your child's food, test it yourself before spooning it up to him to make sure the food's not scalding hot.

✔ You'll need a highchair, a lot of bibs and some sort of protective plastic matting for your floor — unless you like orange patterns on your carpet.

✔ You can buy plastic feeding spoons which are gentler on baby's gums and smaller than teaspoons. They look huge compared to your little one's tiny mouth.

✔ As your baby gets older, food can become more textured and less runny.

Once your baby has the hang of solid food, try mixing different foods for a range of flavours. Introduce meat into her diet, because at six months old she needs more iron than you to support the growth of her rapidly developing brain. Cooked liver can be given to boost her iron supply, but only once a week as it contains a lot of vitamin A which your baby can get too much of.

Try adding these foods to the menu:

✔ Cooked meat like beef mince, chicken, liver and lamb. Meat must be pureed, minced or served as a broth so it's soft and fine enough for an infant to eat.

✔ Cooked parsnips, broccoli, courgettes/zucchinis, green beans

✔ Egg yolks (from a hard boiled egg)

✔ Uncooked melon, plum and nectarine

✔ White toast, rusks and crackers.

Try each food out for three to five days to make sure your champ isn't allergic to it. If he is, he'll have a bloated tummy, a rash, or a hard time breathing. Call your GP or an ambulance right away if he's having a severe reaction.

Honey is potentially lethal for babies up to 12 months of age. Honey can contain bacteria that release botulinum toxin, a neurotoxin which can lead to severe food poisoning. Honey is safe to eat by toddlers from about one year of age because their digestive system is fully developed and can neutralise the toxins.

After eight months you can introduce these foods into baby's diet:

- ✔ Cooked creamed corn, peas, silverbeet, cabbage and spinach
- ✔ Fish, unless your family has a history of fish allergy, in which case wait until your champ is a year old
- ✔ Pasta and rice
- ✔ Smooth peanut butter, unless there's a family history of nut allergy, in which case wait until bub is three years old
- ✔ Soy foods like tofu and tempeh
- ✔ Uncooked kiwifruit, orange, berries, pineapple and tomatoes
- ✔ Yoghurt, cheese, custard and ice-cream, unless there's a strong family allergy to dairy, in which case wait until your baby is a year old.

At eight months, your baby can also start exploring finger foods such as slices of soft fruit, cooked vegetable pieces, slices of toast, grated cheese, cooked pasta pieces and crackers. Avoid anything small and hard that may choke your baby, like hard nuts, popcorn and lollies.

After eight months, solid food takes on more importance in baby's diet and can be given before a milk feed. Move baby onto three meals a day, with breastmilk or formula snacks at morning and afternoon tea time.

Encourage family meals from the start. Pull the highchair up to the dining table so the three of you can enjoy your meals together. Your champ learns the mechanics of eating from you by copying, and you teach her that eating is about sharing a meal and eating healthy food together.

If you're not sure about when a particular food, such as traditional Maori, Pacific Islander or Aboriginal foods, is okay to feed to your baby, check with your child health nurse or Well Child provider.

Don't pass your food preferences to your baby. For example, if you don't like broccoli you needn't put it in front of your baby in a way that makes it obvious you don't like it. Why should he like broccoli if you present it poorly? Make encouraging noises, like 'Yummy yummy broccoli', when you serve food.

Don't forget the toothbrush

In the coming months your baby gets her first teeth (see later in this chapter for information about teething), so you need a new piece of equipment — a wee toothbrush. You can instil healthy oral hygiene early by making tooth brushing time good fun.

Special low-fluoride toothpaste and soft toothbrushes for babies are available. You need only a pea-size dot of paste at the moment, if for nothing else than it provides a bit of taste for baby to think about while you brush his gnashers.

Brushing teeth with the little one is another perfect dad job. If you're a working dad you can integrate brushing teeth into your champ's bed routine. That way you get even more daddy–baby time in your day.

Your little explorer

From rolling over, to crawling, to pulling up, to cruising to walking — the next six months are characterised by your baby's growing mobility and all the challenges that brings for us dads. Of course, you followed our baby-proofing instructions in Chapter 7 to the letter, and your house is a place where your baby can free range and explore to his heart's content once he's mobile. But you can't just let him loose on your house to do his exploring. Instead, help his exploration by exposing him to all sorts of different materials and textures. Use plenty of chatting about what's he experiencing to help develop his language at the same time.

The routines, they're a-changing

All babies are different, but you may be surprised to wake one morning and find the sun's up and bub hasn't even made a whimper. This can be terrifying — you rush into her room to make sure nothing is wrong, to be met by a sweetly sleeping baby who wakes just as you enter and greets you with a smile. Yep, your baby has slept through the night — a miracle!

If your baby hasn't slept through the night after six months, don't worry. Teething, getting enough to eat and not having a developed sense of sleep yet can keep her waking up at night. Also bear in mind that sleeping through the night can mean from 10.00 pm to 5.00 am. Don't get stressed about getting your baby to sleep for 12 hours at a time — this may or may not happen with your little one.

You may also notice that baby is awake more and more during the day, and is settling into having two naps a day, one in the morning and one in the afternoon. At six months, your baby needs about 14 hours of sleep in a 24-hour period. By one year of age, she may be giving up one of her naps in favour of a nap in the late morning or early afternoon. Let her decide when she naps by reading her tired signs.

A change in routine can be messy and may result in things being unsettled for a while, but if you roll with it and remember that everything is just a phase, things settle in no time at all. Some health professionals say that pretty much any routine can be changed over a period of two weeks (consistency is important), so don't worry that you're being locked into a schedule you can't change.

With the rate of development your baby is going through right now and all the new skills he's picking up, you may find he's too excited for sleep and tries out his new party tricks at sleep time, such as pulling up on the side of his cot or crawling around his bed. Some babies pull up on their cot and find they can't get down again, so cry out for your help. Just ease him back down with your well-practised settling techniques and wait for this phase to blow over. One sure thing about parenting and dealing with babies and kids is that things change frequently.

Parenting styles

As your baby becomes an active toddler, the way you manage her behaviour comes to the fore. The researcher Diana Baumrind defines four different styles of parenting; *authoritarian*, *authoritative*, *neglectful* and *permissive*. These parenting styles influence the relationship you have with your child, including how you manage discipline and behaviour.

Each style has its own characteristics:

- ✔ **Authoritarian:** A kind of parenting in which children are 'seen and not heard' and the carer has high expectations that the child follow rules. Parents don't allow for dialogue between themselves and their children, and are not responsive to children's wishes. It's the parents' way or the highway.

- ✔ **Authoritative:** This style of parenting also has high demands on the children to follow rules, but the parents also respond to their children, explain boundaries and limits, and encourage the child's independence. Children know where they stand and are encouraged to have an open dialogue with their parents.

- ✔ **Neglectful:** Also known as detached or uninvolved parenting. The title says it all — carers don't engage with children, children don't have limits or boundaries and parents are not responsive to children's needs. This style of parenting has been linked to truancy and delinquency in teenage years.

- ✔ **Permissive:** Also known as indulgent parenting, parents have low expectations of the children but are highly responsive to them. The carers may be loving and nurturing, but there are no limits or boundaries for the children. This parenting style is likely to lead to some very difficult behavioural issues when the child is older.

Your child needs your love and nurturing, to feel safe with you and to know she has boundaries, which she will keep pushing at until she's well into her twenties! Have a chat to your partner about the way you would like to parent your child as she grows older. If you're interested in more about parenting styles and discipline, check out Chapter 10 where we talk about the principles of effective discipline.

You're good at this

Seen the way your baby responds to you these days? With smiles and squeals? He knows without doubt you're his dad and he thinks you're a bit of a rock star.

Perhaps you'd like to take the reins for the day and spend a day alone with your baby. Send mum out for the day, or let her have a day lounging in bed while you and your little one get your groove on together. You might even surprise yourself with how naturally being a dad comes to you now. Isn't it amazing how far you have come on your fatherhood journey? Pat yourself on the shoulder and enjoy your new skills.

Playtime with Daddy

The second half of your baby's first year is characterised by his growing mobility, which is great news for dads. Soon you'll be at the park on slides and swings, or kicking a ball around. But you have to learn to walk before you can run and you can help your little champ get the strength he needs to be on his feet.

Sitting, crawling, walking

All babies are different and develop at different rates, but generally you can expect your baby to be:

- ✔ Rolling over from her back to her front between three to six months
- ✔ Sitting unsupported between six to eight months
- ✔ Crawling between 8 and 11 months
- ✔ Walking between 11 and 17 months.

Each stage of mobility is pretty exciting. The first time he rolls over, you may praise him like he's just discovered a cure for cancer and taking his first step is a moment to treasure. Activities and games you play together at all these different levels of mobility encourage your baby's strength and learning.

Your baby is a little parrot and loves to mimic you. You help her move and learn just by being there and having time to play. She watches you sitting, getting up and walking, and wants to copy what you're doing.

Some activities to help your baby get the strength to reach these milestones include:

- ✔ **Sitting:** To sit, your baby needs good head control and good balance, both of which are encouraged by tummy time. By lying on the floor on her tummy, she instinctively lifts her head to see you or any interesting toys nearby. You could even have a mirror in front of her so she can see another baby — and a miracle — two dads! You can encourage her balance with some gentle rolling, which helps develop the *vestibular system* in the ear that controls balance.

✔ **Crawling:** Once your baby is sitting unsupported for a while, he'll start to want to reach out for things around him and then work out how to get back onto his tummy. From here he'll work out how to move his body forward and commando crawl by almost slithering along the floor! As he builds strength in his arms and legs, he'll get up on all fours and work out how to propel himself forward and voila — he's crawling.

You can develop your baby's strength by putting things out of his reach that he can move towards, like blocks, or by rolling a ball near him. When he is crawling confidently, challenge him by giving him tunnels to climb through or chairs to crawl under. Get down on your hands and knees and chase him along — babies love to be chased! Don't forget to give bub lots of different textures to try out, like crawling on grass, lino, your bed, or at the beach.

✔ **Walking:** As she gets stronger, your little lady will figure out that she can pull herself up to standing on solid objects like walls, her highchair, or in her cot. She may want to hold your hands and walk everywhere, using you for balance. After some months of practising, she'll have the confidence and balance to stand by herself and take a few wobbly steps on her own.

No doubt she'll have a lot of falls and there will be tears, but falls and tears are all part of the learning process and she will gain confidence, balance and strength. Be there with a kiss and a cuddle for those bumps and scrapes.

People may say to you that once your baby's walking she'll be into everything and you won't get a moment's peace. That's a very limited view of parenting, because there's a huge upside to it. Your baby can now explore much more of the outdoors, kick balls around in the yard and explore just about everything much more easily, without being dependent on you. This is a huge step towards independence and should be celebrated. When your child is walking, they can do things like greet you at the door when you get home from work, or hold your hand as you walk together to the park, and express their preferences and personality more. Of course this new freedom does come with a need for extra vigilance for parents.

Not all babies develop in the same order. Some miss crawling and shuffle along on their bums, or go straight to walking. If you're concerned about your baby's development, talk to your Well Child provider or child health nurse.

When your child is walking, be prepared for her to run away (and expect you to chase her). Be vigilant — she can disappear in a flash when your back is turned. Take extra care around roads, dogs and water.

Talking the talk

Just as the first year is shaped by baby's growing mobility, the second year's shaped by language and emotional development. But just because junior isn't talking yet doesn't mean she can't understand you. In fact she's soaking up what and how you're saying things to her. When she's figured out how to get her lips and tongue and mouth co-ordinated, language tumbles out of her mouth.

Your baby's babbling and raspberries, shouts and whoops are all attempts to communicate although she hasn't mastered language yet. Observing her attempts at language is often hilarious. She may turn to you with a serious face and deliver a speech in what sounds like Mongolian or Serbo-Croat which you can't make head nor tail of. If you respond with 'really?' or 'is that so?' she'll keep going and eventually words you recognise start emerging.

Babies learn by repetition, so reading the same book over and over, or using the same phrases for activities like changing a nappy or making her cereal, all sink in. Your little champ is learning to associate words or phrases with activities, objects and situations. So don't be surprised if you hear her say things exactly the way you do (and that goes for everything, so if you don't want your child to use certain words hold your tongue when she's around).

Talk to your child and let him know what is happening today: 'Today honey we are going to see Brian, and then we are going to the supermarket and then home for tea'. He may not say anything in response, but he's soaking up those words.

Children use different speech sounds at different ages. When your child will make certain speech sounds depends on how difficult they are to make. For example, some sounds such as 'm' and 'b' are easy to say and these will probably be some of the first sounds your little champ makes.

For more information about when to expect your little one to start using certain speech sounds, go to www.diyfather.com/content/speech-and-language.

Along with 'duck', 'ball' and 'dog', your baby will pick up the less savoury words that he hears around the house. Censor yourself early on — you don't want junior announcing to the world he can swear like a sailor when grandparents come to stay. This also goes for what you say about other people. Kids have a remarkable way of remembering all the things you said about Brian a few days ago and telling Brian about it when he's visiting next.

The life aquatic

One of the joys of having a baby over six months old is that you can go swimming at a public pool together! Before then, his immune system is probably not up to it, he's not able to control his temperature well and his neck muscles aren't strong enough to allow him to control his head. Public pools often have separate pools for babies and toddlers and it can be worthwhile taking swimming lessons with your little one, as much for your own confidence handling your baby in the water as for baby's sake. Instructors can show you how to glide your baby through the water, help him to float on his back and eventually put his head underwater. At this age, being in the pool is all about having fun and becoming confident in the water.

You can buy special swimmer nappies that hold in any wees or poos junior may do while in the pool.

If your baby has had diarrhoea, keep her out of a public pool for at least two weeks. If bub has eczema, chlorine and water may irritate it, so put the swimming on hold until the eczema's cleared up. Avoid going to the pool altogether if your baby is unwell, particularly if he has an ear infection.

Instilling a sense of confidence around water in your child now is a good idea, so start teaching basic water safety. Always supervise your child around water. A child can drown in only four centimetres of water. See www.watersafety.org.nz or www.childsafetyaustralia.com.au/children/water/watersafety.htm.

These tips can help keep your child safe:

- ✔ Empty the bath or paddling pool as soon as you've finished with it.

- ✔ Fence your pool. Check with your local council to check the fencing meets district planning requirements.

- ✔ Stay within arm's reach of your child in or near the water. If the phone rings when junior is in the bath, either ignore it or take your baby with you to answer it. If you have a cordless phone or mobile, take it to the bathroom as you're preparing the bath.

Playgroups

No matter how much fun you're having with your baby at home, there will be days when you just have to get out and see adults. Going along to a playgroup can be a good way to entertain your little one and get some much needed adult company at the same time. One of the great things about playgroup is that there's a whole range of ages and stages, and plenty of other dads and mums to talk with about what's happening in your little one's world and what's coming up next.

Playgroups are usually a group of parents getting together in a community centre or other public space where children can play safely and parents can meet other parents. You can get as involved in the playgroup as you like — taking on responsibilities for running the group or just turning up for a coffee and a chat. You could even start your own playgroup if one isn't in your area. Some playgroups organise musical sessions, have arts and crafts available, and provide morning or afternoon tea for a small donation.

Children love being around other children, even if at this age they don't really interact with each other. Playgroups often have bigger toys, better books and lots more activities than you could fit into your house — all good things for challenging your little one.

Before you join a playgroup in your community, ask yourself these questions:

- ✔ Are there activities suitable for my child's age?
- ✔ How safe are the facilities?
- ✔ Is the playgroup convenient for me? Does it suit bub's sleep time, is it easily accessible for buggies/prams, does it cost much?
- ✔ What is the policy for dealing with other people's children? Am I allowed to pick up another person's child? How is conflict between children handled?
- ✔ Who is running the playgroup? Is there a commercial interest behind it?

Check out www.playgroupaustralia.com.au to find a playgroup in Australia. In New Zealand contact your local parent centre; check out www.parentscentre.org.nz.

Toys you already own

If you like gadgets you'll love the toys that are on the market these days. You may find yourself piling up the shopping cart with battery operated products that do all sorts of funny stuff or claim to turn your child into a genius. As well as the toys you buy, toys also turn up as gifts, your baby inadvertently steals them at playgroup, or you receive toys free with some other baby-related purchase, so you may find gadgetery piling up in your house. But apart from the few toys we mention in Chapter 4 — cloth books, soft toys, teething toys like car keys and rattles — your baby doesn't really need most of the battery operated toys for his development.

You certainly don't need to buy a lot of toys at this age to stimulate development because you already have lots of really cool toys in your house right now. You just may not realise they are toys.

Here are a few examples. Babies love things that they can:

- ✔ **Explore**, like wrapping paper, pieces of cloth, a set of keys (best to use keys you don't actually need) or old books to gnaw on or rip apart

- ✔ **Make noise with**, like pots and pans. Give bub a wooden spoon and let her drum happily away.

- ✔ **Mouth**, like wooden pegs, wooden spoons and those plastic spoons you're feeding him solids with (be vigilant about choking hazards)

- ✔ **Shake**, like a plastic container with a tight-fitting lid half filled with rice, or a plastic milk bottle with pasta shapes inside. Glue the lids on with hot glue or Superglue.

- ✔ **Stack**, such as food containers. Small cardboard boxes or plastic bottles (which you can fill with confetti, rice or pasta) can also be stacked.

Many babies find everyday objects, such as remote controls and mobile phones, far more interesting than their toy version. A toy version will be thrown aside for the real thing any day. Take the batteries out of an old remote or phone and let your little one push all the buttons she likes without risking a call to Brazil.

If the temptation to try lots of different toys takes you, you can avoid spending a small fortune by joining a toy library. Toy libraries cost you a joining fee (around $50 in both New Zealand and Australia), but for just a few dollars you can then rent toys like an exer-saucer (an activity station that you sit your baby in) or dress-up outfits that are too expensive to buy, or will be suitable for your child for only a short time.

Find your local toy library by checking out these sites:

- ✔ Australia www.bubhub.com.au/servicestoyhire.php
- ✔ New Zealand toylibrary.co.nz

Toys with small parts are still off limits for little ones. Anything with parts smaller than a film canister are considered a choking risk, so wait until your baby is at least three years old before letting him play with toys with small parts.

Here Come Some Milestones

As we approach the end of the first year, the stay-at-home parent usually returns to work as obligated under the terms of their employment. Time to sit back and reflect on the past year as your baby approaches her first birthday and becomes a toddler.

Preparing to return to work

Dads are not necessarily the ones bringing home the bacon these days while their baby is small. Increasing numbers of fathers are staying home with their babies while mum goes back to paid employment. But sooner or later most dads also find themselves joining the rat race and returning to work. Check out Chapter 16 for more on stay-at-home dads.

Before you head off with your briefcase though, think about these things:

- ✔ How will you manage days when your child is sick and can't go to day care, or days when her nanny is sick?
- ✔ How will you manage your time? Will you have time to juggle work and family? Will you have time to spend with your partner?
- ✔ Who'll take care of the baby? See Chapter 8 for more about other people taking care of your child, such as day care and nannies.
- ✔ Will the costs of childcare outweigh the benefits of going back to work?

Waiting lists for day care can be up to two years long, so phone around and get yourself on waiting lists as soon as you can. For more about day care options, see Chapter 8.

Keeping work and family time separate is a struggle in our high-tech age, when employees and business associates expect to reach you 24/7. However, you can set a few rules for yourself so that you're not burnt out by work, or short-changing your family. Make it a rule that if you have to bring work home, you wait until your baby is in bed before bringing out the work, or that your phone is switched off when you walk through the front door at night.

Likewise when you're at work, the more productive you are the less likely you may be to have to bring work home. Keeping in mind that time spent working is time you can't be with your child helps to keep you focused and to value the time the two of you have together.

Going on holiday

The idea of taking on holiday a demanding, pooping, sometimes crying child who is wholly dependent on you for his survival sounds a little like an oxymoron. There's nothing holiday-like about looking after a baby! Holidays aren't the same with children, but at some stage in the first year you may want a break from staring at the same old walls.

Going on a short trip isn't such a big deal, but if you're going anywhere further away than a couple of hours drive, you need a few strategies to stop everyone going mental on the journey.

Driving

Imagine if you were strapped into a car seat with a full harness at the front. You'd get pretty uncomfortable after a couple of hours, and if you couldn't stretch and move around of your own free will, you'd get a bit grumpy too. So will your baby if you don't stop every now and then to let him have a breather, some food, or a nappy change.

Here are some more ways to manage a long car trip with your baby.

✔ If you're travelling during summer, keep bub lightly dressed as he can get pretty sticky on his back or anywhere that is touching his car seat. Use visors on windows to keep glare out of his face and to protect him from the sun. Make sure bub has a cup or bottle of water on hand to stop him becoming dehydrated. Avoid driving in the heat of the day if you can.

✔ Make sure you've got some snacks prepared for the trip. You wouldn't want to get caught out miles from anywhere with a hungry baby who won't be satisfied with a breastfeed or bottle. It also means you've got food for bub should you break down, heaven forbid.

✔ Plan your trip around when bub is due to have a sleep because inevitably the motion of the car sends him off to sleepyland.

✔ Take plenty of toys or objects to keep your little one entertained while awake. Books or his favourite teddy bear are also great. If you can, organise a new toy or something he hasn't seen before. That way you can keep him interested for longer.

Drive safely at all times. Your most precious person is in the back with you, so don't take any chances.

Flying

The idea of air travel with a baby can strike fear into the most experienced dads. The perils of confined space and air pressure issues coupled with the idea of sitting within smelling and screeching distance of other passengers aren't to be taken lightly, but they're manageable.

Here are some ways to make flying with your baby easier:

✔ Have plenty of books and toys to keep her entertained. Organise new things that your little one hasn't seen before. A great strategy is to wrap toys, books and other things your baby is used to as if they were presents. Unwrapping the 'present' is fun and adds to the excitement.

✔ If bub's restless, take him for a walk up and down the aisles. Seeing other people cheers him up and gets you out of your seat as well.

✔ If other parents with babies are on board, make contact with them. They may come in very handy if you need an extra pair of hands or for keeping an eye on bub while you eat or go to the toilet. Most parents of young children are quite helpful as they know what travelling with babies is like.

✔ If you get unhelpful cabin crew members, remind them that they can either help you now or clean poo/vomit/baby food off the carpet or other passengers later on. If you're really stressed out because your little one is crying or you haven't had a chance to eat, ask a member of the crew to take care of bub for a few minutes.

✔ If you're travelling on a long flight, book the cot position (called the bulkhead seat) that most major airlines offer when booking your flight. If she's not sleeping in the cot, you at least have extra leg room for her to play on the floor at your feet.

- Pack a drink because the swallowing action helps your baby equalise her ears. If mum's on hand, breastfeeding during takeoff and landing can help too. If mum's not available, give your baby something to drink or eat during takeoff and landing.

- Stay calm. If you're calm, baby will most likely be calm too.

- Take a fully packed nappy bag with nappies, change mat, wipes, plastic bags for dirty nappies, nappy cream or powder, spare clothes and snacks or jars of baby food

- When you check in, ask to hold onto your stroller/pram until you get to the gate (some airlines let you do that; it mostly depends on the size/ model of the pram). Navigating through airports and departure lounges and carrying all the bags is a lot easier when you've got a safe place to put bub. Usually airlines can put your stroller in the hold just before you board.

If you're travelling overseas, your baby needs his own passport.

If you're staying overnight somewhere you need:

- A cot for baby to sleep in, with appropriate bedding. Most hotels and motels have portacots, but check when you make your booking.

- A mini first-aid kit of teething remedies, pain reliever and any lotions and potions your baby needs

- A stroller or baby carrier depending on how much walking you plan to do

- Nappies and nappy changing accessories

- The usual clothes, toys and books.

Wow, that's strange: Addressing your concerns

By now, you know your baby well enough to know when something's not quite right. You may discover something unexpected, such as a rash, or your baby makes a fuss at something specific, or something just doesn't feel right.

Father knows best

Sometimes it may be easy to put up with the problem; ignore it and hope that it goes away. Or you can upskill and deal with your concerns. This doesn't mean buying every book in the store about childhood illness, but observing your baby's body and moods and acting accordingly.

Nobody expects you to know everything about your baby, but you are the best judge if something's not right. Trust your instincts and don't be afraid to ask for help if you need it. Child health nurses and GPs are there to provide help.

Get involved in your child's health care. If something's wrong, don't leave it to mum to work out or take him to the doctor, get in on the act as well. You'll be prepared for when the problem happens again.

Teething

Teething is the biggest issue for babies aged 6 to 12 months. Having a sharp tooth cut through her gum can be very upsetting for your child, especially because she won't understand what's going on.

Signs that bub is teething include the following:

- Her cheeks may be bright red
- She dribbles a lot
- She puts objects in her mouth more than usual
- She may get nappy rash.
- She's more grizzly and clingy.

Here are some simple ways to help relieve her discomfort:

- Amber necklaces are said to help teething babies. These are special necklaces where the beads are individually secured. The beads are also small enough to be swallowed (in a worst case scenario) without being a choking risk. *Note:* There is no scientific evidence for the effectiveness of amber as a pain reliever, but some parents swear by it.
- Chilled apple slices wrapped in a piece of muslin cloth tied with a band are soothing and healthy for her too. Baby sucks and gums the apple, but bits can't come free in her mouth. Chill fruit in the fridge, not the freezer.
- Some parents swear by commercial teething gels and powders, but make sure you're happy with the ingredients in them first.
- Toys with some 'give' in them and texture can help numb pain when baby bites on them by causing counterpressure. Some toys can be filled with liquid and chilled in the fridge.

If all else fails and bub is just too upset with all these remedies, some infant paracetamol or ibuprofen can be given. Check with your child health nurse, Well Child provider or GP about dosage for your child's age and weight.

When bub is teething, he needs more cuddles and may be a bit clingy. He may wake up at night more and be difficult to settle. Try to be patient — teething is not much fun. The love you show your child when he needs you like this builds trust and security in your baby.

As tempting as it may be, don't put teething toys with gels in the freezer. This may make them too cold, which can cause more pain for your little one.

How time flies

Now you're a dad, time seems to evaporate in front of your eyes. Fatherhood is like a whirlwind tour of your favourite places in the shortest time possible. If you don't take photos and keep a diary, you soon forget the journey. So much happens in the first year. Not only does your baby transform into a toddler, you and your partner are transformed into completely awesome parents.

So how can you capture this first year?

- ✔ Keep a diary. You could even do it online with a blog.

- ✔ Pictures paint a thousand words. Take lots of photos of your little one.

- ✔ Start a book for your child where you can record her first words and foods, and the dates when she first rolled over, crawled and walked. You can also keep photos and mementos in the book.

None of this makes any difference if you're not interested in recording these memories. Be interested in contributing to a diary and your photos and spend loads of time having fun with your baby when you take them. When your child becomes interested in his past, he'll really appreciate the effort you put into recording him as a baby.

One today!

What, already?! Your baby isn't a baby anymore — she's a toddler now. How did that happen? Didn't you only just bring her home from the hospital brand-new, like, last week?

Congratulations to you and your partner. Marking this milestone is just as much for you, the parents, as it is for your child — in fact probably more! One year ago your baby was born and turned your lives upside down.

So gather your family and friends and celebrate your baby turning one. A celebration is an excellent way to thank those around you for all the support they've given you over the last year and to cement your child's place in your family.

Your baby won't remember or even understand today's her birthday, but if you want to mark the day with a child's party, here are some tips to make it memorable:

- ✔ Plan well in advance to allow yourself enough time to get everything done.
- ✔ Plastic cups and plates make cleaning up easier and with little ones around make breakages less likely.
- ✔ Provide food for adults as well as safe food for children. Avoid nuts and hard foods that may choke little ones. Have a balance between healthy and treat foods.
- ✔ Take lots of photos! Bub won't turn one again.
- ✔ Time the party around sleep times. You don't want the superstar of the day to be grumpy because he should be sleeping. Other parents will be working around their children's sleep times too so expect people to be late and leave after only an hour or two.

Start the day with quiet family time so you, your partner and your child can look back on the past 12 months and marvel at what you have now in front of you.

Part III
The Toddler Years

Glenn Lumsden

*'It bothered me, too, for the first year
and a half; then the smell just vanished ...'*

In this part ...

Many a father has been warned that once his baby gets up on his feet and starts walking, the real work of being a dad begins. Toddlers can get around quickly, onto the road and into trouble faster than you can imagine. Add to that the ever-increasing need for independence which manifests itself as a volcanic tantrum from time to time, and a toddler is a ticking time bomb. Luckily, we've got a few clues about managing a tempestuous toddler, and in this part, we give you food for thought on discipline and the kind of father you want to be.

The toddler years are also precious ones, as your child speaks real words for the first time, and attempts real skills like putting on her shoes and writing her name. Here, we give you some ideas on how to develop these skills and even broach the subject of toilet training.

Chapter 10

Toddling Towards Two: Months 12–24

In This Chapter

▷ Interacting with a toddler

▷ Helping your toddler develop and grow

▷ Getting to know your toddler's personality

▷ Dealing with setbacks

*H*owever challenging toddlers can be, the second year of life is also a delightful age. Language, social and motor skills are all developing, and toddlers can surprise you with what they understand and repeat back to you as they grow. Your little champ will remember where you hid the biscuits, can figure out what the remote control does, and will mimic your gestures and movements in such a sweet, naïve way that it will make you crack up with laughter.

Your child's first words may be a little predictable — Mum, Dad, ball, dog, more. But be prepared for some unexpected words — noisy, heater, dinosaur or even toothbrush. Kids this age are often called sponges and that's what they are, sucking up knowledge like you wouldn't believe. The kid who just celebrated his first birthday is going to be quite a different boy when he turns two.

In this chapter, you find out all about his development, as well as how to cope as he deals with frustration, anger and all manner of emotions he can't figure out. We also take you through the changes in your child's eating, sleeping, and health and safety needs.

Hey, You've Got a Toddler Now

Once your child starts to walk, she magically transforms from a baby into a toddler. Just the word *toddler* can strike fear into a dad: Toddlers have a reputation for getting into trouble. Your little one is also a ticking tantrum time bomb now. You've probably heard the saying 'terrible twos', meaning that bang on her second birthday your formerly perfectly pleasant baby turns into a monster of unequalled horribleness. It doesn't quite work like that and as your toddler creeps towards being an independent little person she'll be struggling between needing her dad every step of the way and wanting to do things her own way, thank you very much. This means she will sometimes have little meltdowns when what *you* want her to do and what *she* wants to do collide. This can start as early as right now.

If your toddler suddenly starts resisting nappy changes, getting into her car seat or having to sit in a shopping cart, she hasn't turned into a monster, she's just continuing her struggle to become an individual and have her own free will. We talk later on in this chapter about how to deal with taxing toddler behaviour.

Sleeping update

Most dads by now are enjoying a good night's sleep as junior is no longer getting up for feeds in the early hours. That said, don't expect bub to sleep through every night. Teething, colds, being too hot or too cold, having just mastered a new skill or simply needing a cuddle will still have him calling out for you in the night. Often this is just temporary and you'll be getting 40 winks again in no time. Some toddlers will also start to have nightmares and night terrors, where they will wake up screaming or lashing out at you. Be there with a cuddle and some soothing words. Make bed a really happy, attractive place to be with soft toys and special blankets, which toddlers can get very attached to. Make sure there's lots of love and good feelings at bedtime.

Most toddlers go through some sort of *separation anxiety* in the first year and it comes back in the second. Your toddler may cling to you more, need more reassurance and object to you leaving the room. Explain to your toddler that you're not going far, or will be back soon and some other lovely person will look after him while you're gone.

At about the one-year mark, many children go from two naps during the day to one nap, which is usually taken in the middle of the day. Let your child work out how much sleep he needs by watching for his tired signs — yawning, becoming a bit clumsy, gazing into the distance and becoming grizzly — and putting him down for a nap then. At some point he will start missing a nap, needing only one. Sometimes he may seem tired in the afternoon but will resist going for a sleep and by early evening will be exhausted, so you could try moving his bedtime forward a bit until he gets used to his one-nap-a-day routine. For more tips on sleeping check out www.diyfather.com/Sleeping-new.

Eating update

The start of this year will see a change in your little one's diet. As she grows more teeth she'll be able to handle a bigger variety of foods and foods with chunkier textures. With her digestive and immune systems maturing, your toddler can handle foods that were once off the menu such as cow's milk, honey and egg whites. Keep high fibre foods such as bran and wholegrain bread until after her second birthday as they tend to clear the gut too much, stopping nutrients from being absorbed.

Small, hard foods like popcorn and nuts are still off the menu until junior is at least three years old because of the choking risk.

Offer your child a variety of foods. What he doesn't like one day he may love the next so keep trying with things he's turned his nose up at before.

A typical toddler needs:

- At least five servings of fruit and vegetables a day. A serving is the amount that fits into your child's hand. Vitamin C helps your child absorb iron, so include some vitamin C-rich fruits like citrus fruit or kiwifruit.

- Iron from red meat, chicken or fish, or vegetarian options like silverbeet, slivered almonds and broccoli.

- Dairy, but not low fat. Young children need fat to grow, but keep the hot chips and burgers for special treats. Toddlers need about three cups of dairy a day — 600 mL may be given as milk, cheese, yoghurt, etc., but not so much that they fill up on dairy and miss out on other nutrients.

- Breads and cereals, such as bread and Weetbix, but not heavy wholegrains or bran until he's at least two years old.

Limit the number of sweet snacks such as dried fruit, lollies and biscuits because of their tooth-damaging sugar content. Additives and high sugar content in 'junk' food have been linked to altering children's moods and making them potentially even more energetic than they typically are anyway. So if you notice 'sugar highs' or difficult behaviour, such as increased tantrums after your children have eaten certain kinds of food, try to limit intake of those particular foods. Try slices of fresh fruit, sandwiches, rice crackers and vegetables instead.

Now that your toddler is able to experience more texture and variety in her meals, she can have toddler versions of your meals and eat with you. This is a good time to teach your child about the social aspects of eating with all of you around the table talking about your day and about the food in front of you. Make sure the TV is off and just hang out together as a family. Seeing you eat good healthy meals encourages your child to eat healthily too. Check out www.diyfather.com/Food-and-Nutrition for tips on what to give your little champ.

Health update

Try not to forget that your child, even though she's not a baby anymore, still needs to keep up to date with her immunisations. Check www.immunise.health.gov.au for the immunisation schedule in Australia and www.moh.govt.nz/immunisation to see if you're on track in New Zealand, or talk to your GP.

If your child is now at childcare, he's likely to pick up every germ on the planet, and will have between 6 to 12 colds a year. Even kids who aren't in childcare are vulnerable to the viruses flying around and it may sometimes seem as if junior's only just getting over one cold before another one comes along. Children have the same symptoms of a cold as adults — runny nose, cough, fever, headache, sneezing and swollen glands. He'll probably wake up more often in the night for comforting and be a bit miserable during the day. Unfortunately, you can't give your child any cold medication, but you can give extra fluids, the correct dosage of Pamol or Nurofen (by age) and cuddles to make him feel a bit less miserable.

At this age, you can also show your child how to blow her nose, or at least wipe it, or blow it while you hold the tissue. Most children get a great sense of satisfaction and achievement to then put their dirty tissue in the rubbish bin. Give your child heaps of praise when you show her how to do it so blowing her nose is not a chore but a fun thing to do.

You can use non-medicated means to lessen your child's discomfort and congestion. See Chapter 7 for some tips.

Mingling with other children in the wider community also brings your little star into contact with germs that are nastier than the common cold. You may find she's come down with one of the following infections:

- **Bronchiolitis:** An inflammation of the bronchioles (lungs' airways). Your child will have a nasty cough and may have trouble breathing. Take her to your GP.

- **Chickenpox:** Starts with a fever and cold symptoms. After a day or two, your child gets red, itchy blisters on her skin. You can calm the itch with calamine lotion or other lotions available from your pharmacy and give your child lots of soothing baths. A vaccination is available to prevent your child getting chickenpox. Talk to your GP about having her vaccinated.

- **Croup:** A cough caused by a viral infection. It starts out as a cold but becomes a pretty nasty and wheezy cough similar to a barking seal that comes on suddenly. Go to your GP.

- **Ear infection:** If your child has an ear infection she'll be grizzly and tug at her ears, or rub them. A trip to your GP to check your child's ears thoroughly is in order. She may need antibiotics to treat the infection.

- **Gastroenteritis:** Most children have a 'tummy bug' at some stage, which usually involves a lot of vomiting and diarrhoea. A number of common nasties could be responsible for your child's illness. Gastro bugs can cause dehydration, so make sure your child gets plenty to drink. Gastro bugs can take a week to disappear, but if you're concerned, see your GP.

- **Strep throat:** Your child may have a high temperature and be vague and exhausted. Go to your GP.

If you're at all worried about how unwell your child is, take her to your GP. Checking with a health care professional is best, especially if she's running a temperature that doesn't go down after giving her Pamol or Nurofen.

To take care of a child with a fever (a temperature over 37 degrees Celsius), try the following:

- Give her a dose of children's paracetamol or ibuprofen suitable for her age

- Keep her clothing light, and use only a sheet to cover her in bed

- Give her lots of fluids

- Keep her bedroom cool but not cold

If her temperature stays high, or you're worried about her illness, see your GP. You know your child best, so if she seems not to be her usual self — for example, she's less active, quiet or sleepy — checking with your GP is a good idea.

Safety update

Of course you've completely baby-proofed the house by now, as we suggested in Chapter 7, but there's an issue to consider as your baby turns into a toddler to make sure he's safe — the walking issue.

Once toddlers find their feet, they're off — and fast. Leaving the front door open may spell disaster as your child can be out of the house and down to the road in seconds. You may want to invest in safety gates for stairs, making sure back and front yards have toddler-proof fencing, and that any rooms you don't want junior visiting are closed off and out of bounds — at least until he can reach the door handle. Some parents find a playpen handy at this age, but be aware that an 18-month-old can learn pretty quickly how to get out of a playpen.

In the first half of his second year, your little one will be canny enough to use other objects like chairs, fan heaters, boxes and large toys to climb and get into cupboards, benches and other places you assumed were out of reach.

 Pay particular attention to your kitchen. A curious toddler can pull a kettle of boiling water on himself by fiddling with the kettle's cord. He can also work out how to grab at pot handles, so keep handles tucked in towards the stove and away from inquisitive little hands.

 From 12 months of age, your child will be able to sit facing forward in his car seat. Depending on what model you have, he may even need a bigger car seat.

Conscious Fathering

As parents, you have the choice to find out and educate yourselves about your children, or to not bother and rely on what you know from your own parents. In some cases relying on the knowledge of the previous generation may not be such a great option as things have moved on in the last 20–30 years.

You may have heard about *conscious parenting,* which means thinking about what sort of parent you want to be and what you want for your children.

Conscious parenting is also about actively taking part in learning about how children are developing. So for guys this means conscious fathering. We believe being active in your child's life is important so you can understand and manage the different stages she's going through, rather than being dumbfounded by her behaviour.

Parents realise that learning to walk is a great developmental achievement, but so is having a tantrum. Understanding what's behind these developmental milestones makes all the difference. Reacting appropriately to your child's behaviour is much easier when you know what's going on.

If you look at your toddler's new tricks (especially the challenging behaviour) from the point of view that this is a phase of her growth and development, managing the way your child behaves is much easier and less stressful for both of you. That said, the environment and situation plays a big part in your toddler's behaviour as well; for example, toddlers and young children will act up and be difficult to manage when they're tired, hungry, or in pain or discomfort — just like most adults.

Children need:

- ✔ Consistency and consequences
- ✔ Guidance and understanding
- ✔ Limits and boundaries
- ✔ Love and warmth
- ✔ A structured and secure environment
- ✔ To be talked to and listened to

Taking into account your child's developmental stage and temperament when you're interacting with her is also important. Read on to find out about developmental stages for toddlers.

Your toddler is learning that she has her own will and can assert herself. She's a curious little creature who doesn't know yet what the rules about living are, and she needs you to show her what her boundaries and limits are.

A Busy Year for Your Little One

Remember how much your child changed in the first year of life? She may have slowed her rapid rate of physical growth, but not her development. She's speeding towards ever-increasing abilities, skills and independence.

Toddler development

This year is characterised by your little one taking her first steps and speaking her first words, and also by her social and emotional development. By the time she's two she'll be able to say about 50 words, if not more.

At this time, she's developing the following physical skills:

- Being able to see into the distance and spot things like the moon, planes and birds in the sky
- Climbing objects like ladders, steps and chairs to get higher, so watch that safety!
- Feeding herself with a spoon, then a fork, then adding a knife to the equation with much more dexterity and skill than before
- Making attempts to run, albeit with knocked-knees
- Performing little tasks such as 'find dad's slippers'
- Stacking objects on top of each other, such as blocks and little chairs on tables
- Taking her clothes off and putting on some simple clothing, such as her hat and jacket
- Throwing and kicking a ball (however, catching is pretty advanced)

Her language skills are growing too. During this year, she's learning to:

- Listen to and understand conversations
- Say approximately 50-plus words, although not clearly and perhaps not in coherent sentences, but rather like 'Daddy gone' or 'sock where?'
- Understand simple instructions

As for her social and mental development, you'll find that she's:

- Able to feel jealous, and may object if you and your partner show affection for each other, or if you're close to other children.
- Able to remember things, and may talk about them or find things that she's left somewhere (see Chapter 7 for more information about object permanence).
- Able to say 'No' more often than you'd like and can be possessive of favourite toys.
- Excited by presents or events, or the anticipation of seeing someone special like grandparents.

- ✔ Incredibly curious and wants to be involved with everything that you're doing.

- ✔ Involved for longer periods with specific toys. Tell her when you want to start a new activity, such as changing her nappy, because she may not object so loudly then.

- ✔ More interested in books, and will want you to read them over and over again. Repetition is good for children's learning, so even if you've read her *The Gruffalo* 500 times already, just keep reading it if she asks. You may find she also knows the words off by heart and will pull you up if you skip phrases or pages.

- ✔ Objecting to changes in her environment or activity. If she's really enjoying playing with blocks, she may object to having a bath, even though she loves bathing.

- ✔ Perhaps afraid of dogs, water, heights, the dark and all manner of things, including things she used to enjoy.

- ✔ Recognising herself in a mirror, as well as family and friends in photos.

- ✔ Showing more determination to do things her way or the highway. She's also showing her independence by refusing your help with tasks.

- ✔ Well bonded to mum and dad, and will get upset if you leave her alone.

Playing with your child at this age is really fun. Unlike a baby, your toddler can make full use of playgrounds, and go outside and explore the landscape, and you can really talk to each other!

Here are some simple things you two can do together that he'll really love and that will encourage the development of skills:

- ✔ Building blocks fascinate toddlers and help develop fine motor skills. Try making some towers or castles together.

- ✔ Get outdoors. Climb a tree together, get on your bikes, or head to the park or playground.

- ✔ Let the music play. Some toddlers really love listening to music and dancing. He wants to do everything you're doing, so dance along with him. It doesn't matter if the neighbours see you.

- ✔ Let your toddler explore. If he gets into your wardrobe and tries on your shoes, let him go for it! What harm can it do? He may just learn the motor skills to put on his own shoes.

- ✔ Play chase around the house. Stay just a little bit out of his sight so he has to catch you.

- ✔ Play in the sandpit. Sandpit play helps your little champ develop fine motor skills and dexterity, as well as experiencing sand running through his fingers.

✔ Play with water. Toddlers love pouring water into objects, so if you're washing the dishes, he can 'help' by standing on a chair at the sink with you and pouring water from one cup to another.

✔ Read stories together, sometimes dozens of times over. You can change things a bit by reading the story in a silly voice, or asking your child questions about what's on each page as you go along.

✔ Roll around on the floor together. This helps with your toddler's sense of balance and prepares him for rough and tumble play when he gets a bit older.

Toddlers can get pretty excited when rough-housing or playing and forget themselves, so you and mum need to set some rules around play. Some suggestions include no throwing balls in the house, no hitting and no snatching toys from other children. However, children don't fully understand the concept of sharing and inflicting pain until they are much older, so they will still snatch toys and hit other children. Be patient and consistent. When things get a bit out of hand around the playground, remove your child from the scene, distract him or give him a cuddle as a simple intervention.

Talk about everything that you and your little one are doing. His mind is a sponge and he'll soak up every word.

If you announce what you're going to do next or what you'd like your little man to do next, you'll probably encounter less resistance. We all want to feel we're in control (at least a little bit) and know what's happening and toddlers are no different, so commentate everything you're doing and tell him what's going to happen next.

Say 'daddy'

Hearing your child talk for the first time is like your cat suddenly speaking to you. For the whole of your child's life he's done nothing but coo and babble and cry, and then voila! Words! Some of the first words he'll say won't sound like much until a light goes on in your head and you recognise 'ball' or 'truck' or 'dog' — an amazing moment.

Communicating is more than just about words and speech, it's about body language, gestures and the tone of your voice when you speak, which is how you can help your toddler connect ideas with spoken words. For example, the way you say 'hot!' in a sharp tone indicates to your child that hot things are to be avoided, and the way you say 'good boy!' with applause and a kiss helps to connect those words with good feelings. Toddlers understand pointing, gestures and tone before they understand words, so you can help expand your little one's language by connecting those things with words. Try to describe what you're doing so he connects that action with the words you're saying.

Unlike when you tried to learn a language at school, picking up language is really easy for young children. All your child really needs is lots of talking from you and help to connect ideas, like pictures in books, and actions like getting dressed, with words in order to get those language synapses firing.

Toddlers typically go through a *word spurt* from 18 months onward, where they may learn a word from hearing it only once. Children who have been through their word spurts already can deduce or *fast map* what the word for a particular object is by eliminating objects they already know. Show your child three animals, such as a duck, a lion and an animal they've never seen before. Ask him which is the duck, which is the lion and which is the aardvark, and he'll be able to pick the aardvark because it's the animal he doesn't know.

Enthusiasm is infectious. If you're talking about how gorgeous your little petal is, or how well she's put away her toys, your tone communicates how you feel about her, and that's what will hold her attention and motivate her to work out what you're saying.

Repetition of words and phrases is important, so keep pointing at the rabbit picture and saying rabbit. Any day now you'll hear your champ mumble 'wabbit' when you point at the picture.

As we mention in Chapter 7, keep exposing your child to different languages if you can. This exposure helps his pronunciation later in life and he will also enjoy hearing different words that describe the same thing. A great way of exposing your child to different languages is using different words for 'hello'. You can make up a rhyme or a little song using different greetings; for example Talofa, Kia Ora, Hallo, Nihau, Hola and Salut.

Dad, I need a wee

Toilet training is a subject close to the heart of many fathers — those who are cheering for an end to nappy changing and those who can't bear the thought of having to clean poo out of the carpet again.

Toilet training is another of those sticks that people measure their children's success by. Most children are nappy free by 18 months to four years old. Some parents may brag that little Jimmy was toilet trained by two years as if that's some mark of his genius, but some perfectly normal bright children aren't ready to go potty by themselves until they're four. Try not to get too hung up about toilet training by a certain age. Like other milestones such as rolling over and walking, your child will toilet train when she's ready. You can lead her to the toilet but you can't make her wee.

You know your toddler is ready to give the toilet a go when:

- ✔ She's interested in watching you go to the toilet yourself.

- ✔ She has dry nappies for a couple of hours or more. This shows she can 'save up' wee in her bladder.

- ✔ She has the language skills to tell you she has done a wee or a poo, or can tell you she wants to do a wee or a poo.

- ✔ She starts to dislike wearing a nappy and tries to take it off.

- ✔ She can pull up and pull down her trousers or tights.

- ✔ She can walk steadily and sit long enough to wee or poo.

- ✔ Her bowel movements are soft, well formed and fairly predictable.

Your child doesn't need to demonstrate all these signs to show he's ready to toilet train. Like starting solids, starting toilet training is something you can judge and try out. If it doesn't work, just wait and try again when more signs pop up.

In France parents believe you shouldn't start toilet training before the child can walk up and down stairs upright and unassisted. Apparently this means the child's muscles are ready to control bowel movements. See if it works for you!

Some tips for starting toilet training are:

- ✔ Choose a settled time in your child's life to begin toilet training, not the week your parents are coming to stay or an immunisation jab is due.

- ✔ If your child has a regular routine, find a time to try the potty that can become part of that routine.

- ✔ Be prepared for toilet training to take a few months. Have patience if things go backwards. There will be setbacks, but like everything, setbacks are just a phase. If toilet training isn't working after three months, stop and wait a month or so until giving it another shot.

- ✔ If she's watching you use the loo, tell her what you're doing.

- ✔ Let her push the button to make the toilet flush to reduce the fear that comes when she hears the flush.

- ✔ Go slowly. Don't expect junior to be dry at night for a while after she's got the hang of the toilet in the daytime. There will be daytime accidents too, so be a patient dad.

- ✔ Encourage her to eat fruit and drink fluid to avoid constipation.

Forcing your child to toilet train when you want her to is bound to fail. Let her guide you to when she's ready developmentally to go to the toilet.

Here's how to start toilet training:

- ✔ Get a plastic potty or a toilet trainer that sits on the toilet seat.

- ✔ At a specific time of day when you think junior needs to wee or poo, put your champ on the potty with her clothes on so she can get a feel for the potty.

- ✔ When she's used to being on the potty each day, try it with her nappy off.

- ✔ Change to training pants or a combination of training pants and nappies for night time. Training pants are designed so that junior feels wet. The idea is to help your little champ develop a cause–effect link between a soiled nappy and the muscles in her body that are responsible for making a wee or poo.

- ✔ Give a big cheer when she wees or poos in the toilet or potty.

Don't forget to show your little one how to wash and dry her hands after using the toilet. May as well start as you mean to go on.

Can we play football yet?

Any father knows that the possibilities for playing with your toddler have opened up dramatically now that he is mobile. As he develops his throwing, kicking and running, you may be tempted to see him as the next rising star in soccer, or league or rugby or whatever you're into. That's great, as long as you don't pressure your child to perform like Beckham.

The idea that toddlers, not known for their teamwork or sharing, can play team sports seems a little ridiculous on first glance, but not so. Creating structure, rules and team spirit is a great way to introduce your child to sports, not to mention an awesome way to burn off excess energy. And sports are yet another way to encourage some dad-time with your child by giving him encouragement, helping out with practice or even coaching.

Playing in team sports is important because:

- ✔ Children this age love to be around other kids, and being in a group helps them socialise and develop interpersonal skills

- ✔ It encourages your child from an early age to participate in physical activities and learn a skill with other children his age

- ✔ It helps to develop gross motor skills such as throwing and kicking

It's All about Me, Dad!

The newborn who didn't recognise himself in the mirror and had no idea he even had hands has left the building. Your toddler not only knows who he is, but thinks he's the only kid on the block, and will act like nothing else matters — not the instructions you give him, or the cat he's chasing. Now is the time to get serious about discipline. Have a look at `www.diyfather.com/skip` for additional material on disciplining and specific issues like tantrums.

Understanding discipline

Toddlers don't know the rules to the game of life yet, so you dads and your partners need to teach the rules to your children. Another word for this is *discipline*. Discipline's not about laying down the law and punishing your child when he doesn't conform, but about giving your kids the tools to know what's right and wrong and helping them on the way to becoming independent young people. Developing a warm, loving relationship with your child where he feels safe and secure with you is the best place to start, because he'll know you're always there for him and love him, even when he's just painted his room with toothpaste.

Children need boundaries and limits so they know where they stand and know the consequences of crossing those lines. Children are challenging in the respect that part of their nature is to push those boundaries.

Some tips for making discipline work are:

- ✔ Be consistent with your boundaries. If snatching a toy from a friend is not okay one day, but okay the next, junior will be confused. He needs to know from day one that snatching's not okay. At the same time, giving warmth, talking, guidance and encouragement so he doesn't feel alienated as a result of his behaviour is also important. Time-outs and more drastic consequences are more appropriate with slightly older children, such as pre-schoolers.

- ✔ Be realistic about what your child can do. Children can't do everything perfectly straight away and can't control their emotions or understand their bodies the way adults do. We get grumpy when we're hungry or tired, and so do children, but children don't know how to control those emotions yet.

- ✔ Children model the behaviour they see from their parents. If your son sees you punching the wall when you're annoyed, in all likelihood he'll repeat that behaviour when he's annoyed. Saying sorry to your toddler encourages him to say it too when he needs to.

✔ Communicate with your toddler, even if she isn't really speaking well yet. It may take a few explanations to show her the rules, but she'll get there. You don't need to give complicated explanations for why hitting the cat is not okay. Simply telling her he may scratch is enough.

✔ It takes time for toddlers to learn their boundaries and to understand consequences. Try to be patient with your child.

✔ Kids aren't naughty for the sake of it, or to wind you up. There's usually a reason. Your toddler is trying out new things every second of the day, like throwing bits of banana around the car, for the experience of it. She may also be less well behaved when she's tired or hungry, frustrated or shy. Work with your child's routine: Don't go shopping at lunchtime, or to a busy crowded place at nap time.

✔ Remember that your child just wants you to love her and to please you, which may be hard to do on a day when she's thrown bits of banana around the car. Be patient and use distraction to divert her attention while removing the banana from sight.

✔ Reward good behaviour with lots of love and praise, but try not to withhold love when she's behaving badly. Let her know you love *her* (the little person), not the behaviour.

✔ Say more positive than negative things to your child. Reword phrases; for example, 'no running in the house' becomes 'slow down, please'.

✔ You and your partner need to work out what action to take when junior is doing something undesirable. Think about the 'naughty step'. Distracting your child from a behaviour, showing her how to clean up if she's made a mess, or taking away a toy that's being fought over are all techniques to discipline a child. Smacking a child, in our opinion, is not acceptable. Smacking has been found to be ineffective in changing behaviour and it confuses children. How can dad love me when he hits me?

We recommend using a framework for effective discipline which starts before any issues arise. It goes like this:

✔ Be consistent and explain consequences

✔ Establish limits and boundaries

✔ Guide and understand him

✔ Show love and warmth to your child at every opportunity

✔ Talk and listen to him frequently

The result will be a structured and secure environment to grow up in.

If your child is really pushing your buttons with his behaviour, yelling at him won't make things any easier. In fact, it may just make things worse. So try to be calm, take a deep breath and sing a song, like 'Incy Wincy Spider', to yourself.

When you feel yourself getting really wound up, check with yourself how you're feeling and what your day has been like. It may be that the behaviour of your little one isn't actually that bad, you've just had a tough day. It might be a good idea to remove yourself from the situation to let off some steam, or lift your spirits by listening to a good song in the car.

Understand the difference between discipline and punishment. Discipline is derived from 'disciple' and refers to a particular code of conduct given to a person to follow. Punishment is the practice of imposing something unpleasant or aversive on somebody. Punishment doesn't involve any instruction or code of conduct and as a result it is typically not effective in changing behaviour. Use discipline with your children rather than punishment.

Tantrums, biting and hitting

When you first met your seconds-old baby all those months ago, you probably didn't imagine that she'd be having a full-on hissy fit in the middle of the supermarket over not being able to grab a bottle of bleach from the shelf. But it happens to even the nicest babies, with the nicest, most nurturing parents. Not only do children have tantrums, but they hit other children (or you), pull hair, bite and scratch because they aren't yet able to control their emotions, frustrations and physicality.

Tantrums

Although two-year-olds are famous for being tempestuous, even children under two have tantrums. Tantrums can go on into the fifth year and beyond. You've probably seen a child mid-tantrum in the street or shop, with an embarrassed, stressed out parent standing nearby, trying to reason her little one out of it, or ignore the whole thing. You probably said that your kid would never do that. But tantrums are almost inevitable.

Tantrums happen when your child is overloaded with stress or frustration. He has an idea of what he wants to do, such as running around like a crazy thing in the supermarket. If you want him to do otherwise, such as staying by your side as you shop, he's going to get pretty fed up with you holding him back and have a tantrum.

He may also be tired and hungry, or feeling vulnerable or insecure, which makes everyone's tolerance for things they don't want to do much lower, even you big grown up fathers.

Here are some pointers on how to stop tantrums happening:

- ✔ Make sure junior isn't tired or hungry before setting out on an activity.
- ✔ Talk to your child about what you're going to be doing or who you'll be seeing so there aren't surprises for him.
- ✔ If you're at the playground and it's nearly time to leave, let him have plenty of time to get used to the idea, so he understands when it's time to go.
- ✔ Get your child involved in what you're doing so he's engaged with you rather than wanting to behave in a way that requires you telling him off.

If a tantrum is on its way, the best strategy is to ignore it. Keep close by to make sure your little one doesn't feel completely abandoned by you, but trying to reason with or distract him is usually pointless. Just let him get it all out and when the tantrum's over, give him a cuddle and a kiss and keep on with what you were doing. Don't get upset, as that usually just intensifies the tantrum. Keep breathing!

 Chat to your partner about how you plan to manage tantrums and activities that may involve tantrums, like shopping, long car rides, or visiting people. Consistency is important in helping your toddler grow up, so the two of you need a consistent approach to handle tantrums or discipline in general.

Hurting others

Having your child come home from day care with a bite mark or scratches on her face is horrifying. When your child's the person doing the biting and scratching it's also horrifying.

Your toddler hasn't got the hang of *empathy* (the ability to feel how others are feeling) yet and her hitting someone else hasn't registered on her list of things on the 'not okay' list. Hurting others is often a sign of some underlying emotion, such as anger, fear, feeling insecure or frustration. By finding out what is behind this behaviour you can address the problem directly and let her know plainly that hurting another person is never okay. Your little one doesn't necessarily grasp that her hitting or biting hurts the other person. Empathy is a complex concept that most children only master when they are around five years or older.

Labelling your child as a 'biter' or 'hitter' leads to more biting and hitting. Your child is a person, not a behaviour.

Here's how you can deal with your child hitting or scratching another child:

- Acknowledge how your child is feeling — 'I know you're angry ...'
- Explain that's not how we deal with problems — 'but we don't hit people when we're angry. Hitting hurts people.'
- Give her an alternative for dealing with her anger, such as stamping her feet.
- Show her how to touch people, with kindness rather than anger.

Bear in mind that your child is still pretty young. It may be that all the behaviour management is a bit too overwhelming for her at present, so try again in a few months. Be patient and gentle, and keep showing her a better way to handle conflict or frustration. This is another area where you can be a shining example as a dad — show her how it's done.

Sharing — *what a nice idea*

Toddlers are territorial creatures whose favourite word after 'no!' is 'mine!' Your sweet little boy doesn't yet understand the feelings of others and thinks only about himself. Sounds awful, but it's true.

Even kids who are best buddies at day care or cousins who adore each other's company will fight over possession of a favoured toy, and lay claim to what they think is theirs. Play dates, playgroups and childcare can be rife with conflict. This conflict is all part of your toddler becoming independent and learning he has some control over the universe.

But if you want to stop your child turning out like Veruca Salt from *Charlie and the Chocolate Factory*, teach him how to share. Hearing your three-year-old tell you 'we're sharing' and knowing your good fathering got him there is amazing.

Here are some ways to help your child become the sharing type:

- Make it clear that not sharing, such as snatching a toy away or hogging a toy that another child wants, is not okay. Even if your child *owns* the toy, snatching the toy from another is not okay.
- Praise your child whenever she gives a toy to another child and reinforce the behaviour with 'good sharing!'

- ✔ Step in if your child and another child are tussling over a favoured toy. Explain that when we share, we take turns playing with something. Give the toy back to whoever had it first.

- ✔ Show your child how both she and a playmate can use or play with the toy together.

If you're hosting a play date, don't make it too long. An hour or two is long enough. Make sure you keep both children topped up with food and drink. Being hungry or thirsty can make them grumpy and less likely to play nicely.

Sharing is also a complex concept that most children don't fully grasp until they're much older (around five or six years). However, explaining sharing to your little one from an early stage is still important. Patience is required, but eventually she'll understand why sharing is a useful concept.

Setbacks

Dealing with setbacks is a part of fatherhood. All great fathers have setbacks. Your little angel has been glorious company for a week, but one day you come home from work to find he's transformed into a monster, ignoring everything you tell him and chasing the cat like crazy. Letting fly with a few choice words may be easy but won't help anyone.

You'll almost certainly have to face a few setbacks on your fatherhood journey. Maybe setbacks are nature's way of keeping life interesting for parents, or perhaps every so often children have to take a step back to make two steps forward while they're developing. In most cases there don't seem to be any logical explanations for why setbacks occur so you have to take them as they come. Stick with your parenting approach and don't be distracted by temporary setbacks.

These strategies can help:

- ✔ Be consistent with your discipline.

- ✔ Divert the energy of the annoying activity to something else that can be more easily managed, such as introducing a different toy, game or rule.

- ✔ Keep your cool. Take some deep breaths. Think of Monty Python's 'Always look on the bright side of life' and see the funny side of it. Walk outside if you need to.

You're always going to have setbacks — they're part of being a father. Your child, even though he's acting like a demon, really only wants to be loved and to make you happy. Try to remember that when he's smearing jam on your suit jacket.

Chapter 11

Charging Towards Three: Months 24–36

In This Chapter

▶ Helping your little one explore the world

▶ Nurturing talents and helping them develop

▶ Exploring childcare options

*H*aving your child turn two is quite a milestone for a lot of dads — you've put some serious miles between now and when you first met your baby. Now that your little one is two years old, he's no longer an infant, but a fully fledged toddler. At the end of this year when he's three, he'll graduate from toddlerhood and become a preschooler. Your little tyke may have been through a whole lot of firsts in these two years — first smile, first step, first word — but the experience of being a dad just gets better. Now you can have your first kick around, first conversations and first joke together at mum's expense.

Two is also a challenging age. Junior's getting some strong opinions about things and won't hesitate to tell you about them, although the only expression he knows for 'I'm not very fond of this' may be very similar to a full-on scream. Tantrums can also really come to the fore this year.

Luckily for you, in this chapter we're here with tips for talking to your toddler in ways that may bypass the whole tantrum situation, how to encourage his interests with play indoors and out, and how to keep on top of discipline. We also look at kindergarten and changing your work to fit your lifestyle.

Exploring the World with Dad

Your toddler is quickly getting better on her feet and really comes alive in terms of her physical ability around two years old. She'll be up for more sliding, swinging, bike riding and more of everything physical. This increased physical ability is great, because it's good for her learning and also good for you dads to do something other than shake rattles and sing nursery rhymes.

Helping your toddler grow up

You can have all the DVDs in the world to teach your toddler this and that, but what really gets a little person's brain going is contact with other people, most importantly his parents. Children learn best from direct contact with other human beings. The closer the relationship with the person they're learning from, the better they pick up new skills. Even though junior's vocabulary is expanding by leaps and bounds, he's still got a long way to go with his development. Children need stimulation to grow and learn, and the first place they look for stimulation is with parents. Keep challenging your little one to try new things out — even though you may think he's not capable, let him have a go. Learning is about taking risks (within reason) and being challenged.

Everything you do around the house is an opportunity to learn. Even washing the dishes can turn into a chance for your little champ to practise pouring water and wiping down the bench, two simple activities he may be interested in and feel really good about when he masters them. You may find you have a budding chef in the house if you involve him in making his own lunch or getting dinner ready in the evening. Kids this age love having little tasks to do and want to contribute, so let them, even if they make a bit of a mess a times.

When your child is struggling with a task or activity, try to hang back and see what happens rather than stepping in to do it for her. Mums are (generally) more guilty of this than dads, but some dads are also just too keen to step in to help. If you're always stepping in, you deprive your child of the chance to figure things out for herself and overcome obstacles, and enjoy the confidence and self-esteem working out obstacles brings.

Developing skills and confidence

The third year of your child's life is another whirlwind of development. If the second year was all about finding her feet, the third year is about finding her voice, and she will — usually in a shopping mall yelling 'No no no' at you, but that's another topic. Her language skills are growing daily and so are her physical, emotional, social and cognitive skills. You can help develop her skills by:

- **Challenging.** Every day, give your child an opportunity to dress herself, walk up steps by herself, wash her own face and other little steps towards being independent. Of course you can't expect her to master all these skills, but cheering on the progress she makes each day gives her the confidence to keep trying. Not long from now she'll be telling you she can do it all by herself, thank you very much.

- **Drawing.** Junior's fine motor skills are at work when she draws pictures, or rather, scribbles. And there's nothing to stop you joining in. You can have little draw-offs with your child, where you challenge her to draw something for you and in return you draw something for her. Get your child to explain what her pictures are about, rather than giving empty praise for her work. Ask lots of questions about what she's drawing and repeat back to her in your own words what you're looking at; for example, 'Okay, I can see a house, a cat and a dog' (which will probably look like three circles on paper at this stage). Remember — the accuracy of her drawing doesn't matter, the effort and her explanations are what count.

- **Hanging out.** If your child doesn't go to day care, you'll need to arrange some social situations for her to meet other children and play with them. This helps your child learn about sharing, co-operating and language. She'll also see other people her age. See Chapter 9 for information about playgroups and Chapter 10 for tips on handling toddlers' interaction.

- **Making.** How many cereal boxes did you believe were rocket ships when you were a kid? Resurrect your imagination, that thing you gave up when you became an adult, and use it to help your child create all sorts of toys and playthings from everyday objects. See the section 'Fun and games' later in this chapter for some ideas.

✔ **Reading.** You can't read too much to a young child. Bringing your enthusiasm for reading to each story session encourages a love of words, stimulates your child's interest in the topic being read about and creates a warm, secure bond between the two of you. While your toddler wants you to read the same story over and over, mix it up a bit with different authors, styles and topics that challenge her. Buying every *Thomas the Tank Engine* title isn't giving your child variety.

✔ **Talking.** Junior learns her language from hearing you talk to her. Though she hasn't mastered getting her lips, mouth and tongue to do exactly what adults can do, she's on her way. Table 11-1 provides a guide to your toddler's speech development for her age.

✔ **Waiting.** Like time, toddlers wait for no man — or anything else. Patience doesn't come naturally, so provide examples of good things that take time, such as food cooking in the oven, or planting seeds and keeping tabs on their growth. Doing jigsaw puzzles is another excellent way to help her develop patience and persistence to complete a task.

Table 11-1	Language Ages and Stages
Age	**Your child can**
Two years	Use two words together; for example, Daddy gone, more drink, no shoes
	Use words to request something, rather than just name it
	Ask questions
	Name objects without prompting
	Do a two-part task, like put the cup on the table
	Say no (a lot)
	Identify parts of the body when asked
Three years	Make a sentence of three or more words, such as 'me wear shoes'
	Use several hundred words (not all at once)
	Talk about things that happened in the past
	Use adjectives like big and fast
	Talk about things that aren't present
	Ask even more questions
	Answer questions, like 'what's Dad up to?'
	Say her whole name
	Listen attentively for short periods

Source: Adapted from Ministry of Education, More than Words, www.minedu.govt.nz/
NZEducation/EducationPolicies/SpecialEducation/PublicationsAndResources/
MuchMoreThanWords.aspx

Try not to get too hung up about having little Jimmy recite the alphabet or count to 100. You'll have plenty of time for all that when he gets closer to school age.

Lots of genuine praise when your toddler does something awesome, like trying to say a new word when you point at a picture, or completing an activity like putting her cup on the bench, builds her self-confidence.

Fun and games

Here are some more ideas for playing and having fun with your little one:

- **Go camping in your living room.** If you've got a tent you can set it up in your living room and fill it with pillows, toys and sleeping bags. Get snuggled up, watch some fun movies and eat some treat food. If you don't have a tent, organise a large cardboard box (your supermarket, retail stores or furniture shops may be able to provide you with one) and make a little house out of it.

- **Make a roll-around bottle together.** Cut two big plastic drink bottles in half and use the top end of each. Put some interesting shapes inside and thread a shoelace through the bottle tops on either end. Seal in the middle with tape. Knot the shoelaces together to make a line that your toddler can drag around.

- **Make lunch.** Toddlers love to help, and seem especially drawn to helping out in the kitchen. If you get your toddler his own stool or box to stand on so he can reach the benchtop, he can help with simple tasks like peeling boiled eggs and move up to using a knife (with your supervision of course) to cut up firm fruit and vegetables like cucumbers and zucchini.

- **Create an obstacle course.** Make tunnels by placing a blanket over the tops of two chairs with their backs facing each other. Add other elements with low tables to crawl under, stairs to climb and boxes to climb over.

- **Get dizzy.** Have your toddler hold onto a towel and spin it around on a slippery floor slowly so that junior doesn't fall. You can also try sitting in a spinning chair like an office chair with junior on your lap whizzing around and around. These activities help your toddler's balance.

- **Play chase.** Toddlers love being chased, peeking through curtains, and a bit of rough and tumble when they're caught.

- **Sing!** There are so many great children's songs and nursery rhymes. Little ones really love songs with hand actions like 'Two Little Dicky Birds', or 'Incy Wincy Spider'.

Some words for worried mums

If your partner has a seriously worried look on her face while watching you muck around with the little one, talk to her about 'rough and tumble play' (she can even look it up on the internet — rough and tumble play is a well-known concept of child play). Dad's natural way to engage with his child is often to challenge him physically and 'muck about'. There's nothing wrong with this as long as junior still has a smile on his face and is squealing with delight. In fact, rough and tumble play is good for kids — it develops their social and physical skills, uses their imaginations, and introduces the ideas of good and bad, justice and courage. Dads, you have to make sure no-one gets too squished in a rough-housing session, and explain it to mum so she's comfortable. And by the way ... why not ask mum to join in?

You've Created a Genius

Your child's brain is constantly developing, and rapidly. Some areas are coming along faster than others. Speaking and motor skills are getting up there, while emotional and social skills develop fully further down the line and over a long period.

Development update

As your child grows, the things he's capable of doing change, along with his behaviour. As great dads you really need to know about your child's development so you understand his behaviour and interests and know how to respond to them.

Between the ages of two and three, your child:

- Can feed himself, remove and put on clothing, and undo zips and large buttons
- Can remember people, places and stories
- Enjoys creating things
- Has a sense of ownership over his toys and belongings, saying things like 'mine!'

✔ Is able to use two- to three-word sentences, ask questions and follow an instruction with two steps

✔ Is confident enough on his feet to try running, jumping and hopping

✔ Is developing a sense of humour

✔ Likes to pretend to be someone else

✔ Knows his full name and gender

✔ Matches objects, such as shoes and animal pictures

The way your toddler behaves is part of his growing up. One of the fundamental aspects of disciplining your child is to have realistic expectations of what he can and can't do. At two years old he can't manage his emotions well, express how he feels or remember all the rules. Consequently during this stage you need to muster some extra patience. He'll get there in his own time!

Giving your toddler choices

Getting tired of saying 'no' yet? No, you can't open that cupboard! No, you can't go outside. Saying no all the time gets boring, doesn't it? Imagine what it sounds like to your toddler, hearing that all day long.

The answer to avoiding being stuck in the 'no' loop is choices. Junior wants to go outside but it's pouring rain? Instead of saying no, offer him a couple of other activities he can do inside, like drawing with crayons or some blocks he's been tinkering away with. Tell him, 'we can't go outside because it's raining, but we can draw'. Offering your child a couple of things to choose from means you still have some control over what he does, but he also feels like he has some say in his life.

Distracting your child by giving him something else to do instead of the thing he can't do is a great technique for stopping the no's.

Say your champ is pulling out clothes from the dresser to put on in the morning. Instead of saying no to the dressing gown he wants to wear to crèche that day, give him the option of a green jersey or a blue one. He'll feel like you take his opinions into account and will be more receptive to putting on a jersey.

Giving your child a choice also works with eating. Instead of plying your toddler with lots of vegetables, give him a choice: Broccoli or carrots? He may even end up eating both. Also, not forcing a decision helps. Sometimes you can simply say 'I'll do something else while you make up your mind whether you'd like broccoli or carrots'. In some cases your little champ might start eating one of the choices when you're not looking — after all, he's hungry.

At bedtime, letting your child choose a couple of stories before bed gets him interested in the idea of stories and what he wants to hear, rather than having him focus on resisting bedtime.

Setting boundaries and rules to match

Imagine you've landed on planet Wafunkle and you have no idea about the local etiquette, the way people talk to each other, what the customs are, or the way people live. You don't know if smiling is considered rude, or doing underarm farts a way of showing appreciation. You also don't speak the language well, so the best you can do is bumble around trying things out and being shown the rules until you get the hang of things.

This is the situation your toddler finds himself in right now. He doesn't know that wrenching your glasses off your face is wrong, or that sticking a knife in an electric socket is dangerous. He needs a guide to show him through the sometimes confusing maze that is modern life and society. And that guide is you. The method by which you guide him through that maze is called discipline. Discipline's about showing him the rules and having patience and strategies to help the rules stick.

Discipline isn't about punishment, but about guiding your child to learn what the boundaries and rules in life are. You and your partner decide what the rules are depending on your personal beliefs, morals and way of life. Discipline is about finding a balance between letting your child run wild exploring things that can be dangerous for her, or inappropriate, like hitting and biting, and not letting her try anything out and hindering her ability to learn.

Here are some ideas for rules and boundaries you may want to instil in your child:

✔ After two stories, it's into bed.

✔ No going on the road without dad or mum.

✔ Plugs and appliances are off limits.

✔ We're gentle to animals and other people.

- ✔ We don't scream or throw balls in the house.
- ✔ When we're upset we use our words rather than our bodies to express how we feel.
- ✔ When we make a mistake or hurt someone, we say sorry.
- ✔ When we ask for something we say please, and when someone is nice to us we say thank you.

You may also like to come up with some rules and boundaries for yourself as a dad, including all of the preceding and a few more.

Be consistent with your rules and boundaries. Although you've told your little lady not to draw on the walls with crayon but only on paper and she keeps drawing on the walls, she'll understand and get the idea one day, so hang in there.

Some parents like to use a strategy called *time out* when their child pushes the rules, such as refusing to say sorry when she's hurt another child or snatched a toy. This means removing her from the situation and putting her in a designated time-out area, like a corner, or her room, for one minute per year of her age. Most toddlers won't stay put, but it breaks the cycle or tantrum that's about to erupt, and lets them know in a non-violent way that their behaviour isn't okay.

Telling your child for the millionth time not to run out onto the road can push your buttons, and make you angry and frustrated that the message isn't getting through. However scared and angry you are, hitting your child isn't the way to deal with it. Find another way to deal with *your* frustration — take a couple of deep breaths and make a mental note to use your favourite way to let off some steam later on. When you raise your voice to say 'STOP' (as she's about to run onto the street) give her a cuddle afterwards and explain to her why running onto the road isn't okay. The message *will* get through!

A key aspect of effective discipline is consistency and appropriateness of your behaviour management to your child's developmental stage and temperament. The older your child gets, the more you can use rational arguments, rules and consequences. So keep talking to your child about the same rules, outline consequences, stick to your rules and follow through with consequences.

Stimulating your toddler's interests

Every child is different and different things will catch his eye. One thing that all children have in common is their interest in playing. If you notice your toddler doing something over and over, he's exploring a new concept and he can become almost obsessive about it. Childcare professionals usually refer to this behaviour as a *schema*. Your child may pour water from one cup to another cup over and over, or paint a picture then cover the whole thing in black paint, or cut up everything he can get his hands on. These are different types of schema.

Some kinds of schema can be destructive or against the boundaries you've set your child and household, such as flicking the switches on power points up and down again and again. From your child's perspective he's exploring a *vertical schema*. If your champ tears pieces of tissue into little pieces, he's exploring *separation schema*. If you aren't happy with the way he's exploring a particular schema, try to offer another way he can explore it. For example, get together a box of things he's allowed to rip up or cut (with your supervision of course), or encourage him to explore vertical schema by bouncing on a trampoline or drawing. You could also demonstrate your DIY skills in front of your child by making a board of old switches (which aren't connected to an electrical source) so your little one can flick switches all day, safely.

You may also like to take an interest in the things he seems to really enjoy playing with, like a Lego project he's been plugging away at, or a favourite set of shoes he's been trying on, and have these at the ready for when you need to offer your child a tantrum-distracting choice.

Talking to your child so he understands

Sometimes it feels as if you're beating your head against a wall as you try to communicate with your toddler. She won't listen, you get angry, and both of you end up frustrated and in a worse spot than you were before. Take heart — here are some techniques you can use now that will help to build good open communication between the two of you as your little one grows.

✔ **Acknowledge how she feels.** You can easily walk all over your little one's objections or opinions with your words when you're talking to her. As fathers, with all good intentions, you frequently think you know best. When your child falls over and cries, you say things like 'oh, it doesn't hurt'. You may offer a cuddle and some comfort, but your words are denying the way your child feels. Kids need to have their feelings acknowledged, just like adults do. By denying your child's feelings, you're kind of setting yourself up against her, rather than encouraging her to open up and find solutions. When your child is upset about something, rather than offer advice or a phrase to downplay her feelings, say something obvious like 'you're upset', or agree with her by saying 'oh really?' and let her do the talking.

✔ **Describe the problem.** This technique avoids laying blame on your child for something she's done. Blaming can make your toddler feel helpless and wrong all the time, and she'll become defiant whenever you open your mouth. Say she's spilt milk on the carpet. Rather than berate her about the mess she's made, tell her there's milk on the carpet, which describes the problem, and that she'd better get a cloth to clean it up.

✔ **Give information.** Junior has just drawn on the wall for the thousandth time. Instead of yelling at her for her misplaced art, show her that drawing is for paper, not walls.

✔ **Offer choices.** You want junior to clear up her toys, but rather than order her to clean up, offer her a choice of which toys to clean up first.

✔ **Use a single word or gesture.** You've already asked every day for a year that toys be cleared up before bedtime, so your toddler should be getting the hang of that concept by now. Instead of a nightly 'clear up your toys, like I've asked you a million times', simply say 'toys'. Leaving out the blaming and ordering should get a better result. Kids dislike long explanations for things. Your tyke still has a very short attention span.

The underlying principle to most of these techniques is to avoid laying blame or criticism on your child. Making her feel wrong will make her defiant and scared, rather than open and willing to take risks. Ridiculing your child for a mistake is also unlikely to get her to take responsibility for her mistakes in the future because she'll be afraid of your mockery.

When talking to your child, imagine the way that you would like to be talked to by your boss, for example. You wouldn't like to be blamed, yelled at, taken the mickey out of, or ordered around. Neither does your toddler.

To find out more about talking to your toddler, check out Adele Faber and Elaine Mazlish's series on communicating with your child at www. fabermazlish.com.

Exploring Different Opportunities

Your role as a dad is simple — be there for your child with love, food and shelter. And until now, that's been enough. Traditionally this may well have meant that you take care of your child by 'bringing home the bacon'. But in our modern lives, there are other avenues you can explore as well.

The fathering road less travelled

If you're finding, like many dads do, that keeping all your plates in the air — work life, home life, time for yourself — is just too much, there are options you can look at to reduce some of the stress. These options include:

✔ Become a stay-at-home dad (SAHD) while your partner works.

✔ Reduce your hours and work a four-day week, or go part-time.

✔ Start your own business, do what you love doing and organise your work life around your family (for example, by having a home office).

✔ Take a break from work, such as three months, especially if you feel you're stuck in a dead end career or job. Many career coaches recommend you change careers if your current job is a dead end, so use this time as a transition phase to spend some more time with the family.

✔ Take up flexible working, which means you can have flexible start and finish times while remaining in work full-time.

Money and your financial position dictate which of these options is available to you, so before you walk into your boss's office with your resignation letter, do your sums and work out what you can afford.

If you work from home, you can already work quite flexibly by scheduling your work around nap times, or times when your partner or family can take care of your toddler.

TV, videos, computers and games

We live in a media age, where there are literally hundreds of TV channels to choose from, where people communicate via email, Twitter and Facebook rather than with an old fashioned letter, and primary school children have mobile phones. Unless you live in a jungle or a cave, the media's impossible to avoid. To deal with the volume of media coming at your child, which at this age she's becoming increasingly aware of, it may be a good idea to think in terms of moderation rather than banning your toddler from the TV. Watching a little bit of The Wiggles for half an hour or so isn't the worst thing in the world and may help keep her out of your hair while you prepare a meal or have a shower, but letting her stare passively at cartoons all morning isn't doing her a whole lot of good. Watching lots of TV isn't encouraging interaction between the two of you or encouraging any of those synapses to keep connecting through movement or using her body, which is what she needs most right now.

Here are some techniques to help prevent your child turning into a telly tubby:

- ✔ As your toddler grows up, he may be interested in computers, handheld games, mobile phones and MP3 players. Establish a media-free time during the day — perhaps at mealtimes — when all devices are off.

- ✔ Have a specific time your child can watch TV, rather than putting on a show anytime he wants. This can be an effective way of limiting the amount of TV he watches.

- ✔ Keep an eye on what programs your child watches on TV and make sure you're happy with the content. That goes for the advertisements that are played as well. You may want to select a few DVDs from the library to screen rather than just flick on the telly and watch whatever is playing. DVDs are also a great way to avoid all the advertisements which increasingly target young children.

- ✔ Keep bedrooms TV-free. Computers should be in a central part of the house too, if space allows.

- ✔ Try to provide alternatives to media that force your child to be a passive observer. Exposing your child to a variety of activities like sport, handicrafts, the natural environment, gardening, food preparation and music can spark an interest that may be lifelong. When The Wiggles sing 'Big Red Car', get your child to do the movements as well.

- ✔ Watch TV with your child, so you can talk about what you're seeing and hearing, and can encourage participation in any of the songs or dances on the screen.

TV is not for children under two years of age says the American Academy of Paediatrics, whose studies show infants who watched TV learned fewer words than those who didn't.

Next stop — kindergarten

As your child gets closer to becoming a preschooler (when he turns three) you may want to start thinking about a more formal learning environment for him. Kindergarten is traditionally the place children go to transition from being at home with a parent or caregiver, or a step on from childcare before starting school. Kindergarten, or prep and pre-prep in parts of Australia, is a place where children continue to explore learning through play.

Kindergartens used to be for just those aged four, but some cater for children as young as 2½ years. Prep is generally for four-year-olds and pre-prep for three-year-olds. Unlike school, kindergarten, prep and pre-prep aren't compulsory.

Session times and charges for kindergarten are different from childcare, so see the New Zealand Kindergarten Association website www.kindergarten.org.nz, or the website of the Kindergarten Association in your state.

Chapter 12

More Babies: Brothers and Sisters

In This Chapter

▶ Deciding whether to have another baby

▶ Managing a household with more than one child

▶ Getting the hang of sibling discipline

*O*ne of the questions fathers of one child are asked the most is, 'so when are you having number two?' Some dads might be ready with an answer — 'I've been planning on having seven children since I was little'. For others, it may be a question of asking whether number two will *ever* happen — one child is quite enough thanks.

Adding another baby to your family changes the dynamic completely and can be a tricky adjustment period as everyone finds their feet. In this chapter, we take you through making the financial adjustment, juggling the needs of two children at demanding times in their development, and work out how to stop World War III from happening as toys, clothes and, most importantly, your love are shared between the two of them.

Having Another Child

Making the decision to have another child is almost a bigger decision than having the first. As well as all your concerns about being a father — the sleepless nights, supporting your partner, the trials and tribulations of daily life with a helpless baby or rambunctious toddler — you also must take into account your first child's needs, such as his need to be stimulated and cared for. You also now know how much time and work a baby takes, so the 'ignorance is bliss' attitude you may have had the first time round is probably gone.

Here's what you need to think about if you want to take the rational approach to making a decision about baby #2:

- ✔ Are you are expecting life to get easier for you because the children can play with one another? This may be true, but not until your youngest child is two years or older.

- ✔ Can you afford for you or your partner to not earn a living while caring for a new baby, as well as buying any new equipment you may need?

- ✔ Do you have enough room in your house for four? Will you need to move? What about your transport and travel arrangements — will you need a larger vehicle?

- ✔ How mentally prepared are you to cope with a new arrival? Would you be excited to have another baby, or is having another baby something you feel you have to do to complete your family?

- ✔ How will the practical aspects, such as sleeping arrangements, routines and childcare, work?

Some parents think that only children are often spoilt, antisocial and lonely. While having only one child creates a situation that can bring out these tendencies in children, parents can easily counterbalance by involving only children in lots of social settings, such as day care, playgroups, sleepovers and team sports. You needn't worry your child will turn into a spoilt brat just because he doesn't have any siblings.

Is having another child worth it?

In the end, this is the question you and your partner have to resolve for yourselves. Having two children may not feel worthwhile when both kids are sick and up all night, and terrorising each other by day. But it may be worth it when they are adults, have children of their own and support each other in a way only family can.

Having a second child also gives you the opportunity to do things with your new baby differently if you feel you haven't done things the way you wanted the first time around, such as sticking to a routine from early on or trying a different approach to settling bub at night.

If your partner had a traumatic birth experience or difficulties breastfeeding early on last time, she'd need your support this time. You now have the opportunity to help your partner to see your second child as an opportunity to have a very different experience this time round.

What to expect

So you've decided you're ready for baby #2. Here's some more information you need to know.

With baby #2 you'll almost feel like a professional — after all, you've been there, done that. Many fathers of two say they don't feel as wound up and anxious about their baby the second time around, and that mothers are often more relaxed and confident. That said, here are some things you need to know:

- Depending on the age gap between #1 and #2, you may need twice as many prams/buggies and car seats, which may mean you need a bigger car.

- Your life will be twice as busy, with both children having different activities and sleep times, and twice as many nappies to change and clothes to wash.

- Your older child will not necessarily be particularly helpful with the younger child until he is a bit older, but will relish the responsibility of being in charge of the baby when the time comes ... even if it's just in name only.

- You'll need to be a lot more organised and may spend time lying in bed at night thinking about the laundry, getting lunch prepared for childcare, and pulling your weight with the housework.

Budgeting and finance

Raising a child is an expensive business. In Australia, raising a child to 18 years is thought to cost an average A$120,000 for a low-income family, while a high-income family spends about $600,000 on one child. On average, raising two children to 18 years of age in Australia costs between $400,000 and $500,000. In New Zealand, it's estimated to cost NZ$215,000 per child. The good news is that after having raised child #1 you now know what is really useful and essential, and what is just fluff. So our suggestion for #2 is cut out the fluff and focus on essentials. You may also take heart from an old Spanish saying: 'Every baby is born with a loaf of bread under their arm'. In other words, you'll find a way to make ends meet.

You can have another baby and not have to get a third job. Here are some ways to do so:

- Stick to the essentials. You don't need another flash Moses basket or $20-a-tub nappy cream. And you didn't need half of all those clothes you had first time around, did you?

- If you haven't still got your first child's stuff sitting in his wardrobe, ask for hand-me-downs, go to shwopping events (where you can swap clothes and toys), or check with friends who have kids.

- Don't buy anything until after the baby shower, or register for baby shower gifts at a store. That way you won't double up on anything you already have.

- Check out sites like www.reachme.co.nz and www.ausfreeze.com for samples and coupons for baby and child-related products. Some supermarkets also have baby clubs you can join to get deals on nappies, food and other baby stuff.

- Keep an eye on specials at supermarkets and baby stores to start stocking up on consumables.

In the coming years childcare costs are going to be a major expense in your household. Think about how you could work flexibly, reduce your hours, enlist friends and family in a kind of group babysitting scheme, or work from home to reduce this cost.

Frugal dad

So you're having another baby and you're strapped for cash? Try these cheap home-made versions of baby stuff that will save you money. Hey, if they were good enough for our grandparents, they're good enough for us.

- **Nappy rash powder:** Fill an old, clean salt or pepper shaker with cornflour. Sprinkle on junior's backside just like ordinary powder.

- **Wipes:** Cut into quarters some cheap, soft facecloths. If you're really crafty, you can sew up the edges with a sewing machine to stop fraying. Fill an old bowl with water and add a little almond oil. Use to clean junior's backside. Pat dry with a clean cloth afterwards. Wash wipes with the nappies (if you're using cloth nappies) and hang out to dry in the sun to kill any bacteria. You could also use kitchen wipes like Chux cloths.

- **Breastfeeding:** Talk to your partner about breastfeeding, which will save you a fortune in formula, bottles, sterilisers and all the accoutrements.

Looking after Another Family Member

So there's another mouth to feed, another body to clothe and another bum to wipe. If you were stretched by one baby, two may seem impossible right now, but it's not.

Taking a practical approach

All babies really need is love, warmth, food, sleep and a clean bum. Though having colour co-ordinated outfits is mum's thing, when you've got two kids, this may no longer be top priority.

Read Chapters 6 to 9 about bub's first year to remind yourself of what's coming up, such as how to avoid nappy rash, how warm your newborn should be kept and which clothes you'll need.

Get into a routine with your new baby as soon as you can, but don't freak out if it all goes a little awry some days. With two children, you certainly won't get everything right every day, but don't beat yourself up about it.

Remember to be as hands-on with this new baby as you were with the last. Remember how time flew by with the first one? Well, here's another chance to savour the unforgettable time when she's tiny.

Keeping two or more healthy and safe

Having a second child is easier — and harder. It's easier in the sense that you have previous experience at handling a newborn, but harder in the sense that you now have to wrestle your toddler into his car seat with a baby demanding your attention at the same time. If you thought one child was enough to keep you occupied, two will show you that you're capable of a lot more!

Here are some ways you can avoid your life becoming a crazy house:

- ✔ **Get organised.** Think about where the new baby will sleep. Do you need to get another cot, or is your older child ready to move into a bed? Organise chests of drawers and car seats, and work out where you're going to change the baby. Most importantly, look into changing your buggy/pram. Some manufacturers offer to swap or upgrade your one-seater pram to a two-seater (there is usually a charge for this service). Some prams can accommodate a two- or three-year-old as well as a newborn baby.

✔ **Get your family and friends involved.** It takes a village to raise a child, so organise someone to take your older child on outings when you need a break, or to cook when you're too exhausted.

✔ **Keep healthy.** The last thing you need with two little ones is to get ill. Inevitably your whole family will get sick and you'll be so busy looking after children all night long that you won't be able to get better yourself. Keep eating well and take every opportunity you can to get some exercise. A fantastic way to find time to exercise is to combine exercise with an activity with child #1.

✔ **Prepare yourself to give child #1 some extra love.** It can be a rough transition for him — suddenly he has to share your attention with another person in the house. You need to compensate for that. Read more about sibling rivalry later in this chapter.

✔ **Try not to change your older child's routines too much.** If you're currently reading him five stories before bed every night, keep doing that. With a new person in the house, he's going through enough upheaval without losing his time with you too.

✔ **Work as a team and make a schedule.** Divvy up chores around the house, talk about when you and your partner can have some time off, and don't forget to exercise!

Juggling activities

With two children now, both at challenging stages in their development, you'll need to fine tune some of the activities you have in your life. It may be time to look at flexible work (see Chapter 6), reducing your hours, or prioritising some of the things you do outside work and family.

You may find life is a bit like a game of Tetris — trying to fit all tasks and people you need to spend time with into a limited amount of space. Scheduling your tasks and making time with your family one of your top jobs helps to ensure you don't lose touch with what is really important — your partner and children.

It may pay to get a calendar or keep a list on the fridge of your tasks, so you don't get swamped by them.

Talk to your children all the time. Let them share in what you do at work and be prepared to spend time reading stories, playing and doing all the dad stuff you've been doing so well anyway.

If you're one of those guys who puts things off all the time, now's the time to break the habit. Leaving things undone will only stress you out and cause you grief when you could be doing something you enjoy.

Sibling Discipline

All children react differently to the news that another baby is coming along to usurp their throne as king or queen. Some rebel and get extremely upset when the new baby is even mentioned. Others relish the chance to meet their new sibling. Some children change overnight from angels into demons and others develop a new-found sense of responsibility and grown-upness that you never would have imagined. Your child may feel threatened, unloved or ignored.

Understanding sibling rivalry

So far, your child has been the only apple of your eye, the centre of your world and the centre of her own world. Suddenly, a new baby is on the scene, taking away time and attention from her. You're busy with the new baby, which means her demands come second and she has to wait when she doesn't want to, share her stuff and have the limelight shine somewhere else. No wonder she's a little grumpy and jealous right now.

She's caught in a place where she's trying to find her own individuality, but she still very much needs you to boost her confidence and show her the way. If you're giving too much of your time and attention to your new little one, she's going to let you know about it by being angry and jealous, and rebelling against you and her new sibling.

To prepare your child for the fact another baby is coming into your family, try these:

- ✔ Break the news to your child when the three of you are together. A good time to do this is when mum's belly is starting to stick out, or during the final trimester. Toddlers don't have a good grasp of time, so you'll be bombarded with cries of 'is the baby coming yet?'

- ✔ Keep involving your little champ in lots of things you do to prepare for the new arrival. For example, you can take her along to the scans and keep explaining things to her about how the baby develops. She may not understand everything but making her feel involved is important.

✔ Offer some choices to your child when it comes to getting kitted out for the new baby, such as asking her to help pick clothes and gear for the new baby.

✔ Let her know that the baby is not just for mum and dad, the baby is *her* brother or sister.

✔ Prepare her for the demands a new baby will place on the family; that is, the baby will cry, will need to be fed (and how that feeding will happen — your child may get upset at mum and bub's new closeness if she's breastfeeding) and that the baby will not be able to play with her for a little while until he grows bigger.

Check out www.diyfather.com/skip for more information about discipline and sibling rivalry.

Coping with jealousy and fighting

No matter how well your older child copes with the news that another baby is on the way and how brilliantly she accepts the new baby's arrival, she's still that same volatile mix of burgeoning independence and emotional immaturity, so inevitably she'll feel resentful and jealous from time to time.

Here are some techniques you can try to minimise bad feelings:

✔ Balance the time that you spend with your newborn and toddler.

✔ Encourage your toddler's pride in her new little brother by showing her how to hold the baby and taking lots of photos. Talk to your older child about when she was a baby and get some pictures out to look at.

✔ Make special time to devote to your toddler that doesn't include the new baby.

✔ Toddlers love to have 'tasks' to do, so you could enlist her help in getting baby's blanket and putting clothes away. Give her lots of praise for doing a good job.

✔ Try to keep your toddler's routine as much as possible, so she doesn't feel lost in all the upheaval and resent her new sibling.

✔ When your older child meets her new sibling, have the baby in a cot or Moses basket rather than in your arms.

If your older child is uninterested in the baby, don't worry. She'll take an interest in her own time.

Fighting and setting boundaries

If you've got your toddler feeling pretty chuffed with his new sister, helping out with nappy changes and helping to settle her at night, you're doing really well. But we're dealing with a toddler who hasn't quite worked out how to handle his emotions just yet. Anger, resentment and fighting are bound to break out at some stage, so here are some suggestions to help manage that:

- ✔ Should conflict break out, act fast. Hitting, snatching and acting roughly are unacceptable. Use your disciplinary action of choice — a stern talking to or taking away the object of dispute (the toy). Distraction may also work well in these situations.

- ✔ Teach your older child how to touch the baby without hurting her, just like you do with a pet or with other children his own age. Use the words gentle and nice, and praise him for his efforts.

- ✔ Until you feel that your toddler can safely be around the baby without incident, keep a close eye on them. Toddlers are notorious for snatching. If bub has a toy he wants, your toddler may snatch it straight out of your baby's mouth, which could result in some distress from bub.

- ✔ Your behaviour is your child's greatest teacher and he'll copy what he sees you doing. If you're quick to anger and treat others with disrespect, he'll learn to do that too.

Behaviour management strategies need to relate to the developmental stage and temperament of your child. Try out a few things (and keep trying them as your child gets older) and use what works best for your child. In general, distraction techniques tend to work better with younger children, whereas time-outs tend to work better with older children.

Discovering different personalities

Take a look at your own siblings, if you have them. Are you into the same stuff? Do you have the same temperament or ideas? Chances are, although you were brought up by the same parents and share a heck of a lot of DNA, you've got your own interests and personality. After all, we're all individuals.

And so it is with your children. Chances are both your kids are quite different kettles of fish and require different things from you as a father. Both your children are going to require different ways of stimulating them, encouraging them and building their confidence. A bit of trial and error may be required.

Rather than seeing different personalities as extra work for you, think of them as a good thing. You get to explore different interests with your children and they can learn from each other as they grow up, drawing on each other's strengths to get them through challenging times. Different personalities also keeps things interesting for you — never a dull day!

Part IV
The Preschool Years

Glenn Lumsden

*'I'll show you how to tie your shoes, then
you can show me how to connect the
Blu-Ray DVD player to a wireless network.'*

In this part . . .

You're quite the father figure now, aren't you? Your little one is speaking in sentences, steady on his feet, throwing himself at the world like a skydiver. It's an exciting time to be a dad: You can now get into all those things you once dreamed of doing with your child, like fishing and bike riding together.

In this part, we look at building self-esteem and independence, getting into sports and learning, and keeping your child healthy and active. We also start to look more at one of the biggest milestones of your child's life — starting school.

Chapter 13

Fun and Games

In This Chapter

▶ Understanding your preschooler's development

▶ Playing with young children

▶ Encouraging your child to learn and grow

*Y*our walking, talking child is quite a different bundle from the newborn you first met three years ago. He's a dynamo of questions, words, stories and kooky ideas. And he needs you to keep up with him. Hang out with your child (a lot) and hang on for the ride!

In this chapter we explore what your preschooler will be doing for the next couple of years as he nears school age. We share our ideas for keeping that inquisitive, explosive little person busy and show you some ways to help your child get ready for learning at school and beyond.

Your Active Preschooler

With his third birthday, your child graduates from being a toddler to a preschooler. Preschooler isn't a great term because it describes what your child isn't, rather than what he is, but that's the most well-worn term to describe ages three and four years old. *Note:* Some people use 'young children' but that applies to a wide age range so we decided to stick with preschooler.

Mapping the next two years

As well as getting more of a grip on his language skills, being able to come up with more complex sentence structures and increasing his vocabulary, your child is developing in these ways:

- ✔ He has more control over his emotions, is able to empathise more and shows concern for others.

- ✔ He is able to express more complex emotions like embarrassment, pride and guilt.

- ✔ He likes to take part in imaginative games, like playing doctor or schools, or pretending boxes are boats and rockets.

- ✔ He can sort shapes, like pegs and shells or buttons.

- ✔ He can use alternate feet when climbing stairs or steps and as he gets closer to five, to skip.

- ✔ He starts understanding abstract concepts like 'being a hero', confidence, or what it means to be the 'good guy/bad guy' in a play.

- ✔ He can perform simple tasks and use scissors.

- ✔ He can serve food, and eat and drink by himself.

- ✔ His friendships become more important as he nears school age.

Your child is also learning to count, the letters of the alphabet, the names of lots of animals, plants, objects and people, and more besides provided you keep stimulating him with books, pictures, outings and opportunities.

Building self-sufficiency and self-esteem

Like an athlete training for a big race, or a gymnast for a competition, practice makes perfect. The more you do something, the better you get at it. In order for a child to master a skill, she must do it again and again with lots of mistakes along the way so that she can improve and feel a sense of accomplishment. As fathers, your role is to provide plenty of opportunities for your child to practise, make mistakes, improve and master a skill in order to build self-esteem and feel pride in her achievements. Letting your child fall, fail and pick herself up again can be difficult at times, especially because you can often see in advance what's going to happen and may not want to deal with the consequences of her fall. But giving her the space to mess up is important and your attitude that you believe she can get better rubs off too.

Between the ages of three and four, let your child take on more tasks that she might not get right at first, but with a little time and practice and patience from you, she will accomplish. A great example is giving your child little jobs around the house, or getting her to do personal hygiene jobs herself, like washing her hands or brushing her teeth.

Giving healthy doses of praise when your child tries really hard or achieves a goal boosts her confidence and makes her feel pretty chuffed with herself.

Praise

Using praise is a tricky one. Tired fathers coming home from work at night or after a long day minding the children can easily give a glib 'that's great darling' without looking at the picture your champ has drawn. She'll know your heart isn't really in it and feel doubtful about her achievements.

Praise should also be non-judgemental; that is, rather than saying about a painting, 'wow, that's fantastic, darling', be specific about what it is you like or which skills you see developing. 'I like the way you used purple', or 'You are really good at colouring her hair' gives your child a sense of her accomplishment and she will use that praise to tell herself 'I'm good at using colour' when she approaches a drawing next time. Also, point out specifics in the painting, such as 'I can see you've painted a house'. Making out what your child has actually drawn can be hard, but guessing correctly isn't important. Your little champ will tell you that the 'house' is actually a 'dog' and you can then discuss with her aspects of how she has drawn her dog.

Active movement

Active movement — that is, getting out there with your child and encouraging physical activities — is an important tool for building self-esteem and confidence.

Children (and adults) learn through repetition. When we do something over and over it seems to become locked in our brains. Learning things like climbing a ladder takes time and practice for little children to master, and there will probably be some falls and spills along the way. But without that practice, how will she ever get the chance to learn to climb a ladder? Some childcare professionals also believe that physical movement is key to helping the brain develop fully.

For examples of active movement activities check out www.diyfather.com/sparc.

Genuine praise for your child's accomplishments as she gains more confidence in her body also encourages her to get physical more often, which can only be good for her and help keep her healthy and confident of her abilities.

Embrace your inner child and get active with your children. Play on swings, go down the slide, do rolly-pollies. As a dad, you're not only a role model for your children, showing them how to master a skill, but if you also become part of the activity and want to give it a try too, they'll love the activity all the more.

Even if you don't have a playground handy to your home where you can let your child practise swinging, jumping, climbing and balancing, you can encourage active movement at your own place. Here are some ideas:

- Create an obstacle course in your living room from chairs with sheets draped over them, and boxes and tables to crawl under.

- Dance in your front room. Keep a note of music your child enjoys; it will come in handy when she's fussy or bored.

- Go on a walk in your area (not too far, you don't want a cranky, tired child) and check out letterboxes, flowers in gardens, birds on telephone wires and cracks in the pavement.

- Play chase. You probably know by now that little kids love to be chased, and will take off, wanting you to follow. Put a scarf in your child's trousers so it sticks out like a tail and chase her while trying to get the scarf.

- Play hide and seek. If your child can't count, use an egg timer to measure the time passed before she comes looking for you.

- Roll down a gentle slope, or play helicopters where you spin around and around until you're dizzy. This helps your child's developing sense of balance, and is really great fun!

- Show your child how to jump off low walls, and on and off surfaces you put on the floor for her, like a towel or piece of carpet. Be prepared for a few tumbles at first!

- Walk like a bear around the house on all fours, play wheelbarrow walk and make a rope swing on a tree in your yard to encourage upper body development.

Classes

You can also consider enrolling your child in classes like junior soccer, swimming and water confidence, singing or music and movement. Follow your child's lead by paying attention to the things she enjoys doing.

Father worries

Dads have been known to be somewhat competitive and to compare and measure children against one another. Raising children, however, is not a competitive sport, and there's no medal for having a child who is first to spell 'encyclopedia' or count to 1,000. Every child moves and develops at his own pace.

Patience with your child's pace is one of the most important things you can give him right now. He's got to have space and time to develop and learn, and expecting him to do what others can do will leave you frustrated, and him less likely to figure it out for himself. It certainly doesn't boost his confidence to say 'Johnny over here can already count to 100 — why can't you do that?'

Take a deep breath when he spills milk on the carpet for the hundredth time as he learns to master drinking from a glass, or drops his knife and fork as he tries to put his plate on the kitchen bench. He'll get there. By helping, encouraging and gently challenging him, rather than getting frustrated and doing it for him, he'll learn he can do it by himself and have more confidence in his abilities.

So you want junior to be a world class golfer and have already got him swinging clubs in the backyard. But he's just not getting golf and wants to water the garden or help with the cooking instead. Follow his lead and ditch the clubs. Remember that old saying 'you can lead a horse to water but you can't make it drink'? It's the same with children. You can buy your child golf clubs but you can't make him like playing golf. You may have to get used to the idea that you've got a potential Jamie Oliver on your hands, not a golf champion.

During the preschool years, many children often switch from being very close to mum if she's been the primary caregiver, to wanting to be with dad all the time. This is great news! It means you have more opportunities to hang out with your kid and deepen that already awesome relationship you have with him. Make more of your time available to your little champ and enjoy the attention you're getting!

Keeping Your Preschooler Busy

Some preschoolers are always on the move, they're always asking questions and always exploring the world. That's a great thing, but it can be a little tiring and on a rainy day, a high-energy preschooler may be a tantrum waiting to happen. We show you some ways to make the most of the time you and your preschooler have together that are fun and a little educational.

'Dad, I'm bored'

For years to come, you'll occasionally hear the refrain all fathers fear — 'Dad, I'm bored'. Not only is she bored, but she wants you to fix the problem. Fobbing off your child with a computer game or putting a movie on is easy, but the best activities for your preschooler are the ones that involve the two of you being together. These are opportunities to read, play, explore and learn together, or to introduce junior to a hobby or passion of yours that she may be interested in.

Here are some ideas for banishing the 'I'm bored' blues:

- Ask a question about a concept your child wouldn't have come across, like 'do you know how bats can fly in the dark without bumping into things?', then offer to find out together with her. Do some research together and make it into a 'solving the mystery' quest.

- Build something together, such as a swing, bird feeder, or a wooden seat, but be clear about safety around tools. Three-year-olds and saws are not a good mix.

- Encourage a love of gardening and growing her own food by starting a wee garden in the backyard. Pumpkins and peas are pretty easy to grow and your child will be encouraged to eat them at dinnertime knowing she's grown the food herself!

- Hide something in the house or garden that she has to find by asking you for clues.

- Involve your child in a chore you have to do, like vacuuming or washing the car. Let her be in charge of washing the tyres, or lifting rugs for you to clean under. Helping with tasks like hanging out the washing develops fine motor skills and makes a dull job more enjoyable.

✔ Rather than just flicking on the telly, make a point of selecting what your child is going to watch and involve her in the decision making. For example, go to the library to select a DVD, then watch it together.

✔ Read some books. If you're sick of reading the same books over and over, head to the library for some new ones.

✔ Remember all the games you used to play as a child like 'I spy with my little eye'? Play them with your child.

✔ Take a trip to the beach to play in the sand, go for a bike ride, visit the local playground, take a child-friendly bush walk, or wander around the botanic gardens, museum, sportsground, or zoo. Keep talking with your child all the time about what you see and hear, and ask her questions about what she thinks about things you come across.

✔ Visit a local farm. Many farmers are more than happy to open the gates and show you round (provided you arrange a suitable time with them beforehand).

✔ Visit some pals. Arrange a play date with other kids your child's age from crèche, your antenatal group or other friends with children.

Sometimes saying she's bored is your child's code for 'I want to watch TV or play on the computer'. It can be easy just to let her, especially if you have chores you need to do or you're tired. But try to resist. Perhaps just a quick trip to the local park will give her enough lift to come home and be entertained with doing her own thing for the rest of the afternoon.

Encourage your child to come up with activities she would like to try to keep on hand when the 'I'm bored' blues hit.

Bad weather busters

Adults find it difficult not to go stir-crazy with cabin fever when it's raining and cold outside. For children, who have energy to burn, not going mad is even harder.

So what can you do about it? Here are some ideas:

✔ Board games are always good fun for an emergency. Perhaps invite some friends over to play.

✔ Find out about open days at your local fire station, police station, city council or a large factory nearby, such as a beer brewery or cheese processing plant, or ask about public tours of places that your child shows interest in.

- ✔ Get hands-on by getting out the craft supplies or playing with play dough, all cheap and cheerful activities that encourage creativity and fine motor skills. See the sidebar 'How to make your own play dough' for a play dough recipe.

- ✔ Get out some old photos from when you were a child, teen or student. Organise a family photo session, which can be even better if you have some old slides and a projector. Create a fabulous home cinema experience for your child.

- ✔ Get your little champ involved in baking and cooking.

- ✔ Have a singing and dancing competition in your lounge.

- ✔ Make up stories, then draw pictures to go with them.

- ✔ Organise a trip to a nearby airport, train station, harbour or docks. Young children are typically fascinated by the hustle and bustle that can be observed at these places.

- ✔ Pretend you're outdoors by making a tent out of chairs or a table and some sheets. You could camp out all day in your tent, with snacks, toys, books and pillows for lounging on.

- ✔ Visit the local museum or indoor play centre.

Bringing out your child's talents without going OTT

Expecting your child to be super-skilled at something at this age is unreasonable, although you may think the way she kicks a ball means she's the next female David Beckham. Rather, this is a time for giving your child lots of opportunities for her to discover what she's good at and what she enjoys doing. How will your child discover if she loves gardening if she never sees a garden, or enjoys fishing if you never show her what fishing is all about? We don't mean spending thousands on fishing gear, but by exposing your child to ideas, telling her what others are doing and showing her in books, you'll see what your child takes a fancy to.

Sometimes you can use this opportunity to try out something new yourself and share that experience with your little one. Remember the saying 'do something that scares you every day'. Doing something new with your children is a great way to step outside your own comfort zone.

How to make your own play dough

Here's everything you need to make play dough:

2 cups plain flour
2 cups warm water
1 cup salt
2 tablespoons vegetable oil
1 tablespoon cream of tartar
Food colouring

1. Mix all the ingredients together in a pot over a low heat. Stir.

2. When the mixtures thickens, clumps in the middle and feels dry rather than sticky, remove from the heat and allow to cool.

3. Turn out onto a bench or tray and knead until the dough's silky smooth.

4. Divide into as many balls as you want to make colours.

5. Poke a finger into each ball and add a drop of your desired colour into the hole. This protects your hands from coming into contact with the concentrated food colouring, which can stain your skin. Knead the colour through the ball.

This dough keeps for a few days and is best kept in the fridge. Wrap the dough in cling film to stop it drying out. If the dough does dry out, it can be dampened with a little water.

Voila! Now you can get really creative. Watch out Michelangelo!

Being a dad is also about showing your children that you too have to learn new things and that you're keen to try something new. Take a keen interest in what your children like doing, even if they're not interested in your favourite sport or activity.

 Follow your child's interests. Let her choose which books she's interested in, what games she likes and which activities she's into. Forcing your values on her or making her decisions for her isn't going to help build her relationship with you, or let her become her own person.

Being a good sport

Preschoolers are more interested in other people than toddlers are, but still struggle to control their emotions and impulses. While your child may love playing with others, it can be hard for her to accept not having her own way all the time, and playing sports or games where there are winners and losers can be really tricky for a preschooler to deal with. Learning to lose without losing your cool is a skill, like learning to ride a bike. Being able to cope with losing is a step towards being able to admit making mistakes, or accepting not getting your way, which are emotions that even adults struggle with. Being a good winner and not gloating is also an important skill to learn.

Here are some ideas you can instil in your child to help her become a good sport:

- **Be a good sport as a father.** You're a role model and accepting defeat gracefully encourages the same behaviour in your child.

- **Congratulate the winner.** It takes grace to admit someone else played better on the day. If you're the winner, be gracious about winning by not rubbing it in the other team's face.

- **Focus on the fact that the performance, not the person, lost.** Your child is not a 'loser' because she lost. She's the same person and may beat her opponent next time. She lost because of the way she played, not because of who she is.

- **Don't make excuses for why your child lost.** Blaming others like referees or cheating from the other side only makes you look desperate, and means your child has no chance to analyse why she lost and improve on her performance for next time.

Social skills and an understanding of team work take a long time to develop. Younger children can generally only focus on one thing at a time (that's why three-year-olds playing football all chase after the ball and don't keep their positions). So be realistic about your expectations when it comes to team sports.

The great outdoors

Preschoolers are naturally curious, active and imaginative. And what better place to hook into all those parts of themselves than out in nature?

For a fun day out that will charge his batteries and get those brain connections whirring, try taking your child to:

- **The beach.** There's a reason why parks and crèches have sandpits — sand is a blank canvas for a child to play on. Your child can create castles, words, faces and shapes. Or he can just feel the sand and scoop it up for hours. Most little kids also love the water, so keep a look out to make sure he's safe — and remember the sun block.

- **The bush.** Try taking a walk through the bush for a few hours to get your child's body and mind fit and healthy. Take along a book about native plants or birds and animals and see what you can find.

Another great thing about using the outdoors and nature is that they're usually free of charge.

Encouraging an appreciation of the great outdoors also encourages an appreciation of our environment. Remember to take only pictures and leave only footprints when you're out and about.

Lifelong Learning Starts Here

The first years of a child's life are critical to his development as a thinking, feeling human being. Forming an attachment to you and your partner, and forming connections between different parts of his brain is your child's main function at this age.

School is on your child's horizon, and with it comes a more formal way of learning than you've been practising at home with books, toys and talk.

Fathers as first teachers

As a father, you are your child's role model and teacher. He'll learn more from you than how to tie his shoelace or use a knife and fork. Giving your child the opportunity to spend time with you, doing puzzles, climbing trees and reading together, all makes you his first teacher.

Parents as First Teachers

Parents as First Teachers (PAFT) is an international organisation offering an individualised program designed to support and advise parents as their children's first and most important teacher. In New Zealand PAFT is part of the Ministry of Social Development and Family and Community Services. PAFT parent educators visit you at home and talk about your child's development and early learning needs, but you can also go to group meetings. PAFT can link you to other community programs that may be helpful for your family.

Taking part in the PAFT program can help your child to develop:

- ✔ Language skills
- ✔ Problem solving skills
- ✔ Social skills

It also helps fathers and mothers gain confidence in their parenting, and picks up any problems your child may have developmentally, or with hearing or vision, along the way. To contact PAFT in New Zealand, visit www.familyservices.govt.nz/working-with-us/programmes-services/positive-parenting/paft-in-new-zealand.html.

The teaching and example you set now shapes how your child respects other people, manages his emotions, takes winning and losing with dignity, treats the environment and manages relationships with those around him.

Your values, attitudes and beliefs filter down to him, and if you've had a rough upbringing or your experience with schools and authority was not a happy one, you may want to think about ways you can change that for your child, so he has a fresh start.

Kindergarten happiness

If your child hasn't gone to crèche or day care, the first time he leaves home for periods of time away from you may be to go to kindergarten. In Chapter 11 we discuss how kindergartens prepare your child for school and teach children skills through play.

If your child is already in day care or a crèche, have a chat with the teachers there about whether they have sessions that prepare children for school as they turn three and four. Many centres will already have something in place.

When selecting a kindergarten or preschool for your child, ask yourself these questions:

- ✔ What are the staff like? Do I feel confident in their abilities?
- ✔ What is the kindergarten's philosophy on learning? What skills do they encourage the children to have?
- ✔ How will the kindergarten's style of learning suit my child?
- ✔ What preparation is there for going to school?

If your child is used to a specific routine, you need to work kindergarten or preschool into it. Most centres have morning and afternoon sessions rather than all-day sessions, so you may need to change your work hours or make other arrangements to suit. If your child hasn't been to a crèche or centre before, the stimulation at kindergarten or preschool may tire him, so be flexible about bedtimes and naps, perhaps putting him to bed a little earlier at night.

Leaving your child at a kindergarten or preschool can be tough at first as she settles in, but don't feel guilty. Feel confident that the staff have seen it all before and know how to handle it. If your child is upset about you leaving, give her to a teacher, give her a kiss, tell her you love her and you'll see her later. Give her a wave and let the staff get on with their job. If you come back two minutes later you may find your child happily absorbed in an activity, having completely forgotten you were ever there.

Learning objectives

Finding out what your child is capable of learning at this age is a bit tricky as all children develop at their own speed. But you can encourage her learning by stimulating her with books and images, and with one-on-one time with you.

Here are some objectives you can aim for:

- ✔ **Learning the alphabet.** Use jigsaw puzzles and point out letters when you're reading; for example, 'that's A for apple'. Use a chalkboard or drawing paper to practise the shapes of letters.

- ✔ **Learning to count.** Lots of books with numbers are available, and when you're at the shop, or out and about, you can count together the number of things you see. Take it slowly at first. Getting to ten is a major achievement!

- ✔ **Learning about time and the seasons.** Use pictures on your child's bedroom wall, books and your own backyard to show how time passes and seasons change.

As your child approaches school age, talk to your local school about things they might expect a new entrant to know and what skills will make going off to school easier. You may also want to talk to your day care or kindergarten teacher about your child's progress and which areas he may need help with.

Learning for the whole family

Even though you're the father and you're the one role modelling and passing on your knowledge to your kids, learning is a two-way street. You can learn a lot from your child too. Your child can teach you:

- ✔ **How to be totally in the moment.** Watch your son's delight at running sand through his fingers.

- ✔ **How to see the world for the first time again.** Enjoy the moment with your son when he sees an animal at the zoo he's never seen before.

- ✔ **Later in life your child will be able to translate the world for you.** Just like you did for your parents, your child will be able to explain why what's in fashion looks good and why music on the radio is popular.

✔ **How to make the best out of every situation.** For example, you'll learn how unimportant your son rubbing his snotty nose on your suit pants before work is.

✔ **Patience.** When your little champ thinks there's a dragon under his bed at 3.00 am, you can muster the patience to convince him he's going to be okay.

✔ **What really matters in life.** Is it impressing the boss with long hours, or being home in time to read *Green Eggs and Ham* with your son?

Another fun activity is to switch roles with your children: Ask them to play 'dad' and you play 'child'. The outcome can be hilarious as they play back your own behaviour to you. It can also give you interesting clues about what you might want to change in how you treat your child. You can of course also get your own back by throwing yourself on the floor, screaming and shouting to explain what your son looks like when he's in tantrum mode.

Chapter 14

Health and Nutrition

In This Chapter
- Getting your child to eat healthily
- Staying fit with your preschooler
- Looking after your little one when he gets sick

Your health is the most important thing you have. Surely the health of your child is equally important or even more important to you? She doesn't yet know how to maintain her health, so you need to ensure that she stays in tiptop shape. The health she enjoys now, and the healthy eating and exercise she does, are good habits to instil in the early years and will stay with her for life.

In this chapter we show you how to encourage and maintain those good habits, not just for her but for you too. We guide you through the difficulties of picky eaters, allergies and introducing new foods. We also bring you up to speed with the multiple bugs and illnesses your child will inevitably pick up from her environment, which is a rather challenging part of fatherhood.

Food, Nutritious Food

Like you, young children need three meals a day plus snacks and plenty to drink every day to keep healthy and active.

Your child needs a variety of foods from each of these groups:

- Breads and cereals — at least four servings a day
- Dairy products and milk — two to three servings a day
- Meat, pulses, and other sources of protein like eggs or tofu — one to two servings a day
- Vegetables and fruit — at least five servings a day (two fruit, three vegetable)

A serving is usually the size of your child's palm, or a piece of bread, glass of milk or tub of yoghurt.

Cooking and baking for busy dads

Getting all these 'servings' into your child may seem daunting, but it's not. Don't panic if junior hasn't had exactly what's in the guidelines, his appetite will guide you for the most part. It's important to not force feed your child because he may develop an aversion to the food you're trying to get into him. He may also get very upset and throw up, which means you've achieved the opposite of what you were trying to do.

If you're stuck for ideas, try these:

- **Breads and cereals:** Muffins, sandwiches, fried rice, risotto, pikelets, filled rolls, pasta, couscous or quinoa in a salad
- **Fruit and vegetables:** Try dried fruit (only occasionally, as the sugars in them can harm teeth); frozen or tinned fruit and vegetables, which are just as nutritious as fresh; fruit and vegetables in muffins or sandwiches
- **Meat, pulses and protein:** Sliced lunch meats, baked beans, kidney or pinto beans, nuts (only if he's three years or older) or nut spread, tuna in a sandwich or salad, tofu, chickpeas
- **Milk and dairy products:** Cheese slices in a sandwich, yoghurt, a fruit smoothie or milkshake

A simple strategy to inspire kids to eat a variety of fruit and veg is to point out the colours to them; for example, 'you've eaten lots of orange food, how about some green (peas), red (tomatoes) and yellow (sweet corn) food?'

Kids need fluid just like we do, so keep your tyke topped up with cartons of milk or soy milk, or water in a bottle.

Drinking juice is not recommended because the sugar content is very high. If you do want to give your child juice, dilute it, and avoid giving it after he's brushed his teeth at night.

You'll find more recipes, dietary guidelines and nutrition information on www.nutritionaustralia.org.

Avoiding the wrong foods

We're all familiar with the healthy food pyramid, but just in case the rigours of parenting have ousted them from your memory, foods high in salt, sugar and fat are right at the top of the pyramid, which means you should have them only as treats. Just as foods at the top of the healthy food pyramid are 'sometimes' foods for dads, so they are 'sometimes' foods for your children and should be eaten a few times a week at the most.

Occasional treat foods include foods that are:

- ✔ Heavy in sugars like lollies, biscuits, chocolate and dried fruit
- ✔ Heavily processed like microwave ready-meals, frozen ready-meals such as pizza or pies, fruit roll-ups and sweet cereals
- ✔ Laden with saturated fats like fish and chips, or burgers
- ✔ High in salt and flavourings such as crackers and chips

We've also become increasingly aware of how food additives, flavourings and colourings can affect our children; how processing can take away nutritional value; and how cruel some farming practices can be to animals. There's a movement towards eating more organic, less processed foods in order to avoid pesticide residues and get more nutritional value from what we eat. You may want to consider doing the same.

If your child is under three, avoid foods that may choke him, such as nuts, olives or popcorn. Even after three, discourage eating while on the move, watching TV or doing anything that may distract him. Keep cutting food into small pieces to avoid an airway blockage.

Telling your child 'no' for the hundredth time to the lollies or biscuits you have stashed in the pantry is easier said than done, and even if you don't have a private supply that junior knows about, he's going to discover treat foods at crèche or kindy, or at friends' houses. So you probably won't be able to keep your child as pure as the day he was born. That's okay. A few animal crackers every now and then isn't going to turn him into Fat Albert. Just keep remembering to fill him full of good stuff whenever you can and encourage him to get active.

Completely banning 'bad' foods makes them objects of desire, so let him have a few treats now and then, just like you would treat yourself. Children need fat in their diet, but things like chips should be limited to once a week.

Introducing different foods

Putting a plate of never-seen-before food in front of her can be a little disconcerting for your child. She may turn her nose up at something you think she'll love just because it looks funny. So take some time to introduce new tastes and textures thoughtfully. Here are some ideas:

- **Do it yourself.** You are your child's role model, and if you tuck into your food with gusto, chances are she will too.

- **Get creative with your presentation.** Make a face, shapes or patterns with food.

- **Give her something to dip into.** Low-fat dressing, tomato sauce or a mild salsa, hummus and yoghurt dip all provide a fun way of testing out new foods.

- **Get sneaky.** Put finely chopped pieces of new foods into stews, omelettes, mashed spuds or rice.

- **Grow your own.** One way to get children into fruits and vegetables is to take part in growing it themselves. She'll be enormously proud to tuck into those beans she's seen grow from seed and watered every night.

Forcing children to eat something they don't like is counterproductive. If she tries a new meal and doesn't like it, that's okay. She'll make up for it by eating others. Punishing your child for not eating makes her more defiant. Remember also that children take time to develop a taste for something. The fact that she turned down broccoli the first time she tried it doesn't mean she'll never like it.

Leading by example

You are your child's role model, and what you eat and how you live sets the scene for how your child will eat and live.

Children who have one obese parent have a 40 per cent chance of becoming obese themselves, and children with two obese parents have an 80 per cent chance of facing obesity. That's a poor legacy to leave a child. If you've already fallen into the trap of giving your child whatever sugary and fatty processed foods she wants, now's an opportunity to consider a change of course and swap unhealthy food options with healthy ones. Check out www.diyfather.com/content/Simple-breakfast-swaps-for-children for a simple list of 'food swaps'.

Simple ways to make meals healthier include:

✔ **Avoid processed and pre-prepared foods.** Generally, the less time food's spent going through a factory, the better it is for you. This also goes for basic ingredients like sugar, flour or rice. Use raw or brown sugar, wholemeal flour and brown rice.

✔ **Eat meals as a family when you can.** Turn off the TV and use dinner time to catch up on your day and enjoy each other's company. Sharing food is an important social interaction for humans and enjoying food together should be special.

✔ **Exercise restraint.** If you habitually have dessert, keep the portions small.

✔ **Find out about healthy substitutes to sugar and fat-laden foods.** Try natural yoghurt with fruit added rather than tubs of sweetened yoghurt, for example. Honey (especially Manuka honey) is an excellent replacement for refined, white sugar. Honey is a natural product and complex food that is easier to digest and produces less of a 'sugar high' than white sugar.

✔ **Prepare meals together.** Let your child have some responsibility over what goes into her food. Get her involved in where your food comes from and how easy it is to prepare. As we get older, making food for each other is another social interaction that shows our family and friends how much we love and care for each other, and this can be a positive activity for your child to enjoy right now.

Curbing fussy eaters

Children may go through a fussy eating period. This stage is annoying and frustrating, and all you want your child to do is eat! It's enough to make a grown man cry. There can sometimes be a reason behind it, such as mealtimes falling at a time when she's tired, too much distraction when she should be eating, or snacking before mealtimes. In all circumstances patience with fussy eating results in better eating than getting angry and annoyed.

Here are some ways to deal with fussy eaters:

✔ Avoid arguing about food. Forcing your child to eat mushrooms is unlikely to encourage a love of them in the future, so you're no further ahead next time you serve them up.

✔ Avoid giving snacks in the hour before a meal, as she won't be hungry when mealtime arrives.

✔ Offer a variety of small servings of food in a meal, with lots of vegetables and other goodies to choose from, so if she doesn't like one food she has others to choose from.

✔ Praise your child when she eats, especially when she tries something new and different.

✔ Try some of the suggestions from the section 'Leading by example' earlier in this chapter, such as getting your child involved in food preparation, making meal times a family time and growing your own vegies. Polish off your plate whenever you eat. If you leave lots of food on your plate and walk away halfway through a meal your little one will copy exactly what you do.

Try to avoid:

✔ Cooking another meal to feed her if she turns up her nose at the first

✔ Giving your child a treat to make her stop whining

✔ Having meals in front of TV or while doing something else, such as reading, playing games or walking around the house

If you're concerned your fussy eater isn't getting enough to eat to grow, play and be active, talk to your GP.

Coping with special dietary requirements

More and more children seem to be developing allergies to certain foods, such as wheat, gluten, eggs, nuts, milk, shellfish and even some types of fruits and vegetables. Some children may grow out of them, others won't. Managing an allergy can be a matter of life or death.

The recommended practice of introducing new foods one at a time helps with detecting reactions to certain foods. If your baby shows symptoms of an allergic reaction take him to your GP to have him tested.

What is an allergy?

An *allergy* is a reaction by the immune system when it thinks the food you're eating is harmful. It produces *histamines*, which can cause hives, breathing difficulties, a tight throat, nausea, vomiting and diarrhoea. The most dangerous reaction the body can have is called *anaphylaxis* in which the tongue swells, air passages narrow and blood pressure drops. Anaphylaxis can cause death.

How do you manage an allergy?

Avoiding the foods that cause the body to overreact is the best way to avoid an allergic reaction. The jury is still out on what causes allergies, but most thinking seems to be that the later potentially harmful foods are introduced, the less likely your child is to develop a reaction to them.

Luckily, more people are learning about food allergies and food producers are hopping on the bandwagon too. You can now find many substitutes for common food *allergens*, those foods that cause an allergy. Wheat-free breads, pastas and baking products are available, you can buy egg substitute for baking, and cow's milk can be easily replaced by soy or rice milk. Many day care centres, kindergartens and schools have banned nuts and nut products from the premises in a move to ensure the safety of children with nut allergies.

It can be hard to work out whether your child is in fact allergic to certain foods. Talk to your GP — you may be able to have your child tested for the most common allergies.

If your child is allergic to certain foods you'll have to be more vigilant about reading labels on food packets, as well as making other parents and caregivers aware of your child's allergy so that at day care, on play dates or at birthday parties, your child isn't given food that may cause a reaction.

Some people think that just having a small amount of an allergen is okay, but this has been shown to be very dangerous. Small amounts or even being in the same room as an allergen is enough to make some children seriously ill. For severe cases of allergies children may have to carry an EpiPen, which administers medicine in the event of an allergic reaction. Talk to your GP about allergies, and discuss ways of managing your child's allergy, including EpiPens. It may also be helpful to speak with a dietitian who can help manage the allergy and teach you and your child what you need to do to avoid allergic reactions.

Smooth peanut butter can be given to children from eight to nine months of age, but watch them closely for any signs of a reaction. If your family has a strong history of nut allergies, wait until your child is three before trying nuts. If your child has any breathing difficulties, call an ambulance.

Being informed about what you're dealing with when your child has a food allergy helps you stay on top of it. See these sites for tips on managing your child's allergy and contacting support networks:

- ✔ Allergy New Zealand www.allergy.org.nz
- ✔ Anaphylaxis Australia www.allergyfacts.org.au

Vegetarian children

A vegetarian diet is becoming a lifestyle choice for more and more parents, be it to save the planet or on moral grounds. If you want to bring up your child on a vegetarian diet you have to pay a bit more attention to where he gets his iron and protein from, especially because children have higher iron needs than adults. Good sources of iron include:

- ✔ Most dark green (leafy) vegetables such as broccoli, spinach, silverbeet and kale
- ✔ Dried fruit such as prunes and raisins
- ✔ Lentils, chickpeas and dried peas
- ✔ Wholegrain cereal and bread

Vitamin C helps the body absorb iron, so make having fruit such as citrus or kiwifruit with a meal part of your routine.

You can help your child get plenty of protein by feeding him:

- ✔ Dairy products
- ✔ Eggs
- ✔ Grains like brown rice, oatmeal, buckwheat and millet
- ✔ Hummus, chickpeas and most legumes, such as soy beans and lentils
- ✔ Peanut butter and nuts (for children aged three years and over)
- ✔ Tofu and tempeh
- ✔ Vegetables like eggplant, courgettes (zucchini), beetroot, cabbage

A great way of getting protein into your child is adding puffed-up grains to muesli or cereal. Puffed-up grains that are available include millet, rye or quinoa (they're all healthy alternatives to wheat).

A vegetarian diet can be bulkier and more filling than a non-vegetarian diet, so your child may feel fuller with less food. Offer smaller meals more frequently throughout the day to ensure he gets enough energy and nutrients to get through his day.

Exercise

We've talked a lot about how being active from birth helps to develop your child's brain. And, this may not be earth-shattering news — exercise is quite good for her body too!

Getting your child (and yourself) into exercise

An amazing fact of human biology is that, just by being active with our bodies, we grow our brains. So keeping active and exercising can help your child develop her mental powers!

But the balancing act of life at work, home and getting time for yourself may mean exercise falls to the bottom of the priority list, never to be seen again. When it comes to your body, you either use it or lose it.

Yes, you've grown a gut and your partner may be teasing you about potential man boobs. Getting back at her by pointing out her saggy boobs and stretch marks may boost your ego (temporarily) but won't do anything to help you get fit now. So time once more to man up to a big task and get on with it.

Try the following:

✔ Check out gyms that offer childcare.

✔ Get off the bus a few stops early and walk the rest of the way home. Park your car further away from work, or walk or cycle to work. Skip the elevator and walk up and down the stairs.

✔ Involve your child in your exercise program. Stroller jogs, swimming lessons at the local pool, or exercising at home using your child as a weight, sitting on you while you do sit-ups or push-ups are all great ways to incorporate her into your exercise program.

✔ Schedule some time into your week for exercise. Make exercise a priority, a promise to yourself that you can't break. Take turns with your partner; one day she goes for a run, next day you do.

✔ Team up with a few other mates and get a personal trainer. There's nothing like peer pressure and professional advice from a coach to get you in shape.

You are your child's role model, so by making exercise and activity normal and high priority in your own life, you're making exercise normal and high priority in her life.

Exercise with your little champ by:

- ✔ Clambering over the monkey bars and climbing walls at your local playground with her.

- ✔ Doing chores around the house. Vacuuming, mowing the lawn and washing the car can help you get a sweat up. Get your child to help.

- ✔ Getting a trampoline for the backyard. Jumping around for 15 minutes gets your pulse up.

- ✔ Going for walks (short ones at the beginning). Encourage your child to walk by themselves rather than be carried.

- ✔ Having a pillow fight or a bit of rough-housing to get all the muscles working!

- ✔ Showing her how to climb trees.

- ✔ Signing up to coach a sport at your local school and having your child come along to play too.

Working-out routines

Can you imagine your toddler or preschooler doing aerobics, or being able to follow what a weights class instructor is saying? Not likely. Working out with your child should be fun, not a stream of complicated instructions to follow. You can use the activities listed earlier as your workout routines, or try for more traditional exercises with weights (for you, teddies for your child) and set moves. Here are some tips to make working out work out smoothly:

- ✔ Don't eat just before exercise and especially not before swimming.

- ✔ Explain how important it is to warm up, stretch and drink water.

- ✔ Give lots of praise and encouragement. If he can't master an exercise yet, show him how and encourage him to do it himself. Helping his body through an exercise shows him he can do it.

✔ Make doing exercise together a regular activity, say, after day care or before dinner, so that your child looks forward to exercise and it becomes part of his routine.

✔ Start off slowly. You don't want to have junior bench pressing 60 kilograms straight off. A quarter of an hour of exercise is a good way to start.

Practising yoga and meditation

Yoga is an ancient method of not only strengthening the body and maintaining physical wellbeing, but also maintaining mental wellbeing. The practice consists of moving into *poses* by using breath and movement. Yoga encourages flexibility, stamina and relaxation for general good health, including stress relief.

And what better time to start practising yoga than when you have a frisky toddler or preschooler to entertain? Though a young child's attention span may not cater for long sessions of yoga or deep meditation, there are a lot of poses you and your tyke can do at home, or you may want to enrol her in a class specialising in children's yoga.

Many yoga poses are named after animals or things found in nature. Children often enjoy imagining they really are a dolphin when doing the dolphin pose, or have the roots of a thousand year old oak when practising the tree pose.

The best way to get started is by enrolling in a yoga-for-children course. And don't think for a minute that yoga for children is too easy for you. You can do lots of poses along with your child and they are just as challenging for you to do. In fact your child will probably do many poses better than you, which is a great source of motivation. Keep up with your toddler so he doesn't call you 'old man' (just yet).

Common Health Problems

There's no more scary time than when your little one comes down with something and you're not sure what's happening. Before your child can speak and tell you what the matter is, you have only your innate dad-sense to tell you what the trouble is. So we've made it a little easier, by laying out for you some basic health issues you'll probably have to delve into sometime or another.

For a checklist of signs of an unwell child, hop on to www.diyfather.com/unwell-child.

Childhood illnesses

At times it may seem that every couple of weeks your child is struck down with a cold, or worse, an ear or chest infection. As your child's immunity is still developing and he spends more time in the company of other children, he's going to pick up a lot of nasties. The list in this chapter covers the 'usual suspects' of childhood illnesses. Chapter 17 examines what to do when you find out your child may have a serious or rare illness.

Following are some of the most common childhood illnesses to watch out for and what you can do about them.

Bronchiolitis

An acute (usually viral) chest infection, bronchiolitis usually comes after a cold, ear infection or tonsillitis. It affects the small airways in the lungs called *bronchioles*.

- ✔ Symptoms: A hacking cough, difficulty breathing and wheezing. Sometimes a child's lips or tongue turn blue. Some children vomit. Children can be ill for seven to ten days.

- ✔ Treatment: Keep your child well hydrated. Because bronchiolitis is viral, in mild cases there is no drug treatment. Severe cases may require hospitalisation. See your doctor if you're concerned.

- ✔ Precautions: Watch for secondary bacterial infections, which can be treated with antibiotics. If the bronchiolitis symptoms don't go away as quickly as predicted by your GP, or new symptoms, such as flu symptoms, appear, go back to your GP or hospital. They may diagnose a secondary infection.

Chickenpox

Chickenpox usually affects children and is a viral illness that can be transmitted through coughing and sneezing, or from touching one of the fluid blisters that appear on the skin of a patient. Having chickenpox usually provides long-lasting immunity to the disease and only rarely have people had chickenpox twice. In adults, chickenpox can result in complications such as shingles.

- ✔ Symptoms: Cold and flu-like symptoms — runny nose, cough, tiredness and fever. A rash of small round lumps appears which a few days later are replaced by itchy, fluid-filled blisters. The blisters tend to appear more on the torso, stomach and back, but can also form on the inside of the mouth, scalp and face.

- ✔ Treatment: Applying topical lotions to the blisters can help with the itch, but bed rest, paracetamol for pain and fever and not scratching are recommended.

- ✔ Precautions: Let your day care or preschool, friends and family know that your child has chickenpox because it's contagious for about five days before the first symptoms appear.

You can now get your child immunised against chickenpox. Looking after a child with chickenpox is horrendous and is quite a nasty experience for her too, so consider having her immunised, even if you have to pay for it.

You may have heard of the concepts of a 'chickenpox party'. The idea behind chickenpox parties is to purposefully expose children to another child who has chickenpox to get the inevitable infection out of the way. We don't believe this is a fantastic idea as chickenpox can be very severe so should not be treated light-heartedly. Immunisation may be a better alternative.

Common cold

A cold is a viral infection, mainly affecting the nose and throat and lasting from two to three days to a week.

- ✔ Symptoms: Runny nose, nasal congestion, weepy eyes, sore throat, tiredness, cough, sneezing and fever.

- ✔ Treatment: Bed rest and fluids. You can help nasal congestion by placing a few drops of eucalyptus oil in the bath (use as per label or chemist's advice). Lots of cuddles, rest and keeping fluids up are also recommended. Paracetamol can be used for pain and fever. Chest rubs can be used in children over two years old to alleviate coughing.

- ✔ Precautions: If your child doesn't get better over three to four days, see your GP. There may be a secondary infection like an ear infection or worse on the way. If your child has a high fever (more than 37.4 degrees Celsius when measured under the arm or 38 degrees Celsius measured elsewhere, such as in the ear), a strange cry or a very sore throat, go to the GP straight away.

Conjunctivitis

Also known as pink eye, conjunctivitis is an inflammation of the tissue that lines the eyes. A range of things cause conjunctivitis — allergens in the air, bacterial or viral infection, food allergies or a blocked tear duct. If your child's case of conjunctivitis is caused by an infection, it can be very contagious, so wash your hands after touching your child so you don't come down with it as well! Keep your child away from day care and tell staff about the infection.

- ✔ Symptoms: Red, sore eyes and possibly green or yellow mucus at the corners.

- ✔ Treatment: Wash your child's eyes with a disposable cotton bud dipped in cooled, boiled water. Wash and dry your hands after doing this to curb infection spreading to you. A doctor can prescribe eye drops or ointment.

- ✔ Precautions: Wash bedding, clothing, towels and flannels in hot water with some disinfectant to curb further infection or reinfection.

Ear infection

Children under seven years old are particularly prone to ear infections, which occur when germs get into the middle ear. Pus and fluid can build up in the eardrum, making your wee champ pretty miserable.

Deal with ear infections promptly because fluid can remain in the ear, causing a condition known as 'glue ear', which can make it hard for your child to hear, and therefore listen and learn.

- ✔ Symptoms: Ear infections are pretty distressing for young ones. Your child will be cranky, rub his ears and not want to lie down for sleeps or nappy changes. Ear infections can coincide with colds, flu and chest infections. Older children will tell you the ear feels full and in severe cases the eardrum can burst. Don't waste time — see your GP because you need to get confirmation of an ear infection from a health care professional.

- ✔ Treatment: Pain relief like ibuprofen and paracetamol can help. Antibiotics can help when the infection is caused by bacteria, but not with viral ear infections, so see your GP. Raising the head of the bed slightly can help too. Your child won't be able to hear well, so keep background noise down so he can hear you.

- ✔ Precautions: Recurring ear infections may mean more drastic action needs to be taken. Doctors can put *grommets* in children's ears to prevent fluid build-up. Grommets are small tubes inserted in the eardrum to allow airflow and drainage between the inner and outer ear.

Gastroenteritis

Bacteria and viruses can attack the gut, causing a tummy bug. Gastroenteritis can happen because of a range of causes, from not washing hands properly after using the toilet or changing a nappy, to food poisoning.

- ✔ Symptoms: Vomiting, diarrhoea, stomach cramps, body pains, fever, nausea, and in extreme cases, diarrhoea with blood or mucus.

- ✔ Treatment: Losing fluids through vomiting and diarrhoea means you have to be careful dehydration doesn't occur, so make sure your child is drinking plenty of fluids.

- ✔ Precautions: Refusing to eat is less of a worry (in medical terms) than dehydration. However, refusing to eat is an indicator that something may not be right. Monitoring your child's temperature and ensuring she has plenty of fluid intake when she's ill is always the priority.

See your doctor straight away if your child becomes very weak, is overly sleepy, has difficulty breathing, vomits, develops a high fever, has very dry skin, sunken eyes, doesn't want to eat her favourite food or stops passing urine.

Meningitis

Meningitis is a very serious disease in which the *meninges*, or protective membranes of the brain and spinal cord, become infected and inflamed (swollen). Meningitis often comes on very fast and can be fatal or cause severe disability if not treated. There are different kinds of meningitis, but the most well-known is caused by the meningococcal bacteria. Meningitis is passed through coughing, sharing eating utensils or cups and glasses, or being in close contact with a carrier. Many people carry the meningococcal bacteria, but don't develop symptoms. Familiarise yourself with the symptoms of meningitis. You'll need to constantly be on the watch for these symptoms because the disease develops so quickly and is potentially fatal.

✔ Symptoms: Severe headache, neck stiffness, sensitivity to light and loud noises, frequent crying with high-pitched cry, refusing food or feeds, vomiting, fever, rash with blotchy skin or red and purple spots. The onset of symptoms can be very fast. Your child may have an unusual cry, or be very sleepy.

✔ Treatment: See your doctor immediately if you suspect meningitis. Call an ambulance if you can't see your doctor immediately. Your child can become seriously ill very quickly, so don't second-guess yourself — get to the doctor or hospital!

✔ Precautions: Check out www.kiwifamilies.co.nz/Topics/Health/Other+Illnesses/Meningitis.html or www.meningitis.com.au/. There are also helplines for meningitis — call 1800 250 223 in Australia and 0800 611 116 in New Zealand.

Pneumonia

Pneumonia is a disease in which the air sacs of the lungs become infected.

✔ Symptoms: Wheezy or rattly cough, rapid breathing, making a noise when breathing, or having a hard time breathing. Your child may be very tired and look really unwell. Viral pneumonia starts out like a cold, while bacterial pneumonia can cause a fever as well.

✔ Treatment: Go to your GP. Keep your child hydrated with fluids.

✔ Precautions: Pneumonia makes it hard for people suffering from the disease to get oxygen, so your child may look very pale, even a little blue, and be very sleepy. If this happens, see your doctor immediately, because your child needs more oxygen urgently.

Tonsillitis

This is an inflammation of the tonsils, which are two little slits at the back of the throat, one on each side. Tonsils can become extremely sore and covered in pus. Symptoms can go on for four to six days. Tonsillitis can be caused by the streptococcus bacteria and can be highly contagious.

- ✔ Symptoms: Tonsils become red, sore, swollen and sometimes secrete pus. Your child may also have flu symptoms like tiredness, fever, muscle aches and swollen glands in the neck.

- ✔ Treatment: Visit your GP. Antibiotics can sort out a case of strep-caused tonsillitis. However, if the disease is viral, bed rest, fluids and paracetamol for pain relief are your best bet. Since your child's throat will be very sore, eating cold soft foods like jelly is best. Gargling with warm salt water can clear any pus build-up.

- ✔ Precautions: Some children have recurring bouts of tonsillitis, which may result in having their tonsils removed surgically.

Whooping cough

Also known as pertussis, this disease is easily preventable because vaccines have been available in most communities for years. Whooping cough has three stages and can last many weeks, even up to three months. The defining characteristic of whooping cough is the cough with a 'whoop' at the end, but it's no whooping matter — the cough is nasty and will make your child pretty miserable for the duration of the illness.

- ✔ Symptoms: The first stage, which lasts about a week, includes a hacking cough at night, loss of appetite, sneezing and possibly a slight fever. The second stage lasts about another week and is characterised by the horrendous coughing spells ending with the loud 'whoop'. Your child may cough up lots of mucus, which may make her vomit. Sometimes children can stop breathing during these spells, so keep them close to you for monitoring. The third stage is usually when things are on the mend, though watch for secondary infections like ear and chest infections.

- ✔ Treatment: Go to the GP. Some children need to be hospitalised. Small meals and lots of fluids are important, as is lots of love for your little one while she gets through the illness. Antibiotics may be prescribed. Steam and humidifiers can be used, but talk to your doctor.

- ✔ Precautions: Keep your child at home for three weeks from the start of the illness, or for five days after starting antibiotics to prevent infecting other children.

Infants too young to have been vaccinated against whooping cough may become very ill, so if your child or someone else in your family has whooping cough, stay away from infants.

If your child is treated at home, take turns with family and friends to stay up at night to monitor your child because the cough is often worse at night.

Recurring health problems: Where to from here?

Children under five have an average of six to eight respiratory tract infections (or colds) a year. The range in the number of infections children will have is huge though; while some children can get away with no infections at all, other children can have many.

Kids get sick so often because they:

- ✔ Catch bugs from other children, and their immune system is still developing and getting up to speed trying to fight all the bugs around

- ✔ Could have an overactive or an underactive immune system

- ✔ May have problems with the way they are put together anatomically, such as circulation problems, broken skin, and obstructions in the ears and lungs

You can't influence some of the factors cited previously, but you can do your bit to help your little one stay healthy. For example:

- ✔ Check that your child is adequately dressed for the weather when playing outside. For example, in windy weather make sure she wears a hat. Take an extra set of clothes so you can change them quickly if they get wet or put on an extra layer if the temperature drops suddenly.

- ✔ Ensure room temperatures at home (and in her bedroom) are close to the World Health Organization (WHO) recommendation — 19 degrees Celsius. Go easy on air conditioning near children and avoid drafts.

- ✔ Keep up general hygiene standards such as washing hands after going to the toilet or petting animals, especially before touching food or eating. Teach your child not to pick up things from the floor and put them in her mouth.

If you think the number of times your child is ill, or the severity of your child's recurring illness is unusual or excessive, talk to your GP. There may be an anatomical or immune issue here that you can treat.

Alternative medicines and remedies

Some dads seeking help with their children's illnesses sometimes turn to the less beaten track by checking out alternative medicine. Many of these treatments look at preventing illness, or curing illness through looking at the whole person rather than just the disease. Types of alternative care include:

- ✔ **Acupuncture:** An ancient Chinese technique where special needles are inserted at pressure points in the body
- ✔ **Homeopathy:** Using plant extracts to treat illness and promote wellbeing
- ✔ **Massage:** Using touch to relax muscles and stimulate blood flow around the body
- ✔ **Naturopathy:** An alternative medical system that uses the body's ability to heal itself
- ✔ **Osteopathy:** Treats the body using manipulation of the musculoskeletal system

Many of these techniques can be beneficial for your child. However, they're generally not designed to replace primary care, so a trip to your GP is still a good idea even if you swear by the benefits of the various alternative approaches. There are also some things to be aware of when turning to alternative medicine to treat your child:

- ✔ Check the use of alternative medicine beforehand with your GP or hospital. Many alternative therapies are unproven and unregulated.
- ✔ Some herbal remedies may contain allergens. Read labels carefully. Some can cause high blood pressure and liver damage. Check with a GP if in doubt.

We have listed the previous techniques and remedies for the sake of completeness and because some of them are very common. The effectiveness of alternative medicines and remedies in many cases has not been scientifically proven.

Child obesity: Honey, we're spoiling the kid

A 2007 study of nearly 5000 Australian four- to five-year-old children revealed dads play a crucial role in their kids becoming obese. About 15 per cent of the children studied were overweight, another 5 per cent were obese. Parents in the study were classified according to their parenting styles (see Chapter 9 for more details on parenting styles):

- ✔ **Authoritarian:** The old 'children are seen but not heard' style of parenting.
- ✔ **Authoritative:** Warm but with high expectations for their children's behaviour.
- ✔ **Permissive or indulgent:** What little princess wants, she gets. Children aren't given clear boundaries for their behaviour.
- ✔ **Neglectful:** The child is not loved, not cared for and not seen.

Children of authoritarian dads — that's 'eat what you're given and don't leave anything on the plate' parenting — were 11 per cent more likely to become obese or overweight than children of authoritative dads. Children of permissive fathers were 59 per cent more likely to be obese or overweight, while children of neglectful fathers were 35 per cent more likely to be overweight or obese. The parenting style of mothers appeared to have little or no influence on whether their child was obese or overweight.

A word on health insurance

Health care in New Zealand and Australia is technically 'free' for young children. However, you may want to investigate health insurance for your child. This means you pay a premium to an insurance company and in return, you can claim certain medical expenses and have access to private hospital care, avoiding the waiting lists of the public health-care system. Health insurance can cover treatments like putting in ear grommets (see the section earlier on ear infections), depending on the type of policy.

If you have medical insurance for yourself already, talk to your insurer about adding your child to your policy. You may also want to check what cover you can get if your child is seriously ill and you need to take time off work to look after him.

Chapter 15

Education

In This Chapter

▶ Understanding different schooling philosophies

▶ Getting your child ready for school

▶ Finding out about complementary education

*S*chool is a major part of your child's life for the next 13 years. Into adulthood, her school days shape her decisions, her values and her way of thinking, not just the qualifications she earns or the things she knows. As dads you obviously want to get the best schooling for your children. This may mean a focus on academic achievement, on a holistic view of the child as a well-rounded individual, or on spiritual and religious elements important to your culture or ethnic background.

Your child's school should also be somewhere you feel comfortable so that you can stay connected to your child and involved in her school life as much as possible. Research shows that the better the student's family support and involvement, the better she performs at school.

In this chapter we lay out all the options you have in navigating the education landscape, from single-sex schools to Rudolf Steiner (based on imagination and creative thinking), and give you some tools to help decide which is best for your child.

Exploring Education Philosophies

When you were a kid, wasn't school just a place that you went to down the road? These days we know a lot more about how a good education determines the path your life will take, and therefore there's a lot more pressure on parents, and in some cases on dads, to get it right.

Getting your head around education choices

Lots of choices in schools are available and trying to pick the best school for your child can be baffling. Here's a look at what there is to choose from.

In Australia, you have a choice of:

- **Alternative schools:** Schools in the government and non-government categories such as Montessori or Waldorf/Rudolf Steiner.
- **Government schools:** Publicly funded schools in your local area.
- **Non-government schools:** Schools where you pay fees for your child's tuition. The majority are Catholic schools, the rest are called independent schools but can also have a special religious character to them. Aboriginal schools generally fall into this category.
- **Single-sex** (either all-boys or all-girls schools) or **co-educational** (both girls and boys at the same school).

In New Zealand, there are:

- **Kura kaupapa Maori:** Publicly funded schools where all teaching and learning is done in Te Reo Maori and embraces a Maori philosophy of teaching and learning.
- **Private schools:** Schools where you pay fees for your child's tuition. Many have a religious affiliation, most usually Protestant.
- **Single-sex** (either all-boys or all-girls schools) or **co-educational** (both girls and boys at the same school).
- **State schools:** Publicly funded schools in your local area. Some may have enrolment zones, so you can go to that school only if you live in the school's zone.
- **State-integrated schools:** Publicly funded schools that have a special character, usually Catholic. Some Montessori and Rudolf Steiner schools are in this category.

To help you make your decision about which school your child should go to, it may help to ask yourself these questions:

- Besides getting good marks, what else is important at this school? Are there sports teams, language classes or music facilities that you would like to encourage your child to get involved with?
- Can you afford to send your child to a private school?

✔ Do you feel happy and confident about coming in to talk to teachers and the principal?

✔ How practical is it to get your child to the school and back? Are long journeys by car, bus or train involved? Is the school en route to work or a long way out of your work travel route?

✔ What are the school's values and teaching philosophies? Do they match your values and philosophies?

Spend some time at the school if you can. Ask yourself if you like the atmosphere, the way the teachers and children respond to each other and if you like the children there. Are the children precocious, spoiled, respectful, or meek? Ask teachers why they became a teacher. Is teaching their 'calling' or is it simply a job they ended up in because other career options didn't work out?

To find a school in your area, see www.australianschoolsdirectory.com. au for Australia, or www.schoolzones.co.nz/enrolmentzones/Search. aspx for New Zealand.

Go to www.ero.govt.nz to see an independent review of schools in New Zealand, or check the school performance reports on your state or territory's department of education website.

Alternative education philosophies

If public school philosophies, with their emphasis on reading, writing and 'rithmetic, aren't your thing, you do have alternatives. Both Montessori and Rudolf Steiner methods aim to educate children in an holistic way, shaping the child to be a good person with strong values and senses of themselves.

Montessori

Developed by Dr Maria Montessori in 1907, this approach involves observing and following the child's interests and encouraging him to explore and learn at his own pace.

✔ Children are separated into age groups 0–3, 3–6, 6–9, 9–12 and 12–14 years.

✔ Learning environments are designed so children can explore and have lots of specially designed materials to encourage skills and development that are easily manipulated by children. Classrooms are very calm, ordered places, where children learn to respect the space and needs of their classmates. Children are taught to put things back where they belong so others can use them.

- Montessori believed that with the right environment and freedom to explore, children develop a love of work, order and silence, and grow to become independent, self-disciplined adults who are true to their natures.

- Older children are encouraged to be role models and support younger children.

- Montessori Australia www.montessori.org.au

- Montessori Aotearoa New Zealand www.montessori.org.nz

Waldorf/Rudolf Steiner

Rudolf Steiner was an Austrian philosopher who founded the school of thought called anthroposophy. Without getting too technical here, Steiner's schools (sometimes called Waldorf because that was the name of the first school) use the concept of imagination and creative thinking to develop children into free-thinking adults. Steiner schools regard the child's inner life as important as learning to read, write and do maths.

- Childhood is divided into three parts: Early childhood, where emphasis is put on learning through experience; elementary age, where emphasis is put on the child's spirit; and adolescence, where emphasis is on developing analytical and abstract thinking skills.

- Foreign languages and crafts like knitting, art and artistic movement are used to teach staple subjects like reading, maths and science.

- The first lesson of the day is called main lesson and it lasts for about two hours. During main lesson, a particular curriculum area is taught using art, stories, recitation or physical movement. Main lesson has a theme, which continues for about a month.

- The same teacher stays with children as they progress through school for the first six years.

- Steiner Schools in Australia www.steiner-australia.org

- The Anthroposophical Society in New Zealand www.anthroposophy.org.nz/~anthropo/education.htm

Private versus public

For some fathers, whether you send your child to private or public school will be all down to finances — you can either afford the fees, or you can't.

An Australian 2004 study showed there are many factors that affect a child's performance at school. The most important factor is the child's background — the place he comes from, and the support he receives from family and the community. More children from well-off backgrounds went to independent schools and those schools performed better than some government schools. Independent schools had a better record for children going onto tertiary education, whereas government schools had higher rates of students entering the workforce and taking up apprenticeships.

When considering which school to send your child to, ask yourself these questions:

- ✔ Do I want my child to be educated in a religious setting? If yes, private schools (or state-integrated schools in New Zealand) of your denomination are for you.

- ✔ Do I want my child to have access to a large range of extracurricular activities? If yes, a private school may be for you. Private schools tend to have more emphasis on extracurricular activities and sports, and may have scholarships for young people who excel in sports.

- ✔ What value do I place on cultural diversity? Private schools are unlikely to have many Aboriginal, Maori or Pacific Island students, but higher numbers of international students.

Talk to other parents and students at the school you're looking at. They are the best gauge of a school.

Take a look at your potential school's results in Australia at www.myschool. edu.au. In New Zealand go to www.nzqa.govt.nz or the school's Education Review Office report on www.ero.govt.nz.

Same-sex versus co-ed

Girls and boys learn in different ways. Boys learn better when they stand up and are active, girls learn well in a structured/formal setting. Remember what it was like for you when you were young? A little bundle of activity just bursting to get out of the classroom and onto the footy field? So the idea of separating boys and girls to have a more effective learning experience seems pretty straightforward.

That said, experts are divided on the effectiveness of single-sex schools. In New Zealand, girls tend to do better at NCEA (secondary qualifications) than boys, and better than their co-educational counterparts, but adjusted for social background, the variances are minimal. Principals at single-sex schools claim that without the distraction of the opposite sex around, students get on with learning and girls are more likely to come out of their shells a bit. Those who champion co-educational schools say that there are social advantages in having the opposite sex around on a daily basis.

That doesn't help you dads though, does it? Perhaps this is something you'd like to talk about with your child. She may have a preference and you can always check with parents whose children attend single-sex or co-ed schools. Ask yourself the same questions we suggested for checking out schools in general: Does this school reflect your family values? How comfortable are you about this school?

School Begins This Summer

Welcome to a whole new world — the world of school! Going to school is a big milestone in any child's life. Be sure to take lots of pictures and enjoy seeing your child in his new environment. As his role model, if you enjoy school and being there with him, he'll love it too.

In Australia and New Zealand, the school year runs from late January or early February to December, and the academic year is divided into three or four terms depending on where you live. There are short breaks between terms, with a longer break of roughly six weeks over the summer.

Preparing for school

If your child has been to day care, kindergarten or preschool, he has some experience with being around lots of other children and teachers without you, and the transition to school may be quite straightforward. On the other hand, going to school is also a new environment. Bigger kids will be there and your child may be quite scared about all the changes in his life right now. There's also the fact that this is *school*, which is such a big milestone in his life that you'll undoubtedly be feeling all sorts of emotions — your little man is growing up!

Many day care centres, preschools and kindergartens have contacts with local schools and will take a part in getting your child prepared for school. They may initiate visits to the school with other children in your child's peer group so that your child will feel this is an adventure like an outing, rather than a big scary institution. Just like when you were settling your child into day care or kindy, taking your child to school and staying with him for visits will help him adjust and become familiar with his new surroundings. Talking together about what happens at school, what playtime is, what happens at lunchtime and where his bag goes will also help him be less overwhelmed by the change in his life.

Tell your little one what it was like for you when you were in school (hopefully you still remember some details!). Show him photos if you have some and get him excited about school by telling a few tall tales of your own school days.

Most schools have an orientation day for new entrants in the last term of the year before your child starts school. As well as helping your child, the orientation day also helps you be more at home in his new school, which is important. Studies show that fathers who are comfortable at a school are more likely to be actively involved in their child's education.

School holidays come round quickly and you will need a plan for when your little champ doesn't have to go to school for a while. Plan well ahead by arranging with your partner or family who will look after junior during the holidays.

Checklist: Things kids need to know

Imagine you're starting a new job. You turn up at your new office and are shown your desk and a stack of work to do. And that's it. You don't know where the loos are, where to make a cup of coffee, what time lunch is, where meetings are held, or what time you knock off for the day. You'd be feeling pretty out to sea if this happened to you, and your child will feel the same. She may find going to school and settling into a new environment overwhelming if she doesn't get a heads-up from you about what's going to happen, so here are a few things you may have overlooked that your child needs to know:

- ✔ Let her know that asking questions if she's not sure of anything is okay. There are always teachers and teacher aides around who can help.

- ✔ Explain the school rules — no hitting, running with scissors, stealing and other good rules.

- ✔ Give your child a rough guide to the day's structure: There'll be a playtime and lunchtime, and play lunch (morning tea) should be eaten at playtime, not lunch!

- ✔ Explain that only the people she knows well, such as dad, mum and special relatives and friends, should take her home from school.

- ✔ Tell her that school is on every day except weekends.

- ✔ Make sure she knows that looking after her bag, clothing and lunch box is her responsibility. Dad won't be able to run around finding stuff for her at going-home time.

- ✔ Show her how to go to the toilet and wash her hands by herself.

- Show her how to put on her uniform and how to look after it.

- Be sure she understands that the teacher is in charge of the class. If she needs something, your little one should ask the teacher.

You can help the transition to school by saying hello to the teacher every morning, and stopping to talk to any children or parents that you know. Goodbyes should be short, however. Say 'goodbye' and 'I love you', give a quick kiss, and let the teacher — a trained professional in these matters — take over.

Your child will be really tired from school in the first few weeks, so let her have some time to herself and a snack after school before making her do any chores. Show lots of interest though and be prepared to listen when your little champ is ready to tell you about her exciting day at school.

Just as when you leave your child with a babysitter, or when you've taken her to day care or kindergarten, your child may be a bit clingy when you leave her at school on the first day. To get around this 'return of the separation anxiety', make sure your child is with an adult, such as a teacher or teacher aide, or an older child like a cousin or friend when you leave. Give her a big kiss and a cuddle, and tell her you love her. Say something like 'I'll be back after school', or 'see you later' and walk away. Don't draw out the goodbye. Your child is in good hands in school and she'll be just fine starting her journey to becoming an independent adult. Be there for your child when she needs you — walk her into class and be there to pick her up.

Homework with dad

Along with schoolwork comes homework, where the day's learning is reinforced. Just like when your child was a baby and you repeated things over and over for him to learn, your child needs a second go at what he learnt that day to make it stick in his head. But finding a child that likes doing his homework is as rare as hens' teeth, so here are some ways to make homework less of a battle and more conducive to learning:

- If he's using the internet to research for a project, monitor where he's getting his information from. There are a lot of unreliable sites out there.

- Let your child do his homework independently, but let him know you're there to help should he need it. If reading books is part of the homework, read them with him to help him with new words.

- ✔ Let your child have some down time after school and before homework starts. Go outside and have a kick around, or water the garden together. Then get stuck into the homework.

- ✔ Make a set time for homework. Homework isn't finished until he has it in his bag, ready to go to school tomorrow.

- ✔ Set aside a quiet space where your child can do his homework. Turn off the TV or music — they are distractions.

You remember what doing homework was like, so don't be too hard on your child. If you see him struggling with something, spend some extra time with him. You don't need to do the homework for him (and in fact that would be detrimental to the learning objectives), but inspire him by looking at different approaches to overcoming an obstacle he may be facing. Doing homework with your child is really no different to coaching — help him to do a good job himself without doing the job for him.

Special dads for special needs

The term 'special needs' covers a wide range of issues that some children face, from physical difficulties such as disease or disability, to mental, behavioural and emotional issues that affect the way they learn. Just as all children are unique, so the problems they may face are unique and there is no one-size-fits-all approach when it comes to children with special needs.

Some examples of disorders and disabilities that may require special education include:

- ✔ Children who are hearing or visually impaired, who are wheelchair bound, or who have chronic illnesses like cystic fibrosis

- ✔ Children with autism, attention deficit disorder, foetal alcohol syndrome, developmental delay, Down Syndrome or Tourette Syndrome

For some fathers, it will be obvious that your child needs special help with her education. For others, it may just be a feeling that something isn't quite right. As always, talk to your Well Child provider or child health nurse, your GP or teachers.

Recognising that your child needs special help with her education doesn't mean she'll be packed off to a Dickensian school where she'll be left to languish. In some instances, children can attend mainstream school with the help of a teacher aide, while others may flourish at a special needs school.

Fathers must be strong advocates for their children — be informed and willing to go the extra distance to get your child the educational opportunities she deserves.

If you're concerned about your child's education and feel she may need access to special education services, here are some places to start.

- ✔ ACT www.det.act.gov.au/school_education/special_education
- ✔ New South Wales www.schools.nsw.edu.au/studentsupport/programs/lrngdifficulty.php
- ✔ Northern Territory www.det.nt.gov.au/parents-community/students-learning/special-education-disability
- ✔ Queensland http://education.qld.gov.au/studentservices/learning/index.html
- ✔ South Australia www.decs.sa.gov.au/speced/pages/specialneeds/intro
- ✔ Tasmania www.education.tas.gov.au/school/parents/taught
- ✔ Victoria www.education.vic.gov.au/healthwellbeing/wellbeing/disability/default.htm
- ✔ Western Australia www.det.wa.edu.au/inclusiveeducation/detcms/portal
- ✔ New Zealand www.minedu.govt.nz

When schools don't meet your expectations

If you have any concerns about the education your child is receiving, there are issues with how your child is settling in, or any concerns at all with your child's school, make an appointment to see his teacher or principal. Talking it through may bring to light some issues you weren't aware of that you can address, or vice versa for the school.

If issues such as bullying or questionable standards of teaching continue and you still aren't happy with the school, it may be time to look at what other schooling options are out there that may be a better fit for your child.

Wherever your child goes to school, your attitude and role modelling are most important as a father. Keep reading to your child and encouraging him to do his homework, talk about his day and become a part of your child's education. You're still the most important part of his learning.

Complementary Education

Many people had a whole lot of extracurricular activities going on when they were growing up. Today there are more and more classes and courses that your child can do to complement the learning she does at school.

The best time to start on subjects like language and music is now. As they get older and don't have the absorbent brain they used to have, many adults have regretted not learning in their youth an extra skill such as music. But before you enrol junior into every class under the sun, ask her what she would like to do and follow whatever her interests are, rather than your own.

Languages

Languages other than English form part of the school curriculum depending on where you live. But the languages taught at your school may not be what your little champ wants to learn, or you may have a passion for a particular place and will be visiting there a lot, making learning that language important.

Depending on where you live, private tutors are available to teach your child a language other than English. Check with the following organisations if they conduct classes near you or can point you in the right direction:

- Te Reo Maori — Maori Language Commission www.koreromaori.co.nz
- French — Alliance Francaise
- Spanish — Instituto Cervantes
- German — Goethe Institute
- Embassies and high commissions
- The Correspondence School (in New Zealand)

Music

Starting school age is a great time to start learning to play an instrument. Your local paper or community noticeboard may have listings for local teachers.

✔ Australian Music Teacher Register www.amtr.com.au

✔ The Institute of Registered Music Teachers New Zealand www.irmt.org.nz

Start small. Don't expect your child to be able to handle a full drum kit or stand-up double bass just yet. Piano, guitar, violin and wind instruments may be up your child's alley. See what he would like to play. A great way to inspire junior is to go into a music store and show him the various instruments. Get the sales assistant to put on a show so he gets to see them in action.

Sport

Getting your child involved in the sport of his choice is a great way to keep him active, give him goals and show him how to play with others. Your child should decide which sport he wants to get involved with, because the main thing at this age is to enjoy the sport. If he's not sure or can't decide, watch some games, research the sport on the internet, or if you happen to know how, show him how the sport's played.

Sports can be organised through schools, or through the clubs in your town.

Get inspired by these sites:

✔ School Sport Australia www.schoolsport.edu.au

✔ Sport and Recreation (New Zealand) www.sparc.org.nz

Religious education

Some Australian states have an hour a week of non-compulsory special religious education. If your child's not going to a school associated with a particular religious denomination, you may want him to have religious education outside the school environment. These classes are generally organised by local churches or faiths, so they should be your first port of call.

Part V
What Happens When

Glenn Lumsden

'It used to worry me that my family didn't exactly fit the traditional mould ... until I realised that no-one else's family did either.'

In this part ...

Along with all the good things that come with being a father, you also need to know that sometimes fatherhood can put you in extraordinary circumstances. You may have decided to stay home with the kids, or your baby has an illness or injury, or you've separated from your partner and may be sharing care of your child.

Even more difficult is being faced with losing your baby to miscarriage, stillbirth, or a terminal disease or condition.

In this part, we guide you through coping with each of these extraordinary situations and offer you ways to manage the hardest problems a father has to face.

Chapter 16

Stay-at-home Dad

In This Chapter

▶ Understanding why stay-at-home dads are awesome

▶ Doing the hard yards as the number one caregiver

▶ Juggling working from home with your other full-time job of being a stay-at-home dad

*Y*ou and your partner have made a decision — and it's pretty radical. You're going to stay home with the baby while your partner heads back to work or study. You'll be the number one caregiver, taking care of your baby's needs for the majority of the time. You're about to board a new, scary rollercoaster and as any stay-at-home mum will tell you, a really rewarding one.

Stay-at-home dads (SAHDs) have yet to get much respect. Millions of years of mums being primary caregivers means some people may still find it a little weird for dads to stay home and look after bub. But the times, they are a-changin', and just as women pursue careers and take on formerly male-dominated roles, men can make a change to what was once firmly female territory.

In this chapter we give you a list of the reasons why dads make great primary caregivers — you may want to carry it around with you to shoot down any naysayers — and give you some food for thought on balancing your new full-time job with a little paid work on the side. We also give you the low-down on making the transition into your new role as smooth a ride as possible.

Daddy's in Da House

According to the Australian Bureau of Statistics, in 1983, 2.7 per cent of males aged 15–64 years who weren't employed said that their main activity was 'childcare/home duties'. Twenty years later in 2003, this proportion had risen to 6.6 per cent. Over the same period, the proportion of couple families where the husband was not in paid work while the wife was more than doubled, from 1.6 per cent to 4.0 per cent. Those numbers are still relatively low, but show that the phenomenon of the SAHD is on the increase.

Debunking some myths about guys as primary caregivers

Stay-at-home dads are a recent phenomenon and lots of people don't really understand what 'stay-at-home dad' means. They'll make judgements about you and your family, which can be hard to swallow sometimes. Here are some of the myths you may encounter:

✔ Fathers can't parent as well as mothers until their child is older.

✔ Fathers can't breastfeed babies, so the baby will miss out on breastmilk.

✔ Fathers can't handle looking after a baby without causing chaos in the house and leaving a mess wherever they go.

✔ Fathers won't be able to handle being a SAHD at all.

✔ Fathers will forget practical things like food, nappy changes and appropriate clothing.

✔ Fathers don't have a 'mother's intuition' and won't be able to tell if their child is unwell.

We say this is rubbish. Although fathers parent differently from mothers, it doesn't mean dad's way is wrong. To the sceptics, we say this:

✔ Showing love and wanting the best for their kids makes fathers just as qualified to look after their little ones as their mothers.

✔ Mothers can express breastmilk for dad to give feeds, or top up with formula if appropriate.

✔ Fathers can do everything mums can do, such as looking after the household in addition to looking after bub, even if they haven't been doing it for as long as mums.

✔ Dads make fantastic parents. Active father involvement has been linked to improved performance at school and fewer problems during teen years such as teen pregnancy or binge drinking.

✔ Fathers aren't thick. We can remember nappy changes and to do the washing. Nutting out our own way of doing things may take some work, but we get there.

✔ Fathers who spend time with their babies will learn everything there is to know about their little ones, and will be able to use their commonsense and the tips they learn in this book to tell when baby is ill.

✔ Guys are very practical and often good at things that mums struggle with (and vice versa of course). So dads have got lots of useful skills they can transfer to raising their offspring from an early age.

Coping with your new career

As dads in the 21st century, chances are you were brought up to be the breadwinner and to provide financially for your children. This gender role goes right back to the days of the caveman — men went out to bring home the mammoth. Going from a full-on career to staying home with a baby is a big change — ask any first-time mum how she coped with it! And as guys you don't have the physical changes of pregnancy to prepare for how weird the whole parenthood thing is. But that could also be a blessing of course!

Having a support system in place helps when it comes to your new career. Family, friends who have children and other men who can remind you it's not all about nappies, bottles and crying can all provide support.

Being out of the politics of your office, without a demanding boss or several people to report to, can be nice. You don't have any deadlines for reports or projects to manage. But on the other hand, the small new boss is a pretty demanding one, and if you don't get the work done right — if you don't burp that gas out, if you let her get overtired, or if you don't have enough formula on hand — you're going to be rapped over the knuckles pretty quickly. There is no clocking off at five o'clock, no-one to take over the late shift, and hardest of all, no sick leave. When you're the primary caregiver, the buck stops with you.

So how do you go from being a career man to being the main man? Remember that what you're doing is a privilege and doing so will bring you much closer to your little person than you could ever have imagined. Why would you ever want to go back to work? The time that your child is small is so short and he'll never be this age again. Looking after a baby or toddler is tough work and your career may have been important to you; however, there aren't many men out there who have the same opportunity to be this close to their children. Enjoy it!

You're never alone. Set up your own group of fathers and create a network of people you can call on. See our tips later in this chapter for networking as a SAHD. As a first port of call, check out www.diyfather.com/sahd.

Getting organised

Being organised when you have a child is essential. Having systems and routines in place that save you time and effort make life a lot easier, giving you time for the things you like to do rather than have to do.

Use your mobile phone to keep track of baby supplies, to-do lists, appointments and other jobs around the house. Most phones come with all the tools you need or you can download specific applications to keep track. Nothing like a gadget to keep you focused!

Checking every night at bedtime that you've got the essentials for the next day will prevent you finding you've run out of something really important.

Here's a quick run-down on the essentials that you may want to have on hand:

- ✔ Clean nappies
- ✔ Food, whether it be expressed breastmilk or formula for babies under six months, or solids and finger food for older babies
- ✔ Wipes or cloths for nappy changing
- ✔ Bum cream
- ✔ Any medicine or ointments your child needs
- ✔ At least two changes of clothes

If you get out and about a lot, which we recommend, keep the nappy bag stocked at all times so loading up the buggy and going isn't a big deal.

Always take your nappy bag with you everywhere. Even a short trip to do the grocery shopping may require a nappy change, or circumstances may mean you're away longer than you planned.

In the first few weeks of life, your baby may have a very busy appointment book — checkups with your midwife or doctor, vaccinations, child health nurse visits, or trips to a specialist. Keep a list or calendar of appointments in the early weeks so you don't forget. You'll be too tired to remember your own name, let alone when the nurse is coming.

Some SAHDs plan out their weeks well in advance with activities such as swimming, playgroup and music at the local library. Use technology, such as your computer, laptop or phone, to plan your activities. Mum will be very impressed when you show her the schedule on your iPhone or BlackBerry!

All that organisation may sound boring right now, but children keep things interesting and generally respond well to a change of plan. Even if you're adhering to a strict routine or schedule, children like to mix things up a bit. So what if you miss a swim lesson or don't make it to music? If something else turns up that means you'll have to change plans. It's not worth panicking over.

My Daddy Just Cares for Me

If you're the primary caregiver, the buck stops with you. Being primary caregiver is like being the head of a major corporation, only you have one very demanding, unforgiving, but utterly cute client who pays you in smiles and love.

Upskilling

Trying to figure out what your baby is saying to you when he arches his back, or screws up his face in a certain way, is daunting. It can be baffling when he's grumpy and cranky and nothing seems to settle him. You're not a bad father, you just don't have the skills to deal with each stage of your child's life yet. By the way, stay-at-home mums face the same challenges.

Figuring out what your baby is trying to communicate is a matter of finding out what you don't yet know. Fortunately, this is relatively easy these days! Parenting classes are available to help you decipher your baby's many cues and help you act on them. Parenting classes can also be an invaluable support network. You'll meet other dads, hear what they've been experiencing and get tips on how to deal with any issues you have with your fatherhood experience.

Another great way to upskill is to use our *Dad in a Minute* video tutorials at www.diyfather.com/diam. In addition to the video tutorial there are heaps of links to other useful sites that help you improve your skills. And of course, the many incredibly helpful chapters of this book will come in handy!

To find out about parenting courses in Australia go to www.community.gov.au/Internet/MFMC/Community.nsf/pages/section?opendocument&Section=Parenting%20Skills. For parenting courses in New Zealand check out www.plunket.org.nz/plunket-you/what-we-offer/parenting-education or www.parentscentre.org.nz/parenteducation/default.asp.

Healthy bodies and active minds

Just as your child needs food to grow her body, active movement and experiences feed her mind. When she was first born, her brain was about 15 per cent developed, but by three years of age, her brain's well on its way to being fully developed. The first three years in particular shape your child's life like no other period. By making a great connection with your child, giving her lots of opportunities to explore and learn, and lots of physical encouragement, you're doing the best job a dad can do.

All those little things children do when they play — feeling textures, judging distances, figuring out what's hot and cold, pouring water from one cup to another, and making those raucous noises and squeals — is all about practising skills that we adults have (almost) perfected. By offering lots of things to touch and play with, you're giving your child lots of opportunities to get some practice in for the real deal — growing up and adulthood. See our other chapters on specific age groups for ways to get active with kids.

To ensure your child's body stays as healthy as it can be, give your child lots of healthy and nutritious foods. You may also need to improve your cooking and baking skills in case you're not the natural-born Naked Chef. Remember the basics — avoid fatty, sugary foods, establish a feeding and eating routine, avoid distractions during eating and ensure bub gets lots of rest and good sleep. For more on nutrition see Chapter 14.

Keeping mum in the loop

In a busy household, where you're at home with your child and your partner is out at work, it's easy to fall into a trap where you're so absorbed by the hectic lives you lead you have no time for each other. You're tired from chasing after junior all day and can't wait to hand her over to your partner, who's exhausted from meetings and deadlines. You may fall into a trap of thinking that spending time with your child is a chore.

Remembering that the three of you need to spend time together as a family and enjoy each other's company is really important. If your partner is away at the office and your child does something that would be of interest to her, let her know — send her a text message or text an image of your child to her. Have the video camera around to capture any new words or milestones your child reaches when your partner isn't there. And when she comes home, rather than plonking the child on her lap the instant she walks through the door, have a family meal or a general catch-up on what the three of you have been doing all day.

As your child gets older, encourage him to do something special for his mum when she gets home, such as bringing her slippers or showing her a drawing he made.

Working from home

You may decide to be a SAHD who works from home. If you're used to working with a lot of people or in a busy environment, suddenly finding yourself at home with a child and a laptop to work with can be strange, lonely and a little boring. You may be tempted to make yourself a cup of coffee every ten minutes, or feel unmotivated because you don't have a work environment around you to keep that energy going. If you're not self-disciplined or motivated, chances are working from home is not going to be easy for you.

You can do things to stop yourself going mental, or being so lonely you invite the meter reader in for coffee:

- ✔ Have a routine for you and your child, so you can slot work in around when she sleeps. Having a structured routine allows you to more easily make appointments, schedule phone calls or take part in online meetings. If possible, be flexible to allow for those days when your child's unsettled.

- ✔ Don't be too ambitious with what you can achieve. You'll have days when you can't get any work done and other days when your princess is a dream who sleeps for hours at a time. Overcommitting yourself to your boss will just stress you out and make your fathering life more difficult.

- ✔ Give yourself a few hours each day to get out and about — go to a Babes in Arms movie session, go for a walk, or attend a planned activity like playgroup or swimming lessons. Most of all, use that time to see other people!

- ✔ If you have face-to-face meetings to attend, check ahead to see if you can take your child, or arrange for a sitter, friend or relative to cover for you.

- ✔ Be enthusiastic about the work you're doing. Otherwise you have to ask yourself is it worth the stress of trying to do your job *and* be a SAHD (which is also a full-time job)?

- ✔ Make a work space in your house that's just for your work. By having your own work space, you don't have to set up your gear every time you want to work. You're more likely to settle into productive work if you don't have to clear the breakfast dishes away from the dining table to work at it while bub is sleeping. When your child gets older, explain to him that this is daddy's office and not an indoor playground.

The Brotherhood of Dads

There's a reason why men in the armed services tend to call themselves bands of brothers — they look after one another as if they were blood relatives. The same can be kind of said about SAHDs — we're on the front line of parenting, taking the hits (dirty nappies), outwitting the enemy (playing chase), fighting the good fight (rough-housing) and going the extra mile (in the buggy, when junior won't go to sleep). The Brotherhood of Dads is all about camaraderie between fathers and ensuring that dads gather together and get through any good and bad times they might be experiencing.

Being at home means that you might become slightly isolated, but you can call on your brothers. See the following section for the various ways you can get in touch with the brotherhood.

Networking as a SAHD

So how do you find these mythical brothers, who are going to be your rocks when you need them? SAHDs are more common than they used to be, but they're still a rare beast, so keep your eyes peeled at the local library, music sessions, playgroups, coffee groups, or just stroll up to other blokes pushing buggies — you don't need an excuse to start a conversation. You can also ask your midwife or child health nurse if they have other SAHDs on their books.

Basically, just do what the mums do (but in a man kind of way). Get together with other SAHDs at a local coffee shop, go to child-friendly movie sessions, or take turns for meeting at home. Mums do this all the time and they are pretty good at it — no reason why dads can't network too. In fact many SAHDs are meeting all over the world. Check out our directory for SAHD and father support groups at www.diyfather.com/directories/global-fathers-support-group-directory.

Being the only guy in the room

As most primary caregivers are women, most of the activities that you take your child to, especially in his first year of life, are bound to be full of mums and babies. Being the only guy in the room can be a bit weird. Then again ... it can be really cool because you'll get lots of attention and in our experience, most mums love the fact that there is a SAHD in the group to add some variety and dad-perspective. You may even be overrun with mums keen to find out about the male approach to parenting. Single mums may be especially grateful for exposure to male parenting. So enjoy the attention and show you can keep up with the best of the mums!

Chapter 17

Serious Illness and Losing Your Baby

In This Chapter

▶ Giving your baby the best start in life

▶ Dealing with serious illness and injury

▶ Shedding light on terminal illness

▶ Getting through — how to cope when a child dies

*I*n an ideal world, we wouldn't be writing this chapter and you wouldn't be reading it. Your child should always be well, happy and carefree. But unfortunately, life's not that simple. Children do get ill, they get hurt and sometimes they die.

When a person close to you dies, it's heartbreaking. But it just doesn't seem right that children should die before their parents — it's not the natural order of things. In our culture, we tend to measure the impact of a tragedy against others — that a sudden death is worse than a gradual one, that a miscarriage is less painful than losing a child at birth. In reality, that child's loss will be felt greatly by his parents, no matter what the age or how it happens.

Sometimes illness is unavoidable, sometimes it isn't. In this chapter, we show you ways to minimise the risk of illness, starting with pregnancy, and how to cope should serious illness strike. Lastly, we discuss terminal illness and getting through the unthinkable — when a child dies.

Avoiding Health Problems

What you put in your body plays a big part in your health. Making your home a smoke-free environment and eating nutritious meals go a long way towards staying healthy (see Chapter 3 for more about healthy eating during pregnancy).

Protecting against diseases

Having your child immunised against diseases like whooping cough, meningitis and diphtheria protects her from these illnesses, which can cause death or serious long-term harm to a child. Talk to your child's GP about the right ages to have her vaccinated.

Providing a violence-free home

Shaking your baby or hitting your young child may cause serious physical harm or death in extreme cases. The message is simple — never, ever shake your baby and consider smack-free discipline.

Beyond the physical harm shaking and hitting can cause, in the first years of your child's life he's learning to form a safe and secure attachment to you, his father, and this attachment plays a big part in how well he'll act and form relationships as an adult. If you're violent towards him, chances are he'll be a violent person himself.

If you're at the end of your tether and just feel like making your baby or child shut up, take a deep breath and count to ten, or leave him in a safe place and get some air for a minute. Stress is the distance between the situation in front of you and how well you think you can deal with that situation. Tell yourself you can do it and see how much better you'll feel.

If you're often angry at your child, your partner, or the situations you're in, it may be time to get help dealing with your emotions.

In Australia, see Relationships Australia www.relationships.com.au who have links to courses in your state or territory. In New Zealand, contact Relationship Services www.relate.org.nz who can counsel you in anger management techniques.

Keeping accidents at bay

Keeping your child physically safe around your home, in the street and in your car is also really important. See Chapter 7 on child-proofing your home and Chapter 4 for car seat safety.

Keep your child safe around roads by teaching her to hold your hand crossing the road on footpath crossings, when you're near driveways and to never go on the road without an adult.

A healthy start to life

Doesn't every child deserve the best start in life you can possibly give them? Keeping mum tanked up with healthy food, lots of fresh air and gentle exercise from when you first know you're going to be a dad goes a long way towards keeping your baby healthy in the long run.

Risks during pregnancy

Creating a whole new person is an enormous task and pregnancy can make a woman's body vulnerable to infection and conditions such as high blood pressure. It's also important to consider the effects on the developing baby of what your partner eats and is exposed to.

If your partner has any chronic health issues, such as diabetes or asthma, make sure both of you are happy with the way that your carer is monitoring the progress of the pregnancy. If not, find a carer you *are* happy with.

These are some of the things your partner should be aware of during her pregnancy:

- ✔ **Smoking:** Pregnancy is a great time to take the plunge and quit smoking. Poisons from the smoke are passed to the baby through the placenta. Babies born to mothers who smoke are at risk of developing breathing problems, having a lower birth weight and being twice as likely to die from SIDS (Sudden Infant Death Syndrome, also known as cot death). However, quitting smoking is tough and not made much easier by having a preachy dad-to-be around, or one who is continuing to smoke himself. Instead, give your partner your wholehearted support and contact a helpline in your area, not just for your partner, but for both of you to quit smoking.

  If you want to give up smoking, call these numbers for help and advice:

  • Quitline in Australia www.quitnow.info.au or phone 131 848

  • Quitline in New Zealand www.quit.org.nz or phone 0800 778 778

✔ **Alcohol:** Experts are unsure of what a 'safe' level of alcohol is for pregnant mums, so it's best to avoid all alcohol. *Foetal alcohol syndrome* is caused by alcohol crossing the placenta and affecting the baby's developing brain. Children with foetal alcohol syndrome can have problems with learning, concentration, hyperactivity and speech.

✔ **Chickenpox:** When we're kids, chickenpox (also called varicella) is much like any other illness, and the only long-lasting effect of the disease may be a few pock scars. But in adults, chickenpox is a serious illness. If your partner gets chickenpox when she's pregnant, it can be transmitted to your growing baby. Though rare, the baby's development can be affected, causing limb deformities, mental retardation, or even miscarriage or stillbirth. If you haven't had chickenpox, consider being vaccinated now.

✔ **Listeriosis:** Pregnant women are much more vulnerable to an infection from bacteria living in certain foods, called listeria. The infection, listeriosis, can be caused by eating deli meats, soft cheeses, unpasteurised milk, unwashed fruit and vegetables, raw meat, pâté, ready-made salads, smoked seafood and smoked shellfish. It's best to avoid these foods while pregnant. Listeriosis can cause miscarriage and stillbirth.

✔ **Rubella (German measles):** If a pregnant woman contracts rubella it can seriously harm the developing baby, including severe mental retardation and blindness. Most women are vaccinated against rubella as teenagers, but if your partner hasn't been vaccinated and you're planning to get pregnant, talk to your GP about being vaccinated now.

Being vaccinated against rubella doesn't always guarantee a lifetime immunity against the virus. Women planning pregnancy should have their immunity status checked.

✔ **Toxoplasmosis:** This is an infection that can be caused by a bacteria living in the guts of animals. It can be carried in raw meat and in cat poo, so pregnant women should avoid dealing with kitty litter boxes, and take care when gardening as cats may have used the soil for a toilet. Cook all meat thoroughly.

It may be hard to find the right words if someone close to you experiences the loss of a child. Have a look at www.diyfather.com/content/miscarriage-what-to-say.

Breastfeeding

Encouraging and supporting breastfeeding in the first months of life boosts your baby's immunity and gives her the very best nutrition she needs to grow and thrive. Breastfeeding's difficult in the beginning, and your partner may be pretty exhausted and frustrated at times, so give her all the help you can.

Miscarriage

A miscarriage is the death of a baby before 20 weeks gestation. Many women don't even know they're pregnant when they miscarry, but many others lose much-wanted and cherished babies. In the past, people have had the attitude that miscarriages are something to be gotten over, that everything will be fixed by trying for another baby. Fathers in particular, who can often seem withdrawn or uncaring about the loss because men can be more private about the way they deal with grief, are encouraged to 'just get over it'. But for parents who lose babies it can often be devastating. You also feel you have to be strong for your partner and in a sense you do — you need to advocate for your partner at a time when she's confused, angry, vulnerable and grieving. But you also need to be empathetic and caring, and one way to do that is to talk openly about your feelings with your partner. You also need to acknowledge your feelings of loss and sadness, rather than pretend to keep a stiff upper lip.

Having a ceremony or funeral for your lost baby may be comforting and give you a chance to express your grief and let others support you. The ceremony can be anything from a few people lighting a candle, to a funeral with a minister. Just do what comes naturally to you and your partner. Naming your baby can also help you heal — acknowledging your baby as a real person, not a 'loss' or an 'it' can really help.

If you need to talk to someone outside your family and friends, support is available. You just have to ask for it.

In Australia:

The Bonnie Babes Foundation www.bbf. org.au or call 1300 266 643 to get in touch with a grief counsellor.

In New Zealand:

Miscarriage Support Auckland is a voluntary organisation working with families affected by miscarriage in Auckland www.mis carriagesupport.org.nz and has links to support groups in other parts of the country www.miscarriagesupport.org.nz/ contacts.html#nzgroup.

Birth options to reduce the risk of fatality

Approximately one per cent of babies die between 20 weeks gestation and up to 28 days after birth. This is referred to as a *perinatal* death. Most of these babies die because they're born too early and their bodies aren't developed enough for life outside the womb. Others die from congenital abnormalities and in some cases, there is no known reason. Completely normal, healthy pregnancies can end in stillbirths.

The World Health Organization and various UN agencies estimate that 11 in 1,000 Australian mothers die because of complications in pregnancy and childbirth. In New Zealand, the number is 5 in 1,000. We're lucky that we have access to good health-care facilities, skilled maternity carers and plenty of nutritious food for pregnant women and their growing babies.

To reduce the risk of complications during pregnancy and childbirth, find a carer you trust, whether it be an obstetrician, GP or midwife, and attend regular checkups with them. Your carer will monitor for conditions such as pre-eclampsia, gestational diabetes and other factors that may cause complications during pregnancy and childbirth. If you're not familiar with these terms, check the Glossary and read up on them.

Home birth

You may be wondering whether having your baby at home is riskier than having your baby in a hospital. While being nearer to medical facilities should something go wrong during your child's birth may help, babies can still die in hospitals with experienced carers, even after mum-to-be took great care of her health during pregnancy and excellent health care was provided to her during her pregnancy. We don't mean to put you off or frighten you, but there's no absolutely certain way to eliminate all risks.

Studies quoted by Home Birth Aotearoa have shown home births are just as safe, if not safer in some cases, for women who have had low-risk pregnancies. Home birth is a contentious issue in Australia. Talk with your carer about your birthing options.

But women with high-risk pregnancies, who are at risk of pre-term labour, have pre-eclampsia, gestational diabetes or any other medical complication during pregnancy are not advised to have a planned home birth.

Caesarean birth

You may think that avoiding a vaginal birth and the stress on baby and the mother's body may be the way to go, but there are risks associated with elective caesareans too. After all, a caesarean is major surgery and the mother may experience haemorrhaging and infection.

A 2007 British study also showed that babies born by caesarean can have breathing difficulties because fluid in the lungs is not squeezed out as it is in a vaginal birth. Emergency caesareans are performed when the condition of the baby or mother is deteriorating, such as *cord prolapse*, when the umbilical cord comes out of the uterus before the baby, blocking off his lifeline. In those cases you often don't have a choice about having an emergency caesarean because the life of the mother or child is at risk.

If your partner has had a textbook pregnancy, we suggest *not* worrying about the risks of fatality. Concentrate instead on creating a peaceful and calm environment for your baby to be born into, with lots of support for your partner. Relax and enjoy this momentous time in your life.

Reducing the risk of SUDI and SIDS

SUDI stands for Sudden Unexplained Death of Infants. In some cases, death is caused by smothering or some other known cause. SIDS is a type of SUDI and stands for Sudden Infant Death Syndrome, where the baby, for reasons unknown, stops breathing. It's thought babies who have been around cigarette smoke are more at risk. SIDS used to be commonly known as cot death.

There are some simple ways you can reduce your baby's risk of SUDI/SIDS:

- Keep your baby's environment smoke-free. If you both gave up smoking when your partner was pregnant your home will be smoke-free. If you still need help with quitting the habit, call the Quit helpline in your area (the contact details are earlier in this chapter).
- Sleep your baby on her back, not on her side or front.
- Keep your baby's cot or bassinet free from bumpers, duvets and doonas, cuddly toys and sheepskins that could smother her.
- If you do share your bed with your baby (known as co-sleeping) only do so when neither you nor your partner has been drinking or is excessively tired to avoid the risk of rolling onto your baby. Co-sleeping is also safe only if you haven't been smoking because exposure to smoke puts your baby at risk.

You can buy baskets that allow you to co-sleep with your child and prevent you rolling onto her or smothering her with a blanket. Check with your local baby supply store.

If you're worried about your baby's risk of SUDI or SIDS consider buying an advanced baby monitor that constantly checks the baby's heartbeat and breathing. Check your local baby supply store for these monitors.

The following sites have more about SUDI and SIDS:

- Change for our children www.changeforourchildren.co.nz
- DIYFather www.diyfather.com/SUDI
- SIDS and Kids www.sidsandkids.org

Calling all dads — creating a healthy and safe home

Keeping up to date with household chores while looking after a small child can sometimes seem like taking one step forward, two steps back. You wash and clean all the nappies, only to have junior need changing twice as often. Or he's suddenly power-spewing all over the place. You may have your hands full just tending to bub. But washing your hands after nappy changes, cleaning up spew or dealing with laundry is absolutely essential, and will help cut down the risk of bacterial infection from nappies and stomach bugs. You can also:

- Have a bottle of hand steriliser in your nappy bag.
- Empty rubbish bins with disposable nappies and wipes in them regularly — at least once a day.
- Wash toys regularly. Most plastic toys can be scrubbed in a basin, while soft toys can go in the washing machine.
- To reduce the risk of respiratory infections caused by damp, dusty houses, air your rooms regularly.
- Keep baby's room at a temperature of 19 degrees Celsius, as recommended by the World Health Organization, and avoid any draughts.
- Avoid tummy bugs by not reheating food for your child that's been in the fridge more than 24 hours. Cook fresh food, or food that's been safely frozen and thawed. If you need to keep food in the fridge, make sure it's covered; for example, with cling wrap.
- Check the child-proofing you've made in your house (see Chapter 7 for more).

Coping with Illness and Injury

Having a sick or injured baby or child is no fun. As well as feeling pretty darn terrible, your child may have trouble understanding what's wrong with him, not be able to communicate well with you about what's wrong, and be scared of the treatments he's receiving.

Spotting injury

It can be hard when your child is constantly getting bumps and bruises to tell when something is going on that can't just be fixed with a plaster and a cuddle. So how do you figure it out? And what do you do if it's more serious than you first thought?

First of all, stay calm. Reach for the first aid kit and let us show you the way.

- ✔ **Broken bones:** Your child will let you know he's snapped something because he'll be in a lot of pain — much more than usual. You may even be able to see how the limb is broken. The area may swell or bruise immediately. Keep your child as still as possible and support the broken limb. Weight on the limb will make it more painful. Get to the accident and emergency department of your local hospital as soon as you can. If your child can't move, or you think he shouldn't be moved, such as in the case of a spine or neck fracture, call an ambulance.

- ✔ **Burns and scalds:** Run cold water on a burn for 20 minutes. If your child has scalded himself with hot liquid, take his wet clothes off as the heat in the liquid will continue to burn his skin. If material is sticking to the skin, don't try to take it off. If the burn is serious and you see redness and blistering, get someone to call an ambulance while you take care of your child. Once you've finished pouring cold water over the area, cover it with a clean cloth or tea towel and see your doctor. Your child will probably be very cold from the cold water, so make sure they're dressed warmly.

- ✔ **Concussion:** A bump to the head can result in more than just a lump and bruise. Concussion is a temporary loss of brain function, from the brain banging against the skull. Your child may have hit his head so hard he lost consciousness, or has a headache, seems disoriented and may vomit repeatedly. Being irritable and sensitive to light can also be a sign of concussion. Take your child to the hospital immediately.

If in doubt about anything to do with your child's health, it's better to be safe than sorry, so visit your GP. For any of the following injuries, get yourself to the hospital quickly:

- ✔ Anaphylactic shock from food or bee sting, where the face or mouth swells and your child has trouble breathing

- ✔ Bite from a snake, spider or another animal

- ✔ Car accident

- ✔ Convulsions

- ✔ Eye injuries

- ✔ Electric shocks

- ✔ Swallowing poisons, toxic material or prescription medicines that were not prescribed for your child

Emergency phone numbers

In Australia:

- ✔ Ambulance 000 or 112 from a mobile

- ✔ HealthDirect (ACT, NSW, NT, SA, TAS, WA) 1800 022 222 (24 hours, seven days a week)

- ✔ Nurse-on-call (VIC) 1300 60 60 24 (24 hours, seven days a week)

- ✔ 13 HEALTH (QLD) dial 13 HEALTH or 12 43 25 84 (24 hours, seven days a week)

- ✔ Poisons Information Hotline 13 11 26 (24 hours, seven days a week)

- ✔ Parentline (NT and QLD only) 13 22 89 www.parentline.com.au (8.00 am to 10.00 pm, seven days a week) to talk about any concerns regarding parenting and children. This line is completely anonymous.

- ✔ Swine Flu Emergency Hotline 18 02 007 (24 hours, seven days a week) www.healthemergency.gov.au

In New Zealand:

- ✔ Ambulance 111

- ✔ Healthline 0800 611 116 (24-hour health service)

- ✔ Plunketline 0800 933 922 (24-hour phone service for parents and caregivers of young children)

First aid kit

Keep a well-stocked first aid kit to deal with injuries. If you haven't got a first aid kit, see Chapter 4, where we give you a run-down on first aid essentials.

If you haven't done so, consider taking an infant and child first aid and CPR course. It can literally save the life of your child or the lives of others. If you haven't done a general CPR course for a while, getting a refresher by attending an infant and baby CPR course may also be a good idea.

Diagnosing a serious illness

All some children have to deal with health-wise are colds, the odd ear infection or a tummy bug. But some unfortunate children have to cope with much worse. As an involved dad you'll probably spot the first signs of a serious illness, because you know your child inside out and can tell when something's not right.

It takes a doctor's diagnosis to confirm when your child has a *chronic* illness, such as asthma and diabetes, a genetic disorder, or a disease such as cancer. Seeing your little child being admitted to hospital is stressful and heartbreaking, but fortunately lots of support is available.

Your child may be very frightened or blaming herself for the chaos her illness is causing in your lives. Try to be as open and honest with her as you can about her health and how you feel, and be available to answer any questions she puts to you.

The following organisations can help you in the event of your child being diagnosed with a serious illness. Don't be afraid to ask for help if you need it — think of the good it might do your child.

In Australia:

- ✔ Cancer Connection 13 11 20 www.cancerconnections.com.au
- ✔ Kids with Asthma www.kidswithasthma.com.au

In New Zealand:

- ✔ Child Cancer Foundation www.childcancer.org.nz
- ✔ Asthma Foundation www.asthmafoundation.org.nz/children.php
- ✔ Diabetes New Zealand www.diabetes.org.nz/home
- ✔ Cystic Fibrosis New Zealand www.cfnz.org.nz

Preparing for the End

To learn that your precious child has a life-limiting illness is possibly the toughest thing you may have to go through in your life. Anger, confusion, denial, helplessness, despair — you may experience every negative emotion you can imagine. Staying strong for your child when you feel like falling apart will be hard, but with little steps you *can* do it. Take things one day at a time.

Taking care till the end

Some may think it's a good idea not to frighten a child with a terminal illness with the knowledge that he's going to die. But *palliative care* professionals — those who care for people at the end of their lives — say communicating with your child honestly and openly will help allay some of his fears rather than cause them. Your child may be very confused about what's going on, and talking honestly and planning for the future can help put your child's mind at rest. He may be concerned about why you and your partner are so sad, may blame himself for your sadness, or be worried about his pets or schoolwork. Reassure him that it's not his fault that you're upset and be open to answering any questions he may have.

For inspiration, have a look at an amazing blog that documents the journey of Kyah, who passed away after a 500-day battle against cancer at the age of nearly three: kyahsjourney.livejournal.com.

Talk to your health care team about palliative care options for your child. Care can be at home, in hospital or in a children's hospice (in Australia only). These health professionals can help you talk to your child about what he's facing in an age-appropriate manner.

These ideas may also help you get through this seemingly impossible time:

- ✔ Enlist the support of family and friends to help with tasks like laundry, food preparation, feeding pets and so on. They can also babysit your other children if you have them, when you need to be at the hospital or hospice.

- ✔ Look after yourself, rest and eat well when you can.

- ✔ Talk to counsellors or chaplains at your hospital. Your care team can put you in touch with them. Involve your partner and other children if you like.

✔ Find out if there are any special activities your child would like to do. Perhaps you can take a trip to the beach together as a family, or visit a special place together.

✔ Write in a journal, take photographs and revisit old photographs with your child. Make memories.

✔ Cry, shout, stamp your feet. It's okay to be angry, to need time to yourself and to grieve.

✔ Don't let anyone hurry you into making any decisions about anything. Take your time and do things at your own pace.

Where to care for your little one

Palliative care is specialised care for people who have a terminal or life-limiting illness. Palliative care professionals not only take into account the stages that the body goes through as it shuts down, but also how the patient and her family are coping and dealing with this most traumatic event. For adults, most palliative care takes place in a hospital or hospice, which is a special facility for palliative care.

Hospices

Hospices sound like they are scary places, but the staff make every effort to make them comfortable, safe places for families in times of great stress, and crying out loud in a corridor is considered quite normal!

There are two hospices in Australia just for children — Bear Cottage in Sydney and Very Special Kids in Melbourne. Both are specially set up to deal with children and their families in a warm, loving environment where kids' needs come first. They often organise activities for kids with their families. At the time of writing, there are no hospice facilities specifically for children in New Zealand.

See more about these hospices at their websites:

✔ Bear Cottage www.bearcottage.chw.edu.au

✔ Very Special Kids www.vsk.org.au

The Cancer Society of New Zealand (www.cancernz.org.nz) and Cancer Council Australia (www.cancer.org.au) can provide information and support. In New Zealand, general health information, as well as specific information about palliative care for children, can be found at kidshealth.org.nz.

Home

Of course, you can also consider caring for your child at home, with assistance from palliative care workers, depending on the type of illness or injury your child has, and which services are available to you.

You may be overwhelmed by having to make a decision about where your child will spend her last days. Take your time. Talk it through with your partner. Don't hurry into a decision.

Letting family and friends know

Dealing with the devastating news that your child has a life-limiting illness is hard enough without having to tell friends and family. Ultimately this is something only you'll know how to do and when the time is right to tell others.

Once you have told them, people will usually be only too happy to help out with any errands that need to be done, cooking, laundry and the like, which may be in the too-hard basket for you right now.

If it's just too hard to tell people, perhaps you could tell someone in your immediate family who can do this for you. Don't force yourself to do anything you don't want to do right now. Just getting through each moment is challenging enough.

You may have to break the news to your other children or nieces and nephews, and here we give you some pointers:

- ✔ Be honest. Only tell your children what you believe to be true.

- ✔ Be somewhere safe, with the mobile phone off, the phone off the hook and with the children's full attention.

- ✔ Anticipate that there will be tough questions to answer, but answer them as honestly as you can. Trying to soften the blow may mean your children are upset even more when things get messy.

- ✔ Give small pieces of information that the children can chew over. They don't need to know all the ins and outs of cancer treatment, or anything too detailed.

- ✔ It may take a while for the information to get through. Give the children time to digest what they've heard, and be available to answer any other questions they may have in the coming days and weeks.

- ✔ Give lots of cuddles, and let your children know it's okay to be upset.

- ✔ Reassure your children that it's not their fault that this is happening to their sibling or cousin.

Seeking help

You'll have a lot of questions and be feeling all over the place. Knowing there's someone there who can guide you and your partner through your grief helps. While everyone grieves in a different way, it can help to talk it through with people who can share their knowledge and help you on your journey.

These organisations can help:

In Australia:

- ✔ The Compassionate Friends in Sydney www.thecompassionate friends.org.au; 02 9290 2355

- ✔ Healing Heart for Bereaved Parents www.healingheart.net

- ✔ The Bonnie Babes Foundation www.bbf.org.au

- ✔ SANDS (Stillbirth and Newborn Death Support) www.sands.org.au

- ✔ SIDS and Kids www.sidsandkids.org

- ✔ National Association of Loss and Grief www.nalag.org.au

In New Zealand:

- ✔ Skylight 0800 299 100; www.skylight.org.nz

- ✔ National Association of Loss and Grief www.nalag.org.nz

- ✔ SANDS (Stillbirth and Newborn Death Support) www.sands.org.nz

Dealing with the Unthinkable

When a child dies, we lose more than a person we loved — we lose the promise that person brought with him. It can threaten our identity as fathers. We blame ourselves, because as fathers we're supposed to protect our children and look after them, ensuring they're well. The death of a child cannot be approached rationally. You can only acknowledge your feelings and thoughts, many of which may not make any sense.

What to do, what not to do

Men grieve differently from women, so while our partners may find it easy to go to friends or family for support, it may not be so easy for you (or vice versa). It may take a little longer for some dads to really process feelings or some may not know how life is supposed to carry on without their child. Here are some suggestions for getting through this difficult time:

- ✔ Talk to your partner — even if it's just to say you don't want to talk. Let her know you need some space, or a hug, or to just sit together.

- ✔ Being physical can help. Go for a long walk, a bike ride, or play some sport. Being outdoors close to nature can be restorative and help you process your feelings too.

- ✔ Try not to let yourself become isolated. Sure, you want space, but shutting everyone out is not going to help you in the long run. Let people know you need space for a bit.

- ✔ Keeping busy really works for some guys who are grieving. Creating a memorial, or starting a project can distract you from the all-encompassing nature of grief.

- ✔ Try to look after yourself. Eat, sleep and shower. Though they may make you feel good in the short term, avoid drugs and alcohol.

Saying goodbye

Take time with your baby to say goodbye, to hold him, and to let other members of your family see and hold him too. You can ask your funeral director to arrange to have photographs of your baby taken by a tasteful, sensitive photographer. You'll probably feel a bit hesitant about this, but it can be a healing experience for you to look back and remember holding your child.

There's a good reason most cultures have a funeral tradition — the ritual of saying goodbye to a loved one who has died is a very powerful and healing process. Funerals encourage us to confront our grief and to express how we feel about our loved one. A funeral also marks that child's place among her family.

When a baby is stillborn (dies *in utero* after 20 weeks gestation) or dies shortly after birth, the law requires that a funeral must take place and that the baby be buried in a cemetery or cremated. In Australia, some hospitals can arrange the funeral for you, but SANDS (Stillbirth And Newborn Death Support) recommend having a family arranged funeral as hospital arranged funerals sometimes take control out of the family's hands, leaving the family little choice about what happens at the funeral, or even when the funeral's held.

For your baby's funeral, consider music to be played, songs, readings and poems to be read. You can have your baby's funeral at home, and can transport your baby from the hospital, home and to the cemetery.

There's no hurry to do anything. Don't feel forced into doing anything you don't want to do. Take your time and decide when you feel you're ready.

For more help, see www.sands.org.au in Australia, or www.sands.org.nz in New Zealand. The organisation provides peer-to-peer counselling — that's people who have been through the death of a baby supporting others.

Is there such a thing as 'moving on'?

Each parent and person grieves differently for the child they've lost. The term 'moving on' implies that the intensity of feeling you had for the child you've lost fades and the significance of that child also fades. Organisations helping parents grieve report that no parent ever forgets the loss of a child. Some parents report that for them, they haven't moved on, but the way they feel is different. The child they've lost, whether he be 12 weeks gestation, stillborn, or a teenager when he died, is still a big part of his parents' lives and a part of their family, and they celebrate the impact he had on their hearts.

Chapter 18

Disabilities, Disorders and Special Conditions

In This Chapter

▷ Discovering your child has a disability

▷ Starting your journey as dad to a child with a disability

▷ Adapting to living with a child with a disability

*E*very father wants his child to be happy and healthy. Fathers want their children to experience everything, to have every opportunity and to be able to do anything they want to do. But for some children, that world of possibilities is limited by illness, injury, or an inherited disorder or condition.

Although medical science and technology can help improve the mobility, hearing and sight of a disabled child, and our more enlightened society can give children with disabilities the same rights and advantages that non-disabled children have, it's still a hard road for many dads.

But where to start? How do you discover your child has a disability? And what do you do about it? Once you have a diagnosis, what do you do then? In this chapter, we offer some suggestions along the way, with tips for finding help, knowing your speech pathologist from your occupational therapist, and give you a heads-up on how having a child with a disability may change your lifestyle.

What Is a Disability, Anyway?

A *disability* is a condition, disorder or disease that disables the person from taking part in one or more life activities. The disability stops the person from doing what other people can do, whether it be walking, listening, grasping ideas, or talking. Disabilities can be physical or mental. Children with disabilities are sometimes called *special needs* children.

Knowing when something is wrong with your baby

Some children are born with a noticeable disability. Congenital abnormalities (also known as birth defects) or genetic disorders that manifest themselves physically, such as Down Syndrome, will be pretty obvious when the child is born. These problems may have been picked up during the pregnancy.

But other disabilities aren't so obvious and it may be a while before they make themselves known. Disabilities such as visual and hearing impairment, learning disabilities and autism won't be apparent for months, sometimes years.

Sometimes you can just tell when something's not right. Perhaps your baby doesn't recognise toys or shapes, perhaps he doesn't seem to hear or respond to your voice the way other babies respond to their dads. Perhaps he doesn't try to crawl or move when other kids his age are already running. Or perhaps it's just a feeling you get, your intuition telling you things aren't quite right.

Your first port of call should be your child health nurse, Well Child provider, or GP. Discuss your concerns and see if you can be referred to a specialist such as a paediatrician or psychologist to pinpoint what the problem might be. If your GP or child nurse tries to fob you off with an 'I think he looks fine', and you're sure he's not, stand your ground. Your child isn't able to stick up for himself the way you are. Your job is to advocate for your child and get him the help you feel he needs. If you don't trust and have confidence in your GP or child nurse to take your concerns seriously, try another GP until you find one you feel comfortable with.

It may pay to track your child's progress before going to see your child nurse or GP, so you have something concrete to show them when you have your appointment. Keep doing this until you've spoken to a specialist and have decided on a course of action or had a diagnosis made.

Waiting for a diagnosis can be incredibly stressful, but try to stay positive for your little one. Don't blame yourself or your partner for any perceived problems — neither of you is at fault.

Once a diagnosis is made, you and your specialist can decide on a course of action and get your child started on medication or treatment if required.

Physical disabilities

A physical disability is a permanent disability that restricts body movement or mobility in some way. Some physical disabilities are caused by genetic disorders, a *congenital abnormality* or birth defect that has developed while growing in the womb, an illness such as meningitis, or as the result of an injury to the spine, brain or limbs.

The main forms of physical disability include:

- **Brain and spinal injuries:** These injuries are mainly caused by an accident which breaks or damages the spinal cord, or causes damage to the brain. They can cause paralysis or mental impairment.

- **Cerebral palsy:** This is a condition where parts of the brain are damaged either during pregnancy, during birth, or as the result of a lack of oxygen.

- **Disabilities of the senses:** Children can be born with visual or hearing impairments because of congenital abnormality or a genetic disorder. These senses can also be affected by disease after birth.

- **Muscular dystrophy:** This is a genetic disorder in which muscle strength and function deteriorate over time. Most commonly seen in babies and young boys, some forms aren't diagnosed until early adulthood. Duchenne muscular dystrophy is the most common form and it affects mainly boys (Duchenne muscular dystrophy is rare in girls). About one-third of those affected also have some sort of learning difficulty. Not only are muscles in the limbs affected, but also heart muscles, which eventually affects life expectancy.

- **Spina bifida:** A congenital abnormality, which means it happens while the baby is growing in the womb, spina bifida literally means 'split spine' and happens in the early weeks of pregnancy. As the spine develops, vertebrae grow and close around the spinal cord, protecting it. In the case of spina bifida, the vertebrae don't close completely and in some types of spina bifida, the spinal cord and *meninges* (a system of membranes which envelop the central nervous system) protrude from the back. As a result, the spinal cord can be damaged and messages sent to and from the brain get confused. Paralysis, incontinence, loss of sensation and a build-up of fluid on the brain called *hydrocephalus* can occur.

To find out more about any of these physical disabilities, see these websites.

In Australia:

- ✔ Cerebral Palsy Australia www.cpaustralia.com.au
- ✔ Muscular Dystrophy Foundation Australia mdaustralia.org.au
- ✔ Vision Australia www.visionaustralia.org/info.aspx?
- ✔ Deaf Children Australia www.deafchildrenaustralia.org.au
- ✔ Australian Association for Families of Children with a Disability www.aafcd.org.au

In New Zealand:

- ✔ What Everybody Keeps Asking About Disability Information www.weka.net.nz — a general website for people with disabilities and their carers
- ✔ Royal New Zealand Foundation of the Blind www.rnzfb.org.nz
- ✔ National Foundation for the Deaf www.nfd.org.nz
- ✔ Parents of the Visually Impaired www.pvi.org.nz
- ✔ CCS Disability Action www.ccsdisabilityaction.org.nz

Australia also has associations in individual states and territories that you can find on the internet using a search engine.

Intellectual disabilities

Just as congenital abnormalities and genetic disorders can affect a child's body, so they can also affect a child's intellectual abilities — the ability to think, reason, communicate, control emotions and grasp ideas. Increasingly people with intellectual disabilities are being integrated into mainstream society, where they're appreciated for their individual attributes rather than judged by their disability.

Some intellectual disabilities can be diagnosed at birth, or even before. Others won't be obvious until your child is a few years old, or at school.

Some of the most common syndromes and disorders that can cause intellectual disability include the following.

✔ **Autism**, which is also known as autism spectrum disorder because the range of severity differs from person to person. A person with autism may have trouble making sense of the world, and find it difficult to communicate, cope in social situations, or control his emotions. Autism New Zealand estimates that autism is four times as common as cerebral palsy and 17 times as common as Down Syndrome. The causes of autism are unknown.

✔ **Down Syndrome**, which is caused by an extra bit of chromosome being replicated in cell division very early on after the mother's ovum has been fertilised, means that a child with Down Syndrome has an extra chromosome in his body. Children with Down Syndrome have varying degrees of mental and sometimes physical disability.

Intellectual disability can also be caused by drinking, drug abuse or illness during pregnancy, an infection like meningitis, head injuries, a lack of oxygen during birth or during an accident like a near-drowning. There are also other rare genetic conditions like Prader-Willi Syndrome that cause intellectual disability.

With a very small child, doctors and health professionals often use the term *developmental delay* rather than labelling the child as intellectually disabled.

For more about specific intellectual disabilities, see these websites.

In Australia:

✔ Autism Spectrum Australia `www.autismspectrum.org.au`

✔ The Brain Foundation site has links to common and not so common brain disorders, with support information. `www.brainaustralia.org.au/AZ_of_Brain_Disorders`

In New Zealand:

✔ Autism New Zealand `www.autismnz.org.nz`

✔ Down Syndrome Association `www.nzdsa.org.nz/index.htm`

✔ IHC, a general organisation for those with an intellectual disability `www.ihc.org.nz`

Multiple disabilities

Most disorders, illnesses or injuries are rarely limited to only one part of the body, so in some cases a child with a particular problem will have more than one disability. For example, Down Syndrome affects cognitive abilities as well as physical growth. Children with Down Syndrome also have a higher risk of having congenital heart defects, recurrent ear infections and thyroid dysfunctions as well as other conditions.

Getting formal confirmation

In some cases, the specialist you've been referred to will be able to tell you if your child has a specific disability or a range of disabilities and may be able to tell you how the disabilities were caused.

In other cases, a diagnosis isn't clear and your child may continue to undergo tests, which can be a fairly traumatic time.

Once you have confirmation about a disability it's time to put a plan in place to manage the condition, through medication, physical treatment or getting any equipment you may need like a wheelchair. In some situations you'll be given a case worker to help you.

Support groups and organisations for almost every condition, illness and disability that exists are available. Contact the organisations listed earlier in this chapter, or consult your specialist or care worker. Having support from people who've been through what you're going through now, who may be able to share information and strategies, or help you get access to specialist services is invaluable. Sometimes even just knowing that you are not alone with a condition and discussing what it was like for other parents can be a huge help.

What comes next?

You're in for yet another journey as part of your fatherhood experience. Treatment, therapy and learning about the fathering your special needs child will probably require takes some extra effort. This is also a huge opportunity for your own personal growth and development to become an amazing father.

We've come across a number of inspiring stories from fathers with disabled children and some are published on DIYFather.com. They generally all say that looking after a disabled baby and child in many ways is no different from looking after a non-disabled child. Babies and children with disabilities all cry, laugh, eat, soil their nappies and want to be loved. When dealing with the limiting factors of their children's condition, these dads have often challenged doctors or therapists about their expectations of what children with a particular disability may or may not be able to do. Often parents have managed to achieve amazing results with their children by finding alternative ways around barriers that have allowed their children to participate in what life has to offer, just like any other child would.

Here are some general tips on living with a child with a disability for both you and your family:

- Work with your child's strengths and likes. What does your child like doing? You can incorporate dancing, art, footy and water play into your child's therapy or treatment plan. Does she like to be hands-on? Or does your child need a strict routine to give her security? Being aware of the way your child learns best and the routines she needs is a key dad-skill to develop.

- Involve your child whenever you can with simple tasks like food preparation, doing the vacuuming, or making the bed. Break instructions down into simple bite-sized pieces and give heaps of praise for her efforts.

- Get support. There are a lot of support organisations out there that can put you in touch with other fathers and guide you to find funding, treatments and even respite care.

- Give lots of praise for your child when she accomplishes a new skill or takes on a new challenge.

- Focus on the things your child can do, rather than what she can't.

- Learn as much as you can about your child's disability. Knowledge is power.

- Have realistic expectations about your child's development, but challenge any preconceived limitations people place on your child about what she can and can't do. Perhaps there's a way she can accomplish a task — after all, you know your child best.

Help, My Child is Disabled!

You've had confirmation that your child is disabled. This can bring out all sorts of frustrations and disappointments and you may keep these emotions pretty tightly under wraps for the moment. That's fine, but it may also feel good to let it all out with someone who has been in a similar situation.

Imagining the hard road ahead of you can be devastating and you may even blame yourself for whatever the problem is. But another way to look at your child's disability is as a way to motivate yourself to help your child develop to her full potential.

Adjusting your expectations

When you first find out you're going to be a father, thinking of your child as a way to fix all the things that went wrong in your own life, or wanting your child to have more opportunities or career options than you did, is tempting. Perhaps you imagined your child becoming an astronaut, concert pianist or anything that she may dream of being.

So it takes a bit of getting used to the idea that your blind child will never see the world, your face or his own children (unless there are amazing leaps forward in technology). But then again, would Stevie Wonder have become the amazing artist he is if he wasn't blind? You never know what's in store for your offspring, which is really no different from the experience all other parents have.

Going into fatherhood, we also expect that our children will grow up and one day leave home. It may not be possible for children with a severe intellectual disability who need one-on-one care, 24 hours a day, to live an independent life. This can take quite a while to sink in, so cut yourself some slack and allow emotions and frustration to come and go.

Disabled in one way — very able in others

Disabled is a misleading term. For one thing, it defines a person by what he's not able to do.

What do we most remember about Beethoven, Louis Braille, or Stephen Hawking? They've all achieved incredible things, far beyond what many able-bodied folk have done! The great composer Beethoven gradually went deaf, but was still able to create incredible music without any sense of hearing. Louis Braille was blinded by an accident as a young child and went on to create a way for the blind to read with their fingers. Stephen Hawking has a form of motor neurone disease called *amyotrophic lateral sclerosis* and was given only a few years to live when his condition was diagnosed in his early twenties (he's now in his late sixties). Hawking is wheelchair bound and needs a computer to communicate. Despite these limitations, he has produced groundbreaking work in the field of theoretical physics. Hawking writes about his experience of disability on his website www.hawking.org.uk.

Other famous people who have shown disability is no barrier to success include actress Marlee Matlin, who went deaf from a childhood illness; Helen Keller, who proved being deaf, blind and mute couldn't stop her getting a university degree; and though his legs were paralysed from polio, Franklin Roosevelt still became President of the United States.

But there are incredible things to be said for accomplishing things that are relevant to your child's world. The triumph of an autistic child who, with time, patience and the right support, is able to communicate her needs and ideas to a range of people, feels like a huge achievement, on par with any other milestone parents see their children accomplish.

And who's to say that your child won't be able to do what most experts think he can't do? You may find that your little one completely shatters your ideas of what it means to have a disability and achieves much more than you ever imagined.

Finding help, assistance and resources

Knowing where to go to find assistance is a minefield. Start with your case worker, paediatrician or GP, the support organisations listed earlier in this chapter, and the following resources.

In Australia:

- ✔ To find out about allowances for carers of children with disabilities, go to www.centrelink.gov.au/internet/internet.nsf/ payments/ca_child_eligible.htm. To learn about inclusion support programs and subsidies, check out www.mychild.gov.au/ inclusionsupportprogram.htm.
- ✔ Association for Children with a Disability is an organisation based in Victoria, but their advice is universal www.acd.org.au.
- ✔ My Time supports parents of children with disabilities through forums and links to specific sites for disabilities www.mytime.net.au.
- ✔ The Raising Children Network, supported by the Australian government and other agencies, has some great resources on bringing up a child with a disability raisingchildren.net.au/articles/raising_a_ child_with_a_disability.html.

Also see the health department in your state or territory for more information.

In New Zealand:

- ✔ To check if your child qualifies for subsidised help go to www.disabilityfunding.co.nz, or the Ministry of Health website NZ Support entitlements www.moh.govt.nz/disability.
- ✔ See the Office of Disability Issues for more about the government's approach to disability www.odi.govt.nz.
- ✔ Get in touch with other parents through this website for parents caring for a special needs child www.parent2parent.org.nz/start.htm.

Access for People with Disabilities

Now that you know what you're dealing with, it's time to get into solution mode — something dads are great at! You can shine as dad for your disabled child in numerous ways, such as by making a little ramp for the wheelchair or coming up with a computer program that assists your child's communication. No doubt you'll have many skills you can readily use to create a better experience for your baby and child.

Your special baby

You're bringing your baby home from the hospital for the first time. It should be a time of great excitement, but you're probably overwhelmed with the challenges of not only looking after a new, small human being, but a new small human being with special needs. These tips may help you get through this time:

✔ While you may still experience an emotional rollercoaster, try not to forget that you have a small child who needs all the love and nurturing you can give him as he becomes aware of his world. As for any newborn child, this time is fleeting, so take some time to admire those little fingers, those chubby little legs, and enjoy the new addition to your lives.

✔ Get family or close friends to support you, by perhaps fending off unwanted visitors, organising appointments with health workers, or just doing your laundry. Let someone look after you for a while, just as you need to look after your baby.

✔ Ask for help if you need it. There's no point in struggling on bravely because you can't ask for a hand. Plenty of people are around to help you.

✔ Keep records of health visits, of your baby's daily progress or any notes you need in one central place so you can grab them next time you need to talk to your health workers.

Working with health professionals

Some of the health professionals you might meet when caring for your special needs child include

✔ An *audiologist*, who assesses your child's hearing and can recommend treatment or hearing aids.

✔ An *occupational therapist*, or OT, who assesses how well your child is able to perform day-to-day tasks, like dressing or brushing teeth. She may also assess how you'll manage getting from place to place if transport is a bit more complicated with your little one. The aim of an OT is to help your child become involved in all aspects of day-to-day life, and increase his independence and wellbeing.

✔ A *psychologist*, who assesses your child's mental health and cognitive skills. Psychologists may help with strategies for managing emotional and behavioural problems.

✔ *Speech therapists* and *speech pathologists*, who assess how well your child can communicate with others, and figure out ways to either improve his speech, or find alternative ways of communicating, such as electronic devices or sign language.

Other health professionals you may need include physiotherapists, neurodevelopmental therapists and dietitians.

Living with a disability

It doesn't matter what the condition, illness, injury or syndrome your child has, finding out that your child is not the child you had hoped he would be can be devastating. On top of managing your own feelings and frustration you may also be sensitive to what other people's reactions are when they see your child. As with all feelings, give yourself time to work through them (rather than ignore or suppress them) and seek help if you need to. Most importantly, keep communicating with your partner, who's likely to be feeling the same thing.

Be aware of what triggers negative feelings, such as going to doctor's appointments or seeing friends' children. Then you can prepare yourself and work out strategies for coping with any negative emotions.

Living with a disabled child is often a bit more involved than living with an able-bodied child, but there are things you can do to make it easier.

✔ Do your own research. Knowledge is power. These days practically everyone has access to an amazing information resource — the internet. Find out if there are any devices, techniques or therapies that could help your child (or you) become more independent or make life easier.

✔ Set small achievable goals for your child, as you would any child. Pushing him too hard will only leave both of you frustrated.

✔ If your child is going to day care or school, talk to teachers and administration staff well in advance, so they can build ramps, obtain resources and apply for any special teacher aide staff that may be required.

✔ Keep in touch with teaching staff about your child's progress. This helps you, your child and the teachers, who can personalise a program for your child.

Changing your lifestyle

Having a child with a disability will probably mean you have to adjust your lifestyle to suit his needs.

✔ Depending on the level of care your child needs, you or your partner may have to give up working outside the home.

✔ If your child uses a wheelchair, you'll need to renovate your home to make doors wide enough to get the wheelchair through, install ramps rather than steps, and fit equipment for lifting the chair in and out of vehicles.

✔ With one less income and more expenses, your family may be under extra financial pressure, so seek out any subsidies or allowances you can from government agencies. See 'Finding help, assistance and resources' earlier in this chapter for links.

✔ You may need to go to more doctors' appointments and trips to the hospital. If you live far from a hospital, it may mean you need to move house to be closer to medical facilities.

✔ Some children need 24-hour, seven days a week care, which is hard work. You may need a dedicated carer or specialist assistance to organise care in your home.

If your child is disabled and needs a lot of care, you must take some time to take care of yourself and your partner. Talk to your health workers about respite care, or get support from family and friends so you have a little time off every now and then.

Sharing the love

If there's one word we've used over and over again in this book, it's *support*. Nothing beats having people to help share not only your problems, but also the love. When your child is disabled, small victories are to be had along the way. With other parents in similar situations, you have a whole lot more people to share those successes with.

Chapter 19

Divorce and Separation

. . . .

In This Chapter

▶ Saving a failing relationship — what you can do

▶ Realising that your marriage has gone under — what next?

▶ Coping as a single dad

▶ Looking after your children as the primary caregiver

▶ Explaining a new love in your life to your kids

. . . .

*H*aving a relationship these days is hard. You're expected to be all things to all people — your partners, families, friends, employers and children. This puts a lot of strain on you and your relationships. As a result some marriages and relationships won't survive the stresses of parenting, financial worry, the frenetic pace of life and the need for your own space.

A relationship failure is devastating, even more so when children are involved. As a father in this situation, life can feel pretty rough and frustrating. But being a great father doesn't end with your relationship.

You're the adult here, the dad, and where you have control and the power to make decisions for your family, your children don't. They may be confused, blaming themselves and frightened about what the future brings for them. They may be hoping you and their mother can patch things up. It's important to tread carefully, for their sakes.

In this chapter, we offer some ways to help save an ailing marriage or relationship and avoid the devastation a breakup causes. But if your relationship's beyond help and it's time to call it a day, we guide you through the separation and divorce process in terms of how it impacts you as a dad. And we give you some advice on surviving your new life as a single dad, whether you're primary caregiver or not.

Marriage on the Rocks!

Every relationship goes through difficult times, but knowing what you can do about it can mean the difference between calling it quits or building a better relationship than you and your partner had before.

What you can do

If your marriage or relationship is going through a rough patch, you need to take a close look at yourself and your part in the difficulties the two of you are experiencing. It's true that it takes two to tango and two to make a relationship work, but here we need to focus on the part you as an individual play in it. You need to be able to take full responsibility for your actions in the relationship. Ultimately you have full control only over your own actions. You can't make someone else do what you want. So to avoid further frustration, start looking at the man in the mirror to see what he can change before pointing the finger at your partner.

To be able to look at your role in the relationship objectively, let go of negative emotions like anger and blame. Being righteously indignant, or holding on to the feeling that you've been wronged, doesn't help you fix whatever the problem is. If you're feeling guilty or ashamed, try to let it go. Clear your head, sit down and make a list of what you really want from your relationship. It can help to put some thought into what your partner wants from the relationship and whether you're able to provide that for her. Ideally, ask your partner if she wants to do the same exercise as well.

Look at what you've written, and consider and keep this in mind as an inspirational goal for your relationship. Once you're clear about what you want, discuss your list (and her list) with your partner. Remember that you and your partner are on the same side of the mediation table and the 'problem' in your relationship is on the other side. The process of getting your relationship back on track is much more productive if you work together, rather than getting wound up in a blame game.

Asking others for some feedback may also help. This can be pretty tough but a close friend will tell you straight up how he sees things. Keeping a clear head and seeing things objectively when your relationship is in a tailspin can be tricky. A third-party perspective may give you a more unbiased view of yourself and your relationship.

Repairing a marriage takes time. Try to be patient and realise things aren't going to magically happen overnight. Be conscious of, and patient about, how things are changing as a result of your efforts.

You're an adult and a dad who is in the process of bringing up a child or children to be responsible, able to deal with their emotions, and have self-control. It therefore makes sense to demonstrate those qualities in yourself and not fight or bad mouth your spouse in front of your children. It places a lot of stress on a child and forces her to take sides, which clearly isn't fair. If you need to let off some steam find a place where you can be alone and do whatever helps you release some tension (in a safe way). Ideally, do something that's physically exhausting.

What you can both do

You can only change yourself — but if you get your partner working with you, the two of you can agree on ways to rebuild your relationship. Both of you have to be willing and able to make changes.

Here are some ideas:

- Talk openly about what is and isn't working in your relationship. Rather than blaming the other person for what's wrong, try to explain things in terms of how you feel or think. If talking between yourselves about the relationship gets you nowhere, consider involving a relationship coach or relationship counsellor.

- As a couple come up with strategies for making things better. Write down your strategy. Assess how well you're sticking to it and figure out if you need to make some adjustments.

- Make it a rule to say three to five positive things for one negative thing about each other.

- Eat together at night, so you have a chance to talk about your day and catch up a little bit. Maybe go out for lunch or dinner every now and then.

- Listen without interrupting your partner, even if you strongly disagree with what she's saying. Ask your partner to do the same when you've got something you want to express.

- If financial stress is an issue, sit down with a calculator and work on remedying your financial problems once and for all. Money is one of the biggest stresses a relationship faces. If you feel lost get a money coach or financial adviser.

- Don't get complacent. Your relationship isn't going to fix itself without a little work from both of you. You both need to work on your relationship and keep at it.

You can get relationship counselling through these organisations. In Australia, contact Family Relationship Services Australia (www.frsa.org.au/site) or Relationships Australia www.relationships.com.au. In New Zealand, contact Relationship Services www.relate.org.nz.

Where to go if all fails

Sometimes, despite all the efforts you've made to hold onto your relationship, it still fails.

The best case scenario when a relationship comes to an end is that your relationship is amicable and you're both a daily feature of your children's lives, with that same loving bond with them.

However, if the relationship has ended badly, or you've been turfed out or had to leave the family home, it can be very easy to slide into despair. Sure, you're not going to be the life of the party right now, and feeling rotten is normal, but if you have trouble getting out of that dark place and feel hopeless, you need to get help climbing back out. Feeling depressed and frustrated only holds you back from moving on and being a great dad. Your kids will be feeling confused, anxious, and if they're still young, potentially blaming themselves for what's happened. They need you right now and your job is to be there for them.

Your role as a lover and partner is over and it may hurt and be embarrassing, but you're still the father of your children and this will always be the case. Your fatherhood journey doesn't end here, although you may have to take a different route.

These are some places you can look to for support and advice when your relationship's gone pear-shaped:

- ✔ **Counsellor:** Get help dealing with the grief and emotions you have about the end of your relationship or marriage.
- ✔ **Lawyer or legal aid:** Find out where you stand legally with regards to seeing your children, and what rights and obligations you have.
- ✔ **Mediator:** Talk to someone who can assist with family group counselling sessions.
- ✔ **Men's group:** Get support from men who have been through the same thing as you. (Men's groups are a bit rare and can be hard to find.)

Splitting Up

Your relationship, sad as it is, is beyond help. You and your partner can't see a way to stay together and have decided to split up. Whether it's amicable or not, the end of a relationship means the start of a whole new world for you, your former partner and your children.

Out the door, with the shirt on your back!

You may find your relationship has taken a turn for the worse and you're out the door with next to nothing. Or, as many men experience, you end up haggling over shared assets and personal possessions and of course the tricky question of how best to manage your children's care.

Sorting out childcare arrangements and the distribution of assets is best done when the dust has settled at bit, not in the heat of the moment, and you and your estranged are able to talk without antagonising each other, or ending the discussion in tears.

Understanding the divorce process

Now that you are separated, you may be thinking about getting divorced or dissolving your civil union, which puts a permanent end to your legal relationship.

In Australia, the Family Law Courts deal with divorce www.familylaw courts.gov.au. In New Zealand, the Family Court deals with divorce and separation. Their website should answer most of your questions about ending the marriage or civil union www.justice.govt.nz/courts/family-court.

Making separation easier on your children

A separation can be quite tough as you struggle with all your feelings about the relationship ending, but your kids also need you. Try to offer them support and continue to nurture that loving relationship you've worked so hard at all this time.

Children react to separation and divorce in different ways. Some act out and will go 'off the rails'. Others are clingy and need reassurance you're not abandoning them. Some children blame themselves for what's happening. Others hide how they really feel and appear to be coping well.

However your child reacts to the news that you and your spouse aren't together any more, these tips will help get them through this traumatic time:

- ✔ **Fighting in front of your kids is not okay.** Fighting in front of your kids is stressful, puts them in the middle of your fight and can dent their trust in you. Leave your kids out of any conflict you have with their mum — don't ask them which parent they'd like to live with, don't ask them to lock her out, and don't ask them for information about what she's doing.

- ✔ **Don't lie to your child.** When you tell your child about what's going on, use neutral language, rather than blaming their mum or getting angry. Take the emotion out of what you're saying. Be honest and genuine with your children.

- ✔ **Let your children know you're there for them.** You may be living away from home right now, but make it clear you're always able to talk to them. Be open and honest with any questions they may have and remember to take the emotion — anger, frustration, animosity — out of what you're saying, so you leave your children out of the conflict you're having.

In Australia, the Supporting Children after Separation Program helps kids whose parents are separating or splitting up www.familyrelationships. gov.au. The Family Court in New Zealand runs a program called Parenting Through Separation. Learn about it at www.justice.govt.nz/courts/ family-court/what-family-court-does/parenting.

You're not just another statistic

Marriage breakdown is, sadly, extremely common. In New Zealand, one in three marriages, and in Australia, two in five marriages end in divorce.

With these high rates of divorce, you're clearly on a well-trodden path, but that doesn't mean it hurts any less, or that your kids aren't going to be hurt by it too. It may even help you to know that there are many people going about their ordinary day having gotten over a divorce and having found great solutions to what was once a very messy situation for them.

On the other hand, even though separation and divorce aren't uncommon, every relationship breakdown, just like every relationship itself, is unique. The way that you cope with, and help your kids cope with, this tricky time in your lives are unique to your family.

You may be able to find a support group near you. However, it's important that the group is a positive influence and not just an angry men's club. As tempting as it may be to rant and see yourself as a victim, it generally does nothing towards being a successful role model for your children. Separation and divorce are yet another opportunity for you to be the bigger man and for your own personal growth.

Finding good support

It's essential you find someone to support you through this time — a kind of 'breakup buddy'. You're probably getting all sorts of advice from all sorts of people, but they don't necessarily know what's best for you or your kids. You need someone who:

- Can be honest with you, perhaps even a bit blunt at times
- Is 100 per cent there for you when you need it
- Isn't vindictive towards your ex
- Knows how important it is you stay a strong role model and loving father to your children

You can also turn to a counsellor or a men's group for advice and support. If you can't find a men's group in your area, try joining an online group.

Avoid any group or professional who makes you feel like you're not being heard. Try to avoid groups who foster negative action towards any or particular organisation such as the family court.

When you find great support, hang onto it. The process of separation and divorce can take several years or more to get through, and you'll need ongoing support to keep you focused and moving forward.

Separating being a husband from being a father

Though the relationship with your partner is over, your relationship with your kids continues and will last for as long as you live. For many years to come, there may be frustrations and difficulties when dealing with your ex, but it helps no-one if you voice these feelings to your kids, who still have a loving relationship and bond with their mum, even if you don't.

At the same time, it's not helpful to lie to your children. They deserve to know what's going on between the two most important people in their lives, but try not to couch the conflict in terms of who's at fault, or what one person did to another.

Instead, try to explain the situation to your kids by taking out the emotion. It's easier said than done and takes some practice. The trick is in choosing your words carefully. You may find it helpful thinking about or even writing down things before you talk to your children. Try hard to describe the situation in neutral terms.

This leaves your children to make up their own minds about what is happening, and it fosters a safe and stress-free environment for them to share their own concerns about what's happening. They'll be more likely to feel comfortable about asking questions and voicing how they feel about the situation.

Are You Still Dad?

With your family split in half you may be asking yourself how you can continue to be the stellar father you've been so far. Now you're either living away from your kids, which is the most common post-breakup situation, or their mother is away from the family home, what new responsibilities and roles do you have?

Who'll look after the kids?

Now that you and your partner are no longer living together, you'll need to work out who the children will live with as their primary caregiver and how the day-to-day care of your children will be managed.

You'll need to think about:

- ✔ Who will your children live with most of the time?
- ✔ How will your children get to and from school and other activities? Who will pick up a younger child from day care or kindergarten?
- ✔ How often will the other parent be able to see the children?
- ✔ Who will look after the children at weekends, school holidays and Christmas?

Day-to-day care, which used to be called custody, can be shared between the two of you, with time spent at both houses equally, or mainly at one parent's house with visits to the other's house.

If you can agree with your former partner amicably about day-to-day care and time spent with the other parent — called *contact* — then you don't need to go to court, you can work it out between you. You can write a non-binding *parenting plan* or *parenting agreement*, so both of you are singing from the same song sheet and your children know what's going on too. The court will also be satisfied as you go through the legal process of divorce that your children are in good hands.

But if you can't agree about day-to-day care and contact that the other parent has with the children, you'll need to get legal advice and take the matter to the Family Court (NZ) or Family Law Court (Australia) and get a *parenting order* or *court order*. This is an order made by the court deciding who will take care of the children on a day-to-day basis, and when other people, which may include you, can see your kids. Even if you and your former partner have agreed amicably about the care of your children with a parenting agreement or parenting plan, you can take it one step further and have it formalised by the court with a parenting order.

Check out www.diyfather.com/singledads for lots of resources for single dads including a simple calendar tool to manage contact arrangements with your ex.

Being a remote or part-time father

An unfortunate consequence of separation and divorce is that a large number of fathers are separated from their children. Separation should be no barrier to continuing to be a great dad and role model for your child or children.

There's very little difference in your responsibilities as a father from being a non-resident father to being a living-at-home father.

You don't have to be going through separation to be regarded as a remote father. Fathers who are away overseas on military service, fathers who are in prison, and dads who are very busy or travel often can also be considered remote fathers.

Here are some tips for continuing to be a great dad, even though you can't be there for every bedtime:

- ✔ Be punctual. If you're expected at noon, be there at 12.00 pm sharp. Waiting around for you can be very hard on a young child, especially one who doesn't understand why you don't live at home anymore.

- ✔ Don't slack off on all those fatherly duties you may have had when you were still living with your kids, such as discipline and encouraging their development. Be consistent with your rules and boundaries. As difficult as it may be, you also need to work hard to agree to some basic principles for disciplining your children with your ex. And of course, keep going with the principles of parenting — provide your child with love and warmth, a secure and safe environment, and do lots of listening and talking with him.

- ✔ Foster a good working relationship with your child's mother. Your child will pick up when things aren't going well between you two, so work hard at putting the anger, bitterness or frustrations behind you.

- ✔ Keep your promises. If you told your champ that you'd be there on Thursday to pick him up after school, then do it.

- ✔ Take care of yourself, mentally and physically. Being positive and happy is rough after separation and divorce, but it makes you a positive role model for your kids. Neglecting your basic needs (eating decent food, showering every day, getting some exercise and keeping your place tidy), or turning your place into a new bachelor pad, is not a great situation for your children to spend time with you.

- ✔ Try to avoid falling into the trap of buying your kids special presents or taking them on special outings all the time in an attempt to be the favourite parent or to ensure they love you. They love you unconditionally and the best gift you can give them is your time, your respect and your unconditional love.

- ✔ When you drop your child back to his mother's house, try not to draw out the goodbyes like you're about to go to the moon for a month. Normalise the situation by saying goodnight, that you love him and you'll see him very soon.

Your child may be feeling abandoned, or resentful that you've left, or just plain confused about when he'll see you again. Being on time and a man of your word means your little one can trust in you and believe in what you say. Remind him that even though you don't live at his home anymore, you'll always be there for him.

Understanding contact arrangements

When you're not granted day-to-day care of your child or children, or it just works out better for your family situation that your children live with their mother, you'll have contact time with your kids.

Contact arrangements range from shared 50/50 (though you're not listed as the primary caregiver) to strict supervised access with time restraints in an enclosed area if the children are believed to be at risk.

At first it can be tough to accept you need to put special time aside to see your kids when you used to be around them all the time. Work hard to make the most of the time you've got with your little ones.

Here are some tips to make contact arrangements work smoothly for both parents and children:

- ✔ Communicate with anyone you need to about how the contact arrangements are working out. If they're not working, talk to your ex or lawyer about changing them.

- ✔ Don't complain to your children about the time or circumstances around your contact arrangements. They can't do anything about the arrangements and your complaining will just make them feel bad.

- ✔ If the time you have together is limited, plan what you're going to do well in advance by asking your children what they would like to do a few days beforehand.

- ✔ If you're going to be late or there's a change of plans, let people affected know as soon as you can.

- ✔ Keep a good working relationship with their mum. Your kids will pick up on any tensions between you and your ex and it will dampen their excitement.

- ✔ Keep your word. Don't let your kids down by not showing up, or by promising something you can't commit to, like a weekend at the beach, or a special gift.

- ✔ Try not to ask your kids to spy on their mother for you. She's getting on with her life and so are you! Asking them to spy puts your kids in the middle of your conflict, which isn't fair for such little people to cope with. Your children love both of you — don't ask them to choose.

✔ Try not to bad mouth your former partner, even if you find our your partner does this about you — again, be the bigger man. Your children still love their mum. Blaming your ex may eventually make your children defend your ex's actions.

✔ When making special arrangements for yourself or your child(ren) remember to notify your ex-partner and any persons or organisation involved in the access arrangements of your intentions. Give them plenty of notice.

The most important thing, whether you're in charge of day-to-day care or have limited contact with your children, is that you enjoy the time you have together.

For the nitty gritty about parenting orders, parenting plans and guardianship of a child or children, see `www.familylawcourts.gov.au/wps/wcm/` `connect/FLC/Home/Children%27s+Matters/` in Australia, or `www.justice.govt.nz/courts/family-court/what-family-court-` `does/care-of-children` in New Zealand.

Paying child support

Though you and your former partner have split up, both of you still have to pay for your children's food, clothes, housing, school fees, and all those other expenses like pocket money and sports fees. It usually falls on the shoulders of the guardian or custodian — that's whoever manages the children's day-to-day care — but between the two of you, you can work out a mechanism so both of you pay your way.

If you're the guardian or custodian of your child or children, ask yourself these things when making a child support agreement with your former partner:

✔ What costs are involved in bringing up children? What special expenses do your children incur, like extracurricular activities, medical expenses, or special dietary requirements?

✔ Have you captured all costs accurately and fairly, such as by keeping receipts, so you can explain how you got to a total figure?

✔ Are you on any benefits that may affect the amount of child support you are entitled to? How will child support payments affect your eligibility for benefits?

In some cases, where there's been a nasty split, or reaching an agreement without resorting to other means isn't possible, the guardian parent can get child support from their ex-partner with the help of government agencies.

Australia

The government agency that deals with child support is the Child Support Agency (CSA). How much child support you'll either pay or receive is usually determined using a formula that takes into account the cost of raising a child at a certain age, both parents' incomes and the amount of time your child is in your care.

CSA publishes a handy guide, *The Parent's Guide to Child Support*, which explains the ins and outs of paying and receiving child support. Download a copy from www.csa.gov.au/publications/pdf/4110.pdf.

New Zealand

In New Zealand, child support payments are administered by Inland Revenue (IRD). Voluntary child support agreements, which are agreements that the parents have worked out between themselves, need to be registered with the IRD, who will work out how this agreement affects your Working For Families tax credits, or benefits. Payments can be made weekly, fortnightly or monthly.

If you can't come to a voluntary agreement, the IRD uses a formula to work out what should be paid to the custodian. Payments must be made monthly. See www.ird.govt.nz/childsupport for more details.

Seeking guardianship of your children

The care of your child used to be called custody, but is now called day-to-day care of your child or children. If you and your former partner can't agree who'll be the main caregiver for your child, and you're determined that it should be you, you'll have to apply for a parenting order through the Family Court (NZ) or the Family Law Court (Australia). If you're successful, you'll be named the guardian or custodian of your child. Applying for a parenting order can be a very challenging, emotional and stressful endeavour, as well as being very time-consuming and expensive. The process of applying for a parenting order depends on your expectations and your former partner's expectations, and the ability to meet an agreement that serves the best interests of the child(ren) involved. You'll need to get a lawyer who specialises in family law.

When you set out to gain guardianship of your children, ask yourself if what you're doing is in the best interests of the kids, or yourself. Be honest about your motivation for doing all this. As tempting as it may seem, try hard not to use guardianship of your child as a way of getting back at your ex. Guardianship and contact arrangements are always done for the maximum benefits of the child(ren), not either of the parents.

Before you start the process to claim guardianship, check the following. Are you:

✔ Able to commit to being in charge of your children by yourself? Bear in mind that at times you'll be sick, have a stressful period at work or start seeing another person. Are you sure you're up for having the day-to-day care of your children?

✔ Concerned about your children's safety if they stay in your former partner's care? Then you're totally justified in attempting to get a parenting order.

✔ Trying to have the children with you because you don't want your ex to have them? This is not a good reason for trying to get a parenting order.

Gaining guardianship of children should only be about what is best for the children and never about personal gain and pride. Be honest and real about your expectations, and try never to lose your cool and get angry during the process.

Also ask yourself these questions:

✔ Have you worked out what child support you might be eligible for? Are you financially able to take care of your children by yourself if child support isn't forthcoming?

✔ How practical is it for you to be guardian? What help do you need from your former partner to pick up your kids from school or day care?

✔ Would your children be happy living with you? Are you living near their friends, other relations and familiar haunts?

The following may help you on your path to guardianship:

✔ Ensure you're well set-up to look after your child or children, with a clean and child-friendly home, close to their school.

✔ Dress well when going to any appointments or hearings with family court judges.

✔ Always keep in mind that you're seeking day-to-day care of your children because it's in the best interests of your kids. That will help you keep motivated when things get rough.

✔ Keep a record of the time you spend with your kids at the moment, with receipts and notes on interactions with your former partner.

If you really think about and decide that being your children's guardian isn't in their best interests after all, don't be afraid to stand up and say it. Be upfront with your lawyer and your former partner. Finding out now is better than when your children do come to live with you. Perhaps after admitting it, you'll be able to reach an amicable voluntary agreement with your former partner about shared arrangements or contact time.

At all times act with dignity and integrity. Think of how your children will remember you during these trying times when they've grown up and have a family of their own.

Getting advice

You probably know from when your child was a newborn baby that every man and his dog likes to give you advice. Sometimes the advice is helpful, sometimes it's not. Ultimately you have to make the decisions. Do what you can to avoid poor choices because you got carried away.

The advice that will be truly useful and beneficial to you is anything that gets you through this time and onto happier, greener pastures, even if the advice is hard to hear, such as being told to get off the couch, stop wallowing in misery and have a shave. Sometimes that's just what you need to hear to move you forward. Anyone who allows you (or encourages you) to keep resenting and blaming your former partner for everything is not doing you any favours.

Counselling and support

If you're struggling to deal with day-to-day tasks or feel hopeless about your future, get some professional help and quick! It's easy — pick up the phone, your yellow pages and call a counsellor.

In Australia:

- ✔ The Mental Health Foundation www.mentalhealth.org.nz/page/mhf_337.php
- ✔ Lone Fathers Association of Australia www.lonefathers.com.au
- ✔ Australian Counselling Association www.theaca.net.au/find_coun/
- ✔ Family Relationship Services Australia www.frsa.org.au/site
- ✔ Dads in Distress www.dadsindistress.asn.au
- ✔ Relationships Australia www.relationships.com.au

In New Zealand, contact Relationship Services www.relate.org.nz.

Finding a lawyer

Navigating the legal system is tricky, but a good lawyer can help you negotiate your way through parenting orders, contact agreements and your divorce. They know the legal system and have experience in dealing with these matters. Many specialise in family matters like parenting orders and divorce.

When looking for a lawyer, ask yourself these things:

✔ Does he explain proceedings and your part in them adequately?

✔ Does he advise you what to do rather than tell you?

✔ Are you bamboozled by what he says or feel fully informed?

This is about the future of your family and you should feel comfortable that your lawyer is representing *you* skilfully in a way you're comfortable with.

If you're looking for legal advice, these sites can help you. In Australia, contact the Law Council of Australia Family Law section at `www.familylaw section.org.au/pages/frmFindLawyer.asp`. In New Zealand, contact the New Zealand Law Society at `www.familylaw.org.nz/public/find_a_ lawyer`.

She Left Me but I Got the Kids

You have either been granted a parenting order by the courts, or negotiated with your former partner that you're primary caregiver. It's more unusual for dads to be primary caregivers than it is for mums, so take pride that you're blazing a trail for dads everywhere! As the primary caregiver, you're in charge of your kids. Whenever you have to make a decision about your family, keep in mind that the kids come first.

Getting to grips with being a primary caregiver

Having day-to-day care of your children on your own can be both exciting and terrifying. Being primary caregiver is a huge responsibility and you need to take a lot into consideration:

- ✔ How do you look after yourself in all this?

- ✔ How will you handle contact arrangements with your former partner? How often will your children see your former partner's family?

- ✔ Where will you find the money for mortgage payments or rent, food, clothes and school uniforms, school fees, doctor's visits, transport, school supplies, extracurricular activities and sports fees? Will you work, or receive welfare or child support payments?

- ✔ How much time will you have for paid employment? How will you juggle your children's school and sports schedules?

- ✔ How are you going to sort out life with your children if you've got a new partner?

At times it may seem daunting to be a single dad, but plenty of single mums are out there looking after children and doing a bang-up job. As we've always maintained, a dad can do just as good a job as mum! Having a routine and making sure your kids know what's happening helps. Enlisting family (both yours and, if practical, your former partner's) to give you some space or help with pick-ups or babysitting from time to time also helps.

See Chapter 16 about stay-at-home dads, a good place to start for more information about all the things you need to know/do/remember when being the primary caregiver.

Being primary caregiver for your children is a great thing, as well as a big responsibility. But just think — your daughter will learn what sort of man she may want in her life and your son will learn what sort of man he wants to be from the examples you provide as you bring them up. How cool is that!

Supporting your children's mother

Even though you're not partners in a romantic sense, you and your children's mother are still partners in a parenting sense. Whatever happened during the marriage or partnership that caused the breakdown and separation, it's time to let go of the negative feelings — the hurt, the resentment, the anger — and get on with raising your children as best as you can.

Your children need their mother around. Although she doesn't live with your children anymore, she can see them all the time and have a close, loving bond with them.

What can you do to support the relationship between your kids and their mum? Here are some ideas:

- Just like bedtime and dinnertime, you might like to make mum time a daily ritual. Mum could call at the same time each night to say goodnight, or read a bedtime story on the phone. If she lives nearby, she could come over for half an hour at the same time each night to tuck the children in.

- Keep your children's mother up to date with your children's progress at school or kindergarten, any special events that are coming up, or parent–teacher evenings she should attend.

- Keep your negative comments about your kids' mum to yourself — bad mouthing her to your children is not okay. They love their mother and have trust in her, and eroding those feelings helps no-one.

- Realise your former partner may be feeling inadequate as a mother, or irresponsible. Appreciate that this arrangement is probably quite tough for her.

- Share pictures and stories, artwork and school successes with your former partner so she still feels a part of what the children are up to when she's not there.

- Try not to be too rigid with contact arrangements. Go easy on your ex-partner if she's a little late. At the beginning she may be a bit nervous, or unsure of how her relationship with her kids is going to work out. Make sure the kids are ready to go when she arrives and pack their bags so she's not caught out without nappies or drink bottles.

Seeking help and assistance

As the primary caregiver of the child(ren) you may require some (or loads) of help and assistance. You shouldn't hold back from making use of what is available. This book, for example, is written with the idea that dads are just as good parents as mums and can do everything mums can do (except breastfeed and be pregnant, of course). No part of this book relies on mum to do anything — you can do it all!

Parenting courses

Should you need hands-on help and the support of talking to real, live other dads, there are parenting courses you can do:

- ✔ Parenting Courses in Australia:
  - www.community.gov.au/Internet/MFMC/Community.nsf/pages/section?opendocument&Section=Parenting%20Skills
- ✔ Parenting Courses in New Zealand:
  - www.parentscentre.org.nz/parenteducation/default.asp
  - www.plunket.org.nz

Financial help

Contact the appropriate government department to see if you're eligible for any benefits or tax credits.

In Australia, Centrelink runs the Family Tax Credit payments, childcare assistance and other payments that help you raise your children (www.centrelink.gov.au).

In New Zealand, Inland Revenue administers the Working for Families scheme (www.ird.govt.nz). Work and Income can tell you if you qualify for a domestic purposes benefit (www.winz.govt.nz).

Getting out and about

Just knowing you're part of a wider network of dads raising their kids alone and well is invaluable. It's also really healthy for your kids to know they're not the only ones dealing with mum and dad apart. If parent's groups or dad's groups are close to where you are, join in so you can network with other parents.

Personal help

The end of a relationship can bring up some personal issues. You may realise you need help with anger management, self-esteem, or managing stress. Don't procrastinate — if you feel you could benefit from a coach, therapist or other specialist, pick up the phone or search the internet. Your kids need you to be the best dad you can be, so if that means getting a bit of help, just do it. See 'Finding good support' and 'Getting advice' earlier in this chapter.

Having fun

Despite everything that's happened, spending time with your children is still generally great fun. But, you may encounter some times when it isn't so much fun. When you're having a rough day in the office, get home to bills in the mail and children who turn their noses up at their dinner, just stop for a moment and clear your head. Take a look at your children's faces. Remember how much you love them, and how they make you smile and laugh. Your children are worth every bit of extra effort in the end.

Your children will bring you more joy than frustration if you're open to it.

Play and interact with your children as much as you can. Read books together, give them lots of cuddles and let yourself be a bit silly with them. Children can learn so much from an involved and caring father.

If you're an older dad, constant playing can take a toll on you, so get other family members involved, set up play dates and share the fun, while you spend time with adults watching the children have fun. Actually, you don't need to be an older parent to do this — it's highly recommended!

Introducing a Stepmum

Wanting to find yourself another partner, or at least have a romantic relationship with someone new, is natural. Your life doesn't have to be all about being a father and working to support your family. But beware — you're not the carefree single man you used to be. You now come with extras.

When you go on dates, or meet someone you'd like to be more than friends with, be honest from the outset that you have children. With the high rates of relationship breakup, it's no longer unusual to be single with kids, so you needn't feel self-conscious about it. By letting this person know you have kids from the outset, you're letting her know how important your children are to you. Some women may not want to get involved with a man who has children — that's okay, their loss.

Talking about a new partner to your children

The idea of a new special person in your life after all the mess and trauma of their parents' breakup may be tough for your children to deal with at first. Initially your children may be confused when they think of how you used to be with their mum and now they're seeing you with another woman. When you start dating or have met someone special, talk to your children about why you want to date and what it means for your family. Take things slowly and don't rush your children into anything they're not comfortable about. Thinking this new person is going to replace their mother may be very painful for your children. The reality is that children are likely to think of their birth mum as 'mum', but over time they can get used to the idea of having two mums.

So give your children lots of time and let them know they can ask you lots of questions about your new partner. Be aware that your children may be resistant to the idea of your new partner. If possible get their ideas for the first meeting and involve them somehow. It may be easier for your children to deal with the situation if they feel they have some sort of say over what happens.

Your children may be secretly hoping that you and their mum are going to get back together. The idea of a new romance in your life will mean that's not going to happen and can be tough for your kids to deal with.

Meet and greet

When you have found the right person, she'll one day need to meet your children and your children will want to meet her. The meeting doesn't have to be stressful, it can be as simple as having any of your friends over to visit. You may want to choose this first meeting to happen in a neutral area, like a park, playground or café. Keep it short, sweet and casual, and don't push your kids into liking this new person.

After a few visits, chances are your children will get used to having your new girlfriend around. Again, never push them into liking her. It can take years for children to accept that a new person is around and that she's going to become part of the family

Make it clear to your kids that your new partner or girlfriend isn't replacing their mother, but is an addition to the family. Continue to support the relationship between your kids and former partner, and make her a priority in your kids' lives. Ask her to do the same if she gets involved with another partner as well.

This situation is probably pretty intense for your new partner too. Listen to the concerns she may have. Just like any good relationship, you should foster an environment of open communication, where all of you can talk openly about anything, including feelings.

Getting remarried

If the time comes that you and your new partner decide to get married, get your kids involved with the whole shebang. Ask them what they would like to do. Tell them that this is a very special day for you and it would be even more special if they helped. Cut them some slack if they're not hugely enthusiastic about you getting remarried. After all they may still be clinging on to the way things used to be with you and their mum being married.

Make sure you don't get so wrapped up in the event on the day that you don't notice your children looking lost and feeling sidelined. It can be helpful to have family dedicated to looking out for them, to give them loads of hugs and kisses, because the wedding's a big day for them too. They now have a stepmum!

Part VI
The Part of Tens

Glenn Lumsden

'I refuse to compromise quality tummy time with mundane household duties.'

In this part ...

*H*ere's where we get down to brass tacks and give you the goods, no-nonsense style. You'll want to bookmark these pages and refer to them often! First, we take you through ten ways to make pregnancy more bearable for your partner (and therefore, for you). We then hand down ten tips for getting to know that most mysterious creature — your newborn child. Lastly we show you how to fire up your toddler's already active mind with activities and strategies for getting in some serious dad-time.

Chapter 20

Ten Ways to Improve Your Partner's Pregnancy Experience

In This Chapter

▶ Being excited about the baby

▶ Earning brownie points by pampering, reassuring and doing the dishes

▶ Letting the good times roll before the baby comes

*P*regnancy looks easy when it's happening to someone else. As men, you don't have to endure what's going on in a pregnant woman's body 24/7 — and there's a lot going on. Media depictions of pregnancy have led us to believe that a woman demurely throws up a few times, then swells elegantly into a glowing, radiant Venus figure, a la Angelina Jolie. Finally, birth is quick with a few screams and ... voila, a beautiful baby is here.

Not so. Read up on Chapter 3 for what really happens when your partner is pregnant, then help her get through it by trying a few of these tips.

Take Care of Your Lady

Growing a baby is hard work and takes quite a physical toll on a woman's body. Sure, some women climb mountains and run marathons up to the day they give birth, but those are exceptions rather than your average woman's pregnancy experience. For starters, morning sickness can be debilitating and for some women the morning sickness never eases off until the pregnancy is over.

The tiredness and carrying all that blood, fluid and an extra person around puts all sorts of strains on the female body. Look after your partner 24/7 if need be, especially if she's having a difficult pregnancy, and do all you can to make life easier for her. It may mean looking after the household for nine months all by yourself and for sure you'll get sick of it. But, let's face it — would you prefer to squeeze a baby out of your body? So, man up and do whatever needs doing in the house. You can take it one step further and really pamper your mum-to-be by painting her toenails, giving her a foot rub or helping her rub oil onto her belly.

Get on the Wagon

Your missus has to stay off alcohol, drugs, cigarettes, blue cheese, seafood and a whole lotta other stuff to keep that baby in there safe and sound. Seeing you downing a pint of beer and enough salami to sink a small ship could be enough to send her over the edge. Staying off alcohol and cigarettes, not to mention anything heavier you may be into, and eating what she can eat is not only better for you, but it sets up a precedent for how you intend to live as a father.

Give Your Partner Some 'Me' Time Every Now and Then

The prospect of becoming a mother, while really exciting for your partner, is also a daunting one, both mentally and physically. For most mothers, the first few months after birth end up being a 24-hour, seven days a week job. Even though they traded in their old life of meetings, schedules, work commitments and deadlines that they may have no sentimental attachment to, for the care of a tiny, helpless baby who they love, the role can be overwhelming.

During pregnancy, your partner is bound to have some trepidation about her new responsibility and how she'll cope. Over the next few years, perhaps until your child has left home, your partner's always going to have one eye on what she's doing and one eye on your child. So in the months before this all kicks off, let her have some time that's just for her.

Be There for the Medical Stuff

Go along to all the medical appointments, scans and meetings with your midwife or obstetrician. Your partner will want you to be there to share in it. The first time you hear your baby's heartbeat through the Doppler or see the faint shadows of your baby moving and bouncing around in your partner's belly during an ultrasound scan, you'll be glad you came along.

Although you're not carrying the baby right now, that tiny growing thing in there is your child too. Your place is to know about how well he's developing, any potential health issues, and what options you as a couple have for welcoming your child into the world.

Going to appointments also supports your partner because, in the event of any unwelcome news, you'll be there to help her.

Get with the Program

Start skilling-up on essential baby knowledge and skills. Mums-to-be love to see their partner getting excited about their new life as parents and what better way to show it than to throw yourself into the preparations? There's so much to learn about looking after a newborn baby and the months after that, so why not find out all you can about it?

Ask your midwife, GP or obstetrician about antenatal classes in your area, and discuss which one you think would suit you and your partner best. Make it a priority to never miss a class, even if there's work to be done at the office, or you've been invited to drinks after work. Let's face it, the office and your work will be there for a long time. Preparing for your first child only happens once in your life.

Go on a Babymoon

As a couple, now is the perfect time to take a relaxing and indulgent holiday somewhere. We're not talking about backpacking through India or somewhere hot, with wild animals and tonnes of people, but somewhere low-key. Somewhere where sun lounges and swimming pools are more common than office blocks, with great restaurants and shops to browse. Somewhere the two of you can just hang out, sleep late, read books and do whatever you want when you want.

Be Excited about Becoming a Dad

Finding out you're going to be a dad is a little scary. You may have some reservations because of your own childhood, your financial situation, or the responsibility you're going to have. Your partner may also share some of those worries and concerns, but burying your head in the sand and pretending the baby's not going to happen won't help. Even if the impending change of lifestyle takes a while to sink in, you can definitely make the pregnancy experience more enjoyable for your partner if you show a bit of excitement about becoming a dad. Showing your partner that you're excited will get her excited and happy about becoming a mum. You want her to be happy and excited.

A lot of parenting is about attitude. The anecdote about dealing with picky eaters really sums this up. One father complains that his daughter is a terrible eater and won't eat anything unless it's got cheese on it. He's really stressed out about it and is pulling his hair out thinking of a solution. On the other hand, another father happily tells the first guy that his son is a terrific eater because as long as it's got cheese on it, he'll eat anything. It's all about attitude.

Celebrate!

In a few months when the baby is born, you'll be celebrating a new person's presence in your life. Not just any new person, but the person who is on this Earth because of you. That's pretty special! But it does come with a price — temporary sleep deprivation and a restricted social life.

So make the most of your quiet nights and unlimited access to the outside world now! Take your lady for a flash dinner somewhere fancy, visit a special place together — do whatever spins your wheels as a couple.

One dad-to-be surprised his partner with a picnic lunch at the local zoo in the weeks before their baby was born. He'd even packed sparkling grape juice to toast their health and a pillow for his lady to sit on. She spent most of her time waddling back and forth from the ladies, but the gesture was most appreciated.

Record That Beautiful Belly

In our great-grandmothers' and grandmothers' days, having a whole litter of children was common, and the pregnant belly was hidden away as if it were some kind of obscenity. These days though, it's rare to have more than five or six children, and more usual that a woman will have one to three children in her lifetime. Celebrating the physical changes that take place during pregnancy (not the heartburn and piles mind you), such as the voluptuous new shape of a pregnant belly and those plus-sized bosoms that you gotta love, is now more usual. Most pregnant women, while despising the weight they put on, love their bellies, so get out your camera from week one and get snapping. You'll laugh when you look back and see how your baby grew even before you got to meet your little champ. Even better, hire a professional photographer to take some shots of your partner's gorgeous shape. Professional photos will help her feel sexy and beautiful and boost her confidence.

Keep Telling Her How Beautiful She Is

For many women, the hardest part of pregnancy is near the due date. Your partner may be having a difficult time getting comfortable at night and suffering from heartburn and piles. She may have stretch marks, and her legs and feet may be sausage-shaped. Your partner's tired all the time but can't sleep. She wants her body back but is frightened about how she's going to handle giving birth.

You, as your partner's great ally, her support and her rock, will earn mega brownie points and endear you to her always if you keep telling her how beautiful she is. She wants to know you still find her attractive and that she's still, despite everything going on in her body, the hot woman you fell in love with, not just because of the way she looks, but because of who she is, and that she's going to make a wonderful mother.

Chapter 21

Ten Ways to Bond with Your Newborn Baby

- -

In This Chapter

▶ Getting to know your baby through day-to-day tasks

▶ Making a commitment to being a great dad

▶ Spending quality time together

- -

*B*onding and attachment to his caregivers allows your child to feel secure so he can focus on growth and development to become independent and self-confident in the world at large. He's half your DNA, so shouldn't bonding be happening by default? Yes and no. Bonding's a process that needs to be worked at, but it's not hard, and since you're the adult, you'll have to lead the way at the beginning. In this chapter, we give you our favourite ways to get to know your baby and let him get to know you.

Be 100 Per Cent Committed

Make a point of totally committing yourself mentally to looking after your little one, not just on a day-to-day basis, but for life. Becoming a father is like getting married — you're in this thing for better or worse, in sickness and in health. But there's one big difference — if things don't work out, there's no divorce. Your child will be your child forever. And since this is your child's one shot at life, give your little one the best shot you can.

It's a little bit like the Dr Seuss book *Horton Hatches the Egg*, which you'll probably come across in the course of your fathering duties. The story tells of a lazy bird that sits on her egg, but gets bored and wants a vacation. So she asks Horton, an elephant, to sit on the egg for her. Horton sits on the nest, enduring snowstorms, being hunted, and the ridicule of his friends because he said he'd be 100 per cent dedicated to sitting on the egg. When the egg hatches, it's Horton the baby bird feels connected to and wants to be with, not the lazy bird who wasn't there for her.

Be at the Birth

The first time you clap eyes on your long-awaited baby is indescribable. Some fathers say the world changes in an instant and the instinct to protect their vulnerable new child is overwhelming. Others say it took them a few weeks to truly feel special about their child. Either way, seeing your baby for the first time is a once-in-a-lifetime event that's not to be missed. It's an exclusive gig that's happening for three people and you've got a backstage pass, so use it!

If you're at the birth, you not only get to see the amazing process of birth itself, but you get to take part! You get to hold your baby (often even before your partner), you get to mop up your partner's blood (just kidding) and you can cut the umbilical cord (if you can muster the courage).

And while mum is having a bit of a rest and some attention from the midwife and other medical staff, you'll have a chance to get to check out your precious new little parcel in detail. Don't forget to take lots of photos!

Up Close and Personal

Newborn babies have spent their entire lives inside a person, so it makes sense that your little champ will still want to be close to the people who love him — that's first and foremost you and your partner. And what better way to be close than skin-to-skin? Your newborn will love snuggling into your chest, be it thick with gorse-like hairs or not, so whip off that shirt and have a wee cuddle. Kangaroo care, as skin-to-skin contact is sometimes known, is a technique used in the care of premature babies to facilitate better breastfeeding, temperature control, bonding and attachment. But your baby doesn't have to be premature to benefit. He'll learn your smell and your sound, and love listening to the gentle thud of your heartbeat putting him to sleep.

Another way to get some close contact with your baby is to have a bath or shower with him. Wait until the belly button is fully healed. You may feel a bit fingers-and-thumbs with a wobbly, tiny baby, but after a few attempts you'll feel more confident. Let your baby rest on your chest in the tub. Have mum nearby to hand you the baby when you're settled in the bath, and give her a call to take bub out when you're finished. Be careful that the water isn't too hot, or the room too chilly, as your baby doesn't have good control over his temperature yet. Some newborns will object loudly to having to take a bath, but by taking them in the bath with you, you can make it much easier for them. Once your little one has got the hang of bathing with you, he'll love bath time even more because it means he gets to hang out with dad.

Ready, Set ... Read!

Your newborn baby loves lots of things. She especially loves spending time with you and everything she can find out about you, such as your smell, the sound of your voice, the shape of your face and the colour of your eyes. Reading to your baby from day one not only encourages closeness, it gives her a chance to see colours and shapes and listen to your voice. Your little tyke can't tell if you're speaking Spanish or Swahili, but she adores the sound of your voice, your smell and being close to you. As your baby grows up and becomes more aware of her surroundings, she'll learn that books are just a normal, everyday part of life that have always been there.

Being read to also helps with language development, which is starting to happen from day one. Before she can speak, she'll be learning through you about the colours, shapes, animals and emotions that she sees on the pages in front of her.

Tummy Time

Tummy time is an important technique in kick-starting your child's development. Simply lay your baby on his tummy (he'll have his knees curled under him to start with) and encourage him to lift his head. This is important because it gets him to use his neck and upper body muscles, as well as encouraging him to look ahead and focus on objects. As he gets older, tummy time helps him develop cross-line movement, which is the action a baby does when he crawls.

Start with just a few minutes a day and build up from there. Most newborns aren't that fond of tummy time. Tummy time's hard work for them, so expect a bit of resistance at first. But keep at it because tummy time helps them develop on many levels.

Be Hands-on — Literally

Baby massage is a technique that every dad should have in his repertoire. Baby massage is easy to learn, and both you and your newborn will love it. Start by bathing your baby, then dry her on her change table or a similar flat surface. Make sure the room you're in is warm, just like when you go for a massage. Get some lovely natural oil, like calendula, and start massaging. Use gentle strokes up and down your baby's limbs, and gently roll her over to rub her back. Use your thumbs to gently knead her legs and feet.

If you want to get more technical about baby massage, a variety of instructional videos and booklets are available.

Be the Paparazzi

In the first year of his life, your baby will change so much you may not recognise pictures taken on the day he was born when you look at them on his first birthday! He'll grow out of his newborn face into a smiley, chubby-cheeked cutie pie, his hair will fall out and grow back again, and his eyes will begin to change into their true colour.

The first year is also populated by so many firsts your head will spin: first smile, first bath, first outing, first swimming lesson, first bump or bruise and (possibly) first steps. So take lots of photos in lots of different settings. Before too long you'll be looking at the photos and getting all nostalgic.

Put the photos on your phone, your work computer, your desk and in your wallet. Immerse yourself in the world of your little one. If you work outside the home, photos can be a great way to remember during the day that you're a dad now and it means you'll look forward to going home to check on your little one. If you're a stay-at-home dad, taking photos can help you remember the good days when you're having some bad ones, and will help keep mum in the loop about what you've been up to with your baby during the day.

Get Creative

Remember that beloved toy truck your granddad carved for you, the one that's gathering dust in your spare room? Or the quilt that an aunt made for you when you were a baby? Things that are handmade by people who love you not only show you how much they care for you, but they can also become precious heirlooms passed down from generation to generation.

Make a future heirloom now by making a mobile, some wooden toys, or decorations like murals for your baby's room. You'll get untold pleasure to see your child using and enjoying whatever you make, or falling in love with a painting you've made for her.

This Stroller Was Made for Walking

You would never have seen a man pushing a buggy or stroller when we were kids, but now pushing a pram is totally the 'in' thing. And as gadget freaks, who doesn't want to show off their buggy with all the adjustable this, that and the other thing buggies come with these days? As you take junior for a stroll, you can check out what models other dads have.

In the early weeks, have your child facing towards you, like an old fashioned pram, so that bub can make out your familiar face and feel comforted by your presence. The more your newborn sees you, the more she'll realise that you're her dad. Some experts believe that all buggies and strollers should face towards the parent, to encourage the two of you to talk more and interact together.

Get Your Hands Dirty

Yep. You're gonna have to change some nappies. Most dads don't exactly relish the idea of dealing with poos and wees several times a day. Neither do mums. Changing nappies is a dirty job but someone's gotta do it. We strongly believe that real men change nappies. If you can't handle a simple nappy change you may have to hand in your man card for real!

But there are also fringe benefits to being a nappy changer. The distance between you and your little tyke when you change a nappy is just perfect for singing and talking together. Many a new dad has seen his baby's first smile while changing a nappy.

Your baby's tiny little feet and gorgeous little tummy are at just the right distance for a little raspberry kiss too (once you've cleaned him and put a fresh nappy on!).

It's the day-to-day care of your baby that tells him you care and can look after him when he needs it. That builds up trust, a connection and an attachment your child needs to grow up feeling loved and secure.

Chapter 22

Ten Ways to Engage with a Toddler

In This Chapter

▶ Turning your living room into an adventure park for toddlers

▶ Helping your little one develop patience and dexterity

▶ Having fun with your toddler in the water

*T*oddlers are funny little creatures. They're curious and cute, interested yet impulsive, and are like little learning sponges soaking up everything they see, hear and do. Playing with toddlers is really fun and interacting with you is great for both of you. One of nature's best tricks is that playing with you is a way of learning and developing for your child. In this chapter we give you lots of great ideas for having fun with your wee one.

Obstacle Course

Our top pick for busting boredom on a rainy day, or just for fun and everything in between, is to set up an obstacle course. Use chairs with a sheet draped over the top, coffee tables to crawl under, big cardboard boxes to crawl through, toys or suitcases to manoeuvre around and bean bags to shimmy over. Of course getting through the obstacle course is all the more fun for having to avoid the dad'o'saurus who threatens to tickle the hide off any toddler who doesn't avoid him in time!

Get Handy

Playing hand games like 'Under the Bam Bushes' and 'Two Little Dicky Birds' are more than just a good time, they encourage the development of hand–eye co-ordination, gross motor skills, language and memory.

Playing Chase and Tag

Have you noticed that your little one loves it when you run after him, and will encourage you to run after him by taking off in the middle of a crowded street, or near a busy road? Near a highway isn't the best place to play tag or chase, but your backyard and home are. Chasing your toddler into another room, then having him hide when you come looking for him is an advanced form of peek-a-boo — it never fails to delight toddlers.

And what's wrong with a little running around the house anyway? Running's good for the heart and lungs and ensures your toddler sleeps well that night. And hey — it may even help you burn a few extra calories!

Jigsaws

Fitting shapes into a jigsaw puzzle is pretty easy for dads, but it wasn't always. A lot's going on in your brain when you do a jigsaw. You need to identify colours and patterns and visualise the piece in a bigger picture, as well as having the motor skills necessary to make that piece fit. Doing a jigsaw is almost like rocket science for toddlers. Best of all, jigsaws help your toddler develop his patience. What many parents don't realise is that patience is a skill that needs to be learnt, just like riding a bike or learning to swim. Patience is not something that some people have and others don't — it needs to be learnt and practised regularly. Doing puzzles with your little one is the perfect way to practise patience.

Balloons

When's the last time you bought a bag of balloons and blew them up? Back in the 1980s at the 99 red luft balloon party? Well, that's about to change. Though your toddler may not understand how to blow up balloons, there's nothing to stop you from doing it, and letting them go so they whiz around the room in a crazy freefall. Toddlers love to look at balloons, play with balloons, have air come out of balloons in their faces, and watch balloons float into the sky. Balloons should be part of every great dad's kit. Same goes for bubbles.

Balls

Like balloons, balls are an endless source of fascination for toddlers. The unpredictability of where a ball is going to bounce, roll or fall can keep a toddler engaged for whole ... minutes. Show your toddler how to throw a ball and watch how excited she becomes. Then try throwing the ball gently to her. She probably won't catch it, but will try again and again. And that's how skills are learned — by repetition. At the beginning you can start engaging with your child by rolling a ball to her and getting her to roll it back to you. As your child gets older you can do trickier stuff with balls, until finally you can teach her (or learn with her) the art of juggling.

Water Games

Who would have thought that an old bucket, some empty drink bottles and a little watering can could be a great investment for engaging with your child? Most children are fascinated by water play — the simple acts of pouring, splashing and swishing develop their motor skills and their spatial awareness. Have a water play 'set' ready to go on warm days, and show bub how to water the garden or the balcony plants.

You may want to take this a step further and enrol your toddler in swimming lessons. Swimming lessons for toddlers are usually just having a play in the water and building up confidence in the pool.

Art

Every culture in the world has a concept of art as a way of expressing themselves. Children do too. Get messy with finger paints, crayons, pencils and felt pens. This lets your children explore *schema* — repetitive patterns and shapes that develop a child's brain. He'll also get the hang of the idea of writing and holding a pen in a certain way, and you'll begin to see more recognisable shapes and themes as he grows up.

Reading

You can't read enough to your child. As time passes, you'll find story time before bed, whether you're perched in bed together or sitting in a favourite armchair, one of the highlights of your day. Many a father knows *The Gruffalo, The Very Hungry Caterpillar,* or *The Cat in the Hat* by heart from his many story times with his children.

Reading together isn't just about the words on the page, just as eating together isn't just about food. Reading together's about spending time together, exploring a new world together, and providing a safe, secure place for your child to be.

Children learn by repetition, and often want you to read to them the same story over and over again. So go with it, and soon your little one will be reciting *The Gruffalo* back to you. Don't forget to stop at each page and see which things your child can point out or name as you go.

Stacking Blocks and Building

Most toddlers are fascinated by textures, colours and stacking things. Sit down with your child on a rainy day with a bucket of blocks, and you may not get up again for an hour or so. Not only will you get a kick out of making the perfect Lego spaceship, but you might also discover that your child has just built the Eiffel Tower.

You can build all sorts of things from basic wooden blocks — garages for toy cars to be parked in, tunnels for trains to rumble through, houses for cuddly toys to sleep in. You're limited only by your imagination.

Resources for Dads

· ·

*T*his Appendix lists helpful resources and contact details of organisations set up to provide general support for dads (parents), or offer assistance for parents in particular circumstances.

Childbirth Education and Parenting Information

Australia

Birth and Beyond Parent Resource Centre

Haaren House, 18 Warburton St, Eastside
PO Box 542, Alice Springs NT 0871
Phone: (08) 8952 0916
Email: birthandbeyondprc@gmail.com
Website: www.ceaalicesprings.asn.au

Childbirth Education Association of Australia

749b Old Princess Highway, Sutherland NSW 2232
Phone: (02) 8539 7188
Email: info@cea-nsw.com.au
Website: www.cea-nsw.com.au

Childbirth Education Association (Brisbane)

PO Box 206, Petrie QLD 4502
Phone/fax: (07) 3285 8233
Email: mail@ceabrisbane.asn.au
Website: www.ceabrisbane.asn.au

Childbirth Education Association (Darwin)

Shop 6, 18 Bauhinia Street, Nightcliff Community Centre, Nightcliff NT 0810
Phone: (08) 8948 3043
Email: ceadarwin@hotkey.net.au
Website: www.ceadarwin.asn.au

Parenting South Australia

295 South Terrace, Adelaide SA 5000
Phone: (08) 8303 1660
Fax: (08) 8303 1653
Email: diana.skott@health.sa.gov.au
Website: www.parenting.sa.gov.au/parentgroups

New Zealand

Parents Centres New Zealand Inc.

Unit 4, Bridgepoint, 13 Marina View, Mana
PO Box 54128, Mana
Phone: (04) 233 2022
Email: info@parentscentre.org.nz
Website: www.parentscentre.org.nz

Royal New Zealand Plunket Society

PO Box 5474, Wellington 6145
Phone: (04) 471 0177
Fax: (04) 471 0190
Plunketline: 0800 933 922 (24 hours)
Email: plunket@plunket.org.nz
Website: www.plunket.org.nz

Childcare and Education

Australia

Australian Schools Directory

Website: www.australianschoolsdirectory.com.au

Montessori Australia

44d Smith Street, Balmain NSW 2041
Phone: (02) 9555 4338
Fax: (02) 9555 6862
Email: info@montessori.org.au
Website: www.montessori.org.au

National Childcare Accreditation Council (NCAC)

Level 3, 418a Elizabeth Street, Surry Hills NSW 2010
Phone: (02) 8260 1900 or 1300 136 554 (for callers outside Sydney)
Fax: (02) 8260 1901
Telephone translating service for calls in languages other than English:
131 450
National relay service for hearing or speech impaired callers: 131 677
Email: qualitycare@ncac.gov.au
Website: www.ncac.gov.au

School Sport Australia

PO Box 4757, Higgins ACT 2615
Phone: (02) 6205 9153
Fax: (02) 6205 9154
Email: assc@bigpond.com
Website: www.schoolsport.edu.au

Special Education

ACT www.det.act.gov.au/school_education/special_education

New South Wales www.schools.nsw.edu.au/studentsupport/programs/
lrngdifficulty.php

Northern Territory www.det.nt.gov.au/parents-community/students-
learning/special-education-disability

Queensland education.qld.gov.au/studentservices/learning/index.
html

South Australia www.decs.sa.gov.au/speced/pages/specialneeds/
intro/

Tasmania www.education.tas.gov.au/school/parents/taught

Victoria www.education.vic.gov.au/healthwellbeing/wellbeing/
disability/default.htm

Western Australia www.det.wa.edu.au/inclusiveeducation/detcms/
portal

Steiner Schools in Australia

Email: webmaster@steiner-australia.org
Website: www.steiner-australia.org

New Zealand

Education Review Office

Level 1 Sybase House, 101 Lambton Quay, Wellington 6011
PO Box 2799, Wellington 6140
Phone: (04) 499 2489
Email: info@ero.govt.nz
Website: www.ero.govt.nz

Ministry of Education

45–47 Pipitea Street, PO Box 1666, Thorndon, Wellington 6011
Phone: (04) 463 8000
Fax: (04) 463 8001
Email: enquiries.national@minedu.govt.nz
Website: www.minedu.govt.nz

Montessori Aotearoa New Zealand

PO Box 2305, Stoke, Nelson 7041
Phone: (03) 544 3273 or 0800 336 612
Email: eo@montessori.org.nz
Website: www.montessori.org.nz

Music Education New Zealand

PO Box 27499, Marion Square, Wellington 6141
Email: admin@menza.org.nz
Website: www.menza.org.nz

New Zealand Kindergartens Inc.

Level 1, 32 The Terrace, PO Box 3058, Wellington
Phone: (04) 495 3744
Fax: (04) 471 0775
Email: contact@nzkindergarten.org.nz
Website: www.nzkindergarten.org.nz

New Zealand Qualifications Authority

Level 13, 125 The Terrace, Wellington 6011
PO Box 160, Wellington 6140
Phone: 0800 697 296
Email: helpdesk@nzqa.govt.nz
Website: www.nzqa.govt.nz

School Enrolment Zones

Website: www.schoolzones.co.nz/enrolmentzones/Search.aspx

SPARC — Sport and Recreation

Ground floor, AMP Building, 86 Customhouse Quay, Wellington 6011
PO Box 2251, Wellington 6140
Phone: (04) 472 8058
Fax: (04) 471 0813
Website: www.sparc.org.nz

The Anthroposophical Society in New Zealand (Steiner and Waldorf schools)

PO Box 8279, Havelock 4157
Phone: (06) 877 6656
Website: www.anthroposophy.org.nz/~anthropo/education.htm

Child Development

Australia

Currently there are no listings for Australia.

New Zealand

SPARC — Sport and Recreation

Ground floor, AMP Building, 86 Customhouse Quay, Wellington 6011
PO Box 2251, Wellington 6140
Phone: (04) 472 8058
Fax: (04) 471 0813
Website: www.sparc.org.nz

Brainwave Trust Aotearoa

PO Box 55206, Mission Bay, Auckland 1744
Phone/fax: (09) 528 3981, Christchurch Administrator: (03) 981 3224
Website: http://brainwave.org.nz

Royal New Zealand Plunket Society

See earlier listing

Child Safety

Australia

Child Safety Australia

PO Box 280, Brooklyn NSW 2083
Email: info@childsafetyaustralia.com.au
Website: www.childsafetyaustralia.com.au

New Zealand

Royal New Zealand Plunket Society

See earlier listing

Water Safety New Zealand

Website: www.watersafety.org.nz

Disability

Australia

Association for Children with a Disability

Suite 2, 98 Morang Road, Hawthorn VIC 3122
Phone: (03) 9818 2000 or 1800 654 013
Email: fionag@acd.org.au
Website: www.acd.org.au

Australian Association for Families of Children with a Disability

Phone: 1800 222 660
Email: mail@aafcd.org.au
Website: www.aafcd.org.au

Centrelink

Phone: 13 2717
Website: www.centrelink.gov.au/internet/internet.nsf/payments/
ca_child_eligible.htm

Deaf Children Australia

597 St Kilda Road, Melbourne VIC 3004
PO Box 6466, St Kilda Road Central, Melbourne VIC 8008
Phone: (03) 9539 5300
Fax: (03) 9525 2595
TTY: (03) 9510 7143
Helpline: 1800 645 916
Email: helpline@deafchildren.org.au
Website: www.deafchildrenaustralia.org.au

My Time

Phone: 1800 889 997
Email: mytime@parentingrc.org.au
Website: www.mytime.net.au

The Raising Children Network

Website: http://raisingchildren.net.au/articles/raising_a_child_
with_a_disability.html

Vision Australia

Phone: 1300 84 74 66
Email: info@visionaustralia.org
Website: www.visionaustralia.org

New Zealand

CCS Disability Action

Level 3, Orbit Systems House, 94 Dixon Street, Wellington 6011
PO Box 6349, Marion Square, Wellington 6141
Phone: (04) 384 5677 or 0800 227 200
Fax: (04) 382 9353
Email: info@ccsdisabilityaction.org.nz
Website: www.ccsdisabilityaction.org.nz

Disability Funding

Phone: 0800 17 19 81
Website: www.disabilityfunding.co.nz

Enable New Zealand (What Everybody Keeps Asking)

69 Malden St, Palmerston North 4414
PO Box 4547, Palmerston North 4442
Phone: 0800 17 1981
Email: weka@enable.co.nz
Website: www.weka.net.nz

IHC

Level 15, Willbank House, 57 Willis Street, Wellington 6011
PO Box 4155, Wellington 6140
Phone: (04) 472 2247 or 0800 442 442
Fax: (04) 472 0429
Website: www.ihc.org.nz

Ministry of Health

Phone: 0800 373 664 (0800 DSD MOH)
Text (free): 373 898
Email: disability@moh.govt.nz
Website: www.moh.govt.nz/disability

National Foundation for the Deaf

205 Parnell Road, PO Box 37729, Parnell, Auckland 1151
Phone: 0800 867 446
Fax: (09) 307 2923
Email: enquiries@nfd.org.nz
Website: www.nfd.org.nz

Office of Disability Issues

PO Box 1556, Wellington 6140
Phone: (04) 916 3300
Fax: (04) 918 0075
Email: odi@msd.govt.nz
Website: www.odi.govt.nz

Parent to Parent

Website: www.parent2parent.org.nz/start.htm

Parents of Vision Impaired

PO Box 366, Waikato Mail Centre, Hamilton 3240
Phone: (07) 838 3439
Fax: (07) 838 3539
Email: paul@pvi.org.nz
Website: www.pvi.org.nz

Royal New Zealand Foundation of the Blind

Phone: (09) 355 6900 or toll-free 0800 24 33 33
Email: general@rnzfb.org.nz
Website: www.rnzfb.org.nz

Divorce and Separation

Australia

Centrelink (child support)

Phone: 136 150
Website: www.centrelink.gov.au

Dads in Distress

Phone: 1300 853 437
Email: dids@nor.com.au
Website: www.dadsindistress.asn.au

Family Relationships

Phone: 1800 050 321
Website: www.familyrelationships.gov.au

Lone Fathers Association of Australia

PO Box 492, Canberra ACT 2601
Phone: (02) 6239 4650
Fax: (02) 6259 2947
Text: 0417 668802
Website: www.lonefathers.com.au

Mensline Australia

Phone: 1300 789 978 (24 hours)
Website: www.menslineaus.org.au

Relationships Australia

15 Napier Close, Deakin ACT 2600
PO Box 313, Curtin ACT 2605
Phone: (02) 6285 4466 or 1300 364 277
Fax: (02) 6285 4722
Website: www.relationships.com.au

Shared Parenting Council of Australia

PO Box 2027, Bunbury WA 6231
Email: secretariat@spca.org.au
Website: www.spca.org.au

Stepfamilies Australia

195 Drummond Street, Carlton VIC 3053
Phone: (03) 9639 6611
Fax: (03) 9639 6644
Email: info@stepfamily.org.au
Website: www.stepfamiliesaustralia.org.au

New Zealand

Family Court

PO Box 180, Wellington 6140
Level 3, Vogel Building, Aitken Street, Wellington 6011
Phone: (04) 918 8800
Fax: (04) 918 8820
Email: family@justice.govt.nz
Website: www.justice.govt.nz/courts/family-court

Inland Revenue Department (child support)

Phone: 0800 221 221
Website: www.ird.govt.nz/childsupport

Relationship Services

Phone: (04) 472 8798 (national office)
Website: www.relate.org.nz

Fun and Games

Australia

Playgroup Australia

Phone: 1800 171 882
Website: www.playgroupaustralia.com.au

New Zealand

SPARC — Sport and Recreation

Ground floor, AMP Building, 86 Customhouse Quay, Wellington 6011
PO Box 2251, Wellington 6140
Phone: (04) 472 8058
Fax: (04) 471 0813
Website: www.sparc.org.nz

General Fatherhood

DIYFather

Email: Stefan@diyfather.com
Website: www.diyfather.com

Australia

Dads in Distress

Phone: 1300 853 437
Email: dids@nor.com.au
Website: www.dadsindistress.asn.au

Fatherhood Support Project

c/– Parenting Network
Parks Community Centre,
Trafford Street, Angle Park SA 5010
Phone (Steve): (08) 8243 5544 or 0401 125 639
Fax: (08) 8243 5549
Email: sheehy.stephen@health.sa.gov.au

Lone Fathers Association of Australia

PO Box 492, Canberra ACT 2601
Phone: (02) 6239 4650
Fax: (02) 6259 2947
Text: 0417 668802
Website: www.lonefathers.com.au

Mensline Australia

Phone: 1300 789 978 (24 hours)
Website: www.menslineaus.org.au

New Zealand

The Father and Child Union

Email: info@fatherandchild.org.nz
Website: http://fatherandchild.org.nz

The Fatherhood Foundation

c/– The Male Room
28 St Vincent Street, Nelson 7001
Email: info@fatherhoodfoundation.org.nz
Website: http://fatherhoodfoundation.org.nz

Grief and Baby Loss

Australia

National Association for Loss and Grief

Phone: (02) 6882 9222
Fax: (02) 6884 9100
Email: info@nalag.org.au
Website: www.nalag.org.au

SANDS Australia

Phone: (03) 9899 0218 (support line)
Email: info@sands.org.au
Website: www.sandsvic.org.au

The Bonnie Babes Foundation

Phone: 1300 266 643
Website: www.bbf.org.au

The Compassionate Friends (NSW)

Phone: (02) 9290 2355
Website: www.thecompassionatefriends.org.au

New Zealand

Miscarriage Support Auckland Inc

PO Box 14 7011 Ponsonby, Auckland 1144
Phone and fax: (09) 360 4034
Helpline: (09) 378 4060
Email: support@miscarriagesupport.org.nz
Website: www.miscarriagesupport.org.nz

National Association for Loss and Grief

1 Yates Street, Otaki Beach 5512
Phone: (06) 364 8416
Email: carriedean@clear.net.nz
Website: www.nalag.org.nz

SANDS New Zealand

Email: contact@sands.org
Website: www.sands.org.nz

Skylight

Phone: 0800 299 100
Website: www.skylight.org.nz

Health

Australia

13 HEALTH (QLD)

Phone: 13 HEALTH or 12 43 25 84 (24 hours)

Anaphylaxis Australia

Phone: 1300 728 000
Email: coordinator@allergyfacts.org.au
Website: www.allergyfacts.org.au

HealthDirect

(ACT, NSW, NT, SA, TAS, WA)
Phone: 1800 022 222 (24 hours)

Immunise Australia Program

Phone: 1800 671 811
Website: immunise.health.gov.au

Nurse-on-call (VIC)

Phone: 1300 60 60 24 (24 hours)

Parentline (NT and QLD only)

Phone: 1300 30 1300 (8.00 am to 10.00 pm, 7 days a week)
Website: www.parentline.com.au

Poisons Information Hotline

Phone: 13 11 26 (24 hours)

Swine Flu Emergency Hotline

Phone: 18 02 007 (24 hours)
Website: www.healthemergency.gov.au

New Zealand

Allergy New Zealand

PO Box 56117, Dominion Road, Auckland 1446
Phone: (09) 623 3912
Fax: (09) 623 0091
Website: www.allergy.org.nz

Healthline

Phone: 0800 611 116 (24 hours)

Ministry of Health

Website: www.moh.govt.nz

Royal New Zealand Plunket Society

See earlier listing

Illnesses and Conditions

Australia

Autism Spectrum Australia

Phone: 1300 978 611 (funding); or 1800 069 978 (NSW)
or (02) 8977 8377 (infoline)
Website: www.autismspectrum.org.au

Cancer Connection

Phone: 13 11 20
Website: www.cancerconnections.com.au

Cerebral Palsy Australia

830 Whitehorse Road, Box Hill VIC 3128
PO Box 608, Box Hill VIC 3182
Phone: (03) 9843 2081
Fax: (03) 9899 2030
Website: www.cpaustralia.com.au

Early Days — children on the autism spectrum

Phone: 1800 334 155
Email: earlydays@parentingrc.org.au
Website: www.earlydays.net.au

Kids with Asthma

Website: www.kidswithasthma.com.au

Muscular Dystrophy Foundation Australia

Suite 101, 7 Bay Drive, Meadowbank NSW 2114
PO Box 1365, Meadowbank NSW 2114
Phone: (02) 9809 2111
Fax: (02) 9809 4177
Website: http://mdaustralia.org.au

Reflux Infants Support Association Inc. (RISA)

Website: www.reflux.org.au

New Zealand

Asthma Foundation

PO Box 1459, Wellington 6140
Phone: (04) 499 4592
Fax: (04) 499 4594
Email: info@asthmafoundation.org.nz
Website: www.asthmafoundation.org.nz/children.php

Autism New Zealand

Phone: 0800 AUTISM (288 476) or (04) 470 7616
Email: info@autismnz.org.nz
Website: www.autismnz.org.nz

Cystic Fibrosis New Zealand

North Island email: sally@cfnz.org.nz
South Island email: susan@cfnz.org.nz
Website: www.cfnz.org.nz

Diabetes New Zealand

Phone: 0800 DIABETES (0800 342 238)
Website: www.diabetes.org.nz/home

Down Syndrome Association

Phone: 0800 693 724 or 0800 NZDSAI, or 0800 693 724 (press 3 for your closest group)
Website: www.nzdsa.org.nz/index.htm

Reflux Support
Website: www.cryingoverspiltmilk.co.nz

Multiple Births

Australia

Australian Multiple Birth Association (AMBA)
PO Box 105, Coogee NSW 2034
Phone: 1300 88 64 99
Email: secretary@amba.com.au
Website: www.amba.org.au

New Zealand

New Zealand Multiple Birth Association
PO Box 1258, Wellington 6140
Phone: 0800 4 TWINS ETC (0800 489 467)
Email: info@nzmba.org
Website: www.nzmba.org

Palliative Care

Australia

Bear Cottage
PO Box 2500, Manly NSW 1655
2 Fairy Bower Road, Manly NSW 2095
Phone: (02) 9976 8300
Website: www.bearcottage.chw.edu.au

Very Special Kids

321 Glenferrie Road, Malvern VIC 3144
Phone: (03) 9804 6222
Fax: (03) 9822 1252
Free call: 1800 888 875
Email: mail@vsk.org.au
Website: www.vsk.org.au

New Zealand

kidshealth

www.kidshealth.org.nz/index.php/ps_pagename/contentpage/
pi_id/370

Ronald McDonald House Charities

PO Box 6644
Wellesley Street
Auckland 1141
New Zealand
Phone: (09) 539 4300
Web: www.rmhc.org.nz

Starship Children's Health

Private Bag 92024
Auckland
New Zealand
Phone: (09) 307 4949
Web: www.starship.org.nz

Postnatal Depression

Australia

Post and Ante Natal Depression Association

Phone: 1300 726 306
Website: www.panda.org.au

SANE Australia
Phone: 1800 18 SANE (7263)
Website: www.sane.org

New Zealand

Mothers Matter (has information for Dads too)
Website: www.mothersmatter.co.nz

Post and Ante-Natal Distress Support Group
PO Box 57198 Mana, Porirua 5247, New Zealand
Phone: (04) 472 3135 for confidential counselling (available 7 days, 9.00 am to 9.00 pm)
Email: pnd.wellington@paradise.net.nz
Website: www.pnd.org.nz

Post Natal Distress Support Network Trust
Phone: (09) 836 6967
Email: info@postnataldistress.org.nz
Website: www.postnataldistress.org.nz

Pregnancy and Birth

Australia

See your local health department for services in your area:
NSW: www.health.nsw.gov.au

NT: www.health.nt.gov.au

QLD: www.health.qld.gov.au

SA: www.health.sa.gov.au

TAS: www.dhhs.tas.gov.au

VIC: www.health.vic.gov.au

WA: www.health.wa.gov.au

The Raising Children Network

Website: http://raisingchildren.net.au

New Zealand

Ministry of Health

Website: www.moh.govt.nz/moh.nsf/indexmh/maternity-pregnantwomen

SIDS and SUDI

Australia

SIDS and Kids

Phone: 1300 308 307
Website: www.sidsandkids.org

New Zealand

Change for our children

PO Box 13 864, Christchurch 8014
Phone: (03) 379 6686
Fax: (03) 353 9269
Website: www.changeforourchildren.co.nz

Glossary

. . . .

*T*o help you understand the medical mumbo jumbo you may be exposed to during pregnancy or when visiting a paediatrician, we've compiled a list of the most commonly used terms.

active movement: Developing your child's fine and gross motor skills, cognitive skills and senses by doing things like rolling on the floor, crawling, playing finger games and climbing.

active phase: A phase of the first stage of labour, in which contractions are increasingly painful as the cervix is nearly completely dilated and getting ready to start pushing your baby out.

acute illness: A short-term illness.

allergens: Substances or materials that cause an allergic reaction or allergy. Examples include certain foods, grass and animals; see also *anaphylaxis*.

allergy: When the body has an overactive immune system and reacts to particular substances, such as certain foods, grass, and animals, which are called *allergens*.

amniocentesis: A test to check for genetic birth defects like Down Syndrome. The test involves inserting a large needle into the amniotic sac and drawing some amniotic fluid for testing. Amniocentesis is usually done around 16–20 weeks into the pregnancy; see also *Down Syndrome*.

amniotic fluid: Also called *liquor amnii,* this is the fluid that your baby floats around in, in the amniotic sac in the womb. When your partner's waters break, amniotic fluid is what comes out.

amniotic sac: The thin membrane that holds the amniotic fluid. When the 'waters break' it's the amniotic sac that leaks fluid.

anaphylaxis: A life-threatening reaction to an allergen, in which parts of the face and body swell up and block airways; see also *allergens*.

antenatal: Also known as pre-natal, this is the period before the baby is born.

Apgar score: A score from one to ten given to a newborn baby at one and five minutes after birth to determine his health and wellbeing.

artificial insemination (AI): Using donor sperm to fertilise a woman's egg inside the uterus.

assisted reproductive technologies: Using technologies such as *IVF* and *AI* to get pregnant

attachment parenting: A style of parenting in which close contact with the child is maintained at all times. Attachment parents co-sleep with their baby, breastfeed and carry their baby in a sling or carrier rather than a buggy or stroller.

Attention Deficit/Hyperactivity Disorder (ADHD): A condition in which children have trouble concentrating, and are easily distracted, hyperactive and impulsive.

authoritarian parenting: A style of parenting in which children are told what to do, parents are to be obeyed and rules must be observed.

authoritative parenting: A style of parenting in which children and parents have a give and take relationship. Parents have high expectations of children, and children have an open and honest relationship with parents.

autism: Also known as *autism spectrum disorder* because the range of severity differs from person to person. A person with autism may have trouble making sense of the world, and find it difficult to communicate, cope in social situations or control his emotions.

baby carrier: A back or front pack in which you carry a baby or small child on the body. Slings are another form of baby carrier.

barrier cream: A cream you apply to a child's bottom and genitals to prevent nappy rash.

bassinet: A kind of mini cot or basket for newborns to sleep in.

birth canal: A term used to describe your partner's vagina during childbirth and labour.

birth centre: A specialised birthing unit run by midwives. Some birth centres are attached to a hospital, others aren't. Birth centres aren't available in all areas.

birth plan: A document in which you and your partner make clear how you intend the birth of your child to go in the best case scenario. A birth plan should also include which forms of pain relief your partner is open to or would like

available, whether or not you want to cut the umbilical cord, who you want to have in the room with you, and which kinds of intervention you're open to, if any.

bodysuit: A T-shirt that does up at the crotch with domes (clips) that's suitable for babies and young children.

Braxton-Hicks contractions: The false contractions that many women experience in the weeks, days or hours leading up to real labour starting.

breech: When your baby is 'upside down', meaning his feet rather than his head are pointing down, ready for birth.

bronchiolitis: An inflammation of the lungs' airways. Your child will develop a nasty cough and may have trouble breathing. Go to your GP.

buggy: A large pram, usually with three or four wheels, that can be folded down either in half or lengthwise.

burp: The process of getting your baby to bring up wind by rubbing or patting her back.

caesarean section: A baby born by caesarean section is removed from the uterus through an incision in your partner's belly. Caesareans are performed when labour has been going on too long, or there is some condition in which the baby must be born immediately, or vaginal birth is too dangerous.

cerebral palsy: A condition where parts of the brain are damaged during pregnancy or birth, or as the result of a lack of oxygen.

cervix: The opening between the uterus and vagina. The cervix is sealed shut during pregnancy and must widen far enough to let the baby through during labour.

chickenpox: An infection that starts with a fever and cold symptoms. After a day or two, your child starts getting red, itchy blisters on her skin. You can calm the itch with calamine lotion from your pharmacy and give your child lots of soothing baths.

chloasma: Darkish patches that appear on a pregnant woman's face, also known as the *mask of pregnancy.*

chronic illness: A long-term illness, such as asthma or diabetes.

cognitive skills: Thinking skills and the ability to grasp concepts.

colic: Persistent crying at certain times of the day, usually the early evening, for babies under three months. The cause of colic is unknown.

conjunctivitis: A highly contagious eye infection in which the linings of the eye are inflamed.

conscious fathering: Actively developing parenting skills and researching information to understand why babies and children behave the way they do. Respond to your children by using these skills and knowledge, rather than with a reaction picked up from your parents or others.

controlled crying: A technique in which a crying baby is comforted at regular intervals in an effort to help her learn to fall asleep on her own.

cord prolapse: A rare event in which the umbilical cord blocks the baby from being born.

cradle cap: A type of dermatitis that causes flakes on the scalp in young babies, similar to dandruff in adults.

crèche: A kind of day care centre.

croup: A viral infection that starts out as a cold but becomes a pretty nasty and wheezy cough that comes on suddenly. Go to your GP.

crowning: A term used to describe the baby's head showing in the birth canal, meaning birth is near.

cry-it-out: A technique in which a baby is left to cry and fall asleep on its own.

cystic fibrosis: An inherited chronic disease affecting the lungs and digestive system.

day care: A facility where children under five years old are cared for, with programs to assist their learning and development. Day care centres are staffed by qualified early childhood teachers and aides.

demand feeding: Feeding a baby when she shows hunger cues such as turning her head to search for a nipple, crying, or sucking her fists.

developmental delay: Professionals say that a child has a developmental delay, rather than labelling the child intellectually disabled, when a child's development lags behind average statistics on developmental milestones.

dilation: A term used to describe the widening of the cervix ready for the baby to leave the uterus and enter the birth canal.

discipline: A term used to describe the way you show your children clear boundaries, rules and consequences. It doesn't mean punishing your child.

dizygotic twins: Twins from two different eggs, also known as fraternal twins. These twins do not share identical genetic material as identical twins do; see also *monozygotic twins*.

Doppler: An instrument that allows you to hear the baby's heart beating in the womb.

doula: A paid attendant, usually a woman, who helps support and coach a woman through labour and childbirth. Doulas are also called childbirth assistants. They're not common in Australia or New Zealand.

Down Syndrome: A genetic disorder caused by an extra bit of chromosome being replicated in cell division very early on after conception. Children with Down Syndrome have varying degrees of mental and sometimes physical disability.

due date: The date your baby should arrive, though this is not for certain, as only five per cent of babies arrive on their due date (get used to the idea that you cannot plan everything by a watch or calendar when you're a dad). In Australia, the due date is technically called an EDC, or expected date of confinement, while in New Zealand, it's called an EDD, or estimated due date.

ear infection: An infection of the ear, in which your child will be grizzly and tug at his ears, or rub them. A trip to your GP to check your child's ears thoroughly and prescribe antibiotics is in order.

eczema: Also known as *dermatitis*. The skin is sensitive to certain materials and can become itchy and blotchy.

elimination communication: Rather than using nappies to catch poos and wees, parents watch their baby for signs they need to go to the toilet. The baby is then held over a potty.

embryo: What your unborn baby is called from the time it implants into the uterine wall to about 8–12 weeks into the pregnancy.

engaging: Engaging is when an unborn baby is getting in position for birth.

epidural: A pain relief method which involves a needle going into the spinal column with local anaesthetic. Epidurals are used in caesareans so that mum can stay awake while the baby is being born; see also *caesarean section*.

episiotomy: Cutting the perineum to make the vaginal opening bigger during labour.

estrogen: Though estrogen's coursing through the bodies of both men and women, it's found in much higher levels in women. Estrogen's known as the female sex hormone in the same way that testosterone is the male sex hormone. It's responsible for the growth of breasts and contributes to the menstrual cycle in women.

extrusion reflex: A reflex in which a young baby pushes an object out of his mouth with his tongue. One of the signs that your baby's ready to eat solids is when he stops automatically pushing things like spoons out of his mouth.

fallopian tubes: The tubes that connect the ovary with the uterus. An egg is often fertilised in one of the fallopian tubes and travels down the uterus to become an embryo.

family day care: (Australia only) A paid carer looking after your child at her home under the supervision of an early childhood organisation. Called *in-home day care* in New Zealand.

fertilisation: When sperm meets egg, and the beginnings of a new child are formed.

finger food: When your baby is about eight to nine months old, she becomes interested in small snacks like pieces of toast and crackers that she can eat with her fingers.

foetal alcohol syndrome: Condition caused by a woman drinking alcohol heavily in pregnancy. Foetal alcohol syndrome manifests itself as a number of intellectual and behavioural problems in the child.

foetal monitor: A device that monitors foetal heartbeat, movement and contractions of the uterus to determine the unborn baby's wellbeing. Foetal monitors are used in antenatal checkups and in the early stages of labour.

foetus: What your unborn baby is called from the time it stops being an embryo, about 8–12 weeks into the pregnancy, until birth.

folic acid/folate: A vitamin that helps prevent neural tube defects such as spina bifida.

forceps: An instrument like a pair of tongs designed to help with the baby's birth, easing him out of the birth canal if mum needs help pushing.

formula: A substance, primarily of milk powder, which is given to babies.

fundal height: Measurement of how far the uterus has progressed into the abdomen as your baby grows.

gas: A mix of nitrous oxide and oxygen that can be inhaled during labour as pain relief.

gastroenteritis: Infection of the gastrointestinal tract that can be caused by bacteria from infected water, poor hygiene or bad food.

gestation: Another word for the time your baby spends in the womb. You'll hear your carer say things like 30 weeks gestation, which means 30 weeks in the womb.

gestational diabetes: A form of diabetes that can be contracted during pregnancy. Your midwife, obstetrician or GP will be on the look out for it with tests throughout the pregnancy.

gripe water: A fluid given to babies who have trouble bringing up wind. Depending on the brand, it often has fennel, dill and sodium bicarbonate in it.

group B strep: A life-threatening bacterial infection in newborn babies.

HCG: Also known as *human chorionic gonadotropin*, a hormone made by the embryo to ensure its survival. Most pregnancy tests look for the presence of HCG.

home birth: Your partner labours and gives birth at home rather than in a delivery suite at a hospital.

hospice: A palliative care facility, where people who are in the final stages of a terminal illness are cared for.

hydrocephalus: Also known as 'water on the brain', hydrocephalus is a condition in which fluid collects in the brain. It can cause intellectual disability and death.

hyperemesis gravidarum: Extreme morning sickness, with continual nausea and vomiting, weight loss and dehydration.

hypnobirthing: Using hypnotherapy to control pain during labour.

in utero: Latin for 'in the womb'.

in vitro fertilisation (IVF): A technique in which a harvested egg is fertilised by sperm outside the womb.

induction: The process of artificially starting labour. Substances that mimic the body's natural actions are given to a pregnant woman to kick-start labour.

indulgent parenting: *See* permissive parenting

infant acne: A newborn baby's acne, caused by pregnancy hormones which are still present in the baby's body.

in-home day care: (New Zealand only) A paid carer looking after your child at her home under the supervision of an early childhood organisation. Called *family day care* in Australia.

intracytoplasmic sperm injection: A process in which a harvested egg is injected with sperm to ensure fertilisation outside the womb.

kindergarten: A type of preschool.

lactation consultant: A carer specially trained in breastfeeding who can give one-on-one advice and care in getting breastfeeding up and running. She can also provide support when breastfeeding's not going so well.

last menstrual period: The first day of your partner's period before getting pregnant is the date that the length of the pregnancy is calculated by. So even though you may have conceived your baby on the 15th day after your partner's period, your baby is already considered two weeks along or at two weeks *gestation*.

latent phase: The first phase of the first stage of labour, when the cervix is starting to dilate. Contractions shouldn't be too painful and can be managed with natural techniques such as heat packs and moving around.

linea nigra: A darkish line appearing on a pregnant woman's belly as her pregnancy progresses. It's caused by melanin marking where the abdominal muscles are parting to make way for junior. It fades a few weeks after birth.

listeria: Bacteria that live in some foods, such as soft cheese, cold meats and raw seafood. The illness listeria infection causes, listeriosis, is dangerous to an unborn child and can cause miscarriage or stillbirth.

long day care: (Australia only) A day care facility outside the home, such as a preschool for young children.

meconium: Thick, tar-like poos your baby does in the first few days of life.

meningitis: An illness which can cause death. Symptoms include a severe headache, stiff neck and fever.

midwife: A health professional, usually a woman, who specialises in pregnancy, labour, birth and newborn care.

miscarriage: When an unborn child dies before 20 weeks gestation.

monozygotic twins: Twins who are formed when one fertilised egg splits. These twins are identical; see also *dizygotic twins*.

morning sickness: A side effect of pregnancy, usually in the first trimester, in which your partner feels nauseated and hypersensitive to foods and smells.

moro reflex: A reflex in which newborn babies seem to suddenly flinch in their sleep.

Moses basket: A basket that newborn babies sleep in for the first few months of life.

multiple birth: A set of children born at one time, such as twins, triplets and more.

muscular dystrophy: A genetic disorder, in which muscle strength and function deteriorates over time. Most commonly seen in male babies and young boys, some forms aren't diagnosed until early adulthood.

nanny: A person trained in baby and child care hired to look after children.

nappy rash: A skin condition caused by the ammonia in wees and poos on your baby's bottom and genitals. Nappy rash is usually red, flat and quite sore.

neglectful parenting: A parenting style in which children are ignored, abused, or left to fend for themselves.

neural tube defect: The neural tube is an embryo's developing central nervous system and it closes 15–28 days after conception. If the neural tube doesn't close, it can cause a birth defect such as spina bifida, where the spinal cord is not fully formed or not enclosed by the vertebrae.

nuchal fold test: An ultrasound scan done at about 12 weeks to scan for birth defects like spina bifida by checking how the vertebrae is developing around the spinal cord.

obstetrician: A specialist in reproduction.

obstetrics: The arm of medicine to do with reproduction.

occupational therapist: A specialist in helping people regain skills and mobility.

ovaries: A part of female anatomy where eggs are formed.

overdue: Any date past the baby's due date. Even though only about five per cent of babies are born on their due date, many mums-to-be start to get a little bit cranky the longer their pregnancy goes on past this date.

overtired: When your baby can't get to sleep and is too tired, she'll become overtired and be more difficult to settle.

ovulation: When an egg is released from an ovary, ready for fertilisation from a sperm.

oxytocin: The hormone that causes your partner's uterus to contract, and is responsible for the milk let-down reflex when she's breastfeeding.

paediatrician: A doctor specialising in paediatrics, or care of children.

palliative care: Care of a person in the final stages of a terminal illness.

permissive parenting: Also called *indulgent parenting*. Parents let their children do anything and children have no clear boundaries, rules or understanding of consequences.

pethidine: A commonly used drug in labour, which is similar to morphine.

physical disability: A condition, disease or injury that prevents someone from undertaking normal day-to-day activities, such as dressing themselves, eating or walking.

placenta: The lifeline between your baby and her mum, a dinner plate-sized gloop of blood and tissue that is attached to the uterine wall and absorbs nutrients and toxins from the mother. The placenta's connected to the baby by the umbilical cord, and is 'born' shortly after your baby.

placenta previa: When the placenta covers or is close to the cervix. It can cause bleeding, and your baby will have to be delivered by *caesarean*.

playcentre: Parent and family run day care groups.

playgroup: Parent and family run activities for children held in a community centre or hall that is open to everyone.

pneumonia: An infection of the lungs.

postnatal: Also known as *post partum*. The period after birth, usually one year.

postnatal depression (PND): A kind of mental illness after the birth of a child, usually in the early months. People with PND feel hopeless and detached from their baby.

post partum: The period after your baby is born (usually a year). Also known as *postnatal*.

potty: A small plastic seat and bowl for teaching a baby or young child about going to the toilet.

pre-eclampsia: A very serious condition that can occur during pregnancy, pre-eclampsia can cause stroke, organ failure and seizures in the pregnant woman, or cause the placenta to come away from the uterine wall. Symptoms include high blood pressure and protein in urine, so usually your midwife, obstetrician or GP will test these at each checkup.

premature: A baby born before 37 weeks.

preschooler: A child aged three to four years old.

primigravida: A Latin term for a woman who is pregnant for the first time.

progesterone: Progesterone is a pregnancy hormone that helps prepare tissue on the uterine wall for its special guest star, the egg, to implant. Throughout the pregnancy, progesterone helps get breasts ready for milk production and is probably responsible for your partner's mood swings.

prolactin: The hormone that stimulates milk-making cells in the breast to produce milk.

prostaglandin: A substance that helps to make the cervix soft so that it can dilate and efface (or shorten) during labour.

psychologist: A health professional specialising in mental health.

pull-ups: Nappies that pull up and down like underpants.

reflux: A condition in which a young baby can't keep food in their stomach and brings up painful stomach acid in the throat.

ripening the cervix: When the cervix becomes soft and ready to dilate. Prostaglandins do this job.

round ligament pain: Pain endured by pregnant women as the pelvis widens.

rubella: Also known as German measles. If a pregnant woman contracts rubella, it can cause birth defects in her unborn child.

SAHD: Stay-at-home dad.

schema: Repetitive patterns or shapes that characterise children's play.

separation anxiety: Distress at being away from a parent or main caregiver.

show: During pregnancy the 'show' has plugged up the cervix, keeping the uterus free from infection. The show will come out and make an appearance in the days, or hours, leading up to your child's birth.

SIDS: Sudden Infant Death Syndrome. When a baby dies in his sleep for unknown reasons. Also known as cot death.

sleepsuit: An outfit with trousers and top in one piece, usually with long sleeves and legs.

sling: A piece of material or simple carrier that allows a baby or toddler to be carried around on a caregiver's body.

solids: First foods that babies eat after breastmilk or formula. Solids are usually introduced at about six months of age.

special needs: A term describing children who have a physical or intellectual disability.

spill: When a baby has a milk feed, he may spill, or vomit a small amount.

spina bifida: A congenital abnormality caused by the vertebrae not closing around the spinal cord while in the womb.

spinal block: An American term for an epidural, or spinal anaesthesia during childbirth and labour.

stillbirth: When a child dies in utero after 20 weeks gestation, or dies in childbirth.

strep throat: A throat infection accompanied by a high temperature.

stroller: A pram that can be folded easily widthways, and can be carried by the handle with one hand. The child faces outwards.

SUDI: Sudden Unexplained Death of Infants, which can have a known cause, like smothering, or be unexplained, such as in the case of Sudden Infant Death Syndrome (SIDS), also known as cot death.

swaddle: A term to describe wrapping a baby in a light cloth for sleeping, as well as the name of the cloth used to wrap the baby.

synapses: Connections in the brain.

syntocinon: A synthetic version of oxytocin, a naturally occurring substance that triggers breastmilk let-down and contractions.

teething: The process of baby teeth coming up through the gums.

TENS: A machine that delivers an electric current during labour as pain relief. TENS machines are not commonly used in New Zealand and Australia.

thrush: A fungal infection that babies can get on their bottoms and in their mouths.

toddler: A child who walks, or toddles, up until about age three.

toilet training: The process of teaching your child to use the toilet.

tonsillitis: An infection of the tonsils, which are inside the throat. Can be very painful.

toxoplasmosis: An infection caused by a bacteria that lives in the intestines of animals, particularly cats. Humans can also be infected by eating very rare meat. Pregnant women are particularly vulnerable to toxoplasmosis, so take over cat litter box duty and make that steak medium.

transition: A phase of labour between the cervix dilating (first stage) and pushing the baby out of the birth canal (second stage).

tummy time: Having a baby spend time on her tummy to develop head, neck and back muscles, as well as stimulate her eyes and brain.

ultrasound scan: A handheld scanner is run over your partner's belly to see inside. A picture appears on a TV screen nearby showing a grainy black and white image of your baby in the womb. Scans are used in the *nuchal fold test* to check for the possibility of birth defects, the development of your baby's body at 20 weeks, or the presence of twins, and if you like, you can find out what the baby's sex is before he's born.

umbilical cord: The cord which connects the unborn child to the mother.

uterine wall: The wall of the uterus, in which the fertilised egg nestles.

uterus: The organ in which an unborn child grows.

varicocele: Varicose veins in the scrotum which may lead to male infertility.

ventouse: An instrument with a suction cup to help baby be born.

vernix: A waxy coating that protects baby's skin in the womb.

vitamin K: A substance needed for the body's production of blood clotting agents. Some babies are at risk of a deficiency and can be given a dose at birth.

water birth: When your baby is born in a birthing pool or water.

Well Child provider: (New Zealand only) A child or maternal nurse who monitors the growth and development of your child.

whooping cough: Also known as *pertussis*, this is a serious and distressing respiratory tract illness in babies and young children.

wind: When air becomes trapped in your baby's stomach, you need to get that air out by burping him by rubbing or patting his back. Wind is also the name given to air trapped in the stomach.

word spurt: A stage in toddler development where language skills really take off and seem to progress rapidly.

Index

• A •

active movement, 125, 225–226, 276
active phase (labour), 79
activities. *See also* playtime
  for babies, 125, 143–145
  for preschoolers, 228–230
  information resources, 361
  outdoors, 232–233
  with more than one child, 216–217
acupuncture, 255
adopting, 33
adoption services, 33
Adoption Trust (NZ), 33
afterbirth, 78
air travel, tips for managing babies, 170–171
alcohol, 284, 336
allergens, 243
allergies, 242–243
Allergy New Zealand, 243, 364
almond oil, 69
alternative education philosophies, 259–260
alternative schools, 258
amniotic fluid, 44, 48
amniotic sac, 44, 82
amyotrophic lateral sclerosis, 306
anaphylactic shock, 290
anaphylaxis, 242
Anaphylaxis Australia, 243, 364
anger management, 282
animals, and babies, 66–67
antenatal care
  choosing a carer, 36–37
  nature of, 35
antenatal classes, 49, 71–72, 337
Anthroposophical Society in New Zealand, 260, 355
anthroposophy, 260
antibacterial cream, 69
Apgar score, 90
Apgar tests, 90
arnica cream, 70
art, 350
artificial insemination (AI), 32
Asian slings, 144
assisted reproductive technologies, 32

Association for Children with a Disability, 307, 356
asthma, 291
Asthma Foundation (NZ), 291, 366
attachment parenting, 20, 108, 143
Attention Deficit/Hyperactivity Disorder (ADHD), 265
audiologists, 308
Australian Association for Families of Children with a Disability, 302, 357
Australian Breastfeeding Association, 107
Australian Counselling Association, 325
Australian Multiple Birth Association, 367
Australian Music Teacher Register, 268
Australian Schools Directory, 259, 352
authoritarian parenting style, 161
authoritative parenting style, 161
autism, 303, 365
Autism New Zealand, 303, 366
Autism Spectrum Australia, 303, 365

• B •

babies, massage, 123–124, 141
baby accessories, 63
baby baths, 63
'baby brain', 52
baby capsules, 61, 144
baby carriers, 143–144
baby chairs, 63
baby clothes
  hand-me-downs, 65
  sizes, 58–59
  storage, 65
  tips for dressing, 57–58
  what babies need, 56–57
baby equipment hire, 62, 144
baby loss. *See* death of a child; miscarriage
baby massage, 123–124, 255, 344
baby pouches, 144
baby showers, 75
baby slings. *See* slings
baby-proofing
  the house, 145–146
  room by room, 126–127
babymoon, 337

babysitters, 151
babysitting clubs, 149
back pain, 47, 83
bad weather busters, 229–230
Bali, three-month mark for babies, 137
ball games, 349
balloons, 349
barrier cream, 69, 100, 101, 121
bassinets, 64
bathing babies, 102–103, 110, 141, 343
bathrooms, baby-proofing, 127
Bear Cottage hospice (Aust), 293, 367
bedtime routines, 141–142
behaviour management. *See also* sibling discipline
  dealing with setbacks, 195–196
  discipline, 190–192
  hurting others, 193–194
  offering choices, 203–204
  setting boundaries and rules, 204–205
  sharing, 194–195
  tantrums, 192–193
  time out, 205
Birth and Beyond Parent Resource Centre (NT), 351
birth canal, 87
birth centres, 50
birth certificates, 98
birth plans, 35, 51
birth school. *See* antenatal classes
birthing equipment, 73
birthing options
  attendance at the birth, 342
  availability, 37
  choosing, 50
  to reduce risk of fatality, 286–287
biting, 193–194
blaming, avoiding, 207
blocks, 350
blogs, 173
'blues', 92, 99
bodysuits, 56
bonding with your baby, 97–98, 115–116
Bonnie Babes Foundation (Aust), 285, 363
booster seats, 62
bottle feeding, 105
botulinum toxin, 158
bouncinettes, 63
boundaries, setting, 204–205
bowel motions, before labour, 83
Braille, Louis, 306
brain development
  during first three months, 131–132
  encouraging, 125, 131
  and exercise, 245

Brain Foundation (Aust), 303
brain injuries, 301
Brainwave Trust Aotearoa, 356
Braxton-Hicks contractions, 83
breast tenderness, 43
breastfed babies
  bowel movements, 101
  immunity, 285
breastfeeding, 13, 90, 104, 114, 214
breech position, 51
broken bones, 289
bronchioles, 248
bronchiolitis, 181, 248
brushing teeth, 159
Bub Hub, 71, 134
budgeting, for more than one child, 213–214
buggies, 60–61, 62, 143, 215, 345
building blocks, 350
burns, 289
burping, 106–107

• *C* •

caesarean sections
  elective, 71
  emergency, 87
  risks, 286–287
  role of midwives, 36, 51
calendula oil, 69
cancer, 291
Cancer Connection (Aust), 291, 365
Cancer Council Australia, 293
Cancer Society of New Zealand, 293
car seats, 61–63, 182
car trips
  readiness for trip to hospital, 72–73
  tips for managing with children, 169–170
care routines
  attachment parenting, 20
  clarifying for babysitters, 149
  for babies from six to twelve months, 159–160
  for older children when there is a new baby, 216
  for second babies, 212, 215–216
  importance of, 116–117, 141
  strategies, 19–20
  strict routines, 20
carers' allowances, 307
castor oil, 82
Catholic schools, 258
CCS Disability Action (NZ), 302, 357
Centrelink (Aust), 357

cerebral palsy, 301
Cerebral Palsy Australia, 302, 365
cervix, 28, 48, 51, 78–79, 82, 82–83, 84
Change for our Children (NZ), 288, 370
change tables, 64
chase and tag games, 348
checklists, needs prior to birth of child, 76, 81–82
chickenpox, 181, 249, 284
Child Cancer Foundation (NZ), 291
child car seats, 61–62
Child Care Assistance (NZ), 152
Child Care Benefit (Aust), 152
child development
    and conscious parenting, 182–183
    during first three months, 128–132
    during second year, 184–186
    during six to twelve months, 162
    during third year, 199–201, 202–203
    growth during first three months, 128
    growth during three to six months, 135–142
    information resources, 355–356
    language and emotional development in second
        year, 164
    preschoolers, 224
child health nurses, role, 24
child obesity, 256
child safety, information resources, 356
Child Safety Australia, 165, 356
child support, paying, 322–323
Child Support Agency (Australia), 323
Child, Youth and Family (NZ), 33
childbirth
    advocating for your partner, 89
    cutting the cord, 88, 90
    emotional response, 88
    the first few days, 91–92
    the first few hours, 90–91
    helping your partner, 84–85
    medical interventions, 86–87
    meeting your baby, 88–89
    pain relief options, 49–50
    what happens immediately after birth, 89–90
childbirth education, resources, 351–352
Childbirth Education Association of Australia,
    351–352
childcare, information, 352–355
Childcare Assistance (NZ), 152
childhood illnesses, 248–254
children, deciding to have more than one,
    211–212
choices, offering to toddlers, 203–204
chronic illnesses, 291
classes, for preschoolers, 227

cloth books, 60
cloth nappies, 65, 68
co-educational schools, 258, 261–262
cognitive skills, 199, 309
colds, 120–121, 180, 250
colic, 118, 135
colleagues, as sources of help, 25
common colds, 120–121, 180, 250
communication, talking to your toddler so they
        understand, 206–207
community health organisations, 136
Compassionate Friends (NSW), 295, 363
complementary education, 267–268
computers, 208–209
concussions, 289
confidence, as a father, 21
congenital abnormalities, 300, 301
conjunctivitis, 250
conscious fathering, 182–183
conscious parenting, 182–183
constipation, during pregnancy, 47
contact arrangements, understanding, 321–322
contact (with children), 319
contractions, 78, 79, 83, 84
controlled crying, 108
cord prolapse, 287
cot death. *See* SIDS
cots, 64
counselling
    for personal issues, 330
    when you're not ready for fatherhood, 16–17
counsellors, 314
court orders, 319
cradle cap, 118
crawling, 162, 163
creativity, 21, 199
crèches. *See* day care centres
criticising, avoiding, 207
croup, 181
cry-it-out approach, 108
crying
    how to handle, 22, 110
    in newborns, 109–110
cryingoverspiltmilk.com.nz, 120
custody. *See* day-to-day care
cystic fibrosis, 265
Cystic Fibrosis New Zealand, 291, 366

Dads in Distress (Aust), 325, 359, 361
day care centres, 151–152, 169

day-to-day care, 319, 323
Deaf Children Australia, 302, 357
death of a child. *See also* terminal illnesses
    dealing with, 295–297
    grieving, 296, 297
    in infancy, 13, 297
    information resources, 362–363
    information resources for grief and loss, 362–363
    saying goodbye, 296–297
demand feeding, 107
development. *See* child development
development windows, 131
developmental delay, 303
diabetes, 291
Diabetes New Zealand, 291, 366
diarrhoea, 82, 122–123
dietary needs
    avoiding the wrong foods, 239
    babies from six to twelve months, 156–159
    introducing different foods to preschoolers, 240
    managing an allergy, 243
    mothers-to-be, 40–41
    preschoolers, 237–238
    toddlers, 179–180
    vegetarian children, 244
digital thermometers, 70
dilation, 78
disabilities
    defined, 299
    information resources, 356–359
    intellectual disabilities, 302–303
    multiple disabilities, 303–304
    physical disabilities, 301–302
    and success in life, 306
disability funding, 307
Disability Funding (NZ), 358
disabled children
    adjusting your expectations, 306–307
    adjusting your lifestyle to suit their needs, 310
    caring for, 304–305
    getting assistance and resources, 307
    getting formal confirmation of condition, 304
    getting support, 304–305, 310
    know when something is wrong with your baby, 300
    tips for coping, 308, 309–310
    working with health professionals, 308–309
discipline
    framework for effective discipline, 191, 205
    meaning of, 20
    tips for making it work, 190–191
    understanding, 190–192, 203, 205
    versus punishment, 192

disposable nappies, 68
distractions, offering, 203
divorce
    information resources, 359–360
    understanding the process, 315
divorce rates, 316
DIYFather, 23, 24, 361
dizygotic twins, 45
'dog nose', 42–43
Doppler, 46
Down Syndrome, 45, 300, 303
Down Syndrome Association (NZ), 303, 366
drawing, 199
dressing
    newborns, 103–104
    tips for dressing babies, 57–58
Duchenne muscular dystrophy, 301
due date, 51, 81, 82, 339

ear infections, 181, 250–251
Early Days — children on the autism spectrum, 365
ears, cleaning, 122
eczema, 165
education
    alternative education philosophies, 259–260
    children with special needs, 265–266
    complementary education, 267–268
    information resources, 252–255
    preparing for school, 262–263
    private versus public, 260–261
    same-sex versus co-ed, 261–262
    school results, 261
    selecting schools, 258–259, 261, 262
education choices, 258–259
Education Review Office (NZ), 153, 261, 354
education philosophies, 257–262
elective caesarean, 71
electronic games, 208–209
elimination communication (EC), 68, 102
embryos, 28
emergency caesareans, 87
emergency phone numbers, 290
empathy, 193
Enable New Zealand, 358
endometrium, 28
endurance, need for, 21–22
engaging (position for birth), 51
epidurals, 50, 87
EpiPens, 243

episiotomy, 87
exercise
    and brain development, 245
    importance of, 245
    sport for school children, 268
    working-out routines for preschoolers, 246
    with your child, 246
exhaustion
    during first trimester of pregnancy, 42
    from caring for newborn, 96
expressing milk, 104
extrusion reflex, 156

Faber, Adele, 207
fallopian tubes, 28, 29
family
    as babysitters, 149
    relationship with, 15
    as sources of help, 25
    spending time with, 112
Family Assistance Office (Aust), 152
Family Court (NZ), 319, 323, 360
family day care, 153–154
family law, 315, 323
Family Law Court (Aust), 315, 319, 323
Family Relationships Services Australia, 16, 325, 359
Family Tax Credit payments, 329
fast map, 187
Father & Child Trust (NZ), 133
Father and Child Union (NZ), 362
fatherhood
    average age of first-time fathers, 18
    being 100 per cent committed, 341–342
    being involved, committed and passionate, 18–19
    common factors, 13–14
    common myths, 10–11
    creativity and problem-solving, 21
    information resources, 361–362
    options to reduce stress, 208
    pros and cons, 12–13
    showing commitment, 98
    universal experience, 9
    when you're not ready for it, 16–17
    for young dads, 98
Fatherhood Foundation (NZ), 362
Fatherhood Support Project (Aust), 361
fathers as primary caregivers
    as caregivers, 10, 315
    as first teachers, 233–234

following a relationship breakdown, 326–330
    getting to grips with being, 327
    myths about, 272–273
    remembering to have fun, 330
    seeking help and assistance, 329–330
    supporting the relationship between your children and their mother, 328
feeding babies. *See also* dietary needs
    foods to avoid giving, 158
    newborns, 90, 91, 104–107
    on demand, 107
    starting on solid foods, 140, 156–159
female infertility, 31
fertilisation, 29, 30, 32, 34
fevers, 181–182
fighting
    between siblings, 218
    and setting boundaries, 219
finances
    budgeting for more than one child, 213–214
    managing on less, 15
fine motor skills, 199
finger food, 158, 274
fingernails, trimming, 123
first aid kits, 69–70, 291
first birthdays, celebrating, 173–174
first stage of labour, 79, 80, 83
first trimester of pregnancy
    activities to avoid, 43
    common side effects, 42–43
    development of baby, 44
    dietary needs of mothers-to-be, 40–41
flexible working hours, 113–114
flying, with babies, 170–171
foetal alcohol syndrome, 284
foetal heartbeat monitor, 46
foetuses, 28
    development during first trimester, 44
    development during second trimester, 48
    development during third trimester, 53–54
folate, 41
folic acid, 41
food. *See also* dietary needs; feeding babies
    cooking and baking for preschoolers, 238
    curbing fussy eaters, 241–242
    introducing different foods to preschoolers, 240
    making healthy meals, 240–241
forceps, 87
formula-fed babies
    bowel movements, 101
    breast or formula, 104
    how much and when, 105–106

friends
  as babysitters, 149
  relationships with, 15
  as sources of help, 25
frontpacks, 144
fundal height, 46
funerals, 296–297

• G •

games. *See* playtime
gas (for pain relief), 50
gastroenteritis, 181, 251
genetic disorders, 300
German measles, 284
gestation, 28
gestational diabetes, 35, 286
good sports, 231–232
government assistance
  for carers, 307
  for day care, 152
government schools, 258, 261
GPs
  consulting when child is ill, 25, 71, 83, 121, 122,
    172, 181–182, 242–243, 248, 250–253, 255, 300
  and PND, 132, 137
  role in antenatal care, 16, 34, 35, 36, 37, 41, 42,
    46, 47, 51
grief management, information resources,
  362–363
gripe water, 70, 107
group B strep, 51
growth. *See* child development
guardians, 147
guardianship, 322, 323–325

• H •

haemorrhoids, 52
hand games, 348
Hawking, Steven, 306
HCG (human chorionic gonadotropin), 34
Healing Heart for Bereaved Parents (Aust), 295
health and first aid
  first aid kits, 291
  must-haves for babies, 69–70
health insurance, 146, 256
health problems. *See also* disabilities
  addressing, 171–173
  alternative medicines and remedies, 255
  avoiding, 282–288
  child obesity, 256

childhood illnesses, 248–254
coping with illness and injury, 289–291
diagnosing a serious illness, 291
emergency phone numbers, 290
getting help, 25
information resources, 365–367
recurring illnesses, 254–255
spotting injuries, 289–290
terminal illness, 292–295
for toddlers, 180–182
health and wellbeing
  birth options to reduce risk of fatality,
    286–287
  creating a healthy and safe home, 288
  during pregnancy, 29, 30
  information resources, 363–365
  keeping accidents at bay, 283
  protecting against diseases, 282
  providing a violence-free home, 282
  reducing the risk of SUDI and SIDS, 287–288
  risks during pregnancy, 283–284
  and your behaviour, 15
HealthDirect (Aust), 364
Healthline (NZ), 364
hearing, during first three months, 128
hearing impairment, 301
heartburn, during pregnancy, 47
help for dads. *See also* information resources for
    dads
  from friends, colleagues and family, 25
  internet research, 24–25
  networking with other dads, 26, 274, 278–279, 329
high chairs, 63
Hire for Baby (Aust), 62, 144
hiring baby equipment, 62, 144
histamines, 242
hitting others, 193–194
holidays
  when pregnant, 337
  with a baby, 15, 169–171
home births
  as an option, 50
  birthing equipment, 73
  helping your partner, 84–85
  risks, 286
homeopathy, 255
homework, 264–265
honey, 158
hospices, 293
hospital bags, 73–75
hospital births
  as an option, 50, 76
  going home, 91

items mothers need, 74
  when to go to hospital, 84
human chorionic gonadotropin (HCG), 34
hurting others, 193–194
hybrid nappies, 68
hydrocephalus, 301

IHC (NZ), 303, 358
immunisations, 147, 180
Immunise Australia Program, 364
in utero, 297
in vitro fertilisation (IVF), 32
in-home day care, 153–154
independent schools, 258, 261
induction, 82
indulgent parenting. *See* permissive parenting
    style
infant acne, 121
infant deaths. *See* death of a child
infant mortality, 77
infantile colic, 118
infants. *See* newborns
infertility
  contributing factors in men, 31
  definition, 30
information resources for dads
  child development, 355–356
  child safety, 356
  childbirth education and parenting information,
    351–352
  childcare and education, 352–355
  disability, 356–359
  divorce and separation, 359–360
  fatherhood, 361–362
  fun and games, 361
  grief and baby loss, 362–363
  health, 363–365
  illnesses and conditions, 365–367
  multiple births, 367
  organisations and sources of information, 23–24
  palliative care, 367–368
  postnatal depression, 368–369
  pregnancy and birth, 369–370
  SIDS and SUDI, 370
Inland Revenue Department (NZ), child support,
    323, 360
insect repellent, 70
insomnia, during pregnancy, 52
Institute of Registered Music Teachers New
    Zealand, 268

insurance, 146
intellectual disabilities, 302–303
intracytoplasmic sperm injection (ICSI), 32
iPhone apps, for labour, 81
iron, sources of, 244

● J ●

jaundice, 117
jealousy, between siblings, 218
jigsaw puzzles, 348
juice, 238

● K ●

kangaroo care, 342
Kids with Asthma (Aust), 291, 365
KidsHealth (NZ), 368
kindergarten, 209–210, 234
Kindergarten Association (Aust), 210
kitchens, baby-proofing, 127
Kura kaupapa Maori, 258

● L ●

labour. *See also* childbirth
  bringing it on, 82
  early signs, 83
  inducing, 82
  iPhone apps, 81
  keeping sane, 85–86
  knowing when it's real, 84
  phases of first stage, 79
  role of father-to-be, 79–80
  stages of, 78
  what you need to know, 78–79
lactation consultants, 80
language development
  during second year, 184, 186–187
  during the third year, 200–201
  from six to twelve months, 164
language learning, at school, 267
latent phase (labour), 79, 83
laughing gas, 50
laundries, baby-proofing, 127
Law Council of Australian Family Law, 326
lead maternity carers (LMCs), 36
learning
  and meeting new challenges, 198, 199
  objectives for preschoolers, 235
  for the whole family, 235–236

leg cramps, during pregnancy, 47
legal advice, 319, 326
legal aid, 314
life insurance, 146
lifelong learning, 233–236
lifestyle
  inevitable changes, 14–15
  and risk taking behaviours, 15
ligaments, softening during pregnancy, 47
listeria, 41, 284
listeriosis, 284
living areas, baby-proofing, 126
Lone Fathers Association of Australia, 134, 325, 359
long day care centre, 152

• *M* •

male infertility, 31
marriage. *See also* relationship breakdowns; relationships
  dealing with rough patches, 312–313
  rebuilding your relationship, 313–314
  remarriage, 332
Marriage Guidance Services (NZ), 134
massage, for babies, 123–124, 141, 255, 344
Mazlish, Elaine, 207
meconium, 91, 101
mediators, 314
Medicare (Aust), 147
medication, during pregnancy, 30
medicine, administering to babies, 122
meditation, 247
meninges, 301
meningitis, 252
men's groups, 314, 317
Mensline Australia, 360, 362
menstuff.org, 134
mental development, during second year, 184–185
Mental Health Foundation (Aust), 325
Mental Health Services (Aust), 134
midwives, and antenatal care, 36
Ministry of Education (NZ), 354
Ministry of Health (NZ), 358
miscarriage, 13, 281, 284, 285
Miscarriage Support Auckland, 285, 363
mittens, 122
mobility, stages of, 162
monozygotic twins, 45
Montessori Aotearoa New Zealand, 260, 354
Montessori Australia, 260, 353
Montessori schools, 259–260

moodiness, 43
morning sickness, 42
Moro reflex, 109
Moses baskets, 64
Mothers Matter (NZ), 134, 369
movement, 139
movement classes, 145
mucous plug, 83
multiple births, 45, 367
muscular dystrophy, 301
Muscular Dystrophy Foundation Australia, 302, 366
music classes, 145, 268
Music Education New Zealand, 354
myschool.edu.au, 261
My Time (Aust), 307, 357

• *N* •

nail clippers, 70
nannies, 150–151
nappies, 64–65, 67–68
nappy bags, 274–275
nappy changing, 91, 100–101, 345–346
nappy creams, 69
Nappy Network (NZ), 68
nappy rash, 69, 121
National Association for Loss and Grief (Aust), 295, 362
National Association for Loss and Grief (NZ), 295, 363
National Childcare Accreditation Council (Aust), 153, 353
National Foundation for the Deaf (NZ), 302, 358
'nature vs nurture' debate, 131
naturopathy, 255
neglectful parenting style, 161
'nesting instinct', 46
networking, 26, 274, 278–279, 329
new partners, introducing to your children, 330–332
New Zealand Kindergartens Inc., 210, 354
New Zealand Multiple Birth Association, 367
New Zealand Qualifications Authority, 355
newborns
  baby massage, 123–124, 344
  bathing, 102–103, 110
  being committed to caring for, 341–342
  bonding with, 97–98, 341–346
  burping, 106–107
  caring for, 96–97, 99–100
  clothing needs, 56–57
  crying, 109–110

dealing with the aftershock, 95–99
dealing with visitors, 113
death, 297
dressing, 103–104
feeding, 104–107
getting help with, 97, 99–100
items needed immediately after birth, 75
nappy changing, 100–101
reading to, 343
settling your baby, 108
skin-to-skin contact, 342–343
sleeping, 107–109
solutions to common problems in first few
    months, 117–122
tummy time, 111, 125, 139, 343–344
nightmares, 178
nitrous oxide, 50
'no' loop, avoiding, 203–204
non-government schools, 258
non-resident fathers, responsibilities, 319–320
nuchal fold tests, 45
Nurse-on-call (Vic), 364
nurseries
    decorating, 66
    must-have items, 64–65
nut allergies, 243
Nutrition Australia, 238

• *O* •

obesity, 256
object permanence, 130
obstacle courses, 347
obstetricians, and antenatal care, 36
obstetrics, 36
occupational therapists (OTs), 309
Office of Disability Issues (NZ), 358
only children, 212
Open Adoption New Zealand, 33
optimism, maintaining, 22
orgasmic birth, 85
osteopathy, 255
outdoor activities, 232–233
outdoor areas, baby-proofing, 127
ovaries, 28
overdue, 82
overseas travel, 171
overtiredness, 107, 273
ovulation, 28, 30
ovulation test kits, 30
oxytocin, 82
ozclothnappies.org, 68

• *P* •

paediatricians, 5, 209, 300, 307
pain relief
    options for childbirth, 49–50
    for young children, 70, 71
palliative care, 292–293, 367–368
PANDA. *See* Post and Antenatal Depression
        Association (PANDA) (Aust)
Parent to Parent (NZ), 307, 358
parenting agreements, 319
parenting courses, 276, 329
parenting information resources, 351–352
parenting methods, care routine strategies, 19–20
parenting orders, 319, 322, 323
parenting plans, 319, 322
Parenting South Australia, 352
parenting styles, 160–161
Parenting Through Separation (NZ), 316
Parentline (NT/QLD), 364
Parents Centre New Zealand Inc., 71, 166, 329, 352
Parents as First Teachers (PAFT), 233
Parents of Vision Impaired (NZ), 302, 359
passion, for fatherhood, 22
patience
    developing in toddlers, 200
    parents' need for, 22
perinatal deaths, 286
peritoneal cavity, 87
permissive parenting style, 161
persistence, developing, 200
pethidine, 50
pets, and babies, 66–67
photographs, 173, 344
physical disabilities, 301–302
physical skills, of toddlers, 184
piles, 52
placenta, 78
plastic keys, 60
play dough, making, 231
play gyms, 60
Playgroup Australia, 166, 361
playgroups, 145, 166
playtime
    with new babies, 138–139
    'rough and tumble play', 202
    with six to twelve month old babies, 162–168
    stimulating your toddler's interests, 205–206
    with toddlers, 185–186, 201–202, 347–350
Plunket. *See* Royal New Zealand Plunket Society
PlunketLine, 133
pneumonia, 252

Poisons Information Hotline, 364
positing, 96
Post and Ante-Natal Distress Support Group (NZ), 134, 369
Post and Antenatal Depression Association (PANDA) (Aust), 133, 134, 368
Post Natal Distress Support Network Trust (NZ), 369
post partum period, 36
postnatal depression (PND)
  information resources for dads, 368–369
  in men, 133, 137
  nature of, 92, 99, 132–133
  stress release, 133–134
  support organisations, 134
  supporting suffering partners, 133, 137
postnatal period, 36
potty training, 102
Prader-Wili Syndrome, 303
praise, 225
prams, 60–61, 62, 215, 345
pre-birth care. *See* antenatal care
pre-eclampsia, 32, 47, 286
pre-prep children, 209–210
pregnancy. *See also* childbirth; infertility; labour
  activities to avoid, 43
  announcing, 45
  antenatal or pre-birth care, 35
  assisted conception, 32, 34
  being there for the medical stuff, 337
  conceiving naturally, 28–29
  dietary needs, 40–41
  the first trimester, 40–45
  foods to avoid, 41, 336
  getting confirmation, 34–35
  giving your partner some 'me' time, 336
  going on the wagon with your partner, 336
  recording that beautiful belly, 339
  risks to babies, 283–284
  the second trimester, 45–48
  taking care of your partner, 335–336
  telling your partner she's beautiful, 339
  things to do before morning sickness starts, 37–38
  the third trimester, 49–54
  tips and tricks for improving the odds, 29–30
pregnancy tests, 34
premature babies, 59
premature births, 13
prep, 209–210
preschoolers
  active movement, 226–227
  bad weather busters, 229–230
  banishing boredom, 228–229
  bringing our their talents, 230–231
  building self-esteem and self-sufficiency, 224–227
  classes, 227
  common health problems, 248–254
  development, 224, 227
  dietary needs, 237–238
  exercise, 245–246
  kindergarten happiness, 234
  learning objectives, 235
  learning to be a good sport, 231–232
  using praise, 225
presence, engaging with your child, 23
private schools, 258, 260–261
progesterone, 43, 47, 52
prostaglandins, 82, 83
protein, for vegetarians, 244
psychologists, 309
punishment, versus discipline, 192

• Q •

Quitline, 282

• R •

Raising Children Network (Aust), 25, 307, 357
rattles, 60
reading
  to newborns, 343
  to toddlers, 200, 350
  to your baby, 111, 125
reflux, 107, 119–120
Reflux Infants Support Association Inc. (Aust), 366
Reflux Support (NZ), 367
relationship breakdowns
  being the children's primary care-giver, 326–330
  being a remote or part-time father, 319–320
  counselling and support, 325
  divorce rates, 316
  finding a lawyer, 326
  getting advice, 314–315
  getting support, 317
  making separation easier on your children, 315
  paying child support, 322–323
  seeking guardianship of your children, 323–325
  separating being a husband from being a father, 318
  separation information and resources, 359–360
  sorting out childcare arrangements, 315, 318–319
  understanding contact arrangements, 321–322
  understanding the divorce process, 315

Relationship Services (NZ), 16, 134, 282, 325, 360
relationships. *See also* marriage
  being there for the medical stuff, 337
  giving your partner some 'me' time during
    pregnancy, 336
  looking after your partner during pregnancy, 112,
    335–336
  making time for each other, 148
  sharing your excitement about becoming a dad,
    338
  strains caused by having children, 17
  stresses on, 311
  talking about a new partner to your children, 331
Relationships Australia, 16, 282, 325, 360
religious education, 268
remarriage, 332
remote fathers, responsibilities, 319–320
ripening the cervix, 82
Ronald McDonald House Charities, 368
'rough and tumble play', 202
round ligament pain, 47
routines. *See* care routines
Royal New Zealand Foundation of the Blind, 302,
  359
Royal New Zealand Plunket Society, 25, 62, 71, 100,
  107, 352
rubella, 284
rules, setting, 204

• S •

safety
  around water, 165
  for babies, 125–127, 146
  baby-proofing room by room, 126–127
  creating a healthy and safe home, 288
  for toddlers, 182
  when you have more than one child, 215–216
SAHDs. *See* stay-at-home dads
SANDS (Stillbirth and Newborn Death Support)
  (Aust), 295, 297, 362
SANDS (Stillbirth and Newborn Death Support)
  (NZ), 295, 297, 363
SANE Australia, 134, 369
savings accounts, 147
scalding, 126
scalds, 289
schemas, 206, 350
school
  homework, 264–265
  preparing for, 262–263
  things kids need to know when starting, 263–264

School Enrolment Zones (NZ), 259, 355
school holidays, 263
School Sport Australia, 268, 353
schools
  selecting, 258–259, 261, 262
  when they don't meet your expectations,
    266–267
second stage of labour, 79
second trimester of pregnancy
  development of baby, 48
  medical tests, 46–47
  nuchal fold tests, 45
  side effects, 47
  wellbeing of mothers-to-be, 46
self-esteem, building, 224–227
self-sufficiency, building, 224–227
separation anxiety, 178
separation (relationships), information resources,
  359–360
separation schemas, 206
sex
  after childbirth, 114
  during pregnancy, 13, 46
  as a father, 11
  to bring on labour, 82
  when baby is under six months old, 148
  when trying to conceive, 30
sexually transmitted diseases, 31
shaking babies, 282
Shared Parenting Council of Australia, 360
sharing, 194–195
shoes, buying for toddlers, 59
show (pregnancy), 83
sibling discipline
  coping with jealousy and fighting, 218
  discovering different personalities, 219–220
  fighting and setting boundaries, 219
  and sibling rivalry, 217–218
sibling rivalry, 216, 217–218
sickness. *See* health problems
SIDS and Kids, 288, 370
SIDS (Sudden Infant Death Syndrome), 283,
  287–288, 370
sight, during first three months, 128–129
singing
  to babies, 139
  to newborns, 111
single-sex schools, 258, 261–262
sitting, 162–163
skin irritations and scratching, 122
Skylight (NZ), 295, 363
sleep deprivation, 12, 96, 137–138
sleeping bags, 56

sleeping routines
  newborns, 107–109
  settling your baby, 108
  sleep needs of infants, 160
  swaddling, 109
  for toddlers, 178–179
sleepsuits, 103, 122
slings, 63, 143–144
smell (sense of), during first three months, 129
smoking, 283, 336
social development
  during second year, 184–185
  and need for interaction with other children, 199
social life, as a father, 11
social skills, development, 231–232
soft toy animals, 60
solids (foods), for babies, 140, 156–159
SPARC — Sport and Recreation New Zealand, 125, 355
special education. *See also* disabilities
  information resources, 353
  services, 266
special needs children, 265–266
speech pathologists, 309
speech therapists, 309
spills, 96
spina bifida, 301
spinal block. *See* epidurals
spinal injuries, 301
spontaneity, 15
sport, for school children, 268
Sport and Recreation New Zealand, 268
Starship Children's Health, 368
state schools, 258, 260–261
state-integrated schools, 258
stay-at-home dads (SAHDs)
  coping, 273
  ensuring healthy bodies and active minds, 276–277
  getting organised, 274–275
  myths about men as primary caregivers, 272–273
  networking, 274, 278–279
  number of, 1, 272
  relationship with working mother, 277
  respect for, 271
  upskilling, 275–276
  working from home, 277–278
Steiner schools, 260, 354
Stepfamilies Australia, 360
stepmothers, introducing, 330–332
sticky eye, 123
stillbirth, 13, 297
story time and music sessions, 145

strep throat, 181
stress, managing, 282
stretch-n-grows, 56
strollers, 60–61, 62, 143, 345
successful dads, seven habits of, 21–23
SUDI (Sudden Unexplained Death of Infants), 287–288, 370
'sugar highs', 180
sunscreen, 70
Supporting Children after Separation Program (Aust), 316
swaddling, 109, 142
swimming, for babies, 165
Swine Flu Emergency Hotline, 364
synapses, 125, 131
syntocinon, 82

• *T* •

talking
  so that your toddler understands, 206–207
  to babies, 125, 164
  to toddlers, 186–187, 200
tantrums, 192–193
taste (sense of), during first three months, 130
tax benefits, 147, 329
team sports
  for preschoolers, 231–232
  for toddlers, 189
teenage fathers, 98
teendads.fatherandchild.org.nz, 98
teeth brushing, 159
teething
  relief for, 70, 172–173
  signs of, 172
  timing of, 121, 122
teething toys, 59
television, 208–209, 229
terminal illnesses
  home care, 294
  hospices, 293
  letting family and friends know, 294
  palliative care, 292–293
  preparing for the end, 292–295
  seeking help, 295
third stage of labour, 79
third trimester of pregnancy
  antenatal classes, 49
  birth plans, 51
  considering birthing options, 49–50
  development of baby, 53–54

medical checks, 51
side effects, 51–52
time management
  dealing with visitors, 113
  making time for yourself, 111
  work–life balance, 14, 113–114
time out, 205
toddler-proofing, inside and outside areas of the home, 182
toddlers. *See also* behaviour management
  communicating with, 206–207
  developing patience, 200
  development, 184–186, 199–201, 202–203
  dietary needs, 179–180
  engaging with, 347–350
  language development, 184, 186–187, 200–201
  mental development, 184–185
  offering them choices, 203–204
  physical skills, 184
  playing with, 347–350
  reading to, 200, 350
  reputation, 178
  safety, 182
  social development, 184–185
  stimulating their interests through play, 205–206
  talking to, 186, 200
toenails, trimming, 123
toilet training, 187–189
tonsillitis, 253
touch (sense of), during first three months, 130
toxoplasmosis, 284
toy libraries, 167–168
toys
  for babies, 59–60, 142
  making your own, 345
  using everyday objects, 167
transition phase (labour), 79
transport to hospital, 72–73
tummy time, 111, 125, 139, 343–344
tummy tubs, 63
twins, 45

ultrasound scans
  during second trimester, 46
  first scan, 44
umbilical cord, 48, 88, 90, 103, 287, 342
uterine wall, 32
uterus, 28, 29, 46, 78

varicoceles, 31
varicose veins, 52
vegetarian children, 244
vena cava, 52
ventouse, 87
vernix, 48, 89
vertical schemas, 206
Very Special Kids hospice (Aust), 293, 368
vestibular system, 162
videos, 208–209
violence, 282
Vision Australia, 302, 357
visual impairment, 301
vitamin C, 244
voluntary child support agreements, 323
vomiting. *See* positing

• W •

Waldorf schools, 260
walking, 162, 163
water birth, 50, 51, 74
water games, 349
water safety, 165
Water Safety New Zealand, 165, 356
waters breaking, 79
weight
  child obesity, 256
  during first three months, 128
Well Child providers, 22, 24, 99
whooping cough, 253–254
wills, 147
wind, 118
womb, 28
word spurts, 187
work
  preparing to return, 168–169
  working from home, 277–278
Work and Income (NZ), 152, 329
work–life balance, 14, 113–114, 169
Working for Families scheme (NZ), 329
wraps, 144

• Y •

yoga, 247

FOR DUMMIES®

Pregnancy, Health & Fitness

Baby's First Year FOR DUMMIES

1-74031-042-X
$39.95

Pregnancy FOR DUMMIES

1-74031-103-5
$39.95

IVF & Beyond FOR DUMMIES

1-74216-946-5
$39.95

Menopause FOR DUMMIES

1-74031-140-X
$39.95

Food & Nutrition FOR DUMMIES

0-7314-0596-X
$34.95

Diabetes FOR DUMMIES

1-74031-094-2
$39.95

Living Gluten-Free FOR DUMMIES

0-7314-0760-1
$34.95

Fitness FOR DUMMIES

1-74031-009-8
$39.95

Golf FOR DUMMIES

1-74031-011-X
$39.95

Cricket FOR DUMMIES

1-74031-173-6
$39.95

Aussie Rules FOR DUMMIES

0-7314-0595-1
$34.95

Sailing FOR DUMMIES

0-7314-0644-3
$39.95

FOR DUMMIES

Business & Investment

Starting an Online Business FOR DUMMIES

Melissa Norfolk
Greg Holden

0-7314-0991-4
$39.95

Small Business FOR DUMMIES

Veechi Curtis

1-74216-853-1
$39.95

Marketing Your Small Business FOR DUMMIES

Carolyn Tate

1-74216-852-3
$39.95

Superannuation FOR DUMMIES

Trish Power

0-7314-0715-6
$39.95

DIY Super FOR DUMMIES

1-74216-943-0
$39.95

Investing in Real Estate FOR DUMMIES

0-7314-0724-5
$39.95

Online Share Investing FOR DUMMIES

James Frost
Matt Krantz

0-7314-0940-X
$39.95

Tax for Australians FOR DUMMIES

Jimmy B. Prince, MCPA

1-74216-859-0
$32.95

Australian Wills and Estates FOR DUMMIES

Graham Cooke

1-74031-067-5
$39.95

Sorting Out Your Finances FOR DUMMIES

Barbara Drury

0-7314-0746-6
$29.95

Australian Resumes FOR DUMMIES

Amanda McCarthy

1-74031-091-8
$39.95

Debt Repair Kit FOR DUMMIES

Steve Bucci
Anthony Moore

1-74216-941-4
$36.95

FOR DUMMIES®

Reference

0-7314-0723-7
$34.95

1-74031-157-4
$39.95

1-74216-945-7
$39.95

0-7314-0909-4
$39.95

1-74216-925-2
$29.95

0-7314-0722-9
$29.95

0-7314-0784-9
$34.95

0-7314-0752-0
$34.95

Technology

0-7314-0985-X
$39.95

0-7314-0761-X
$39.95

0-7314-0941-8
$39.95

1-74031-159-0
$39.95